TEXAS VOICES:
DOCUMENTS & BIOGRAPHICAL SKETCHES

Fifth Edition

TEXAS VOICES:
DOCUMENTS & BIOGRAPHICAL SKETCHES

Fifth Edition

Keith J. Volanto
Collin College

Design and Production: Abigail Press
Typesetting: Abigail Press
Typeface: AGaramond
Cover Art: Sam Tolia

TEXAS VOICES:
DOCUMENTS & BIOGRAPHICAL SKETCHES

Fifth Edition, 2018
Printed in the United States of America
Translation rights reserved by the publisher
ISBN 1-890919-95-0   13-digit 978-1-890919-95-5

Table of Contents

Chapter Seven
Texas During the Civil War, 1861-1865

Chapter Eight
Reconstruction in Texas: The Unfinished Civil War, 1865-1874

Chapter Fifteen
World War II and Texas, 1941-1945

Chapter Sixteen
On the Threshold of Modernization, 1945-1959

Chapter Seventeen
The Turbulent Decade: Reform and Reaction, 1960-1972

Chapter Eighteen
A Transitional Decade, 1972-1979

Preface

Texas history is a fascinating field of study that continues to evolve from its standard focus on romantic narratives about pre-twentieth century topics, such as Spanish clashes with Indians, the Texas Revolution, the Civil War, and the Great Texas Cattle Drives. While this tradition continues, modern Texas historiography has increasingly followed the lead of national historians and brought renewed attention to the perspectives of Native Americans, Tejanos, Texas slaves, "average" Texans of all races, and women. In addition, twentieth-century topics of importance are getting their due consideration. I have attempted to synthesize both older and newer trends in this book.

Texas Voices has a two-fold purpose. First, I wished to create a unique supplement to our textbook *Beyond Myths and Legends: A Narrative History of Texas* that would be useful as well as enjoyable to read. Each chapter of this book contains six primary source documents, three compact biographies, and photographs dealing with material located in a corresponding chapter of the textbook. I deliberately chose these manuscripts, pictures, and individuals with the idea of providing interesting ancillary details about certain people, topics, and themes introduced in the textbook. A second purpose of this book is to provide a "stand-alone" work reflective of the current state of the field of Texas history that would be useful and enjoyable for a general reader. Anyone interested in learning about the history of the Lone Star State, from the pre-Columbian period to the present, will learn much from this distinctive compilation.

I cannot thank Phyllis Botterweck at Abigail Press enough for her positive encouragement and tireless efforts to get this book into publication. She has been an outstanding editor and an overall pleasure to work with. Ken Howell also aided me through his selection of many documents and biographical subjects found in the first half of this book. His vision made *Beyond Myths and Legends* and *Texas Voices* a reality.

Keith Volanto
May 10, 2018

Chapter 1

Before European Contact

The Great Spirit is a conception of a supreme being prevalent among many Native American cultures. Native Americans were spiritual people with a deep faith in a "higher power." Profound reverence for the Great Spirit, Father Sky and Great Spirit Mother, Mother Earth, is at the heart of many Native American traditions.

Appeal to the Great Spirit
Photo Credit: Library of Congress

THOUGHT QUESTION:

In what way is the Great Spirit different from the monotheistic religion's concept of God and in what way is it the same?

1

Indians Dancing

**Credit: UTSA's Institute of Texas Cultures,
#073-0310h, Courtesy of John L. Davis**

This pictograph of archaic Native Americans dancing is located at Hueco Tanks, a 860-acre park located 40 miles east of El Paso named for the large natural rock basins or "huecos" found there. For thousands of years, Native Americans camped here and drew designs and human and animal figures on the rocks of the area. Hundreds of paintings—from large panels to small mask-like faces—adorn the canyon walls, overhangs, and ceilings of the shelters.

THOUGHT QUESTION:

What can archeologists and historians learn from these pictographs?

Wichita Mortar

Wichita Mortar
Photo Credit: Library of Congress

This Wichita woman is using a mortar and pestle—tools used to crush, grind, and mix substances. The pestle is a heavy bat shaped stick whose end is used for pounding and grinding, and the mortar is a bowl, typically made of hard wood, marble, clay, or stone. The substance is ground between the pestle and the mortar.

THOUGHT QUESTION:

What important roles did women perform in pre-Columbian Native American cultures?

Metate and Mano

Credit: Library of Congress

In addition to the mortar and pestle, women in many Native American groups beginning in the Archaic Period used the metate (a slightly curved stone) and mano (a rounded stone hand piece) to grind small objects such as seeds, nuts, beans, and corn into a powdery meal. Archaeologists have found variations of these stone tools in all parts of the world and they are still used in many cultures today.

THOUGHT QUESTION:

How could each of the major types of pre-Columbian Native American groups in Texas (nomadic, hunter-gatherer, sedentary) used the mano and metate? Which group might have used them more than the others? Why?

The Tai-me

Credit: UTSA's Institute of Texan Cultures, #070-0163
Source: Mooney, James: "History of the Kiowa Indians," 1898.

The tai-me, a Kiowa Indian religious item, is a feathered wand used in the Sun Dance. The Sun Dance was an important religious ceremony of the Plains Indians of nineteenth-century North America. Though their rituals varied, the Arapaho, Arikara, Asbinboine, Cheyenne, Crow, Gros, Ventre, Hidutsa, Sioux, Plains Cree, Plains Ojibway, Sarasi, Omaha, Ponca, Ute, Shoshone, Kiowa, and Blackfoot tribes all practiced a form of the Sun Dance.

THOUGHT QUESTION:

Discuss the Sun Dance. What was the purpose and what features were included in the ceremony? Who ran the ceremony and instructed the participants? How long did it last?

How They Caught Fish

Credit: Library of Congress

Native men and women in a dugout canoe fish while others in the background stand in the river and spear fish. Dugout canoes were made of tree trunks that were cut in half and hollowed out. From forty to fifty feet long, one canoe could hold an entire family and their few possessions. However, the clumsy and hard-to-maneuver crafts could not be used in the deep gulf waters, only in coastal bays, lagoons and rivers.

THOUGHT QUESTION:

Which Native American groups in Texas relied on canoes for fishing and transportation? How did canoes help them perform these functions?

A Wichita Indian Village

Credit: Library of Congress

The types of domiciles where Native Americans in Texas lived varied widely, but similarities existed among the major types of Native American groups. Nomadic groups such as the Comanche and Apache, for example, used portable leather-covered tepees. The aquatic and hunter-gatherer Karankawa of the Gulf Coast utilized small portable huts covered with moss and hides and made of tree branches that could be assembled and disassembled relatively quickly as they moved about their familiar fishing and hunting grounds. The Caddo and Wichita Indians of Northeastern Texas, however, were sedentary, agricultural peoples who lived in large, stationary thatched-roof huts as depicted in this drawing.

THOUGHT QUESTION:

How did the shelters of various Native American groups reflect the general orientation of their daily lives, impacted most strongly by how they acquired food?

VIGNETTES

The Much-Maligned Karankawas

Among the Native American groups occupying Texas at the time of European arrival, none have been more maligned and misunderstood than the Karankawas of the Gulf Coast. Initiated by the Spanish, rumors and accusations of the Karankawas being nothing but ruthless barbarous savages subsisting on human flesh continued to be spread by Mexican and American settlers. As a result, the wanton destruction of the Karankawas became a justifiable action similar to the way that the Spanish justified the conquest of the Aztecs because of their practice of human sacrifice.

Though the Karankawas (as many Native American groups along the Texas coast) performed a form of ritual cannibalism whereby captured war prisoners might be partially eaten upon the belief that the powers of the captured warrior would transfer to those consuming a portion of his body, they did not perform the practice for subsistence or any other purpose. In fact, before large numbers of invaders began to occupy their lands, the Karankawas (like many other Native Americans) could be friendly to those not perceived as a threat. Many scholars point to the report of Álvar Núñez Cabeza de Vaca, who noted how the Karankawas took pity on the surviving members of the Narváez expedition who washed ashore in their territory. Not only did many natives weep for them, they also brought the castaways to their village for care. Further, Cabeza de Vaca specifically noted how the Karankawas were appalled to find out that some desperate members of the expedition cannibalized dead members of their party in order to survive.

The available evidence, coupled with a better understanding of primitive cultures and more sensible interpretations, now vindicate the Karankawas from their undeserved reputation. In the end, the Karankawas seem to be guilty of nothing more than being physically imposing (their men were typically over six feet tall in an age when most Europeans and Americans averaged a half foot shorter), having their rituals misunderstood, occupying coastal land prized by settlers, and being strongly independent and determined to resist foreign encroachment upon their lands.

The Comanche before Texas

Before the Comanche struck fear into the hearts of Spanish, Mexicans, and Americans in Texas as expert mounted warriors, their ancestors lived a rather humble existence as simple nomadic hunters and gatherers. Oral tradition, backed by linguistic and archeological evidence, links them with the Northern Shoshones.

For hundreds of years, the Shoshone moved within an area encompassing portions of present-day northern Utah and western Wyoming. Their lifestyle revolved around a yearly cycle, spending much of their time attempting to snare rabbits, rodents, lizards, and other small animals in the mountains and meadows of the Great Basin, occasionally fishing along lakes and streams, and gathering nuts, berries, and roots of edible wild plants. During the winters, they traveled through the South Pass to the eastern slopes of the Rocky Mountains to hunt bison and elk while seeking adequate protection against the bitter cold. Overall, their tools, means of hunting and gathering, and types of shelter reveal a very primitive and precarious existence.

During the course of the sixteenth century, many Shoshone began to move eastward onto the Southern Plains of North America, joining some other Native American groups taking advantage of cooler temperatures and heavy rainfall that replenished the grasslands and tremendously bolstered the size of bison herds. They began to transform themselves into nomadic bison hunters. Pursuing the animals on foot, they tried to kill their prey by surrounding the bison or driving them off steep drops. Though extremely dangerous and requiring much planning and energy to execute, these communal hunts paid dividends in the form of increased food and other resources that could be taken from the carcasses.

Sometime in the late seventeenth century, possibly due to an epidemic, threats from other Native American groups, or both, the Comanche separated from the Shoshones and travelled in a southeasterly direction toward the grasslands of present-day eastern Colorado and western Kansas. Another contributing factor posited by some historians is that at some point during the late 1600s, the Comanche encountered horses for the first time as the animals migrated in a northeasterly direction following the Arkansas River. From that moment on, life for the Comanche would never be the same again. Within a short period of time, the Comanche developed into expert horsemen. Their enhanced mobility made their ability to hunt bison to increase exponentially. The horse also formed the basis of Comanche military prowess for the next two hundred years, as Spanish, Mexican, American settlers and many Native American rival would attest. By the 1720s, they had arrived in Texas.

The Lipan Apaches before Comanche and Spanish Dominance in Texas

The Lipan Apaches, who came to dominate the Southern Plains of Texas before Comanche raiders and Spanish settlers moved into Texas, were descendants of a branch of Atahpaskan-speaking peoples residing in Alaska, western Canada, and the Pacific Northwest. Archeological evidence supports the theory that they were hunter-gatherers who moved southward along the eastern slopes of the Rocky Mountains during the thirteenth or fourteenth centuries, settling in the American Southwest by the 1400s. The extended family formed the basis of Apache society, with multiple family groups forming a band that stayed in close proximity to each other and united for military operations and ceremonial occasions. The Lipan Apaches were the easternmost band who resided in the present-day Texas Panhandle region and would have the largest impact on Texas history.

The Lipan Apaches adapted to their new environment in two major ways. First, and foremost, they hunted bison. Before the arrival of horses, they undertook this dangerous task on foot, as did other Plains Indians. The bison provided ample food and resources for their needs but also allowed them to trade surplus items with Pueblo Indians for supplementary materials such as maize, pottery, and woven cotton goods. Second, Apache women gathered edible wild plants and practiced small-scale cultivation of maize, beans, squash, pumpkins, and watermelons to supplement their diets. Because the Lipan Apache dedicated most of their time and energy to the bison hunt, this rudimentary agriculture basically involved planting fields and leaving them during the growing season, then returning to harvest the surviving crops.

The Spanish conquistador Francisco Vásquez de Coronado noted the presence of Lipan Apache in 1541 during his trek through the Southern Plains in search of Quivera. For the next 150 years, the Lipan Apache continued with their traditional way of life.

Then, a few decades before the turn of the eighteenth century, they began to acquire the horse through trade with Pueblo Indians, raids upon settlements, and the gathering of wild mustangs. The changes in lifestyle that this development produced were truly revolutionary. Bison could now be hunted more safely and efficiently, plus the increased mobility allowed the Lipan Apaches to attack rival Native American villages and new Spanish settlements with impunity. However, the same benefits that the Apaches received from the horse also transferred to the Comanche, who proved to be even more adept horsemen. By 1700, the Comanche began forcing the Lipan Apache southward. Within four decades, the Comanche became the supreme people of the Southern Plains of Texas. The Lipan Apaches once again had to adapt to a new environment, this time, the former Coahuiltecan lands of South Texas, which were increasingly occupied by the Spanish, thus laying the foundation for future conflict.

The Three Sisters Arrive in Texas

Though Native American women in Texas were involved in small-scale agriculture by the late Woodland Period (c.100 B.C.-800 A.D.), tending gardens of such plants as sunflowers and squash, great changes would inevitably come that upended the previous ways in which many groups acquired their sustenance. Whereas the relatively small amount of cultivated crops had been used to supplement native diets based on hunting animals and gathering nuts, roots, and berries, after 900 A.D. many peoples began to take in a majority of their food from farming.

These changes came about slowly as corn and beans began to be introduced into Texas. Though maize had been domesticated in Mexico since 4000 B.C. and beans since 2000 B.C., corn domestication did not begin for peoples residing along the Sabine, Neches, Trinity, and Red Rivers of Texas until 700 A.D., with beans coming two hundred years later. Over time, women learned to interplant the "Three Sisters" of the "American Triad"—corn, beans, and squash—which by 1200 A.D. had become absolutely essential to the diets of Northeast Texas natives. Women discovered how to produce crops most efficiently by planting the kernels from the stoutest corn plants into small mounds of dirt. As the corn sprouted, beans and squash were planted nearby. The vines of the beans would then grow and loop around the established corn stalks while the squash leaves covered the mounds to suppress weed growth and lessen soil erosion. In addition to greatly increasing crop yields, the Three Sisters also enhanced the native diet. Corn by itself is often difficult for humans to digest, but the lysine acid in beans aided with the digestion of the corn proteins.

The Agricultural Revolution made possible by the Three Sisters contributed to an elevated status for women in farming societies. While only a few females served as chieftains, and women usually only took control while men were away on a hunt, they often served as influential advisors to the male leaders on important matters pertaining to the group. Though many Indian groups did not engage in agriculture, by 1500 A.D. virtually all Native American communities in Texas were either growing corn or seeking the harvested crop through trade.

Chapter 2

The Spanish Invasion of Texas, 1519-1821

Alvar Nuñez Cabeza de Vaca Encounters Texas Coastal Indians

Alvar Nuñez de Vaca, Andrés Dorantes de Carranza, Alonso Castillo Maldonado, and Estevan (Dorantes's slave) were the sole survivors of the failed Pánfilo de Narváez expedition of 1528. Below are some of Cabeza de Vaca's recollections of their experiences when they came ashore in Texas and first made contact with Native Americans. These remembrances come from his report to Viceroy Antonio de Mendoza, an extremely valuable resource which historians and anthropologists still use to better their understanding of Native American groups in Texas at the time of European arrival.

. . . Near daybreak I fancied to hear the sound of breakers, for as the coast was low, their noise was greater. Surprised at it, I called to the skipper, who said he thought we were near the shore. Sounding, we found seven fathoms, and he was of the opinion that we should keep off shore till dawn. So I took the oar and rowed along the coast, from which we were one league away, and turned the stern to seaward.

Close to shore a wave took us and hurled the barge a horse's length out of water. With the violent shock nearly all the people who lay in the boat like dead came to themselves, and, seeing we were close to land, began to crawl out on all fours. As they took to some rocks, we built a fire and toasted some of our maize. We found rain water, and with the warmth of the fire people revived and began to cheer up. The day we arrived there was the sixth of the month of November.

After the people had eaten I sent Lope de Oviedo, who was the strongest and heartiest of all, to go to some trees nearby and climb to the top of one, examine the surroundings and the country in which we were. He did so and found we were on an island, and that the

11

ground was hollowed out, as if cattle had gone over it, from which it seemed to him that the land belonged to Christians, and so he told us. I sent him again to look and examine more closely if there were any worn trails, and not to go too far so as not to run into danger. He went, found a footpath, followed it for about one-half league, and saw several Indian huts which stood empty because the Indians had gone out into the field.

He took away a cooking pot, a little dag and a few ruffs and turned back, but as he seemed to delay I sent two other Christians to look for him and find out what had happened. They met him nearby and saw that three Indians, with bows and arrows, were following and calling to him, while he did the same to them by signs. So he came to where we were, the Indians remaining behind, seated on the beach. Half an hour after a hundred Indian archers joined them, and our fright was such that, whether tall or little, it made them appear giants to us. They stood still close to the first ones, near where we were.

We could not defend ourselves, as there were scarcely three of us who could stand on their feet. The inspector and I stepped forward and called them. They came, and we tried to quiet them the best we could and save ourselves, giving them beads and bells. Each one of them gave me an arrow in token of friendship, and by signs they gave us to understand that on the following morning they would come back with food, as then they had none.

The next day, at sunrise, which was the hour the Indians had given us to understand, they came as promised and brought us plenty of fish and some roots which they eat that taste like nuts, some bigger, some smaller, most of which are taken out of the water with much trouble.

In the evening they returned and brought us more fish and some of the same roots, and they brought their women and children to look at us. They thought themselves very rich with the little bells and beads we gave them, and thereafter visited us daily with the same things as before. As we saw ourselves provided with fish, roots, water and the other things we had asked for, we concluded to embark again and continue our voyage.

We lifted the barge out of the sand into which it had sunk (for which purpose we all had to take off our clothes) and had great work to set her afloat, as our condition was such that much lighter things would have given us trouble.

Then we embarked. Two crossbow shots from shore a wave swept over us, we all got wet, and being naked and the cold very great, the oars dropped out of our hands. The next wave overturned the barge. The inspector and two others clung to her to save themselves, but the contrary happened; they got underneath the barge and were drowned.

The shore being very rough, the sea took the others and thrust them, half dead, on the beach of the same island again, less the three that had perished underneath the barge. The rest of us, as naked as we had been born, had lost everything, and while it was not worth much, to us it meant a great deal. It was in November, bitterly cold, and we in such a state that every bone could easily be counted, and we looked like death itself. . . .

At sunset the Indians, thinking we had not left, came to bring us food, but when they saw us in such a different attire from before and so strange-looking, they were so frightened as to turn back. I went to call them, and in great fear they came. I then gave them to understand by signs how we had lost a barge and three of our men had been drowned, while before them there lay two of our men dead, with the others about to go the same way.

Upon seeing the disaster we had suffered, our misery and distress, the Indians sat down with us and all began to weep out of compassion for our misfortune, and for more than half an hour they wept so loud and so sincerely that it could be heard far away.

Verily, to see beings so devoid of reason, untutored, so like unto brutes, yet so deeply moved by pity for us, it increased my feelings and those of others in my company for our own misfortune. When the lament was over, I spoke to the Christians and asked them if they would like me to beg the Indians to take us to their homes. Some of the men, who had been to New Spain, answered that it would be unwise, as, once at their abode, they might sacrifice us to their idols.

Still, seeing there was no remedy and that in any other way death was surer and nearer, I did not mind what they said, but begged the Indians to take us to their dwellings, at which they showed great pleasure, telling us to tarry yet a little, but that they would do what we wished. Soon thirty of them loaded themselves with firewood and went to their lodges, which were far away, while we stayed with the others until it was almost dark. Then they took hold of us and carried us along hurriedly to where they lived. . . .

Against the cold, and lest on the way some one of us might faint or die, they had provided four or five big fires on the road, at each one of which they warmed us. As soon as they saw we had regained a little warmth and strength they would carry us to the next fire with such haste that our feet barely touched the ground.

So we got to their dwellings, where we saw they had built a hut for us with many fires in it. About one hour after our arrival began to dance and to make a great celebration (which lasted the whole night), although there was neither pleasure, feast nor sleep in it for us, since we expected to be sacrificed. In the morning they again gave us fish and roots, and treated us so well that we became reassured, losing somewhat our apprehension of being butchered.

Source: Alvar Nuñez Cabeza de Vaca, Marco da Niza, Antonio de Mendoza, *The Journey of Alvar Nuñez Cabeza de Vaca and his companions from Florida to the Pacific, 1528-1536*, trans. Fanny Bandelier, and Adolph Francis Alphonse (New York: A.S. Barnes & Company, 1905)

THOUGHT QUESTIONS:

1. What hardships did Cabeza de Vaca and his companions suffer upon their arrival to Texas?

2. How did the Native Americans react to the Spanish castaways?

3. Was Cabeza de Vaca and the other Spaniards surprised by the natives' reaction to them? Why or why not?

Coronado's Report to Viceroy Antonio de Mendoza Sent From Cíbola, August 3, 1540

In the early 1540s, Francisco Vásquez de Coronado led a Spanish expedition into Texas and the Southwest seeking the fabled Seven Cities, a cluster of fictitious wealthy settlements supposedly laden with gold, which seven Portuguese bishops founded after leaving their homeland in the eighth century due to the Muslim invasion of the Iberian Peninsula. Below are excerpts from Coronado's account of the expedition to Viceroy Mendoza and the actual "cities" he discovered.

Of the situation and condition of the Seven Cities called the kingdom of Cevola, and the sort of people and their customs, and of the animals which are found there. . . .

The Seven Cities are seven little villages, all having the kind of houses I have described. They are all within a radius of five leagues. They are all called the kingdom of Cevola, and each has its own name and no single one is called Cevola, but all together are called Cevola. This one which I have called a city I have named Granada, partly because it has some similarity to it, as well as out of regard for Your Lordship. In this place where I am now lodged there are perhaps 200 houses, all surrounded by a wall, and it seems to me that with the other houses, which are not so surrounded, there might be altogether 500 families. There is another town nearby, which is one of the seven, but somewhat larger than this, and another of the same size as this, & the other four are somewhat smaller. I send them all to Your Lordship, painted with the route. The skin on which the painting is made was found here with other skins.

The people of the towns seem to me to be of ordinary size and intelligent, although I do not think that they have the judgment & intelligence which they ought to have to build these houses in the way in which they have, for most of them are entirely naked except the covering of their privy parts, and they have painted mantles like the one which I send to Your Lordship. They do not raise cotton, because the country is very cold, but they wear mantles, as may be seen by the exhibit which I send. It is also true that some cotton thread was found in their houses. They wear the hair on their heads like the Mexicans. They all have good figures, and are well bred. I think that they have a quantity of turquoises, which they had removed with the rest of their goods, except the corn, when I arrived, because I did not find any women here nor any men under 15 years or over 60, except two or three old men who remained in command of all the other men and the warriors. . . .

The climate of this country and the temperature of the air is almost like that of Mexico, because it is sometimes hot and sometimes it rains. I have not yet seen it rain, however, except once when there fell a little shower with wind, such as often falls in Spain. The snow and the cold are usually very great, according to what the natives of the country all say. This may very probably be so, both because of the nature of the country and the sort of houses they build and the skins and other things which these people have to protect them from the cold. There are no kinds of fruit or fruit trees. The country is all level, & is nowhere shut in by high mountains, although there are some hills and rough passages. There are not many birds, probably because of the cold, and because there are no mountains near. There are no trees fit for firewood here, because they can bring enough for their needs from a clump of very small cedars four leagues distant. Very good grass is found a quarter of a league away, where there is a pasturage for our horses as well as mowing for hay, of which we had great need, because our horses were so weak and feeble when they arrived.

The food which they eat in this country is corn, of which they have a great abundance, & beans & venison, which they probably eat (although they say that they do not), because we found many skins of deer and hares and rabbits. They make the best corn cakes I have ever seen anywhere, and this is what everybody ordinarily eats. They have the very best arrangement and machinery for grinding that was ever seen. One of these Indian women here will grind as much as four of the Mexicans. They have very good salt in crystals, which they bring from a lake a day's journey distant from here. . . .

. . . They have many animals—bears, tigers, lions, porcupines, and some sheep as big as a horse, with very large horns and little tails. I have seen some of their horns the size of which was something to marvel at. There are also wild goats, whose heads I have seen, and the paws of the bears and the skins of the wild boars. For game they have deer, leopards, & very large deer, & everyone thinks that some of them are larger than that animal which Your Lordship favored me with, which belonged to Juan Melaz. They inhabit some plains eight day's journey toward the north. They have some of their skins here very well dressed, & they prepare and paint them where they kill the cows, according to what they tell me.

I send you a cow skin, some turquoises, and two earrings of the same, and fifteen of the Indian combs, and some plates decorated with these turquoises, and two baskets made of wicker, of which the Indians have a large supply. I also send two rolls, such as the women usually wear on their heads when they bring water from the spring, the same way that they do in Spain. One of these Indian women, with one of these rolls on her head, will carry a jar of water up a ladder without touching it with her hands. And, lastly, I send you samples of the weapons with which the natives of this country fight, a shield, a hammer, and a bow with some arrows, among which there are two with bone points, the like of which have never been seen, according to what these conquerors say. As far as I can judge, it does not appear to me that there is any hope of getting gold or silver, but I trust in God that, if there is any, we shall get our share of it, and it shall not escape us through any lack of diligence in the search. I am unable to give Your Lordship any certain information about the dress of the women, because the Indians keep them guarded so carefully that I have not seen any, except two old women. These had on two long skirts reaching down to their feet and open in front, & a girdle, & they are tied together with some cotton strings. I asked the Indians to give me one of those which they wore, to send to you, since they were not willing to show me the women. They brought me two mantles, which are these that I send, almost painted over. They have two tassels, like the women of Spain, which hang somewhat over their shoulders.

Some gold & silver has been found in this place, which those who know about minerals say is not bad. I have not yet been able to learn from these people where they got it. I perceive that they refuse to tell me the truth in everything, because they think that I shall have to depart from here in a short time, as I have said. But I trust in God that they will not be able to avoid answering much longer. . . .

Source: George Parker Winship, ed., *The Coronado Expedition, 1540-1542* (Washington, D.C.: Government Printing Office, 1896), 552-563.

THOUGHT QUESTIONS:

1. How does Coronado describe the people that he encountered, as well as their food and their customs?

2. How does Coronado describe the climate and terrain that the Native Americans inhabited?

3. What forms of wealth did Coronado find, and not find, in the region that he explored?

The Adventures of Luis de Moscoso Alvarado in Texas

Unlike other expeditions that originated in Mexico City, Hernando de Soto's expedition reached present-day Texas from the east. With an army of 600, De Soto landed at Tampa Bay, Florida on May 25, 1539. After cutting a swath through the present-day southeastern portion of the United States, killing hundreds of Native Americans along the way, the expedition arrived at the Mississippi River, where de Soto died of a fever on May 21, 1542. Command of the expedition shifted to Luis de Moscoso Alvarado, who led the Spaniards into southeastern Oklahoma and then circled back into East Texas where the Spaniards encountered the Hasinai, a Caddoan tribe. The expedition traveled as far south as the Trinity River and may have reached the Brazos River before turning back to the Mississippi River. Below is what many scholars believe to be an account of the expedition's travels through Texas.

The Governor [Moscoso] set out from Nondacao for Soacatino, and on the fifth day came to a province called Aays. The inhabitants had never heard of the Christians. So soon as they observed them entering the territory the people were called out, who, as fast as they could get together, came by fifties and hundreds on the road, to give battle. While some encountered us, others fell upon our rear; and when we followed up those, these pursued us. The attack continued during the greater part of the day, until we arrived at their town. Some men were injured, and some horses, but nothing so as to hinder travel, there being not one dangerous wound among all. The Indians suffered great slaughter.

The day on which the Governor departed, the guide told him he had heard it said in Nondacao, that the Indians of Soacatino [possibly northeastern Texas] had seen other Christians; at which we were all delighted, thinking it might be true, and that they could have come by the way of New Spain; for if it were so, finding nothing in Florida of value, we should be able to go out of it, there being fear we might perish in some wilderness. The Governor, having been led for two days out of the way, ordered that the Indian be put to the torture, when he confessed that his master, the Cacique of Nondacao, had ordered him to take them in that manner, we being his enemies, and he, as his vassal, was bound to obey him. He was commanded to be cast to the dogs, and another Indian guided us to Soacatino, where we came the following day.

The country was very poor, and the want of maize was greatly felt. The natives being asked if they had any knowledge of other Christians, said they had heard that near there, towards the south, such men were moving about. For twenty days the march was through a very thinly peopled country, where great privation and toil were endured; the little maize there was, the Indians having buried in the scrub, where the Christians, at the close of the day's march, when they were well weary, went trailing, to seek for what they had need of it to eat.

Arrived at a province called Guasco [probably near the Brazos River], they found maize, with which they loaded the horses and the Indians; thence they went to another settlement, called Naquiscoça, the inhabitants of which said that they had no knowledge of any other Christians. The Governor ordered them put to torture, when they stated that farther on, in the territories of another chief, called Naçacahoz, the Christians had arrived, and gone back toward the west, whence they came. He reached there in two days, and took some women, among whom was one who said that she had seen Christians, and, having been in their hands, had made her escape from them. The Governor sent a captain with fifteen cavalry to where she said they were seen, to discover if there were any marks of horses, or signs of any Christians having been there; and after travelling three or four leagues, she who was the guide declared that all she had said was false; and so it was deemed of everything else the Indians had told of having seen Christians in [Texas].

As the region thereabout was scarce of maize, and no information could be got of any inhabited country to the west, the Governor went back to Guasco. The residents stated, that ten days' journey from there, toward the sunset, was a river called Daycao, whither they sometimes went to drive and kill deer, and whence they had seen persons on the other bank, but without knowing what people they were. The Christians took as much maize as they could find, to carry with them; and journeying ten days through a wilderness, they arrived at the river of which the Indians had spoken. Ten horsemen sent in advance by the Governor had crossed; and, following a road leading up from the bank, they came upon an encampment of Indians living in very small huts, who, directly as they saw the Christians, took to flight, leaving what they had, indications only of poverty and misery. So wretched was the country, that what was found everywhere, put together, was not half an alqueire of maize. Taking two natives, they went back to the river, where the Governor waited; and on coming to question the captives, to ascertain what towns there might be to the west, no Indian was found in the camp who knew their language.

The Governor commanded the captains and principal personages to be called together that he might determine now by their opinions what was best to do. The majority declared it their judgment to return to the River, Grande of Guachoya, because in Anilco and thereabout was much maize; that during the winter they would build brigantines, and the following spring go down the river in them in quest of the sea, where having arrived, they would follow the coast thence along to New Spain,—an enterprise which, although it appeared to be one difficult to accomplish, yet from their experience it offered the only course to be pursued. They could not travel by land, for want of an interpreter; and they considered the country farther on, beyond the River Daycao, on which they were, to be that which Cabeza de Vaca had said in his narrative should have to be traversed, where the Indians wandered like Arabs, having no settled place of residence, living on prickly pears, the roots of plants, and game ; and that if this should be so, and they, entering upon that tract, found no provision for sustenance during winter, they must inevitably perish, it being already the beginning of October ; and if they remained any longer where they were, what with rains and snow, they should neither be able to fall back, nor, in a land so poor as that, to subsist.

The Governor, who longed to be again where he could get his full measure of sleep, rather than govern and go conquering a country so beset for him with hardships, directly returned, getting back from whence he came.

Source: Luys Hernandez de Biedma, *Narratives of the Career of Hernado de Soto in the Conquest of Florida as Told by a Knight of Elvas*, trans. Buckingham Smith (New York: A.S. Barnes & Company, 1904), 176-180

THOUGHT QUESTIONS:

1. How did the Spaniards of the DeSoto-Moscoso Expedition treat the Native Americans that they encountered?

2. How did the Native Americans react to the members of the expedition?

3. How does this account compare with that of Cabeza de Vaca and Coronado?

The De León Expedition Finds the Ruins of Fort St. Louis, 1689

*In 1685, René-Robert Cavelier, Sieur de La Salle, led a French expedition to plant a colony at the mouth of the Mississippi River to control that mighty waterway and to begin the occupation of the Louisiana Territory that he recently claimed for France. After overshooting his intended target, La Salle's group wound up instead in Matagorda Bay on the Texas Gulf Coast. Upon building a stockade that he called Fort St. Louis, La Salle spent much of his time trying to ascertain his bearings to see how far his colony's location was from the Mississippi. After two years, with supplies dwindling, hostile Karankawa natives looming nearby, and his situation increasingly desperate after a storm sunk **La Belle**, his last ship, La Salle was leading a small expedition northward in search of the great river when a mutinous soldier murdered him. Not long afterward, the Karankawas launched a final raid upon Fort St. Louis, killing the remaining twenty adults and hauling away five children. [The wreckage of **La Belle** was found in Matagorda Bay in 1995. The following year, archeologists finally discovered the site of Fort St. Louis and began extensive excavations.]*

When rumors first swirled that the French were encroaching on lands to the north of Mexico, Spanish authorities responded by sending multiple reconnaissance expeditions but did not find anything until a party led by Alonso De León stumbled upon the remnants of Fort St. Louis in early 1689. The following excerpt of a report from that expedition, probably authored by De León himself, relays what the soldiers found upon their arrival at the destroyed outpost several months after the attack. The confirmation of the French presence soon led Spanish of-ficials to authorize the commencement of missionary operations in Texas beginning with the establishment of Mission San Francisco de los Tejas among the Caddo Indians in 1690.

Friday the 22nd [of April], as we were near the settlement, our party set out, though the day dawned rainy. Three leagues down the creek we found it. Having halted with the forces about an arquebus-shot away, we went to see it, and found all the houses sacked, all the chests, bottle-cases, and all the rest of the settler's furniture broken; apparently more than two hundred books, torn apart, and with the rotten leaves scattered through the patios---all in French. We noted that the perpetrators of this massacre had pulled every-thing that the colonists had out of their chests, and divided the booty among themselves; and that what they had not cared for they had torn to pieces, making a frightful sack of all the French possessed; for besides the evidence involved in our finding everything in this condition, further proof was found in the fact that in the rancherías through which we had passed before our arrival at the settlement, we had found in the possession of the Indians some French books in very good condition, with other articles of very little value. These books were recovered and their titles committed to memory. The Indians had done this damage not only to the furnishings, but also to the arms; for we found more than a hundred stocks of flintlock arquebuses, without locks or barrels. They must have carried these off, as was proved by an [arquebus] barrel found at some distance from the houses.

We found three dead bodies scattered over the plain. One of these, from the dress that still clung to the bones, appeared to be that of a woman. We took the bodies up, chanted mass with the bodies present, and buried them. We looked for the other dead bodies, but could not find them; whence we supposed that they had been thrown into the creek and had been eaten by alligators, of which there are many. The principal house of this settlement is in the form of a fort, made of ship's timber, with a second story, also made of ship's timber, and with a slope to turn off water. Next to it, without any parti-tion, is another apartment, not so strong, which must have served as a chapel where mass was said. The other five houses are of stakes, covered with mud inside and out; their roofs are covered with buffalo-hides. All are quite useless for any defense. In and about the fort and the houses were eight pieces of artillery, iron, of medium bore (four or five-pounders), and three very old swivels whose chambers were lacking. Some iron bars were also found, and some ship's nails, estimated as altogether about five hundredweight. Some of the guns were scattered over the ground and some were on their broken carriages. There were some casks with their heads knocked in and their contents spilled out so that nothing was worth anything. Around the building was also some tackle, much the worse for wear. The settlement was on a beautiful, level site, so as to be capable of defense in any event. On the frame of the principal door of the fort was inscribed the date of the settlement....

Source: Translated and cited in Elizabeth Howard West, "De León's Expedition of 1689: An Annotated Translation," *The Quarterly of the Texas State Historical Association*, Vol. 8, No. 3 (Jan., 1905), 216-218.

THOUGHT QUESTIONS:

1. According to the Spanish writer, what had the Karankawa attackers done to the property of the French after their attack?

2. How many bodies did the Spanish find at the fort? What did they do with them? Where did most of the bodies of the other French probably end up, according to the writer?

3. In what condition did the Spanish expedition find the buildings inside Fort St. Louis? How suitable for defense did the writer find the fort's location in general?

The 1783 Census of Texas

The Spanish regularly gathered annual census data for their provinces. The Center for American History at the University of Texas preserves microfilmed copies of Texas census data taken from the 1770s through the Mexican period of the mid-1830s. Below are the findings [translated from Spanish] for 1783.

Statement that manifests the number of vassals and inhabitants which the King has in this province, with distinction as to class, condition and race of all the persons of both sexes, including the children.

Names of the Populations	Men	Women	Boys	Girls	Male Slaves	Female Slaves
Presidio of San Antonio de Béxar and Village of San Fernando	331	311	321	264	8	13
Mission of:						
San José	41	31	26	25		
San Juan Capistrano	53	26	13	7		
San Francisco de la Espada	32	28	30	6		
Nuestra Señora de la Concepción	32	29	18	8		
San Antonio de Valero	49	35	36	29		
Presidio of La Bahía del Espíritu Santo	193	147	68	45	1	
Mission of La Bahía del Espíritu Santo	75	66	33	40		
Town of Nuestra Señora del Pilar de los Nacogdoches	129	104	52	50	8	6
Totals of the present year	935	777	597	474	17	19
Totals for last year	947	786	597	474	17	19
Decrease	12	9				
General Summary:						
Of Spaniards	488	373	376	340		
Of Indians	290	241	70	76		
Of Mestizos	43	38	32	12		
Of Mulattos [*de Color Quebrado*]	114	125	119	46		
Of Slaves					17	19
Totals	935	777	597	474	17	19

General Summary:

Of secular ecclesiastics	3					
Of regular clergy	8					
Of those married	655	655				
Of widows and widowers	61	122				
Of single persons	208					
Totals	935	777	597	474	17	19

Royal Presidio of San Antonio de Béxar, December 31, 1783
[Signed] Domingo Cabello [Governor]

THOUGHT QUESTIONS:

1. How many major population centers (for the times) existed in Texas in 1783? Where were they located and what was their size?

2. Describe the racial makeup of the Texas population in 1783.

3. With regard to the data provided, what information surprised you the most? Which information surprised you the least? Why?

The Neutral Ground Agreement

When Napoleon Bonaparte sold the Louisiana Territory to the United States in 1803, a potential for conflict arose between the U.S. and Spain due to a lack of specificity concerning the territory's western borders. While Americans began to claim that the boundary line should exist west of the Sabine River, Spanish authorities asserted that the region began and ended with the Arroyo Hondo, a tributary of the Red River in Louisiana to the east of the Sabine.

While never officially accepted by the Spanish or American governments, the Neutral Ground Agreement emerged as an informal understanding between the American governor of Louisiana, General James Wilkinson, and the Spanish General Simon Herrera to avoid conflict by refusing to enforce claims to the region between the Sabine River and the Arroyo Hondo. Settlers and troops from both countries were to avoid the area, but the region became a haven for political exiles, refugees, military deserters, and criminals. The Adams-Onís Treaty, ratified in 1821, finally established the border between Texas and the United States at the Sabine and Red rivers.

The following letter is Wilkinson's offer, addressed to the Spanish governor of Texas, which General Herrera accepted.

Letter, dated October 29, 1806, from U. S. General James Wilkinson to Governor of Texas, Antonio Cordero y Bustamente:

Sir, . . . In my letter to your Excellency the 24th ultimo, . . . I emphatically remarked to your Excellency, "that the ultimate decision of the competent authority had been taken, that my orders were absolute, and my determination first to assert and, under God, to sustain the jurisdiction of the United States to the Sabine River, against any force which may be opposed to me"...

Your Excellency appears to lay much stress on the letter of Captain General Salcedo [Don Nemecio Salcedo, Commandant-General of the Interior Provinces] to Governor [William] Claiborne [Governor of Louisiana Territory], but as that letter treats generally on subjects of civil import, and as my functions are purely Military, it does not fall within my province to take particular cognizance of it. I will however beg leave to observe that his Excellency's exposition of the grounds on which he asserts the Arroyo Honda [sic] to be the line of provincial demarcation, carries with it an air of much plausibility, but being diametrically opposed to the sense of Expression of my Government, I cannot respect it; ...

Your Excellency is sensible to the extreme delicacy with which a Military man may exercise his discretion, when shackled with specific orders, yet such instances have occurred even on the field of Battle and must frequently become necessary, where operations are at issue a thousand miles from the source of authority. Believing that the controversy in which we are engaged presents a case precisely in point, I am willing to risque [sic] the approbations of my Government to perpetuate the tranquility of the inhospitable wilds, where waving the point of Honor, the subject of our test is scarcely worth the blood of one brave man.

Permit me then in the true spirit of reconciliation to propose to your Excellency, without yielding a Pretension, ceding a right, or interfering with the discussions which, belong to our superiors, to restore the "Status quo" at the delivery of the Province of Lousiana [sic] to the United States, by the withdrawal of our troops from the points they at present occupy to the post of Nacogdoches and Natchitoches respectively; your Excellency's assent to this proposition shall be conclusive on my conduct, and I will commence my retrograde, on the day you break up your Camp on the right bank of the Sabine; under the joint stipulation that the troops of my Command shall not cross the Arroyo Honda, so long as those under your orders are restrained from crossing the Sabine, or until we may receive further instruction from our respective Governments ...

Source: U.S. War Department Records, National Archives

THOUGHT QUESTIONS:

1. According to Wilkinson, why did he undertake the proposed agreement?

2. On what authority did the general say he had to make such a deal?

3. What problems might Wilkinson have encountered if President Thomas Jefferson or other superiors in the U.S. government disapproved of his actions?

Spanish Map

**Credit: UTSA's Institute of Texas Cultures, #070-0173,
Source: Yoakum, H.: "History of Texas," 1856.**

This map of Spanish Texas shows locations of various Native American tribes, settlements, missions, and various roads: Presidio Road, La Bahia Road, Herrera's Road, Atascosito Road, and Old Comanche Trail.

THOUGHT QUESTION:

Locate "The Neutral Ground" on the map. Why was this area established?

James Long's Cannon

**Credit: UTSA's Institute of Texan Cultures, #068-2060,
Courtesy of La Bahía Presidio, Goliad, TX**

James Long led an early filibustering adventure, one related to the western boundary of the Louisiana Territory. The expedition began in Natchez, Mississippi, where local leaders condemned the boundary set by the Adams-Onís Treaty of 1819 because it excluded Texas. Long's force captured Nacogdoches on June 21, 1819, set up a provisional government, and declared Texas independent. However, a Spanish expedition soon routed Long and his followers, chasing them out of East Texas. Long later sailed southward to capture Spanish fortifications on the Gulf Coast but was found and arrested. Sent to a prison in Mexico City, Long was accidentally shot by a guard and died.

THOUGHT QUESTION:

What were the motives of "filibusters"? Were they working for the interests of Spain? What were their intentions and ultimate purpose?

BIOGRAPHIES

ESTEVAN (?-1539) Estevan, the first person of African origin to enter Texas and one of the earliest non-indigenous explorers of the region, was born in Azemmour, a port city on the Atlantic coast of Morrocco. In 1513, Portuguese soldiers under orders of King Manuel I captured Azemmour and subjugated its people. During a severe drought in 1520-21, the Portuguese decided that it was more profitable to sell the citizens of Azemmour into slavery in Europe rather than use the Moroccans as forced laborers in their own country. As a result, Estevan became the personal servant of Andrés Dorantes de Carranza, a native of the Castilian town of Gibraleón.

In 1527, Dorantes and his servant accompanied Pánfilo de Narváez on an ill-fated expedition to conquer Florida. After a lengthy temporary stay in Cuba, the expedition arrived on the coast of Florida, near present-day Tampa Bay, on April 12, 1528. After enduring frequent hardships associated with the uninviting terrain of the peninsula and suffering numerous casualties resulting from armed clashes with the indigenous population, Narváez decided to abandon their original mission and to make their way to the safety of the Spanish settlements at the mouth of the Pánuco River on the Gulf Coast of Mexico. Believing that the expedition could reach their destination by sea, Narváez ordered his men to slaughter their horses for food and build five crude barges. The 250 survivors set sail from Florida in September 1528.

All seemed to go well during the first month of their journey, but soon the Spaniards' food and water supplies ran short and their small vessels became separated after sailing through several coastal storms. Eventually, the small crafts ran aground at different locations on the Texas coast, with Estevan's raft coming ashore near Galveston Island. Setting out on foot, Estevan, Dorantes, and Castillo made their way to Matagorda Bay. During the next few years, the men were made captives of local Native American tribes. Their continued survival rested on the fact that the indigenous people believed that castaways were gifted healers who could treat the native population's infirmed and injured. Six years after landing on the Texas coast, a fourth survivor of the Narváez expedition, Álvar Núñez Cabaza de Vaca, joined them. After enduring two more years of hardship, the four men successfully escaped from the natives who had enslaved them and made their way inland, beginning a two-year journey across southern Texas and northern Mexico.

Reaching Culiacán near the Pacific coast of Mexico in early 1536, Estevan and his companions had traveled approximately two thousand miles on foot. During their journey, Estevan proved invaluable to the group's survival. He was able to quickly learn the sign language of the native people and was able to communicate with the indigenous population. As a result, the four survivors were able to learn which trails to follow and which ones to avoid during their journey through unfamiliar territories. After arriving in Culiacán, the survivors were sent to Mexico City in July 1536 where Estevan was recognized as a fluent translator and for supposedly knowing the location of the legendary golden Seven Cities which, according to Spanish folklore, were settled by seven Portuguese bishops who left their homeland after the Muslim invasion of the Iberian Peninsula in the eighth century.

In the spring of 1539, Viceroy Antonio de Mendoza organized an expedition to explore the unsettled area of northern New Spain and to find the cities of gold. Mendoza named Fray Marcos de Niza as the leader of the expedition and assigned Estevan (whom Mendoza had earlier purchased from Dorantes) to Niza as a guide. By March 1539, the expedition reached the Río Mayo, near present-day Sonora. There, Estevan grew weary of the slow progress of the other members in the expedition and received Niza's permission to serve as an advance scout. Estevan was several days ahead of the main body of the expedition when he reached a Zuñi Indian settlement (Hawikuh) located in present-day western New Mexico. The village elders were very distrustful of the stranger's presence, believing that his medicine gourd decorated with owl feathers signified death. Apparently, Estevan was not aware of certain cultural differences between the Native Americans that he had encountered in Texas and those living in New Mexico. It proved a fatal mistake. Not only did the Zuñis deny Estevan and the small group of scouts in his advance party food, water, and shelter upon arrival to their pueblo, the next morning they attacked Estevan's encampment outside of the village. Estevan and his companions were killed trying to flee the Zuñi warriors. Fray Niza, who later claimed to view the pueblo from a distance, returned to Mexico City and reported to the viceroy that he had seen one of the fabled golden cities. Niza may have allowed his eyes to deceive him, or possibly he invented his observation in order to lure the Spanish northward with tales of wealth in order to spur on missionary work in the region. Not until Francisco Vásquez de Coronado led another expedition into the region in 1540 did the Spaniards realize that the village's buildings were not made of gold but rather were constructed of adobe, a sundried mixture of straw and clay.

JANE HERBERT WILKINSON LONG (1798-1880). Often revered as the first English-speaking woman to give birth in Texas (though not true), Jane Herbert Wilkinson Long was born on July 23, 1798 in Charles County, Maryland. Her father died a year after her birth. In 1811, she moved with her mother and nine siblings to Washington in the Mississippi Territory. Two years later, her mother died. Jane began to reside with her older sister, Barbara, the wife of Alexander Calvit who owned a plantation near Natchez. In 1815, while living with the Calvit family, she met and married James Long, a veteran of the Battle of New Orleans. The couple lived in Natchez for the next four years, with James working as a physician and merchant. When her husband joined a filibuster expedition seeking to separate Texas from Spanish rule in June 1819, Jane remained behind because she was in the late stages of her second pregnancy. Shortly after giving birth, Jane joined her husband, leaving her two children and a slave named Kian with the Cavits. Less than three months after arriving, Spanish troops from San Antonio threatened the headquarters that Long's expedition established in Nacogdoches, forcing Jane and others to retreat toward the Louisiana-Texas border. At the Sabine River, James Long caught up with Jane and instructed her to return to the Cavit family who had relocated to Alexandria, Louisiana. When Jane arrived there, she learned that her second child had died from an illness.

By 1821, the Longs lived with other expedition members and their families next to their new headquarters, a makeshift fort located on Bolivar Peninsula in Galveston Bay. In September 1821, James left for La Bahía and elsewhere in Texas to gain support for the cause. During his journey, he was taken prisoner in San Antonio and sent to Mexico City. After a six-month incarceration, a guard reportedly shot him by accident. Not knowing that her husband had been killed, Jane waited for James to return even after the other families began to leave the Bolivar Peninsula community. Pregnant again, she was alone except for her daughter and Kian. On December 21, 1821, she gave birth to her third daughter, Mary James, which earned her the accolade of "Mother of Texas." This moniker is incorrect, however, because census records dated between 1807 and 1821 show that a number of children in Texas were born to Anglo-American mothers prior to 1821.

In early 1822, suffering from the harsh environment on the peninsula, Jane decided to join a family of incoming immigrants planning to reside along the San Jacinto River. By mid-summer, she discovered the fate of her husband. She left for Alexandria in September 1823. Following Mary James' death, Jane returned to Texas with the Calvit family in June 1824. Empresario Stephen F. Austin soon granted her title to lands in Fort Bend and Waller counties. Jane preferred to live in San Felipe until 1830, when she escorted her surviving daughter to school in Mississippi. After her daughter married, Jane returned to Texas with the couple and engaged in a number of business pursuits, including operating a boarding house, running a plantation (with nineteen slaves by 1861), raising some cattle, and buying and selling land. She remained in Texas for the rest of her life and died on December 30, 1880.

JOSÉ BERNARDO MAXIMILIANO GUTIÉRREZ DE LARA (1774-1841). José Bernardo Gutiérrez de Lara, the Mexican revolutionary leader of the Gutiérrez-Magee Expedition, was born on August 20, 1774 in Revilla, a small town planned by José Escandón on the southern side of the Rio Grande in Nuevo Santander, which Gutiérrez's family had helped to establish twenty-five years earlier. As a young adult, he married a cousin and prospered for many years as a local merchant and manager of the hacienda that he inherited from his father.

When Miguel Hidalgo's revolt erupted in September 1810, Gutiérrez was sympathetic to the movement. Like many creoles influenced by the American and French Revolutions, he held nationalist views and resented Spanish colonial rule. He committed to the cause in December 1810 by writing, publishing, and circulating numerous pamphlets promoting independence in Nuevo Santander, Coahuila, and Texas. Gutiérrez also encouraged soldiers to defect to the Hidalgistas.

After a major defeat of the Hidalgo forces in January 1811, and subsequent flight northward, Gutiérrez made direct contact with rebel leaders at Saltillo in March. Needing strong allies in northern Mexico, believing Gutiérrez's zeal, and thankful for his efforts thus far, Hidalgo and the other leaders named him a lieutenant colonel in their forces and charged him with returning to Nuevo Santander in order to rally the province's populace against Spanish authority. However, word soon reached the revolutionaries that diplomats sent to the United States to drum up support for the cause had been seized in Texas. Gutiérrez volunteered to replace them, but before departing for Louisiana, he worked to build up resistance forces along the Rio Grande. In April, he heard the disastrous news of Hidalgo's capture and execution. Fearing for his safety, Gutiérrez accelerated his travel preparations and departed for the United States by early August, arriving in Washington, D.C. by mid-December 1811. There he visited Secretary of State James Monroe and the ministers of several European countries who displayed sympathy but provided no firm commitments. He also met with José Alvarez de Toledo, a Cuban creole revolutionary who was forming his own plans to liberate portions of the Americas from Spain. A diary kept during his stay reveals that Gutiérrez devoted some time to sightseeing. He reflected positively on his observations of America—marveling, for example, at water-powered factories in northern Virginia and praising humane treatment of prisoners at a Philadelphia reform penitentiary that he visited.

Gutiérrez returned to Louisiana in March 1812 and soon met with William Shaler, a U.S. special agent ordered to establish friendly ties with Mexican revolutionary leaders to create a basis for strong ties between the United States and Mexico if a successful revolt took place. Over the next several months, Shaler helped Gutiérrez recruit and organize the "Republican Army of the North"–a force primarily composed of U.S. volunteers and French Louisianans later to be supplemented with a mixture of Tejanos and Mexicans that would launch the Gutiérrez-Magee Expedition into Texas. The filibusters entered Texas in August 1812, easily capturing Nacogdoches and soon marching on La Bahía. Following La Bahía's capture, royalist forces besieged the Republican Army for three months until driven off. After the Battle of Salado on March 29, 1813, the expeditionary forces triumphantly entered San Antonio.

Discontent among Anglo members of the Republican Army began to spread after Gutiérrez sanctioned the execution of Governor Manuel Salcedo (who had tried and executed Hidalgo) and other royalist prisoners. Further, while the new Texas Constitution that Gutiérrez promulgated offered a league of land for every six months' service in the fight for Texas independence, the document also created a provisional government that centralized much power in the hands of a junta and an appointed governor (Gutiérrez). These developments played into the hands of William Shaler, who came to oppose Gutiérrez because of the latter's refusal to make firm commitments with respect to American territorial interests in Texas plus the agent's belief that José Alvarez de Toledo was a better man for the job based on his political skills, refinement, and overall temperament. Through propaganda publications designed to undermine the leader's base of support (including the *Gaceta de Tejas*—the first Texas newspaper, probably created in Nacogdoches) with allegations of corruption and authoritarian tendencies, plus envoys sent to San Antonio touting Toledo's credentials, Shaler and Toledo began to place doubts about Gutiérrez in the minds of many Republican Army fighters. When Toledo boldly arrived in San Antonio on August 1, 1813, the junta asked Gutiérrez to step aside, paving the way for Toledo to become the newly appointed governor. The shunned leader left for exile in Louisiana a few days later, a move that may have saved his life after the forces of Joaquín de Arredondo crushed the Republican Army at the Battle of the Medina River on August 18.

From Louisiana, Gutiérrez continued to seek American support for a new liberation fight against Spain. In 1821, he rejoiced following Mexico's successful bid for independence, throwing his support behind Emperor Augustín de Íturbide. Gutiérrez continued to favor the idea of centralized authority at the primitive stage of nation building, as he had attempted to do in Texas, by maintaining support for Íturbide after the emperor disbanded the first Mexican Congress. He returned to his hometown of Revilla where he became governor of Tamaulipas in July 1824. A year later, he was appointed Commandant General of Tamaulipas and later served as Commandant General of the Eastern Division of the Provincias Internas until late 1826. Gutiérrez spent much of his later years out of the turbulent Mexican political spotlight. In 1839, however, at age sixty-five, he helped defend northern Tamaulipas from Federalist rebels but then witnessed the sacking of his home after his garrison surrendered after a bitter fight. In the years following Mexican independence until his death on May 13, 1841, Gutiérrez remained a firm believer in national unity and the territorial integrity of Mexico. Though he observed that Mexico and the United States had common interests when it came to keeping a watchful eye on European intrusion into Western Hemispheric affairs, he also frequently warned his countrymen, who often did not need reminding, to be weary of American encroachment upon Mexican soil.

MANUEL MARÍA DE SALCEDO (1776-1813). Manuel María de Salcedo, the ill-fated governor of Texas during the War for Mexican Independence, was born in Málaga, Spain on April 3, 1776. The son of a Spanish military officer, Salcedo was educated at the Royal Academy of Ocaña and the Royal Seminary of Nobles before joining the Spanish army at the age of seventeen and serving as an infantry lieutenant under his father's command in the Canary Islands. In 1801, he moved to New Orleans after his father became the new governor of Spanish Louisiana. After marrying a local woman of Spanish and French extraction in 1803, he returned to Spain the following year when Louisiana became part of the United States as a result of the Louisiana Purchase. In 1807, Salcedo learned that he had been appointed governor of Texas, under the overall supervision of his uncle, Nemesio Salcedo, the Commandant General of the Interior Provinces. Accompanied by his wife and young daughter, Salcedo left for North America in May 1807, landed in New England, and made the long overland journey across the United States, reaching San Antonio by early November.

Upon his arrival, the new governor was beset with a host of military and civic matters. As the military commander of the province, he oversaw the deployment of troops and regularly digested status reports from subordinate commanders stationed at various outposts within the province, paying particular attention to those received from the Louisiana border area where bandits, immigrants, and runaway slaves occasionally crossed into Texas. As the primary civil administrator, he was responsible for providing instructions for local elections and certifying winners. Salcedo also spent much time overseeing a military hospital on the grounds of the Alamo mission in San Antonio, as well as attempting to improve the efficiency of the extensive postal system that facilitated essential communications within the province. In September 1810, the governor embarked on a major inspection tour of Texas just as the revolution initiated by Father Miguel Hidalgo commenced in Mexico.

Concern over the Hidalgo revolt led the governor to restrict civilian movements in Texas, censor the mail, and send his family to the relative safety of New Orleans. Nevertheless, the upheaval came to San Antonio on the morning of January 22, 1811, when a retired creole army captain by the name of Juan Batista de Las Casas led a group of mutinous soldiers in a coup against Salcedo, arresting the governor and his entire staff. Proclaiming allegiance to the Hidalgo movement, Las Casas sent forces to La Bahia and Nacogdoches, soon declaring the liberation of Texas. Meanwhile, the governor and his staff were sent in chains to Monclova in Coahuila. Disenchanted with Las Casas's arbitrary actions, royalist citizens and elements of the army garrison in San Antonio rose up to mount a countercoup against him, capturing the captain after 39 days in power, and sending word to the insurgents in Monclova holding the governor. After receiving word from San Antonio, Salcedo's captors freed him and his staff, in part due to promises of promotions and other benefits that the governor made if he was released. Salcedo and his officers were soon able to obtain documents detailing the movements of Father Hidalgo after the defeat of his forces in central Mexico and subsequent flight northward. This information enabled Salcedo to capture Hidalgo and many other rebel leaders. After transporting them to his uncle's headquarters in Chihuahua, Salcedo was named to head a tribunal that condemned the rebels to death by firing squad.

Returning to San Antonio in September 1811, Salcedo would soon face another threat in the form of the Republican Army of the North. Organized in Louisiana by Hidalgo sympathizer José Bernardo Gutiérrez de Lara with the tacit help of American officials, the filibuster force of over 750 men under the military command of Augustus Magee entered Texas in early August 1812, quickly capturing Nacogdoches before moving on to La Bahia. Salcedo quickly reacted by moving a sizeable force to the area and instituting a prolonged siege. Unable to force a surrender, Salcedo lifted the siege and pulled back towards San Antonio, losing many men to desertions along the way. Forced to make a stand outside of his capital, the governor's forces were routed at the Battle of Rosillo Creek. Salcedo soon capitulated after receiving promises of no reprisals against him or his troops, who would soon be paroled. When the American officers in the victorious expedition refused to accept his sword at a surrender ceremony in San Antonio's military plaza, Salcedo drove the weapon into the ground rather than hand it to Gutiérrez. Instead of paroling Salcedo and his staff officers, however, Gutiérrez and some appointed cohorts held a secret trial where they convicted them of treachery in the deaths of Hidalgo and other rebel leaders, including the father of Captain Antonio Delgado whose son wished to carry out the death sentences. Told that they were being exiled from Texas, Salcedo and his officers were marched out of San Antonio. As the party stopped near the site of the Rosillo Creek, the governor and his men were bound, made to kneel, and after some general taunting, Delgado methodically slit their throats. The governor's dishonorable treatment after promises of parole so shocked many of the American adventurers that Gutiérrez was soon forced from power. Nevertheless, many decided at that point to leave Texas, irreparably weakening the expedition. Within a month, Salcedo's murder would be avenged when the remnants of the Republican Army were destroyed by royalist forces under the command of General Joaquín de Arredondo at the Battle of Medina—the largest battle ever fought on Texas soil.

Chapter 3

Mexican Texas, 1821-1835

Green DeWitt's Empresario Contract, April 15, 1825

Green DeWitt proved to be one of the most successful empresarios in Texas. The terms of his land grant originated under the 1825 colonization law. Below is an excerpt from the contract that DeWitt signed with Mexican officials.

Conditions upon which is allowed the projected introduction by Green DeWitt, a citizen of the United States of North America, of four hundred families as colonists into the department of Texas.

1st. Inasmuch as the plan presented in the preceding memorial by the person concerned conforms to the colonization law of the honorable congress of the state, adopted March 24, the government consents to it, and, therefore, in fulfillment of article 8 [of this colonization law], and in consideration of his petition, assigns to him the land for which he asks, contained within these limits: Beginning on the right bank of the Arroyo de la Vaca at a distance of the reserved ten leagues from the coast, adjoining the colony of Stephen Austin, the line shall go up this *arroyo* as far as the Bejar-Nacogdoches road; it shall follow this road toward the west until it reaches a point two leagues west of the Guadalupe River; from there it shall run parallel with the river south toward the coast until it reaches the ten-league coast reservation; thence it shall run along the inner edge of this reservation toward the east to the place of beginning.

2nd. The *empresario* shall respect the rights of individuals legally possessed of lands within this district.

3rd. In accordance with the above-mentioned colonization law of March 24, the *empresario*, Green DeWitt, shall be obliged under penalty of losing the rights and privileges guaranteed by article 8 of this law, to introduce the four hundred families within the term of six years beginning from to-day.

4th. The families that shall compose this colony, besides being Catholic, as the *empresario* promises in his petition, must also be able to prove, by certificates from the authorities of the localities from which they come, their good moral character.

5th. The *empresario* shall not introduce into his colony criminals, vagrants, or persons of bad morals, and if such be found there he shall cause them to leave the republic, by force of arms if necessary.

6th. To this end he shall organize, in accordance with law, the national militia, and he shall be commanding officer of it until other arrangements shall be made.

7th. When he shall have introduced at least one hundred families he must advise the government, in order that a commissioner may be sent to put the colonists in possession of their lands according to law, and to establish towns, for which he shall carry competent instructions.

8th. Official correspondence with the government or with the state authorities, legal instruments, and other public documents must be written in Spanish, and when towns shall have been formed, it shall be the duty of the *empresario* to establish schools in that language.

9th. It shall also be his duty to erect churches in the new towns; to provide them with ornaments, sacred vessels, and other adornments dedicated to divine worship; and to apply in due time for the priests needed for the administration of spiritual instruction.

10th. In all matters not here referred to he shall be governed by the constitution, the general laws of the nation, and the special laws of the state . . .

Source: Ethel Ziveley Rather, "De Witt's Colony," *Southwestern Historical Quarterly* (October 1904), 173-175

THOUGHT QUESTIONS:

1. Where was DeWitt's colony to be located? What portions of modern Texas did this colony encompass?

2. What obligations did DeWitt have to fulfill according to this contract?

3. What kind of families was DeWitt supposed to settle in his colony? Why do you think they were chosen?

The Fredonian Declaration of Independence, December 21, 1826

Mexican authorities and Haden Edwards agreed to the terms of an empresario contract on April 14, 1825. The contract called on Edwards to settle 800 families in eastern Texas, with Nacogdoches serving as the main urban area. Haden sent his brother Benjamin to run the colony's affairs. Soon after Ben arrived in Nacogdoches, trouble escalated over competing land claims between Edwards and Mexican settlers who had inhabited the region before the empresario's arrival. Government officials sided with the Mexican settlers and ultimately voided the contract, prompting Haden, his brother, and their recruited families to declare that they were seceding from Mexico and creating what they called the "Republic of Fredonia." Their republic was a short-lived enterprise. The Mexican government sent a military force to Nacogdoches, forcing the brothers and their cohorts to retreat to the safety of Louisiana. Below is the document that proclaimed Fredonia's independence.

Whereas, the Government of the Mexican United States, have by repeated insults, treachery and oppression, reduced the White and Red emigrants from the United States of North America, now living in the Province of Texas, within the Territory of the said Government, into which they have been deluded by promises solemnly made, and most basely broken, to the dreadful alternative of either submitting their freeborn necks to the yoke of an imbecile, faithless, and despotic government, miscalled a Republic; or of taking up arms in defense of their unalienable rights and asserting their Independence; They —viz:—The White emigrants now assembled in the town of Nacogdoches, around the Independent Standard, on the. One part, and the Red emigrants who have espoused the same Holy Cause, on the other, in order to prosecute more speedily and effectually the War of Independence, they have mutually undertaken, to a successful issue, and to bind themselves by the ligaments of reciprocal interests and obligations, have resolved to form a Treaty of Union, League and Confederation.

For the illustrious object, BENJAMIN W. EDWARDS and HARMAN B. MAYO, Agents of the Committee of Independence, and RICHARD FIELDS and JOHN D. HUNTER, the Agents of the Red people, being respectively furnished with due powers, have agreed to the following Articles.

1. The above named contracting parties, bind themselves to a solemn Union, League and Confederation, in Peace and War, to establish and defend their mutual independence of the Mexican United States.

2. The contracting parties guaranty, mutually, to the extent of their power, the integrity of their respective Territories, as now agreed upon and described, viz: The Territory apportioned to the Red people, shall begin at the Sandy Spring, where Bradley's road takes off from the road leading from Nacogdoches to the Plantation of Joseph Dust, from thence West, by the Compass, without regard to variation, to the Rio Grande, thence to

the head of the Rio Grande, thence with the mountains to the head of Big Red River, thence north to the boundary of the United States of North America, thence with the same line to the mouth of Sulphur Fork, thence in a right line to the beginning. The territory apportioned to the White people, shall comprehend all the residue of the Province of Texas, and of such other portions of the Mexican United States, as the contracting parties, by their mutual efforts and resources, may render Independent, provided the same shall not extend further west than the Rio Grande.

3. The contracting parties mutually guaranty the rights of Empressarios to their premium lands only, and the rights of all other individuals, acquired under the Mexican Government, and relating or appertaining to the above described Territories, provided the said Empresarios and individuals do not forfeit the same by an opposition to the Independence of the said Territories, or by withdrawing their aid and support to its accomplishment.

4. It is distinctly understood by the contracting parties, that the Territory apportioned to the Red people, is intended as well for the benefit of the Tribes now settled within the Territory apportioned to the White people, as for those living in the former Territory, and that is incumbent upon the contracting parties for the Red people to offer the said Tribes a participation in the same.

5. It is also mutually agreed by the contracting parties, that every individual, Red and White, who has made improvement within either of the Respective Allied Territories and lives upon the same, shall have a fee simple of a section of land including his improvement, as well as the protection of the government under which he may reside.

6. The contracting parties mutually agree, that all roads, navigable streams, and all other channels of conveyance within each Territory, shall be open and free to the use of the inhabitants of the other.

7. The contracting parties mutually stipulate that they will direct all their resources to the prosecution of the Heaven-inspired cause which has given birth to this solemn Union, League and Confederation, firmly relying upon their united efforts, and the strong arm of Heaven, for success.

In faith whereof the Agents of the respective contracting parties hereunto affix their names. Done in the Town of Nacogdoches, this twenty-first day of December, in the year of our Lord one thousand eight hundred and twenty-six.

B. W. EDWARDS,
H. B. MAYO,
RICHARD FIELDS,
JOHN D. HUNTER,

We, the Committee of Independence, and the Committee of Red People, do ratify the above Treaty, and do pledge ourselves to maintain it in good faith. Done on the day and date above mentioned.

MARTIN FARMER, President
RICHARD FIELDS,
JOHN D. HUNTER,
NE-KO-LAKE,
JOHN BAGS,
CUK-TO-KEH,
HADEN EDWARDS,
W. B. LEGON,
JNO. SPROW,
B. P. THOMPSON,
JOS. A. HUBER,
B. W. EDWARDS,
H. B. MAYO.

Source: H. P. N. Gammel, *The Laws of Texas, 1822-1897,* 10 vols. (Austin, 1898), I, 107-110

THOUGHT QUESTIONS:

1. According to the document, why were the "Fredonians" declaring their independence?

2. What provisions does the declaration make for Native Americans?

3. What did the Edwards brothers stand to gain by declaring independence?

Stephen Austin Reacts to the Fredonian Rebellion

The creation of the "Republic of Fredonia" in Nacogdoches by the empresario Haden Edwards and his supporters placed Stephen Austin in an incredibly awkward position. Though previously working with Edwards to secure the latter's land grant and frequently advised him on how best to deal with the Mexican government, the Fredonians' secessionist actions compelled Austin to take sides against Edwards. After his efforts to quell the situation by diplomatic overtures to the Fredonians were rebuffed, Austin issued this open letter to the residents of his colony on January 22, 1827, condemning the rebels and rallying his people to join in the suppression of the revolt. On February 8, Mexican troops arrived in Nacogdoches to find that the Fredonians had fled to Louisiana.

TO THE INHABITANTS OF THE COLONY,

The persons who were sent on from this colony by the Chief of Department & Military Commandant to offer peace to the Nacogdoches madmen have returned without affecting anything. The Olive Branch of peace that was magnanimously held out to them has been insultingly refused, and that party have denounced massacre and desolation on this Colony. They are trying to excite all the Northern Indians to murder and plunder, and it appears as though they had no other object than the ruin of the Country. They are no longer Americans, for they have forfeited all title to that high name by their unnatural and bloody alliance with Savages. They openly threaten us with Indian massacre and the plunder of our property. Ought we to hesitate at such a moment? Shall we hesitate because they were once our countrymen? No. They are our countrymen no longer. They have by a solemn treaty united and identified themselves with Indians -- made common cause with savages, and pledged their faith to carry on a war of murder and plunder against the peacible [sic] inhabitants of Texas. They are worse than the Natives of the forest with whom they are allied, and it is our duty as men, as Americans, and as adopted Mexicans to prove to these infatuated criminals and to the world that we have not forgotten the Land of our birth, nor the principles of honor & patriotism we inherited from our fathers, and that we are not to be dictated to & driven into crime and anarchy by a handful of desperate renegadoes [sic]. The civil and military chiefs of Texas accompanied by a chosen band of national troops march with us, who in union with the brave and patriotic Militia of the Colony will be fully able to crush in its infancy this mad unjust and unnatural rebellion.

To arms Fellow Citizens! To arms in the cause of liberty, of virtue and justice; To arms in defense of your adopted Government, and hurl back the thunder upon the head, of those base & degraded apostates from the name of Americans who have dared to insult you by a threatening to join them in their mad and criminal schemes.

Every man able to bear arms is now wanted. Temporary inconvenience and loss must and ought to yield to necessity and duty; you will receive pay allowed by law to National Troops of the same class, and the commander will see that it is punctually discharged as soon as possible.

The people of the Colony after a full understanding of the pretended cause of complaint on the part of the rebels as well as of the mild and magnanimous course of the government in offering them a full and unreserved amnesty and an impartial and public investigation of their alleged greivances [sic], have unanimously, solomny [sic], and voluntarily pledged themselves in writing to the Government, to oppose the factionists by force of arms. You are bound in honor to redeem the sacred pledge.

To arms then my friends and fellow citizens, and hasten to the standard of our Country -- Hasten to the field of honor and of duty -- Hasten to the protection of your property and families and all that you hold dear and sacred upon earth. The approbation of every honest & honorable man in your native country of your adopted Govt, and of a just and omnipresent God, and the conciousness [sic] that you will have done your duty & saved yourselves will be your reward.

The first hundred men who were called out from this Colony will march on the 26th inst. and I now call on you to turn out in Mass, and join us as soon as possible.

The necessary orders for Mustering into service and other purposes will be issued to the commanding officers.

Union and Mexico
San Felipe de Austin, 22d January, 1827
Stephen F. Austin

THOUGHT QUESTIONS:

1. What do you think were some of the more damning words and phrases that Austin used to describe the Fredonian rebels and their cause?

2. How did Austin try to use the Fredonians' alliance with some Cherokee Indians to rally his people to end the revolt?

3. What motivations do you think Austin had for refusing to join the Fredonian Rebellion and for supporting the Mexican government's efforts to suppress it?

General Manuel Mier y Terán's Letter to President Guadalupe Victoria, June 30, 1828

While visiting Texas to survey the boundary areas with the United States and to investigate the possible need for more military posts in the region, General Manuel Mier y Terán wrote a lengthy letter to Mexican President Guadalupe Victoria from Nacogdoches in which he not only bemoaned waning Mexican influence on the province but also provided specific recommendations about how the government could regain control. This letter (excerpts shown below) and other reports would directly lead to the policy laid out in the Law of April 6, 1830:

... As one covers the distance from Béjar to this town, he will note that Mexican influence is proportionately diminished until on arriving in this place he will see that it is almost nothing. And indeed, whence could such influence come? Hardly from superior numbers in population, since the ratio of Mexicans to foreigners is one to ten; certainly not from the superior character of the Mexican population, for exactly the opposite is true, the Mexicans of this town comprising what in all countries is called the lowest class—the very poor and very ignorant. The naturalized North Americans in the town maintain an English school, and send their children north for further education; the poor Mexicans not only do not have sufficient means to establish schools, but they are not of the type that take any thought for the improvement of its public institutions or the betterment of its degraded condition. Neither are there civil authorities or magistrates; one insignificant little man—not to say more—who is called an *alcalde*, and an *ayuntamiento* that does not convene once is a lifetime is the most that we have here at this important point on our frontier; yet, wherever I have looked, in the short time that I have been here, I have witnessed grave occurrences, both political and judicial. It would cause you the same chagrin that it has caused me to see the opinion that is held of our nation by these foreign colonists, since, with the exception of some few who have journeyed to our capital, they know no other Mexicans than the inhabitants about here, and excepting the authorities necessary to any form of society, the said inhabitants are the most ignorant of negroes and Indians, among whom I pass for a man of culture. Thus, I tell myself that it could not be otherwise than that from such a state of affairs should arise an antagonism between the Mexicans and foreigners, which is not the least of the smoldering fires which I have discovered. Therefore, I am warning you to take timely measures. Texas could throw the whole nation into revolution.

The colonists murmur against the political disorganization of the frontier, and the Mexicans complain of the superiority and better education of the colonists; the colonists find it unendurable that they must go three hundred leagues to lodge a complaint against the petty pickpocketing that they suffer from a venal and ignorant *alcalde*, and the Mexicans with no knowledge of the laws of their own country, nor those regulating colonization, set themselves against the foreigners, deliberately setting nets to deprive them of the right of franchise and to exclude them from the *ayuntamiento*. Meanwhile, the incoming stream of new settlers is unceasing; the first news of these comes by discovering them on land already under cultivation, where they have been located for many months; the old inhabitants set up a claim to the property, basing their titles of doubtful priority, and for which there are no records, on a law of the Spanish government; and thus arises a lawsuit in which the *alcalde* has a chance to come out with some money. In this state of affairs, the town where there are no magistrates is the one in which lawsuits abound, and it is at once evident that in Nacogdoches and its vicinity, being most distant from the seat of the general government, the primitive order of things should take its course, which is to say that this section is being settled up without the consent of anybody.

The majority of the North Americans established here under the Spanish government—and these are few—are of two classes. First, those who are fugitives from our neighbor republic and bear the unmistakable earmarks of thieves and criminals; these are located between Nacogdoches and the Sabine, ready to cross and recross this river as they see the necessity of separating themselves from the country in which they have just committed some crime; however, some of these have reformed and settled down to an industrious life in the new country. The other class of early settlers are poor laborers who lack the four or five thousand dollars necessary to buy a *sitio* of land in the north, but having the ambition to become landholders—one of the strong virtues of our neighbors—have come to Texas. Of such as this latter class is Austin's colony composed. They are for the most part industrious and honest, and appreciate this country. Most of them own at least one or two slaves. Unfortunately the emigration of such is made under difficulties, because they lack the means of transportation, and to accomplish this emigration it has become necessary to do what was not necessary until lately: there are empresarios of wealth who advance them the means for their transportation and establishment. . . .

That which most impressed me in view of all these conditions is the necessity of effective government in Nacogdoches at least, since it is the frontier with which the Republic is most in contact. Every officer of the federal government has immense districts under his jurisdiction, and to distribute these effectively it is necessary to give attention to economy as well as to government and security. The whole population here is a mixture of strange and incoherent parts without parallel in our federation: numerous tribes of Indians, now at peace, but armed and at any moment ready for war, whose steps toward civilization should be taken under the close supervision of a strong and intelligent government; colonists of another people, more progressive and better informed than the Mexican inhabitants, but also more shrewd and unruly; among these foreigners are fugitives from justice, honest laborers, vagabonds and criminals, but honorable and dishonorable alike travel with their political constitution in their pockets, demanding the privileges, authority and officers which such a constitution guarantees. The most of them have slaves, and these slaves are beginning to learn the favorable intent of the Mexican law toward their unfortunate condition and are becoming restless under their yoke, and the masters, in the effort to retain them, are making that yoke even heavier; they extract their teeth, set on the dogs to tear them in pieces, the most lenient being he who but flogs his slaves until they are flayed.

In short, the growing population, its unusual class, the prosperity and safety of the nation, all seem to me to demand the placing at this point of a *jefe politico* subordinate to the one at Béjar, and also a court of appeals. This done, I do not believe so radical a step as the separation of Texas from Coahuila, now desired by the inhabitants, would be necessary.

I must ask your forbearance for this long letter, but I desire to forward to you at once my observations of this country and not withhold them until the day when I make full report to the government, for fear the time for remedy will be past.

Source: Translated and cited in Alleine Howren, "Causes and Origin of the Decree of April 6, 1830," *Southwestern Historical Quarterly*, XVI (April, 1913), 395-98.

THOUGHT QUESTIONS:

1. What specific reasons does the general cite for waning Mexican influence in Texas?

2. How does he describe the people who then made up the population of Texas?

3. What suggestions does Mier y Terán make to improve conditions in Texas?

The Law of April 6, 1830

Following the recommendations of General Manuel Mier y Terán, Mexican officials passed the Law of April 6, 1830 in an effort to strengthen Mexican sovereignty over Texas by limiting Anglo-American immigration into the region, among other important changes. Below is a reprint of this important legislation.

The Vice President of the Mexican United States, to the inhabitants of the Republic, KNOW YE, that the General Congress has decreed, as follows:—

Article 1. Cotton goods excluded in the Law of May 22, 1829, may be introduced through the ports of the Republic until January 1, 1831, and through the ports of the South Sea until June 30, 1831.

Art. 2. The duties received on the above mentioned goods shall be used to maintain the integrity of Mexican territory, to form a reserve fund against the event of Spanish invasion, and to promote the development of national industries in the branch of cotton manufacturers.

Art. 3. The government is authorized to name one or more commissioners who shall visit the colonies of the frontier states and contract with the legislatures, of said states for the purchase, in behalf of the federal government, of lands deemed suitable for the establishment of colonies of Mexicans and other nationalities; and the said commissioners shall make with the existing colonies whatever arrangements seem expedient for the security of the Republic. The said commissioners shall supervise the introduction of new colonists and the fulfilling of their contracts for settlement, and shall ascertain to what extent the existing contracts have been completed.

Art. 4. The chief executive is authorized to take such lands as are deemed suitable for fortifications or arsenals and for the new colonies, indemnifying the states for same, in proportion to their assessments due the federal government.

Art. 5. The government is authorized to transport the convict-soldiers destined for Vera Cruz and other points to the colonies, there to establish them as is deemed fit; the government will furnish free transportation to the families of the soldiers, should they desire to go.

Art. 6. The convict-soldiers shall be employed in constructing the fortifications, public works and roads which the commissioners may deem necessary, and when the time of their imprisonment is terminated, if they should desire to remain as colonists, they shall be given lands and agricultural implements, and their provisions shall be continued through the year of their colonization.

Art. 7. Mexican families who voluntarily express a desire to become colonists will be furnished transportation, maintained for one year, and assigned the best of agricultural lands.

Art. 8. All the individuals above mentioned shall be subject to both the federal and state colonization laws.

Art. 9. The introduction of foreigners across the northern frontier is prohibited under any pretext whatever, unless the said foreigners are provided with a passport issued by the agents of this Republic at the point whence the said foreigners set out.

Art. 10. No change shall be made with respect to the slaves now in the states, but the federal government and the government of each state shall most strictly en force the colonization laws and prevent the further introduction of slaves.

Art. 11. In accordance with the right reserved by the general congress in the seventh article of the Law of August 18, 1824, it is prohibited that emigrants from nations bordering on this Republic shall settle in the states or territory adjacent to their own nation. Consequently, all contracts not already completed and not in harmony with this law are suspended.

Art. 12. Coastwide trade shall be free to all foreigners for the term of four years, with the object of turning colonial trade to the ports of Matamoras, Tampico, and Vera Cruz.

Art. 13. Frame houses and all classes of foreign food products may be introduced through the ports of Galveston and Matagorda, free of duty, for a period of two years.

Art. 14. The government is authorized to expend five hundred thousand dollars (*pesos*) in the construction of fortifications and settlements on the frontier, in the transportation of the convict-soldiers and Mexican families to same and their maintenance for one year, on agricultural implements, on expenses of the commissioners, on the transportation of troops, on premiums to such farmers among the colonists as may distinguish themselves in agriculture, and on all the other expedients conducive to progress and security as set forth in the foregoing articles.

Art. 15. To obtain at once one-half of the above sum, the government is authorized to negotiate a loan on the customs proceeds which will be derived from the ordinary classes of cotton goods, said loan to pay a premium of three per cent monthly, payable at the expiration of the periods fixed in the tariff schedule.

Art. 16. One-twentieth of the said customs receipts shall be used in the promotion of cotton manufactures, such as in the purchase of machines and looms, small sums being set aside for the installing of the machinery, and any other purpose that the government shall deem necessary; the government shall apportion these funds to the states having this form of industry. The said funds shall be under the control of the Minister of Relations for the purpose of promoting industries of such importance.

Art. 17. Also three hundred thousand dollars (*pesos*) of the above mentioned customs receipts shall be set aside as a reserve fund on deposit in the treasury, under the strict responsibility of the government, which shall have power to use the same only in the case of Spanish invasion.

Art. 18. The government shall regulate the establishment of the new colonies, and shall present to Congress within a year a record of the emigrants and immigrants established under the new law. . . .

Source: *Texas Gazette* (Austin), July 3, 1830

THOUGHT QUESTIONS:

1. In what major ways did the law propose to change Texas after 1830?

2. According to the law, what changes regarding slavery would take place?

3. Why do you think Anglo Texans objected to the Law of April 6, 1830?

The Turtle Bayou Resolutions of June 13, 1832

In June 1832, a group of American settlers in the coastal town of Anahuac rebelled against the local Mexican commander, John Davis Bradburn, a Virginia-born mercenary who had fought for the Centralist government and had been appointed by Mexico to establish the town two years earlier to collect tariffs and provide order. William Barret Travis and other locals resented Bradburn's strict enforcement of many statutes. The commander arrested Travis and other opposition leaders after accusing Travis of spreading rumors of an impending assault on his garrison in an effort to compel Bradburn to turn over two runaway slaves. Travis's friends rose up in his defense, capturing some Mexican cavalrymen in order to arrange a prisoner exchange. When Bradburn counterattacked, the rebels withdrew to an area known as Turtle Bayou, released their captives, and waited for reinforcements.

While camping at Turtle Bayou, the settlers drafted a set of resolutions explaining their actions to Federalist colonel José Antonio Mexía, who had recently arrived at Brazoria with 400 troops to quell an alleged secession movement. In the following document, the rebels cast their actions within the broader struggle of Mexican politics, proclaiming themselves for the Federalist (at the moment) Antonio López de Santa Anna in his efforts to challenge the Centralist government of Anastacio Bustamente:

Col Jose Antonio Mexia

Sir

Having understood that the causes which impelled us to take up arms have been misrepresented, or misunderstood, we therefore make you the following representation.

The colonists of Texas have long been convinced of the arbitrary and unconstitutional measures of the administration of Bustamante; as evinced

First: By their repeated violations of the constitution and laws and the total disregard of the civil and political rights of the people.

Second: By their fixing and establishing among us, in the time of peace, military posts, the officers of which, totally disregarding the local civil authorities of the State, have committed various acts evincing opposition to the true interest of the people in the enjoyment of civil liberty.

Third: By arresting the commissioners, especially Juan Francisco Madero, who, on the part of the State government, was to put the inhabitants east of Trinity River in possession of other lands, in conformity with the laws of colonization.

Fourth: By the imposition of military force, preventing the Alcalde of the jurisdiction of Liberty from the exercise of his constitutional functions.

Fifth: By the appointing to the revenue department men whose principles are avowedly to the true interest of the people of Texas; and that, too, when their character for infamy had been repeatedly established.

Sixth: By the military commandant of Anahuac advising and procuring servants to quit the service of their masters, and offering them protection; causing them to labor for his benefits, and refusing to compensate them for the same.

Seventh: By imprisonment of our citizens without lawful cause; and claiming the right of trying said citizens by a military court for offense of a character cognizable by the civil authority alone.

Resolved: That we view with feelings of the deepest regret, the manner in which the government of the Republic of Mexico is administered by the present dynasty. The repeated violation of the constitution; the total disregard of the laws; the entire prostration of the civil power, are grievances of such character as to arouse the feelings of every freeman, and impel him to resistance.

Resolved: That we view with feelings of deepest interest and solicitude, the firm and manly resistance which is made by those patriots under the highly and distinguished chieftain Santa Anna, to the numerous encroachments and infractions which have been made by the present administration upon the laws and constitution of our beloved and adopted country.

Resolved: That as freemen devoted to a correct interpretation and enforcement of the constitution and laws, according to their true spirit, we pledge our lives and fortunes in support of the same, and of those distinguished leaders who are gallantly fighting in defense of civil liberty.

Resolved: That all the people of Texas be united to co-operate with us, in support of the principles incorporated in the foregoing resolutions.

Source: Mirabeau B. Lamar Papers, Texas State Library and Archives Commission

THOUGHT QUESTIONS:

1. How did the settlers attempt to create the sense that they were victims of injustice?

2. How did the rebels try to tie their resentment toward Bradburn to the prevailing Federalist opposition to the Centralists?

3. How would the statements made about Santa Anna seem ironic to Anglos five years later?

An Old-Time Buffalo Hunt

Credit: Library of Congress
Painting by Charles M. Russell,
Illustration in *Field and Stream*, May 1898, p. 65

In this painting, two mounted Indians with bow and arrow and a spear are killing a buffalo. During the Mexican period, many Native American groups residing on the Southern Plains continued to rely on buffalo hunting to provide for most of their needs. Almost all parts of the buffalo were used. In addition to devouring the meat, Plains Indians such as the Comanche and the Apache also used the hides to craft their tepees, blankets, and clothing. Artisans fashioned arrowheads and utensils from bones, while sinews proved to be valuable for making bow strings and lashing material. Bladders made excellent bags and canteens. Surplus items could be traded for luxury items or anything else desired that could not be provided by the buffalo.

THOUGHT QUESTION:

Besides being used for food and clothing, the buffalo provided a "Spiritual Blessing." Native Americans believed in a spiritual concept of nature and wildlife. How do you think the buffalo fit into this concept?

BIOGRAPHIES

LORENZO DE ZAVALA (1788-1836). Manuel Lorenzo Justiniano de Zavala y Saenz, the first vice president of the Republic of Texas, was born in a village near Mérida, Yucatán in Mexico on October 3, 1788. His family sent him to be educated at the Tridentine Seminary of San Idlefonso in Mérida. Upon graduation in 1807, he married Teresa Correa y Correa (with whom he had three children) and founded several newspapers, the first to appear in Yucatan. Zavala's editorship displayed a marked pro-democratic viewpoint. In 1814, his support for various reforms in Mexico led Spanish authorities to imprison the young idealist. While incarcerated for three years in a Veracruz fortress, Zavala passed the time teaching himself English and studying medical textbooks. Upon his release in 1817, he dabbled in the practice of medicine before re-entering politics, agreeing to serve as secretary for Yucatan's provincial assembly. In 1821, Zavala traveled to Madrid to serve as a deputy to the Spanish Cortes. After Mexico achieved independence from Spain, he returned the next year to help establish the Mexican Republic. From 1822 to 1826, Zavala represented Yucatan in the Mexican Congress and Senate. In Mexican politics, he clearly identified himself with the Federalists. When Vicente Guerrero became president in 1829, he appointed Zavala to be Secretary of the Treasury, a position he held for six months before Guerrero was ousted by his Centralist Vice President Anastacio Busta-mente. After a period of house arrest, Zavala went into political exile to New York City in June 1830.

In March 1829, just before assuming his post as Treasury Secretary, Zavala had entered the empresario business when he received a land grant in southeastern Texas and charged with the responsibility of settling 500 families on the large tract. Upon arriving in New York, Zavala sought support from American businessmen to enable him to fulfill his obligations. In October 1830, he transferred rights to his grant over to an entity that named itself the Galveston Bay and Texas Land Company. After his wife died in 1831, Zavala spent time travelling to England and France. By the end of the year he returned to New York, married Emily West (with whom he had three additional children), and published a two-volume history of Mexico from 1808 to 1830 entitled *Ensayo Historico de las Revoluciones de Megico des 1808 hasta 1830*. Zavala returned to Mexico in 1832, serving as governor of the state of Mexico before resuming his role as deputy for Yucatan in the Mexican Congress. In October 1833, President Antonio López de Santa Anna appointed Zavala to serve as minister to France. While residing in Paris, he published a book filled with his observations of Americans based on his time in the United States entitled *Viage los Estados-Unidos del Norte de America*. When he learned that Santa Anna had assumed dictatorial powers, Zavala resigned his post in protest and travelled first to New York City then to Texas, arriving in July 1835.

Zavala attended the Consultation at San Felipe in October 1835. Soon thereafter, he wrote an article attempting to persuade Tejanos to support resistance against Santa Anna, as well as a declaration for all Texas readers that laid out objections to the dictator, supported a federalist Mexican government, and called for separate statehood for Texas. By the time of the March 1836 convention at Washington-on-the-Brazos, he realized that much of Mexico was not going to rise up to challenge Santa Anna, plus Texas public opinion had changed toward the majority supporting the idea of independence. Consequently, Zavala joined the secessionists, signed the Texas Declaration of Independence, and was appointed to the committee established to draft a constitution for the Republic of Texas. Zavala's extensive political experience and linguistic ability earned the respect of his fellow revolutionaries who unanimously elected him to be vice president of the interim government. As Mexican forces approached eastern Texas, Zavala rejoined his fleeing family to Galveston Island. After the Battle of San Jacinto, he agreed to serve as translator and intermediary for the captured Santa Anna.

Like his friend Stephen Austin, Zavala did not long survive the Texas Revolution. In poor health due to frequent bouts with malaria, he gave up the affairs of government, resigning as vice president in October 1836. A month later, while rowing on Buffalo Bayou near his home, Zavala's boat overturned in a storm leaving him soaking wet. After developing pneumonia, he died on November 15, 1836 and was buried in a small cemetery plot that is now submerged under Buffalo Bayou.

HADEN EDWARDS (1771-1849). Haden Edwards, the Texas empresario who insti- gated the Fredonian Rebellion, was born on August 12, 1771 in Stafford County, Vir- ginia. When he was nine years old, his family moved to Bourbon County, Kentucky, where his father acquired over 20,000 acres of land and became one of Kentucky's first two U.S. senators. In 1820 Edwards married Susanna Beall and the couple started a fam- ily that would eventually total thirteen children. Though educated in law, Haden, along with his brother Benjamin, became more interested in land speculation. Aided by their wealthy father, the Edwards brothers moved to Jackson, Mississippi where they acquired a plantation. While in Mississippi, they learned about the Mexican government's plans to encourage Americans to colonize Texas. In 1823, Edwards travelled to Mexico City, where he joined Stephen F. Austin and other potential empresarios in lobbying Mexican officials to authorize American settlements in Texas. Through their efforts, the Mexican government passed a provision in the Constitution of 1824 allowing the states to de- termine land grant issues and the state of Coahulia y Tejas's Colonization Law of 1825, which allowed recognized empresarios to introduce settlers into Texas.

Edwards eventually secured an empresario grant to locate 800 families in the Na- cogdoches area of East Texas, a region already containing an existing population of set- tlers. Like other empresarios, he originally agreed to honor preexisting grants and claims made by Spanish or Mexican officials, though Edwards had a larger number of such claims to contend with than other empresarios who settled families in less populated loca- tions in Texas. In 1825, he posted notices that all potential claimants must come forward and show proof of land claims within his grant. Any inhabitant not showing proper title would have to purchase the land or move. Edwards's announcement angered many local residents—many could not prove their claims because such records were in Spain, while others were squatters without legal claim to the land that they occupied. He also became involved in a nasty dispute over the election of the next alcalde of Nacodoches. While local resident Samuel Norris gained the support of the older settlers, Chichester Chap- lin, Edwards's son-in-law, was favored by the newly arrived colonists. Edwards certified the election in favor of Chaplin, resulting in a protest to the governor by Norris and his supporters. The governor recognized Norris's claim, but Chaplin refused to give up the office. As a growing number of various complaints from the older settlers flowed to the governor, he pressed the Edwards brothers for explanations. When word reached Mexican president Guadalupe Victoria about the condescending and disrespectful tone of the Edwards brothers' replies, the president finally revoked the Edwards grant in October 1826.

Having invested over $50,000 into the colony, the empresario decided that he could not simply walk away from his investment. Additionally, the revocation of his grant would nullify all the claims of the newly arrived settlers. The Edwards brothers and many of their colonists, therefore, began the short-lived revolutionary movement known as the Fredonian Rebellion, so named because after declaring independence from Mexico, they announced that they were establishing the "Republic of Fredonia." After creating a constitution, they named Haden Edwards to be their president. The Edwards brothers also forged an alliance with the Cherokees in East Texas, who held other grievances against the Mexican government. News of the Fredonian Rebellion, however, soon reached the Mexican authorities who immediately sent Lieutenant Colonel Mateo Ahumada to Nacogdoches to arrest the rebels. Aiding Mexican troopers were Anglo militiamen from Stephen Austin's colony. Before the Mexican troops and their American allies arrived, the Fredonians dispersed, fleeing to the safety of Louisiana.

During the Texas Revolution, Edwards returned to Texas and made his home in Nacogdoches. He engaged in the land business until his death on August 14, 1849. Beginning with Edwards's revolt, Mexican officials became increasingly wary of continuing their empresario policy in Texas. This fact was not lost on Stephen Austin, which explains his willingness (and perceived need) to display loyalty to the Mexican government by aiding in the suppression of the Fredonian rebellion. Nevertheless, Mexican authorities began to reconsider their policies, soon leading to a ban on further American immigration into Texas and increased tensions between the Americans residing in Texas and the Mexican government.

JOHN [JUAN] DAVIS BRADBURN (1787-1842). The American mercenary and Mexican military officer John Bradburn was born in Virginia sometime in 1787. His family later moved to Kentucky. Scholars speculate that he might have been a member of the Gutiérrez-Magee expedition because the returned filibusters elected him to be an officer in the Louisiana volunteer regiment that they organized to fight against the British in the War of 1812. Bradburn's unit arrived too late to aid Andrew Jackson's successful defense of New Orleans in January 1815.

Following the war, Bradburn linked up with Henry Perry, a known veteran of the Gutiérrez-Magee expedition, in planning a new filibustering expedition into Texas. Based in Nacogdoches, Bradburn served as a recruiter and a supply officer for the plotters. He and Perry later joined with Francisco Xavier Mina's forces for a successful attack on the Tamaulipas coast in April 1817 before moving inland to assist revolutionary forces active in north-central Mexico. Bradburn remained with Mina's men as second-in-command of the American volunteers until royal forces counterattacked, forcing the survivors to scatter. He continued to participate in local Mexican resistance activities and eventually joined Vicente Guerrero's rebels near Acapulco. After several months with Guerrero, Bradburn learned of a general amnesty for rebels and defected in December 1820 to join the forces of Augstín de Iturbide. When Iturbide sought an alliance with Guerrero in order to aid his planned coup to overthrow Spanish rule in Mexico, Bradburn served as an intermediary between Iturbide and Guerrero.

After Mexico won its independence, Bradburn remained in the Mexican army as a colonel and served as a personal aide to Iturbide, who sent him to Washington, D.C. to establish diplomatic relations. He returned with news of American recognition of an independent Mexico. Bradburn married into a wealthy Mexican family when he wed María Josefa Hurtado de Mendoza, an heiress whose family owned sizeable property on the main square in Mexico City. The couple would later have one son, Andrés, who later became a priest. Politically, Bradburn remained strongly allied with the Centralists in Mexican politics. By 1830, he was living near Matamoros with his wife and son.

After the Mexican government passed the Law of April 6, 1830, General Manuel de Mier y Terán asked for Bradburn's assistance in enforcing the new immigration and customs regulations for Texas. He agreed to command a new Galveston Bay garrison for this purpose that would include a fortification, customhouse, and a new town to be named Anahuac (after the ancient valley home of the Aztecs). Chosen to lead the post because of his familiarity with the area and his bilingual communication skills, Bradburn decided to locate the base on a bluff overlooking the mouth of the Trinity River.

Once established, Bradburn earned the ire of numerous local residents for his collection of tariff duties and strict enforcement of land title regulations. Increasingly suspicious of the American residents in Texas and always watchful for signs of secessionist sentiment, he became involved in a series of quarrels with future Texas revolutionary leader William Barret Travis who was practicing law in Anahuac. After Bradburn granted sanctuary to two fugitive slaves from Louisiana, Travis sought their return for his client who had hired him to work on his behalf. In May 1832, Bradburn received warning that armed men were planning to seize the runaways. After determining that the rumors were false, he suspected Travis's involvement in the ruse and arrested the lawyer for allegedly fomenting an insurrection. Before he could send Travis to Matamoros for a military trial, about 150 outraged locals rose up, marched on Anahuac, skirmished with Bradburn's troops, and then withdrew to await cannon and other reinforcements. They soon crafted the Turtle Bayou Resolutions to openly cast their lot with the Federalists in the ongoing Mexican civil war against the Centralist government. Bradburn sent word to Colonel José de la Piedras in Nacogdoches for help. Piedras arrived quickly but feared that he may be outnumbered. The colonel decided to diffuse the worsening situation (known ever since as the Anahuac Disturbances) by removing Bradburn from his command and freeing all Anglo prisoners, including Travis. Fearing for his life, Bradburn fled to New Orleans in August 1832, but negative news of his previous actions as garrison commander followed him, probably thanks to Travis, so he booked quick passage on a ship for Matamoros.

Bradburn stayed in the Mexican army and remained loyal to the Centralist government. He attained the rank of brigadier general before retiring to Matamoros. After the Texas Revolution began, he agreed to serve under General José de Urrea's command under the condition that he would not have to fight in eastern Texas. Urrea left Bradburn to command the port of Copano, located slightly north of the Nueces River. After Mexican forces left Texas after the Battle of Jacinto, Bradburn made his way back to his Matamoros home. He died at his home on April 20, 1842, and was buried on his ranch at Puertas Verdes, in present-day Hidalgo County, Texas. Few Texans mourned his passing when they heard the news. Though Bradburn believed he was dutifully carrying out his orders at Anahuac, most Texans instead likened his authoritarian ways to those of Antonio López de Santa Anna.

BARON DE BASTROP (1759-1827). Born Philip Hendrik Nering Bögel in Para-maribo, Dutch Guiana, on November 23, 1759, the future Texas colonizer moved to Holland with his parents in 1764, married in 1782, and raised a family of five children while serving as tax collector for the province of Friesland. In 1793, upon accusations of embezzling tax funds, Bögel fled the country to avoid arrest. He surfaced in Spanish-held Louisiana in 1795, portraying himself as a nobleman, sporting the title "Baron de Bastrop," who had fled Holland to escape a recent French invasion. The charismatic and persuasive Dutchman soon became friends with the governor of Louisiana, who at the time was concerned about the increasing encroachment of American settlers into Louisiana. Wishing to create a buffer zone against this advance, the governor signed a deal with Bögel to settle 500 European immigrant families along the Ouachita River in northeast Louisiana. Bögel planned to build grist mills for the colony and expected to make money milling and selling the colonists' wheat crops. In 1797, he brought in a hundred settlers recruited from Kentucky, but the project did not succeed after promised financial aid from the Spanish government was not sustained.

With the Louisiana Purchase transferring Louisiana to American control in 1803, Bögel moved to Texas, and after seeking a permit to establish a colony between San Antonio and the Trinity River, opened a freighting business moving goods locally by mule. His charming demeanor and fluency in English, Spanish, French, and Dutch helped him rise to leadership in San Antonio, where he began serving as *alcalde* in 1810. The Dutchman's presence in San Antonio proved instrumental in the efforts of Moses Austin to have the Spanish government accept his petition to receive an *empresario* grant in Texas. Austin had traveled to San Antonio in late December 1820, but his initial offer was rejected by Antonio Maria Martinez, the last governor of Spanish Texas. Austin then had a chance encounter with Bögel, someone with whom he had briefly met while traveling in Missouri twenty years earlier. After Austin told him of his reason for being in San Antonio and his inability to have his petition advanced past Martinez' office, Bögel returned with him to see the governor to vouch for him and endorse the idea for the colony. A few days after the meeting, Martinez forwarded the proposal, eventually leading to its acceptance by Spanish authorities. Thus, the groundwork was set for the establishment of the colony during the Mexican period under Stephen F. Austin, who benefited greatly from additional assistance provided by Bögel throughout the process.

Appointed commissioner of colonization for the Austin colony in July 1823 by Luciano Garcia, the political chief of the province, Bögel was given the power to issue land titles. In May 1824, he was chosen to represent the colony in the newly created state legislature for Coahuila y Tejas. While representing Texas, Bögel strongly pushed for policies and legislation that promoted immigration and enhanced settlers' rights until his death and burial in the capital of Saltillo on February 23, 1827. Though research by historians in the late twentieth century have conclusively proven his claims to nobility to be false, the "Baron de Bastrop" was nevertheless a respected member of the San Antonio community who played an instrumental role in promoting American immigration into Texas.

Chapter 4

Texas Revolution (October 1, 1835-April 21, 1836)

The Texas Declaration of Causes For Taking Up Arms Against Santa Anna, November 7, 1835

At the Consultation of 1835 held a month after the outbreak of hostilities at the Battle of Gonzales, assembled delegates from twelve Texas municipalities debated the current situation and possible future courses of action. Eventually, the representatives rejected independence by a 33 to 15 vote but supported resistance against Antonio López de Santa Anna plus the creation of a provisional government by a 33 to 14 tally. On November 7, 1835, the delegates approved the wording of a declaration explaining why they had taken up arms against Santa Anna. Below is the declaration of causes, which preceded the Texas Declaration of Independence and the Texas Constitution by five months.

DECLARATION OF THE PEOPLE OF TEXAS IN GENERAL CONVENTION ASSEMBLED.

Whereas, General Antonio Lopez de Santa Anna and other Military Chieftains have, by force of arms, overthrown the Federal Institutions of Mexico, and dissolved the Social Compact which existed between Texas and the other Members of the Mexican Confederacy—Now, the good People of Texas, availing themselves of their natural rights,

SOLEMNLY DECLARE

1st. That they have taken up arms in defense of their rights and Liberties, which were threatened by the encroachments of military despots, and in defense of the Republican Principles of the Federal Constitution of Mexico of eighteen hundred and twenty-four.

2d. That Texas is no longer, morally or civilly, bound by the compact of Union; yet, stimulated by the generosity and sympathy common to a free people they offer their support and assistance to such Mexicans of the Mexican Confederacy as will take up arms against their military despotism.

3d. That they do not acknowledge, that the present authorities of the nominal Mexican Republic have the right to govern within the limits of Texas.

4th. That they will not cease to carry on war against the said authorities, whilst their troops are within the limits of Texas.

5th. That they hold it to be their right, during the disorganization of the Federal System and the reign of despotism, to withdraw from the Union, to establish an independent Government, or to adopt such measures as they may deem best calculated to protect their rights and liberties; but that they will continue faithful to the Mexican Government so long as that nation is governed by the Constitution and Laws that were formed for the government of the Political Association.

6th. That Texas is responsible for the expenses of her Armies now in the field.

7th. That the public faith is pledged for the payment of any debts contracted by her Agents.

8th. That she will reward by donations in Land, all who volunteer their services in her present struggle, and receive them as Citizens.

These *Declarations* we solemnly avow to the world, and call GOD to witness their truth and sincerity; and invoke defeat and disgrace upon our heads should we prove guilty of duplicity.

[P. B. Dexter], *Secretary*

 B. T. Archer, *President*

Source: "Declaration of the People of Texas in General Convention Assembled," *Journals of the Consultation Held at San Felipe De Austin,* October 16, 1835 (Houston, 1838), 21-22

THOUGHT QUESTIONS:

1. According to the document, why did Texas take up arms against Santa Anna?

2. How did Texans plan to reward members of the volunteer army?

3. To what degree did American ideals and principles influence the Texans?

Report of the Committee on Naval Affairs, November 18, 1835

While the exploits of the Army of the Republic during the Texas Revolution have been retold countless times, the story of the small but effective Texas Navy remains almost unknown to modern Texans. Nevertheless, the efforts of the Texas sailors were vital to the revolt in defending the coastline from Mexican invasion, protecting supply lines from New Orleans, and providing revenue from captured Mexican prize ships. One of the major issues considered by the Consultation, which formed the provisional revolutionary government, was the protection of the coast. The rebel leaders eventually followed the general recommendations laid out in the following report of their Naval Affairs Committee and adopted the traditional practice of issuing letters of marque and reprisal to privateers, or privately-owned ships, to guard the coastline, harass Mexican shipping, and bring in prizes that could be sold off, with the Texas government's treasury receiving a percentage of the proceeds. In all, six letters of marque were issued to privateers to patrol the Gulf and to pursue Mexican shipping on the high seas. By the beginning of 1836, the provisional government also undertook another recommendation of the Naval Affairs Committee Report and began the task of creating a formal navy when it purchased four armed schooners in January and February of 1836.

Mr. Perry from the Committee on Naval Affairs, presented the following Report.

Your Committee on Naval Affairs to whom was refered [sic] so much of the Governor's message as relates to the granting of "Letters of Marque and Reprisal" have had the same under consideration and respectfully report.

Your Committee are of opinion that the same should be granted under the following principles and restriction.

1st All persons applying for "Letters of Marque and Reprisal" should be men of known Character, standing and skill as Naval Tacticians and no license to cruise as such should be granted to any vessel under 80 Tons [burden] or carry less than 4 twelve pound cannonades or their equivalent in metal.

2nd All vessels so licensed should cruise in the Gulf of Mexico and in no other waters and should be permitted to war upon, capture or make prize of all vessels sailing under the flag and under commission of the civil and Government of Mexico and on no other.

3rd All prizes so captured should be ordered or brought into the port of Texas, and when there adjudicated and condemned as prizes to the capters [sic] by the competent tribunal. There should be retained out of the monies arising from the sale of said prize or prizes twenty five per cent for the use of Texas and be paid forthwith into the public Treasury accordingly and the balance to be paid over to the Capters [sic] or their assigns or legal representatives.

4th   All persons to whom a license to cruise in the Gulf of Mexico, as a Letter of Marque and reprisal, shall have been given, or may hereafter be given, shall give good and sufficient security, in a bond, in the sum of _____ Thousand Dollars to be approved by the Governor and Council payable to him and his successors in office for the faithful adherence to and fulfilment of the above enumerated restrictions.

5th   That Commissions or license be not granted for a longer time than six months, nor less than three, and in all cases to expire at the conclusion of our War between Texas and the Central Government of Mexico.

Your Committee would further most earnestly represent that the establishment of a small Naval force for the security of our extended Coast and the protection of our own Commerce would seem to them highly necessary and indispensible [sic] and under that conviction would recommend the purchase, arming and equipping [of] Two Schooners of twelve and two Schooners of six guns each to cruise in and about the bays and harbours of our coast.

This arm of the servise [sic] should be confided and entrusted only to men whose nautical skill and experience are well known and established and whose activity and efficiency would with greater certainty accrue the object of its creation and organization.

HG Perry   Chairman
WP Harris
C West   Committee

Source: Texas State Library and Archives Commission

THOUGHT QUESTIONS:

1. Would anyone be allowed to receive a letter of marque or were certain conditions to be considered? How long was each commission recommended to be in effect?

2. Were suggested limits placed on where those receiving letters of marque should be allowed to patrol and who they could attack? What was the recommended percentage of the proceeds of captured prizes that the report's writers believed should be given to the Texas government?

3. What benefits do you think were gained by the Texas provisional government deciding initially to issue letters of marque to individual privateers? What potential risks might be involved with the practice?

William Travis's "Victory or Death" Letter of February 24, 1836

When Santa Anna's forces arrived in San Antonio on February 23, 1836, William Travis quickly wrote a note to the town of Gonzales asking for reinforcements. The next day, he penned this famous "Victory or Death" letter, promising not to relinquish his position but nevertheless calling for immediate aid, which he gave courier Albert Martin to deliver in haste.

Commandancy of the The Alamo
Bejar, Feby. 24th. 1836

To the People of Texas & All Americans in the World—

Fellow Citizens & compatriots—
    I am besieged, by a thousand or more of the Mexicans under Santa Anna—I have sustained a continual Bombardment & cannonade for 24 hours & have not lost a man— The enemy has demanded a surrender at discretion, otherwise, the garrison are to be put to the sword, if the fort is taken—I have answered the demand with a cannon shot, & our flag still waves proudly from the walls—I shall never surrender or retreat. Then, I call on you in the name of Liberty, of patriotism & everything dear to the American character, to come to our aid, with all dispatch—The enemy is receiving reinforcements daily & will no doubt increase to three or four thousand in four or five days. If this call is neglected, I am determined to sustain myself as long as possible & die like a soldier who never forgets what is due to his own honor & that of his country—**Victory or Death.**
William Barret Travis.
Lt. Col. comdt.

P. S. The Lord is on our side—When the enemy appeared in sight we had not three bushels of corn—We have since found in deserted houses 80 or 90 bushels and got into the walls 20 or 30 head of Beeves.

Travis

Source: Texas State Library and Archives Commission

THOUGHT QUESTIONS:

1. How did Travis attempt to create a sense of urgency with this letter?

2. In the name of what did Travis call on his fellow Americans to come to his aid? Why do you think he did so?

3. In your opinion, what was the purpose of Travis's postscript? Explain.

Travis's Last Appeal From the Alamo, March 3, 1836

From inside the walls of the Alamo, William Barret Travis sent at least three dispatches to Gonzales asking for assistance. On March 3, 1836, Santa Anna had gathered the bulk of his forces outside the Alamo and was preparing to attack the Texas defenders. On this same day, Travis sent his final appeal for military aid. Unfortunately for the defenders, help never arrived, leaving their fate to Santa Anna who chose to offer no quarter to those inside. Below is Travis's final dispatch.

Sir,

In the present confusion of the political authorities of the country, and in the absence of the commander-in-chief, I beg leave to communicate to you the situation of this garrison. You have doubtless already seen my official report of the action of the 25th ult., made on that day to Gen. Sam. Houston, together with the various communications heretofore sent by express. I shall therefore confine myself to what has transpired since that date.

From the 25th to the present date, the enemy have kept up a bombardment from two howitzers, (one a five and a half inch, and the other an eight inch,) and a heavy cannonade from two long nine pounders, mounted on a battery on the opposite side of the river, at the distance of four hundred yards from our walls. During this period the enemy have been busily employed in encircling us with entrenched encampments on all sides, at the following distances, to wit:

—in Bejar, four hundred yards west; in Lavilleta, three hundred yards south; at the powder house, one thousand yards east by south; on the ditch, eight hundred yards northeast, and at the old mill, eight hundred yards north. Notwithstanding all this, a company of thirty-two men, from Gonzales, made their way into us on the morning of the 1st inst., at 3 o'clock, and Col. J. B. Bonham (a courier from Gonzales) got in this morning at 11 o'clock, without molestation. I have so fortified this place, that the walls are generally proof against cannon balls; and I still continue to entrench on the inside, and strengthen the walls by throwing up the dirt. At least two hundred shells have fallen inside of our works without having injured a single man: indeed, we have been so fortunate as not to lose a man from any cause; and we have killed many of the enemy. The spirits of my men are still high, although they have had much to depress them. We have contended for ten days against an enemy whose numbers are variously estimated at from fifteen hundred to six thousand men, with Gen. Ramier Siesma and Col. Batres, the aids-de-camps of Santa Anna, at their head. A report was circulated that Santa Anna himself was with the enemy, but I think it was false. A reinforcement of about one thousand men is now entering Bejar from the west, and I think it more than probable that Santa Anna is now in town, from the rejoicing we hear. Col. Fannin is said to be on the march to this place with reinforcements; but I fear it is not true, as I have repeatedly sent to him for aid without receiving any. Colonel Bonham, my special messenger, arrived at La Bahia fourteen days ago, with a request for aid; and on the arrival of the enemy in Bejar ten days ago, I sent an express to Col. Fannin, which arrived at Goliad on the next day, urging him to send us reinforcements—*none have yet arrived.* I look to the *colonies alone* for aid: unless it arrives soon, I shall have to fight the enemy on his own terms. I will, however, do the best I can under the circumstances; and I feel confident that the determined valor, and desperate courage, heretofore evinced by my men, will not fail them in the last struggle: and although they may be sacrificed to the vengeance of a gothic enemy, the victory will cost the enemy so dear, that it will be worse for him than a defeat. I hope your honourable body will hasten on reinforcements, ammunition, and provisions to our aid, as soon as possible. We have provisions for twenty days for the men we have—our supply of ammunition is limited. At least five hundred pounds of cannon powder, and two hundred rounds of six, nine, twelve, and eighteen pound balls—ten kegs of rifle powder, and a supply of lead, should be sent to this place without delay, under a sufficient guard.

If these things are promptly sent and large reinforcements are hastened to this frontier, this neighborhood will be the great and decisive battle ground. The power of Santa Anna is to be met here, or in the colonies; we had better meet them here, than to suffer a war of desolation to rage in our settlements. A blood red banner waves from the church of Bejar, and in the camp above us, in token that the war is one of vengeance against rebels: they have declared us as such, and demanded that we should surrender at discretion, or that this garrison should be put to the sword. Their threats have had no influence on me, or my men, but to make all fight with desperation, and that high souled courage which characterizes the patriot, who is willing to die in defense of his country's liberty and his own honor.

The citizens of this municipality are all our enemies except those who have joined us heretofore; we have but three Mexicans now in the fort; those who have not joined us in this extremity, should be declared public enemies, and their property should aid in paying the expenses of the war.

The bearer of this will give your honorable body, a statement more in detail, should he escape through the enemies lines—*God and Texas—Victory or Death*!

Your obedient servant,

W. BARRET TRAVIS, Lieut Col. Comm.

P.S. The enemies [sic] troops are still arriving, and the reinforcement will probably amount to two or three thousand.

Source: Mary Austin Holley, *Texas* (Lexington, Ky., 1836), 351-53

THOUGHT QUESTIONS:

1. How did Travis characterize the circumstances at the Alamo?

2. Why did Travis believe that fighting Santa Anna in San Antonio was important?

3. According to the document, what did Travis predict would be the outcome if Santa Anna attacked him at the "present time"? Do you think Travis believed that reinforcements would arrive in time to save the Alamo's defenders? Why or why not?

Sam Houston's Treaty with the Cherokee Indians, February 23, 1836

During the Texas Revolution, Sam Houston negotiated with the Cherokee in an effort to guarantee their neutrality during the fight with Mexico. For their part, the Cherokee, led by Duwali (Chief Bowl) sought recognition of the lands they occupied in East Texas. The resulting treaty, excerpted below, was concluded on February 23, 1836, but never ratified by the Texas Senate. Houston always maintained that the treaty was legal even without the Senate's approval based on power given to him by the Consultation and confirmed by the Convention of 1836. President Mirabeau B. Lamar agreed with the Senate's interpretation and would eventually send troops to drive the Cherokee out of Texas.

Article First

The Parties declare, that there shall be a firm and lasting peace forever, and that a friendly intercourse shall be preserved, by the people belonging to both parties.

Article Second

It is agreed and declared that the before named Tribes, or Bands shall form one community, and that they shall have and possess the lands, within the following bounds. To wit,—laying West of the San Antonio road, and beginning on the West, at the point where the said road crosses the River Angeline, and running up said river, until it reaches the mouth of the first large creek, (below the Great Shawanee village) emptying into the said River from the north east, thence running with said creek, to its main source, and from thence, a due north line to the Sabine River, and with said river west-then starting where the San. Antonio road crosses the Angeline river, and with the said road to the point where it crosses the Naches river and thence running up the east side of said river, in a North West direction.

Article Third

All lands granted or settled in good faith previous to the settlement of the Cherokees, within the before described bounds are not conveyed by this treaty, but excepted from its operation. All persons who have once been removed and returned shall be considered as intruders and their settlements, not be respected. . . .

Article Fifth

It is agreed and declared, by the parties aforesaid, that the land, lying and being within the aforesaid limits shall never be sold or alienated to any person or persons, power or Government, whatsoever else than the Government of Texas, and the Commissioners on behalf of the Government of Texas bind themselves, to prevent in future all persons from intruding within the said bounds.—And it is agreed upon the part of the Cherokees, for themselves and their younger Brothers, that no other tribes or Bands of Indians, whatsoever shall settle within the limits aforesaid, but those already named in this Treaty, and now residing in Texas.

Article Sixth

It is declared that no individual person, member of the Tribes before named, shall have power to sell, or lease land to any, person or persons, not a member or members of this community of Indians, nor shall any citizen of Texas, be allowed to lease or buy land from any Indian or Indians.

Article Seventh

That the Indians shall be governed by their own Regulations, and Laws, within their own territory, not contrary to the Laws of the Government of Texas.—all property stolen from the citizens of Texas, or from the Indians shall be restored to the party from whom it was stolen, and the offender or offenders shall be punished by the party to whom he or they may belong.

Article Eighth

The Government of Texas shall have power to regulate Trade, and intercourse, but no Tax shall be laid on the Trade of the Indians. . . .

Done at Colonel Bowls Village on the Twenty third day of February, Eighteen hundred and thirty six, and the first Year of the Provisional Government of Texas.

Source: Texas State Library and Archives Commission

THOUGHT QUESTIONS:

1. Who would be allowed and who would be banned from the Cherokee lands by the terms of this treaty?

2. Who was allowed and who was forbidden to purchase any portion of the Cherokee lands? Why do you think this provision was included?

3. What aspects of interaction between the Texans and the Cherokee were mentioned in the treaty?

The Treaties of Velasco, May 14, 1836

Following the Battle of San Jacinto, the Texans caught Santa Anna and forced him to sign the Treaties of Velasco on May 14, 1836. One of the treaties quickly became public, establishing a cease fire in Texas among other conditions. The other treaty was a private agreement containing other important stipulations. Both treaties were rejected by the Mexican Senate a few days after it was signed. Below is a copy of both the private and public treaty.

PUBLIC AGREEMENT.

Articles of Agreement entered into between His Excellency DAVID G. BURNET, President of the Republic of Texas, of the one part, and His Excellency General ANTONIO LOPEZ DE SANTA ANNA, President-General-in-Chief of the Mexican Army, of the other part:—

ARTICLE 1. General Antonio Lopez de Santa Anna agrees that he will not take up arms, nor will he exercise his influence to cause them to be taken up, against the people of Texas, during the present war of independence.

ARTICLE 2. All hostilities between the Mexican and Texan troops will cease immediately, both on land and water.

ARTICLE 3. The Mexican troops will evacuate the territory of Texas, passing to the other side of the Rio Grande del Norte.

ARTICLE 4. The Mexican army, in its retreat, shall not take the property of any person without his consent and just indemnification, using only such articles as may be necessary for its subsistence, in cases where the owners may not be present, and remitting to the commander of the army of Texas, or to the commissioners to be appointed for the adjustment of such matters, an account of the value of the property consumed, the place where taken, and the name of the owner, if it can be ascertained.

ARTICLE 5. That all private property, including horses, cattle, negro slaves, or indentured persons of whatever denomination, that may have been captured by any portion of the Mexican army, or may have taken refuge in the said army, since the commencement of the late invasion, shall be restored to the commander of the Texan army, or to such other persons as may be appointed by the government of Texas to receive them.

ARTICLE 6. The troops of both armies will refrain from coming into contact with each other; and, to this end, the commander of the army of Texas will be careful not to approach within a shorter distance of the Mexican army than five leagues.

ARTICLE 7. The Mexican army shall not make any other delay on its march than that which is necessary to take up their hospitals, baggage, &c., and to cross the rivers. Any delay, not necessary to these purposes, to be considered an infraction of this agreement.

ARTICLE 8. By express, to be immediately despatched, this agreement shall be sent to General Filisola, and to General T. J. Rusk, commander of the Texan army, in order that they may be apprized of its stipulations; and, to this end, they will exchange engagements to comply with the same.

ARTICLE 9. That all Texan prisoners now in possession of the Mexican army, or its authorities, be forthwith released, and furnished with free passports to return to their homes; in consideration of which a corresponding number of Mexican prisoners, rank and file, now in possession of the government of Texas, shall be immediately released. The remainder of the Mexican prisoners, that continue in possession of the government of Texas, to be treated with due humanity: any extraordinary comforts that may be furnished them to be at the charge of the government of Mexico.

ARTICLE 10. General Antonio Lopez de Santa Anna will be sent to Vera Cruz, as soon as it shall be deemed proper.

The contracting parties sign this instrument for the above-mentioned purposes, by duplicate, at the port of Velasco, this the 14th day of May, 1836.

DAVID G. BURNET,
ANT. LOPEZ DE SANTA ANNA.

PRIVATE AGREEMENT.

ANTONIO LOPEZ DE SANTA ANNA, General-in-Chief of the Army of Operations, and President of the Republic of Mexico, before the Government established in Texas, solemnly pledges himself to fulfil the Stipulations contained in the following Articles, so far as concerns himself:—

ARTICLE 1. He will not take up arms, nor cause them to be taken up, against the people of Texas, during the present war for independence.

ARTICLE 2. He will give his orders that, in the shortest time, the Mexican troops may leave the territory of Texas.

ARTICLE 3. He will so prepare matters in the cabinet of Mexico, that the mission that may be sent thither by the government of Texas may be well received, and that by means of negotiations all differences may be settled, and the independence that has been declared by the convention may be acknowledged.

ARTICLE 4. A treaty of commerce, amity, and limits, will be established between Mexico and Texas, the territory of the latter not to extend beyond the Rio Bravo del Norte.

ARTICLE 5. The present return of General Santa Anna to Vera Cruz being indispensable for the purpose of effecting his solemn engagements, the government of Texas will provide for his immediate embarkation for said port.

ARTICLE 6. This instrument, being obligatory on one part as well as on the other, will be signed in duplicate, remaining folded and sealed until the negotiations shall have been concluded, when it will be restored to his excellency General Santa Anna; no use of it to be made before that time, unless there should be an infraction by either of the contracting parties.

PORT OF VELASCO, *May the 14th*, 1836.

ANT. LOPEZ DE SANTA ANNA,
DAVID G. BURNET.

Source: Henry Yoakum, *History of Texas, 1685-1845*, 2 vols. (New York, 1855), 526-28

THOUGHT QUESTIONS:

1. What military provisions are specified in the public treaty?

2. What were the main differences between the private and public agreements in the treaty?

3. Why do you think Texans demanded that Santa Anna accept the private provisions of the treaty?

Fannin's Cannon

**Credit: UTSA's Institute of Texas Cultures, #071-0691,
Courtesy of Frances Johnston.**

This photograph shows a cannon used by James Fannin's (biography at the end of this chapter) men at Presidio La Bahia. Fannin had received orders from Sam Houston to destroy such weapons and retreat to Victoria, but the colonel disregarded Houston's instructions, which slowed his pace and allowed Mexican cavalry to intercept him at Coleto Creek.

THOUGHT QUESTION:

What were some of the positive merits and the many negative attributes of James Fannin as a military officer during the Texas Revolution?

"Delegates Voting on the Texas Constitution"

**Credit: UTSA's Institute of Texan Cultures, #074-0445,
Courtesy, artist Bruce Marshall.**

The painting depicts delegates voting on the Republic of Texas Constitution on the evening of March 16, 1836 at Washington-on-the-Brazos amidst the "Runaway Scrape."

THOUGHT QUESTION:

Describe the Runaway Scrape. Who took part in the retreat and what precipitated the move?

BIOGRAPHIES

JAMES WALKER FANNIN (1804-1836) Texas revolutionary leader James Walker Fannin was born on January 1, 1804, in Georgia. Illegitimately fathered by a young planter named Isham Fannin, his maternal grandfather, James W. Walker, raised the boy on his plantation near Marion, Georgia. In July 1819 he earned admission to the United States Military Academy at West Point but left in 1821 due to poor performance. Returning home, he became a merchant and married Minerva Fort in 1829 with whom he had two daughters. In the fall of 1834, Fannin moved with his family to Texas, settling near Velasco, where he operated a plantation and engaged in slave trading.

In August 1835, Fannin became involved in the Texas Revolution. He wrote to a United States Army officer in Georgia requesting financial support and recruits for the Texas independence movement then traveled to Gonzales where volunteers chose him to be their captain. Despite his lack of combat experience, many rebels deferred to him because he had some formal military training. He participated in the Battle of Gonzales on October 2, 1835. When Stephen F. Austin prepared to move Texas forces toward San Antonio, he appointed Fannin and James Bowie to lead an advance group of ninety men to locate a suitable defensive position near the town and to determine general conditions between Gonzales and San Antonio. On October 27, they camped near the Nuestra Señora de la Purísima Concepción de Acuña Mission. The next day, Mexican General Martín Perfecto de Cos attacked, but Fannin's force repelled them in a fight known as the Battle of Concepción, the opening engagement of the siege of Bexar. In late November, Sam Houston offered Fannin the position of inspector general, but he desired a field command. Houston commissioned him as a colonel in the regular army and ordered him to procure necessary men and supplies for the campaign against the Mexican forces at San Antonio. Before he could complete his task, General Cos surrendered his remaining forces after the five-day Battle of San Antonio.

Fannin began to recruit men for a planned expedition to capture Matamoros. The regiment's volunteers elected him colonel before learning that a sizeable Mexican force led by José de Urrea had occupied Matamoros. Forced to drop his invasion plans, Fannin ordered his men to strengthen their position at Goliad.

While at Goliad, Fannin's numerous weaknesses as a military commander began to emerge. Most of his men perceived him as arrogant and disliked his penchant for harsh discipline. His indecisiveness became evident with his response to William Travis and James Bowie's desperate pleas for help at the Alamo. Though Fannin quickly organized a 320-man relief expedition to make the one hundred-mile trek to San Antonio, the group did not get far from Goliad before the commander changed his mind. Already without a full heart for the mission, Fannin began to reassess the situation after some supply carts broke down, and the men failed to move their ammunition wagon across the San Antonio River. After camping for the night, several oxen also wandered off. When news arrived that fresh supplies had landed at Matagorda Bay, Fannin called a meeting of his officers who unanimously agreed that they should return to Goliad. Further adding to the case against Fannin's abilities, he questionably divided his command on two occasions in the face of an approaching enemy. He first sent a contingent of men under Captain Amon King to Refugio to help evacuate families located there.

Then, after learning that King had been attacked by General Urrea's cavalry, he sent another force under Lieutenant Colonel William Ward to aid the captain. Men from both units were eventually killed, captured, or scattered, thus further reducing Fannin's numbers.

In addition to diminishing his forces, Fannin's moves cost him valuable time, delaying his withdrawal to Victoria after Houston ordered him to pull back. He compounded these errors with additional miscues, such as wasting time destroying buildings to prevent their use by Urrea. Upon finally getting his men marching, the colonel also slowed their pace considerably when he disregarded Houston's instructions to destroy his cannon and insisted upon bringing along his nine artillery pieces. Fannin's final blunder occurred when he ordered his men to stop for rest on an open prairie five miles short of Coleto Creek's protective tree line. General Urrea's cavalry caught up with the Texans and harassed them throughout the day, buying time for the main portion of the Mexican army to arrive and soon surround the rebels. Though a flawed tactician, Fannin proved his mettle as a fearless combat leader as he directed the Texans' defense despite receiving a painful thigh wound. Nevertheless, he realized by the next morning that their cause was hopeless. Meeting with General Urrea under a white flag of truce, Fannin agreed to surrender with no conditions. Though some historians have brought up the possibility of a misunderstanding due to language barriers, the fact remains that the Mexican military archives in Mexico City house a copy of the unconditional surrender document signed by Fannin. Most probably, he simply told his men that Urrea agreed to treat them as prisoners of war rather than pirates in order to convince them to lay down their arms. In this manner, they might still have a chance for survival.

Urrea marched the prisoners back to Goliad, reported their capture to Santa Anna, and expressed his personal belief that they should be exiled to New Orleans. The captured Texans, however, had no luck as Santa Anna decided to show no mercy, ordering their execution. The subsequent Goliad Massacre took place on March 27, 1836. Fannin and over 340 men (almost twice as many killed defending the Alamo) perished. While Mexican soldiers killed most of the rebels outside the presidio (though some escaped to tell their tale), troops inside the presidio's walls shot the colonel and the other wounded men. Fannin's last requests were to be shot in the chest, to be given a Christian burial, and to have his personal watch delivered to his family. Instead, the officer in charge pocketed his watch, ordered the leader to be shot in the head, and arranged for his body to be thrown into a large fire with the other rebel corpses. Though Fannin's errors directly resulted in his force's elimination, Santa Anna's blunder in ordering the Texans' execution unnecessarily created martyrs that filled Texas insurgents with renewed resolve to triumph over their adversaries.

SUSANNA WILKERSON DICKINSON (1814-1883). Susanna Dickinson, Alamo widow and survivor, was a native of Tennessee born in 1814. Only fifteen years of age when she and twenty-nine-year old Almaron Dickinson eloped in May 1829, the couple migrated with fifty-four other settlers to Green De Witt's colony in 1831. Settling on a league of land along the San Marcos River just above Gonzales, Susanna gave birth to a daughter named Angelina in December 1834. Almaron took part in the October 1835 skirmish at Gonzales against Mexican troopers marking the first shots of the Texas

Revolution before joining Texans besieging San Antonio. After the rebels attacked and captured the town, Susanna arrived in December 1835.

With the approach of Santa Anna's forces, she moved herself and her child into the Alamo where Almaron served as captain in charge of artillery. When Mexican forces finally attacked on March 6, Susanna and Angelina hid in the church sacristy. Susanna later reported that her husband ran to her soon after the Mexican assault commenced to report that the walls has been breached before kissing her goodbye and returning to his post where he was subsequently killed. The rebel failure to destroy the gunpowder magazine stored in the church probably saved Susanna's and Angelina's lives. They were captured near the end of the violence when Mexican forces burst into the sacristy. Susanna was struck in the leg by an errant bullet during the melee when Mexican troops fired upon a rebel within the building. She was later interviewed by Santa Anna before being sent east to Sam Houston's encampment in order to spread word of the Alamo's capture and the slaughter of the rebels.

Susanna Dickinson's less well-known post-Revolution life was filled with instability. At the end of hostilities, she was a twenty-two year old widow with a young daughter to raise and no extended family to provide support. In October 1836, she joined other widows and veterans in petitioning the Texas Congress for aid. The financially strapped government refused her request. She began living with John Williams in June 1837 and married him in November, but they divorced in March 1838 on grounds that he failed to provide proper support and often beat her and young Angelina. For a time Susanna reportedly lived in Pamelia Mann's rowdy Mansion House Hotel in Houston, which had a reputation for tolerating drunkenness and prostitution. In December 1838 she married a water carrier named Francis Herring, but he died after only five years of marriage. Susanna married again in December 1847, this time to a drayman originally from Pennsylvania named Peter Bellows. The 1850 U.S. census lists the couple living together with Angelina, now aged sixteen. The marriage fell apart by 1854, however, when Susanna moved out (Angelina had left when she married in 1851) and perhaps lived once again at the Mansion House Hotel—Bellows' 1857 divorce petition, which was granted, accused Susanna of taking up residence in a "house of ill fame" where she was "in constant habit of committing adultery with various persons."

Susanna's fifth and final marriage endured. After moving to Lockhart where she set up a boarding house to support herself, Susanna married a German immigrant named Joseph W. Hannig in 1857. The couple soon moved to Austin where he ran a cabinet shop, furniture store, and an undertaking business. Meanwhile, Susanna held minor celebrity status throughout her remaining years in Austin. Though never writing about her wartime experiences, she often related her story to inquiring individuals and dutifully appeared at various commemorations for revolutionary heroes when called upon to do so. She died in Austin on October 7, 1883. Though buried next to Hannig at the Oakwood Cemetery in Austin, the Texas State Cemetery contains a cenotaph in her honor.

JOSÉ DE URREA (1797-1849). José de Urrea, the most accomplished Mexican general of the Texas Revolution, was born in 1797 into a military family at the presidio of Tucson, Sonora (present-day Arizona). In 1809 he joined the Spanish army as a cadet. Seven years later, he served as a young lieutenant and participated in the Battles of Jalisco and

Michoacán. In 1821, he supported Agustín de Iturbide's Plan of Iguala but was removed from the Mexican army six years later for assisting a failed coup attempt against Vicente Guerrero. In 1829 he served as a volunteer under General Antonio López de Santa Anna against a Spanish invasion force led by Isidro Barradas. After Anastasio Bustamante came to power, Urrea was reinstated and promoted to the rank of lieutenant colonel. By 1835 he was a brigadier general also serving as governor of Durango.

In 1836, Santa Anna ordered Urrea to aid his suppression of the Texas Revolution. Steadily advancing northward along the coastal Atascosito Road, Urrea easily dispatched rebels at Agua Dulce Creek, San Patricio, and Refugio. After capturing the town and presidio at Goliad, the general steadily pressed on, eventually intercepting James Fannin's retreating garrison near Coleto Creek. Urrea sought and achieved the rebels' unconditional surrender, promising only to recommend clemency to Santa Anna. Objecting on principle to standing orders to kill all prisoners, Urrea wrote the dictator to explain his preference to see Fannin and his men paroled and shipped to New Orleans. Upon hearing that prisoners were alive, Santa Anna delivered a strong rebuke to Urrea and issued direct orders to the presidial commander at Goliad to execute them all. Nevertheless, Urrea managed to spare several prisoners in the form of physicians used to aid wounded Mexican soldiers, as well as various carpenters, artisans, and other "essential personnel" that the general stated were needed to facilitate his advance along the coast. Due to torrential spring rains and heavy mud, however, Urrea's rapid advance stalled at the mouth of the Brazos River.

After the Battle of San Jacinto, Urrea opposed withdrawing Mexican troops out of Texas, but he eventually complied with Santa Anna's orders to withdraw. The next year, he became commandant general of the departments of Sinaloa and Sonora. He led troops against Santa Anna upon the ex-dictator's return to Mexico but was defeated at Mazatlán in 1838. Fleeing to Durango, the general was captured in 1839 and spent time in Veracruz's infamous Perote Prison. When Santa Anna declared adherence to Federalist principles, Urrea supported him and was named governor of Sonora, a post he held until May 1844. Before dying of cholera in 1849, he took part in his last military action leading a cavalry division against American forces during the Mexican War.

JOE (1815-?). For generations, not much was known about the life of Joe, William B. Travis's slave who survived the Battle of the Alamo. Thanks to over ten years of detective work by Ron L. Jackson Jr. and Lee Spencer White, and their findings published in a 2015 book entitled *Joe: The Slave Who Became an Alamo Legend*, we know a lot more about Joe's early life than many thought possible. Born on a farm near Lexington, Kentucky in 1815, Joe and dozens of other slaves were brought to the Missouri Territory the next year by his master, a doctor named John Young. Joe's mother was a mulatto slave named Elizabeth who had seven children, including one of Joe's brothers who Jackson and White determined to be the noted African-American abolitionist William Wells Brown (who had escaped bondage in the mid-1830s). When Young encountered financial trouble, he started selling his slaves, including Joe's mother and her children. In the early 1830s, Joe became the property of Isaac Mansfield, who owned a tin manufacturing plant in St. Louis. When Mansfield suffered money problems of his own, he moved to Texas with Joe and five other slaves, arriving in early 1833. Public records in Austin County show that upon Mansfield's death, Joe was sold again, at a December 1834 auction in San Felipe de Austin for $410 to John Cummings, the brother of William B. Travis's fiancé, Rebecca Cummings. Travis purchased Joe from Cummings prior to their February 1836 arrival at the Alamo.

When Santa Anna broke the siege of the Alamo on the morning of March 6, 1836, Joe later related to listeners how the men grabbed their rifles and ran up an earthen ramp to the north wall. Within minutes, Travis would be killed with a bullet to the head. Joe fled to a building where he was shot and stabbed by Mexican troopers. An officer intervened to save him because he was a slave. After being interrogated by Santa Anna, Joe joined Susannah Dickinson and her daughter on their way to Sam Houston's encampment at Gonzales. On March 20, Joe was questioned by rebel officials about what had transpired at the Alamo. He was then taken to Travis's estate near Columbia, where he remained for over a year working at a tavern and boarding house before being sold by Travis's estate to John Rice Jones, who had recently purchased a plantation near Columbia.

On the night of April 21, 1837, Joe escorted Jones and his wife to a ball held in Houston to commemorate the one-year anniversary of the Battle of San Jacinto. After dropping off the couple, Joe escaped. Jones offered fifty dollars for his return in a notice appearing in the *Telegraph and Texas Register* on May 26, 1837, but he discontinued the advertisement after three months. According to Travis family lore, Joe made the long trek from eastern Texas to southern Alabama in order to relay the news about Travis's fight to his relatives and lived with the family for many years, supposedly returning to the Alamo many decades later with William Travis's brother to show him where his kin had fought and died.

Chapter 5

Birth of a New Republic,
1836-1845

A Report on the New Capital Site

Mirabeau Lamar personally suggested the site for the future permanent capital of the Republic after visiting central Texas in 1838. At the time, a few families had been the sole residents of the location along the north bank of the Colorado River approximately where the Congress Avenue Bridge in Austin stands today. A five-man commission appointed by Lamar in early 1839 originally named the tiny settlement Waterloo, the name under which it was known until the Texas Congress soon officially renamed the new capital town in honor of Stephen F. Austin.

In this letter to Lamar written on April 15, 1839, commission member Thomas Jefferson Jones reports on the proposed site, comments on the frontier situation as he believed it then existed, and mentions his enthusiasm for participation in the upcoming Santa Fe Expedition into New Mexico.

Camp on Wilbarger's Prairie

Dear Gen.

I have just returned from Waterloo, the contemplated new seat of government which I visited in company with Gen. [Edward] Burleson. It is the most beautiful and at the same time the most sublime scene I ever saw. I know you will be delighted with it and I frequently wished that you were present to enjoy the scenery as I saw it in all the majesty of nature and the verdure of Spring. The atmosphere was charged with the most delightful perfume and every shrub and every hill and every flower seemed to extend a welcome to the weary traveller [sic.]. I never expected to realize your eloquent description of Texas till I saw the lanos [llanos: Spanish for plains] of the upper Colorado. There are hundreds of the most beautiful scites [sic.] for building around the town level and Rome itself with all its famous hills could not have surpassed the natural scenery of Waterloo. When I have a better opportunity I will send you a landscape of the spot and the surrounding country.

The frontier is now quiet and perfectly safe. The Valley from La Grange to the mountains presents a bountiful prospect to the eye of the traveller [sic]. All fears of a[n] Indian invasion are dissapated [sic] and the people are actively employed in planting & tending their crops. The inhabitants say they have [illegible] in three years. Burleson has acted like a hero and a skilled officer. He has defeated the Indians and solved the Mexicans and all done without expense to the government or [illegible] to the planting interest.

I envy no man the command of volunteers when in the settlements and not on active duty. I have had a hard task to perform but I never tired. I have had to command my men singly & alone. I have had no help from the subordinate officers. I had to walk to Bastrop myself to get my men to follow me. I have had their murmurings to silence—their discontents to allay and their patriotism to arouse to get them along. I have cursed them. I have shamed them and I have done all that man could do to make soldiers of them. I hope I may have succeeded in part.

Let me hear from you as soon as possible. I must return to Houston before I start on the Santa Fe expedition but I must be ordered to return. That expedition is universally approved and it will be the most glorious event in the history of your political life.

Remember me to all my friends and believe me as ever to be your sincere friend.

T. Jefferson Jones

P.S. Gen Burleson will tell you the disposition I have made of my men.

Source: Texas State Library and Archives Commission

THOUGHT QUESTIONS:

1. What are Jones's general opinions about Waterloo as a location for a capital and settlement? What imagery does he employ to back his claims?

2. How did Jones describe the situation on the central Texas frontier as a result of Lamar's policy toward Native Americans?

3. What attitude did Jones have toward his men now that hostilities had ceased? How did he try to motivate his men?

Hugh McLeod's Description of the Council House Fight

Early in 1840, the Comanches sent word to Texas officials in San Antonio that they wished to negotiate a peace settlement. The Texas government accepted the request as long as the Comanches agreed to cease raiding, returned stolen property, and released all white prisoners captured. On March 19, 1840, at the Council House in San Antonio, Colonel Hugh McLeod and Colonel William G. Cooke planned to negotiate the release of several white captives, mostly women and children who had been taken in earlier raids along the frontier. They were told to order troops to capture the Comanche representatives and hold them as hostages if all of the white captives were not turned over to them. When the Comanche delegation arrived, they only brought one captive (young Matilda Lockhart) to the Council House. Before negotiations could take place, a battle erupted between the Comanches and the Texans present at the meeting. Thirty Comanche warriors along with five women and children were killed. Seven Texans died in the melee. When word reached the other Comanches stationed outside of San Antonio, they killed all of their prisoners and proceeded to initiate a rampage on Texas frontier settlements. Below is McLeod's version of what happened at the Council House.

San Antonio, March 20, 1840. To his Excellency M. B. Lamar:

Sir—On yesterday morning the 19th inst. two runners came into town and announced the arrival of the Comanches, who, about a month since, held a talk at this place, and promised to bring in the Texian prisoners in their camp. The party consisted of 65—men, women, and children. The runners also informed us that they had with them but one prisoner (the daughter of Mr. Lockhart).

They came to town. The little girl was very intelligent, and told us that she had seen several of the other prisoners at the principal camp a few days before she left; and that they brought her in to see if they could get a high price for her, and if so, would bring in the rest, one at a time.

Having ascertained this, it became necessary to execute your orders, and take hostages for the safe return of our own people—and the order was accordingly given by Col. Wm. G. Cooke, acting Secretary of War.

Lieut. Col. Fisher, 1st infantry, was ordered to march up two companies, and place them in the immediate vicinity of the council room. The chiefs were then called together, and were asked "Where are the prisoners you promised to bring to this talk?" One of them, Muke-war-rab, the chief who held the last talk, and made the promise, replied—"We have brought in the only one we had; the others are with other tribes." A pause ensued, because, as this was a palpable lie, and a direct violation of the pledge given scarcely a month since, we had the only alternative left us. He observed the pause, and asked quickly, "How do you like answer?"

The order was now given to march one company into the council room, and the other in the rear of the building, where the warriors were assembled. During the execution of this order, the talk was re-opened, and the terms of a treaty directed by your excellency to be made with them in the case the prisoners were restored, were discussed, and they were told the treaty would be made when they brought in the prisoners. They acknowledged that they had violated all their previous treaties, and yet tauntingly demanded that new confidence should be reposed in another promise to bring in the prisoners.

The troops being now posted, the chiefs and captains were told that they were our prisoners and would be kept as hostages for the safety of our people, then in their hands, and they might send the young men to the tribe, and as soon as our friends were restored they should be liberated.

Capt. Howard, whose company was stationed in the council house, posted sentinels at the doors and drew up his men across the room. We told the chiefs that the soldiers they saw were their guards, and descended from the platform. The chiefs immediately followed. One sprang to the door and attempted to pass the sentinel, who presented his musket, when the chief drew his knife and stabbed him. A rush was then made for the door. Capt. Howard collared one of them, and received a severe stab from him in the side. He ordered the sentinel to fire upon him, which he immediately did, and the Indian fell dead. They now all drew their knives and bows, and evidently resolved to fight to the last. Col. Fisher ordered "fire, if they resist." The Indians rushed on, attacked us desperately, and a general order to fire became necessary. The chiefs in the council house, twelve in number, were immediately shot.

The council house being cleared, Capt. Howard was ordered to form in front, to receive any who might attempt to retreat in that direction. He was subsequently relieved of command, in consequence of the severity of his wound, by Capt. Allen, who commanded the company during the rest of the action.

Capt. Redd, whose company was formed in rear of the council house, was attacked by the warriors in the yard, who fought with desperation. They were repulsed and driven into the stone houses, from which they kept up a galling fire with their bows, and a few rifles. Their arrows, when they struck, were driven to the feather.

A small party succeeded in breaking through, and gained the opposite bank of the river, but were pursued by Col. Wells, with a party of mounted men, and all killed but one, a renegade Mexican.

A single warrior, who threw himself into a very strong stone house, refused every effort of his life, sent to him through the squaws, and after killing and wounding several of our men, was forced out by fire late at night, and fell as he passed the door.

In a melee action, and so unexpected, it was impossible to discriminate between the sexes, so similar in dress, and several women were shot; but when discovered, all were spared, and twenty-nine women and children remain our prisoners.

Our loss was as follows: killed—Lieut. W. M. Dunnington, 1st infantry; private Kaminski, of A. company; private Whitney, of E. company, Judge Thompson, of Houston; Judge Hood, of Bexar; Mr. Casey, of Matagorda county; and a Mexican (name unknown). Total killed 7.

LIST OF WOUNDED.

Capt. George T. Howard, 1st infantry; Capt. Mathew Caldwell, 1st infantry; Lieut. Edward A. Thompson; private Kelly, company I; Judge Robinson; Mr. Higginbotham; Mr. Morgan; and Mr. Carson. Total wounded 8.

Capt. Howard, Lieut. Thompson, and private Kelly, very severely.

Source: From Hugh McLeod to Mirabeau Lamar, March 20, 1840; Texas State Library and Archives Commission

THOUGHT QUESTIONS:

1. According to McLeod, why did the Comanche only bring one captive? What was the source of this information?

2. According to McLeod, how and when did the violence at the Council House meeting start?

3. Keeping in mind the context of this event, who do you think was at fault for this unfortunate incident and why?"

Lamar's Address to the People of Santa Fe

During Mirabeau B. Lamar's administration, the president sought to secure Texas's claim to all lands to the north and east of the Rio Grande, including Santa Fe, though the settlements there had never been considered a part of Texas. Along with the ill-fated Santa Fe Expedition of 1841, Lamar sent three commissioners to establish a government under Texas authority. They brought with them a lengthy letter, excerpts provided below, in which Lamar attempts to persuade the people of Santa Fe that it was in their best interest to accept Texas sovereignty over them:

Executive Department Austin City June 5th, 1841

To the Inhabitants of Santa Fe and of the other portions of New Mexico, to the East of the Rio Grande

FELLOW CITIZENS

Very early after assuming the duties of this official station, the present executive felt it to be his obligation to assert the Jurisdiction of the Government over the inhabited portion of the Republic; and to admit its remotest citizens to an equal participation of the blessings which have been acquired by our late glorious revolution, and made secure by a wise and liberal constitution. But various circumstances having conspired to delay the execution of his purpose until the present auspicious period, he now calls the attention of the people of Santa Fe to the deep interest which they have in the proposed policy, with an earnest hope that it will not only meet their cordial approbation, but that it will, when successfully carried out be attended with all the beneficial consequences which we so fondly anticipate and desire. . . .

Knowing that you have been long subjected to like injuries with those which impelled us to take up arms against the authorities of Mexico, we do not doubt but that you duly appreciate the spirit, that animated our patriots, and sympathized with them in the progress of our struggle in which you were not able to participate—as you probably desired to do—in consequence of your remote and isolated situation. That struggle was brief, bloody and decisive; and terminated in the total discomfiture and expulsion of our foe, and in the establishment of a free, happy, and independent, Republic, extending from the Sabine to the Rio del Norte [Rio Grande], and from the Gulf to the Pacific; embracing within its limits a vast and varied Country, unrivalled in beauty, salubrity, and fertility; and capable of sustaining a population as dense prosperous and powerful as any people on the earth. The boundaries which were thus marked by the sword, and which have been confirmed to us, by the recognition of the most enlightened and influential nations, it is the resolve of this Government, at all hazards to maintain the country has been won by our valor, and is consecrated to civil and religious liberty; and in no portion of it will the enemy who provoked our resentment and received our chastisement, ever be permitted to continue its authority or perpetuate its domination. Knowing such to be the feelings of our people, it is due to candor to apprise you of the fact and to let you know that the position which which [sic] you now occupy towards this government is temporary only and will have to give way to a more enlarged and liberal policy. Although residing within our established limits you are at present paying tribute to our enemies, professing allegiance to them and receiving Laws from their hands a state of things utterly incompatible with out right of sovereignty, and which certainly cannot be permitted to be of long continuance. . . .

Believing that you are the friends of liberty, and will duly appreciate the motives by which we are actuated, we have appointed commissioners to make known to you in a distinct and definite manner, the general desire of the citizens of this Republic to receive the people of Santa Fe, as a portion of the national family, and to give to them all the protection which they themselves enjoy. This union, however, to make it agreeable to this Government, must be altogether voluntary on your part; and based on mutual interest, confidence and affection. Should you, therefore, in view of the whole matter be willing to avail yourselves of this opportunity to secure your own prosperity, as well as that of your descendents, by a prompt, cheerful and unanimous adherence to the Government of this republic we invite you to a full and unreserved intercourse and communication with our commissioners, who are instructed to extend to you every assistance and co-operation to effectuate the object desired; and, at the same time, to assure you that your religion will in no wise be interfered with by this Government. The only change we desire to effect in your affairs, is such as we wrought in our own when we broke our fetters and established our freedom; a change which was well worth the price we paid; and the blessings of which we are ready now to extend to you at the sacrafice [sic] of our own lives and fortunes, if you are ready to receive them; and if not we have ordered our commissioners, not to interrupt you in any of your rights, nor to disturb your tranquility, but to establish with you, if possible such commercial relations as you may deem conducive to your own interests and then peacibly [sic] retire from your city.

MIRABEAU B. LAMAR.

Source: Charles A. Gulick and Katherine Elliott (eds.), *The Papers of Mirabeau Buonaparte Lamar* (6 vols.; Austin, 1922), III, 488-491

THOUGHT QUESTIONS:

1. What is the purpose of Lamar's letter to the people of Santa Fe?

2. Based on this letter, how do you think Lamar truly viewed the citizens of Santa Fe?

3. Does Lamar make any veiled threats in his letter to those who do not subject themselves to Texas authority?

Alexander Somervell Seeks to Aid Juan Seguín

In March 1842, after Mayor Juan Seguín and most of the Hispanic population of San Antonio fled the city in the face of a probing raid ordered by Antonio López de Santa Anna and led by Rafael Vasquez, many Anglo Texans suspected Seguín of favoring the invading Mexican forces. As a result of threats, Seguín and his family fled Texas for northern Mexico on April 18. Six months later, he returned to Texas, forced by Mexican authorities to join another force of Mexican invaders under the command of Adrian Woll. President Sam Houston placed Alexander Somervell in command of a force to chase Woll, but when Somervell ordered his men to return home, many refused and continued into northern Mexico as the ill-fated Mier Expedition.

In this letter sent to Houston less than a month before Seguín fled Texas, Somervell proposed a plan (which never transpired) to allow Seguín to recover lost favor with Texans by acting as an intermediary with Mexican General Mariano Arista, a rival of Santa Anna's.

San Antonio 31st March 1842

Much esteemed Sir

I confess it is with diffidence I approach a subject on which so much may depend and yet such is my firm conviction of the great good that may result from it that I am emboldened to speak and not however in a spirit of obtrusiveness or advice but with due deference and respect and a firm reliance in your well known and truly appreciated better judgment.

This then is the subject on which I would speak. There is a well-known jealousy now existing between Santa Anna and General Arista. Could you not in your own peculiar and felicitous style, foment and excite that jealousy to open rivalry and hostility by tendering to Arista on your part (as it is an executive act) the acknowledgment of the independence of the Government he may establish and also to offer him the services of a thousand or more Texian soldiers to be recruited, officered, and fought under our own flag, subject to his orders while in that service but under the rules and articles of war that govern us, he to pay the expenses of the troops and they to act offensively and defensively against our common enemy Santa Anna and the Southern portion of the Republic of Mexico; if the plan succeed it would have the salutary effect of taking the war out of our own country and erecting a barrier between us and our enemies.

There is a difficulty as to the manner of approaching Arista but that I think can be obviated by the employment of John N. Seguín for that service, he is at present in bad odour [sic.] among the Texians from which circumstance he could frame a good pretext for crossing the Rio Grande and asking an audience of Arista. Whether or not Seguín would accept of such a mission I cannot say, but I should think it would give him an opportunity to retrieve his former standing that he would gladly embrace, for if he be successful it would redound to his credit in an eminent degree and establish his loyalty to Texas and if he be not successful he would be in none the worse condition. Yourself are better acquainted than I of his fitness for such a mission.

I have understood that your Lady has been afflicted with ill health. Be pleased to present her my kind regards and my sincere wishes for her speedy recovery.

Accept the friendship of Yours Truly

A Somervell

Source: Texas State Library and Archives Commission.

THOUGHT QUESTIONS:

1. What specific plan does Somervell want Houston to propose to General Arista?

2. What benefits to Texas did Somervell see coming out of this scheme?

3. How did Somervell believe that Seguín would benefit from delivering the message? Did he think Seguín would accept the offer? Why or why not?

The Black Bean Episode of the Mier Expedition

In response to the Santa Fe expedition, the Mexican government ordered several raids into Texas. In 1842, Mexican General Adrian Woll attacked and occupied San Antonio for nine days. When his army left the city, they carried with them several prominent Texans. Angry Texans quickly answered President Houston's call for volunteers to punish the Mexican invaders. General Alexander Somervell led the volunteers as far as the Rio Grande, but stopped short of pursuing Woll's troops across the river. Houston order the men to disperse and return to their homes, but a select group of men led by Colonel W. S. Fisher decided to disobey orders, cross the Rio Grande, and start attacking border towns, including the village of Mier. On December 26, the Texans lost a desperate battle against Mexican forces in Mier and surrendered. Mexican forces marched the captured Texas troops to the town of Salado, south of Saltillo.

After a failed escaped attempt, Antonio López de Santa Anna originally ordered all of the captured prisoners to be executed, but after intervention by American and British diplomats, a compromise was reached: only one in ten, or seventeen of the 176 total prisoners, would be shot, with their fate chosen by lots in the form of seventeen black beans to be drawn by the prisoners themselves from an earthen pot filled with 176 white and black beans. Survivors of this so-called Black Bean Episode were taken to Mexico City and imprisoned in Castle Perote, housed alongside surviving members of the Santa Fe expedition and those prisoners taken by Woll from San Antonio.

Below is an account of the Black Bean Episode based on a book written by Thomas Jefferson Green, the second in command of the Mier Expedition. Though not present at the time of the execution of the Mier prisoners, Green used a diary from a survivor and other sources to produce this standard description of the event.

Soon after they arrived [at the Salado on March 25, 1843], our men received the melancholy intelligence that they were to be decimated, and each tenth man shot.

It was now too late to resist the horrible order. Our men were closely ironed and drawn up in front of all their guards, with arms in readiness to fire. Could they have known it previously, they would have again charged their guards, and made them dearly pay for this last perfidious breach of national faith. It was now too late! A manly gloom and a proud defiance pervaded all countenances. They had but one alternative, and that was to invoke their country's vengeance upon their murders, consign their souls to God, and die like men. Could these martyrs in liberty's cause, who so proudly yielded up their President had endorsed their execution by the most villainous of all falsehoods, declaring them brigands—great God! What would have been their feelings. . . .

The decimation took place by the drawing of black and white beans from a small earthen mug. The white ones signified *exemption*, and the black *death*. One hundred and fifty-nine white beans were placed in the bottom of the mug, and seventeen black ones placed upon the top of them. The beans were not stirred, and had so slight a shake that it was perfectly clear they had not been mixed together. Such was their anxiety to execute Captain Cameron, and perhaps the balance of the officers, that first Cameron, and afterward they, were made to draw a bean each from the mug in this condition. . . .

[Captain Cameron] said, with his usual coolness, "Well, boys, we have to draw, let's be at it;" so saying, he thrust his hand into the mug, and drew out a white bean. Next came Colonel Win. F. Wilson, who was chained to him; then Captain Wm. Ryan, and then Judge F. M. Gibson, all of whom drew white beans. Next came Captain Eastland, who drew the first black one, and then came the balance of the men. They all drew their beans with that manly dignity and firmness which showed them superior to their condition. Some of lighter temper jested over the bloody tragedy. One would say, "Boys, this beats raffling all to pieces;" another would say that "this is the tallest gambling scrape I ever was in," and such like remarks. None showed changes of countenance; and as the black beans failed to depress, so did the white fail to elate. . . .

Just previous to the firing they were bound together with cords, and their eyes being bandaged, they were set upon a log near the wall, with their backs to their executioners. They all begged the officer to shoot them in front, and at a short distance; that "they were not afraid to look death in the face." This he refused; and, to make his cruelty as refined as possible, fired at several paces, and continued the firing from ten to twelve minutes, lacerating and mangling these heroes in a manner too horrible for description.

Our interpreter, who was permitted to remain with them to the last, says that "fifteen times they wounded that iron-nerved soul, Henry Whaling; and it would seem that Providence had a special care in prolonging his existence, that he might demonstrate to his enemies the national character they had to contend with; for he gritted his teeth at and defied them in terms of withering reproach, until they placed a gun to his head and blew his brains against the wall. Such was the effect of this horrible massacre upon their own soldiers, who were stationed as a guard upon the wall above, that one of them fainted, and near falling over, but was caught by his comrades.

During the martyrdom of these noble patriots, the main body of our men were separated from them by a stone wall of some fifteen feet high, and heard their last agonized groans with feelings of which it would be mockery to attempt the description. The next morning, as they were marched on the road to Mexico, they passed the mangled bodies of their dead comrades, whose bones now lie bleaching upon the plains of Salado, a perishing remembrance of exalted patriotism, but a lasting one of the infamy of their President, Sam Houston, who caused them to be falsely executed as robbers and marauders upon Mexico.

Source: Thomas J. Green, *Journal of the Texian Expedition against Mier* (New York, 1845), 169-175

THOUGHT QUESTIONS:

1. How did Green describe the attitude of the men as they took their turns to draw the beans?

2. How did the prisoners wish to be executed? How were they eventually killed?

3. What is Green's general opinion of Sam Houston? Explain.

Texas Navy Commander A.C. Hinton Seeks to Refit his Vessel

During the Republic period, the Texas Navy had both passionate supporters and harsh detractors. The pro-Navy partisans touted the added protection of the coastline, the revenue brought in by the sale of captured prize ships, and how the existence of a navy helped Texas command respect from the outside world. The Navy's critics, however, decried the seeming independent-mindedness of the flotilla's captains and crews not to mention the high costs associated with procuring ships and maintaining them. In this letter from A.C. Hinton to the Texas Secretary of the Navy Louis P. Cook, the naval commander relates the difficulties that he encountered in trying to refit the **Zavala** *as well as feeding and clothing the crew in New Orleans. Though eventually able to complete the task, he went $14,000 over the budget assigned to him by the government and was relieved of his command.*

Hon L.P. Cooke, Sec. of the Navy, Texas Steamship *Zavala*, New Orleans Nov 29th 1839
Sir.

Prior to my departure from Galveston a requisition was made out, in triplicate for clothing cheifly [sic] for the Firemen of this vessel, signed by myself. Approved by Com[modore Edwin] Moore and given to the Navy Agent for supply. [P]rior to leaving, most of them being almost in a state of nudity—not being supplied there, Com. Moore informed me, Mr. Brannum would meet it here. Mr. Brannum brought the requisition with him—I awaited some days expecting the supply from the agent, but not hearing anything of them, & four of my men having deserted in consequence of their beggared condition, I called on the Navy-agent, two, three, several times to purchase the clothing simply called for in the requisition, as the crew were shivering with cold, and on the eve of general desertion to procure by some other means the clothing necessary to protect them from the severity of the weather, being very cold, windy, and rainy—in this state of things. Mr. Brannum refused positively to furnish the clothing, until all the provisions ordered to be purchased were procured, and paid for, whereupon I deemed it my duty to demand the requisition from the Agent, and procure the necessary clothing in the best manner I could. I have, accordingly ordered Purser Kerr to procure a supply of clothing for all hands. Dr. Dory having reported to me that "unless the crew are supplied with warm clothing immediately the consequences must prove extremely disastrous." The clothing will be purchased upon sufficient time to hear from the Department upon the subject, when I trust the Hon. Sec. of the Navy, will instruct the Navy Agent to take up the bills.

Contrary to my expectation, it will take at least a month from this time to complete the repairs on this vessel, which time has been offered to enable me to get your instructions, & save the necessity of paying for them out of the money for repairs etc. The Navy Agent did supply the Colorado with some clothing, purchased here, & carried down to the Balize, & when called upon to supply a requisition for the same purpose, for this ship, signed, & approved, at Galveston, he refuses to supply me, when my men are giving up, one by one, from want of them, and absolutely going below, unable any longer to bear the cold. As Mr. Brannum is either obstinate or ignorant of the responsibility of his office & the Law upon the subject, I trust the Hon. Sec. of the Navy will instruct him, inasmuch as the refusal on his part to supply a requisition legally made out, has, not only injured the health of the Crew, but, others observing their beggared condition, it has been productive of serious injury to the service, ashore, but, as I have not, & cannot ship any men yet, having received only $400 from Mr. B. for us, & $200 for Capt Parker, being unable to draw the amount of his [drafts] until the latter part of next week, as he informs me. I hope by the time I haul out in the Steamer, the comfortable appearance of my men, will induce a good many others to ship for the service. I would respectfully state to the Department that, at this season of the year, when Seamen are Shipped it will be necessary to give them comfortable clothing to preserve their health, and as regards economy, I have no hesitation in declaring that, on the Old Levee, clothing of the very best kind may be purchased, as cheap as they can be in New York, and I would respectfully suggest that if pursers of vessels were qualified with means, to purchase Slops [clothing] only as they are required, for so many men and no more, at a time, it would save the Govt. the expense of laying up general supplies, subject to dampness & decay by lying in the public store, & of course many articles subject in a very short time, in so humid an atmosphere, to be condemned, & of no use[.]

[T]hese remarks, I apply Sir, only to the article of Slops. In regard Sir, to the $9000 for this vessel, Mr Brannum informs me that he has been ordered, to pay out of it, a [draft] for $1200, leaving $780-$1000 for Capt Parker, & $2200 for shipping men, will leave only $4600 for repairs etc. when the new wheels alone will cost nearly $1500 & Mr Beatty informs me to complete the work in his Department it will cost nearly $1500 more, leaving scarcely anything for the balance, of the work, beside the incidental expenses of the vessel, and that there may be no delay in completing the work, I thus early remind the Department, that I do not confidently believe the amount appropriated sufficient by some 3 or $4000, including all expenses, and I very respectfully suggest to the Hon. Sec. of the Navy the propriety of making some arrangement here to meet these expenses promptly, be they little or much, as much will depend on it[.] [T]his liberty, has been suggested by the circumstance, that many have been heard to remark, "how is Texas going to pay all these expenses, don't trust her, she can't pay."

These suggestions I have thrown out for the consideration of the Hon Secretary of the Navy, deeming them in my humble judgment important ones. I can assure the Department that whatever I may do, under my present very important & responsible engagement, a full detailed account shall be given of it. I suggested in my first communication from this place, the propriety of giving the Officers & men, available funds while here. I would state to the Dept. that the officers have not been paid off, & are here literally without a cent[.] [T]he men, all that are left, at least, have a good deal of money due them, and, if, after being well clothed, they were paid, one, or even half a months [sic] pay, in good money, it would be productive of incalculable advantage towards keeping good seamen. I hope, upon this subject, I may hear from you Sir, as soon as practicable; in the meantime, to keep the men in good spirits, being now small in number, I will order Purser Kerr to let them have a few dollars each, as soon as Mr Brannum pays over the whole amount he has for this vessel, at present. The work Sir, is going on slowly, on account of the bad weather but will be done well. The amount of clothing to be procured will be say $5 or 600, at present of which a full account will be given. An immediate answer is most respectfully requested.

I am Sir Your Obt Servt
A.C. Hinton, Commander

Source: Texas State Library and Archives Commission

THOUGHT QUESTIONS:

1. How did Commander Hinton describe the state of his crew's clothing and pay? What did he say might result if this condition continued?

2. How much did the commander believe needed to be expended to have the ship seaworthy? Did he believe that he had enough funds on hand to complete the task?

3. Not surprisingly, the subject of the Texas Navy became yet another issue that divided Sam Houston and Mirabeau Lamar. On which side of this issue do you think each Texas leader took and why?

Battle of Plum Creek

Credit: UTSA's Institute of Texan Cultures, #068-0071,
Source: Wilbarger, J.W. "Indian Depredations in Texas,"
Austin, Hutchings Printing House, 1889.

This photograph shows O. Henry's woodcut of the Battle of Plum Creek, August 10, 1840, in the vicinity of present-day Lockhart, Texas. The Battle of Plum Creek was a consequence of the Council House Fight, in which many Comanche were killed. In retaliation, the Comanche launched a new wave of attacks on frontier settlements. Approximately one thousand Comanche warriors raided Victoria and Linnville. Rangers under Benjamin McCulloch struck and pursued the Comanche raiders, delivering them two major defeats, the most famous at Plum Creek.

THOUGHT QUESTION:

How did Lamar's administration differ from Houston's policy towards Native Americans?

Escape from Perote Castle

**Credit: UTSA's Institute of Texan Cultures, #076-0166,
Source: Green, Gen. Thomas J.; Journal of the Texian Expedition Against Mier. N.Y.,
Harper & Bros., 1845.**

This engraving shows the Texan soldiers escaping from Perote Castle. Santa Anna considered the Texans in the Mier Expedition to be criminals and ordered them to be executed. The "Black Bean Episode" eventually determined who lived and who died. The survivors became prisoners at the Fortress of San Carlos located in the city of Perote in the Mexican state of Veracruz. Over the next two years, numerous Texans escaped from their imprisonment.

THOUGHT QUESTION:

Describe the Black Bean Episode. How were the men shown escaping in this engraving excluded from execution before reaching Perote Castle?

BIOGRAPHIES

JUAN NEPOMUCENO SEGUÍN (1806-1890). The Tejano political and military leader Juan Seguín was born in San Antonio to local political figure Juan José María Erasmo Seguín and his wife María Josefa Becerra on October 27, 1806. At age nineteen he married María Gertrudis Flores de Abrego, the daughter of a prominent local rancher. They eventually had ten children. In 1828, the people of San Antonio elected him as an alderman. Five year later, they chose him to be the town's alcalde. For most of 1834, he served as acting political chief for the Department of Bexar.

Seguín's military career began in 1835 when he cast his lot with the Federalist cause against Santa Anna. In October 1835, Stephen F. Austin commissioned Seguín as a captain and charged him with the duty to raise a company of volunteers to serve as scouts for the Texas revolutionaries. He participated in the Battle of San Antonio against General Martín Perfecto de Cos in December 1835. In late February 1836, Seguín entered the Alamo with other Texans upon the arrival of Santa Anna's army but left as a courier before the Mexican forces attacked the mission. Upon reaching Gonzales, he organized another company of Tejanos who joined Sam Houston's army. Before taking part in the Battle of San Jacinto, Seguín and his men pinned colored pieces of cardboard on their clothes to remind Houston's Anglo fighters on the battlefield that they were on the same side. On June 4, Seguín accepted the surrender of Mexican troops at San Antonio and served as the city's military commander until late 1837 when he resigned his post upon election to the Texas Senate.

Seguín had the distinction of being the only Tejano to serve in the Senate of the Republic of Texas, serving as Chairman of the Military Affairs Committee despite his inability to speak English fluently. He left the Senate in 1840 to assist Antonio Canales, a Mexican Federalist, in an unsuccessful campaign against the Centralist government in Mexico. He soon returned to San Antonio to learn that voters had elected him mayor.

Seguín became increasingly disillusioned with developments in the years after the Texas Revolution. While serving as mayor, he found himself in the midst of growing hostilities between Anglos and Tejanos living in the city. Many Texas towns sought to remove Tejano residents and many Anglos in San Antonio considered doing the same. Most troubling of all, however, was the false allegation that he was a loyal Mexican subject who aided General Rafael Vásquez's occupation of San Antonio in March 1842. The Mexican commander himself spread these rumors in an effort to discredit Seguín. The ruse had the desired effect—many Anglos soon turned on the mayor and accused him of treason. In April 1842, fearing for his life, Seguín resigned and fled with his family to northern Mexico.

Upon his arrival, Mexican authorities arrested him and gave him the choice of imprisonment or military service in the Mexican army. Not wishing to go to jail for an extended period of time and needing to care for his family, he chose to command a unit of Tejanos who fled after the Texas Revolution. Seguín's reputation among Texans became further tarnished when his unit aided General Adrián Woll's invasion of Texas in September 1842. Afterwards, his company helped to defend the northern Mexico frontier, occasionally fighting Native American bands. During the Mexican War, his unit fought against United States troops at Buena Vista among other engagements. At the end of the war, looking "careworn and threadbare," he made contact with Texans at Presidio Rio Grande desiring permission to return to Texas. He also wrote Sam Houston for a personal recommendation that might allow him to more easily reestablish himself in Texas. His efforts bore fruit as he and his family soon returned to his father's San Antonio-area ranch. During the 1850s, he became involved in local politics once again, serving as a Bexar County constable and a Democratic Party precinct chairman. He viewed the Democrats as the best bulwark against the spread of the anti-Catholic, anti-immigration Know Nothing Party. In 1858 he penned his memoirs, in part to protect his reputation and defend himself against the scurrilous attacks that he still occasionally encountered. Feeling a growing sense of alienation from Texas society, however, Seguín retired from business and politics and moved with his wife to Nuevo Laredo to live with one of his sons. He died on August 27, 1890. Originally buried in Nuevo Laredo, his remains were returned to Texas in 1974, and he was buried on the outskirts of Seguín, Texas as part of the United States Bicentennial celebrations on July 4, 1976.

DUWALI [CHIEF BOWL] (1756-1839) Duwali, the East Texas Cherokee leader also known as Chief Bowl or Bowles due to the English translation of his name, was born in western North Carolina in 1756 to a Scottish immigrant trader and a full-blooded Cherokee mother. By the early 1790s, he was a village leader, one of several chiefs to sign the Treaty of Holston in 1791, which, though eventually violated, established territorial boundaries and trading terms between the United States and the Cherokees. Ten years later he began to lead his people westward across the Mississippi River in an effort to find better hunting grounds and to escape white encroachment on their ancestral lands. In early 1810, Duwali's band settled in the St. Francis River Valley near New Madrid, Missouri. For a time, they enjoyed the rich soil, abundant game, and scarcity of white settlers, but after several devastating earthquakes, they abandoned the area and moved to northwestern Arkansas. In 1819, Duwali finally relocated his people to the forks of the Trinity River in eastern Texas.

After arriving in Texas, Duwali became the leading chief of a council created to unite several Cherokee villages established in the region. In 1822, he sent an envoy to Mexico City to secure title to their settled lands, but these efforts proved fruitless given the confusion and turmoil following Mexican independence. In early 1827, Duwali hoped to find favor with the Mexican government by opposing the Fredonian Rebellion. Further attempts to secure a land grant from Mexican officials, however, were futile.

In 1836, Duwali sensed an opportunity to take advantage of the Texas Revolution and agreed to sign a treaty with Sam Houston (acting on behalf of the provisional government) that promised to guarantee the Cherokee people title to the lands that they occupied if they remained neutral in the fight with Mexico. Following the Revolution and the formation of the Texas Republic, Houston sought to have the treaty formally validated by the Texas Senate but that body refused to ratify the agreement. Renewed efforts to hammer out a new deal suffered when some Cherokee joined other Indians and Tejanos under Vicente Córdova in disclaiming their allegiance to the Republic. After Texas militia dispersed the force, Duwali claimed to have no association with Córdova's rebels.

Though Houston pardoned any Cherokees and other Native Americans who may have been involved in the Córdova affair, Texas government policy took a sharp turn after

Mirabeau Lamar became president. Lamar denied that the Cherokees had any legitimate claims to east Texas lands and told them in no uncertain terms to begin allowing white settlers to take possession of lands in their midst or prepare to move. After Texas Rangers intercepted and killed Mexican agent Manuel Flores leading a group of Cherokees near Austin, letters addressed to Duwali were found on the emissary indicating that the Mexican government wished to foment rebellion among the Cherokees, promising land in exchange for an uprising that might aid a future Mexican reinvasion of Texas. Though Flores probably did not establish direct contact with Duwali, these documents prompted the Texas president to order all Cherokees to vacate Texas or face destruction.

In July 1839, Lamar sent representatives to meet with Duwali and dictate removal terms. Though the eighty-three year old chief wished to avoid conflict, he was overruled by most of the tribal council. Indeed, a majority of the younger warriors wanted to fight for their land. When negotiations reached an impasse, Texas troops approached the Cherokee village but found it abandoned. Pursued to the headwaters of the Neches River, Duwali finally made a stand against Texas troops under the command of Thomas Rusk and Edward Burleson on July 16, 1839. In the Battle of the Neches near present-day Tyler, the Texans soundly defeated five hundred Cherokee, Delaware, Shawnee, and Kickapoo warriors. As the battle ended, Duwali was shot in the head, scalped, and stripped of his hat and the ceremonial sword given to him by Sam Houston in 1836. After the engagement, the surviving Cherokees fled to the Indian Territory (Oklahoma) north of Texas. Though a majority of Texans supported Lamar's Indian policy, Sam Houston railed against the government's attack on the Cherokees in vociferous terms on the floor of the Texas Congress. Responding to Houston's repeated tirades on the subject, Edward Burleson insolently sent him Duwali's hat, which he had taken from the fallen leader as a souvenir.

MARGARET MOFFETTE LEA HOUSTON (1819-1867). Margaret Lea, the future wife of Sam Houston, was born near Marion, Alabama on April 11, 1819. She grew up on a cotton plantation with fifty slaves that her mother, Nancy Moffette Lea, had purchased with inheritance money. Margaret's father, Temple Lea, devoted much of his time to being a lay Baptist preacher. Spending much of her early years reading books, Margaret was described by others as a beautiful, gentle-natured, and scholarly young woman. At age fifteen, she was devastated by the death of her father who she greatly adored. The family soon moved to Marion to live in the home of her oldest brother Henry, who by this time had become a successful businessman and state legislator. Already a very religious young woman due to the influence of her father, she became more devout after her formal education at two Baptist institutions—Pleasant Valley Academy and Judson Female Institute.

In May 1839, Margaret met Sam Houston in Mobile, Alabama at a soiree held by her sister Antoinette in honor of their mother. After finishing his term as President of the Texas Republic, Houston had traveled to Mobile where he met Margaret's brother Martin, a well-known city promoter. Martin Lea invited Houston to the party so his mother could talk to him about investment opportunities in Texas. While Houston met regularly with Nancy Lea after wards to discuss business matters, he also spent much time courting Margaret, a turn of events of which Nancy strongly disapproved because of the age difference (Houston was forty-six years old while Margaret was only twenty) and his reputation as a hard drinker. Nevertheless, the couple married on May 9, 1840 and subsequently moved to Houston's farm at Cedar Point on Trinity Bay. Nancy rented a home in nearby Galveston to manage her Texas investments but regularly lived with the Houstons.

Margaret provided Houston with the desired domestic stability that had eluded him for so long. She would eventually have eight children with Houston and provide him with a haven from the outside world of politics—not that the family stayed in one location for very long, or were even together consistently. When Houston lived in Texas, the Houstons and their fourteen slaves frequently traveled between homes that he owned in central and eastern Texas. While spending nearly every summer at Cedar Point, Houston liked to reside in his Huntsville and Independence homes at other times of the year. The couple also spent much time apart during his many years in the U.S. Senate. Due to severe bouts with asthma and her frequent pregnancies, Margaret never visited him in Washington, D.C. nor did she usually follow him on the campaign trail. She seemed content with taking care of the children, reading religious tracts, writing poetry, and corresponding with her husband. The existing letters between the two reveal their deep love for one another and their children. She waged constant battle with Houston over his drinking, largely by reminding him how much the practice hurt her and disrupted their home. Houston finally cleaned up his act, pledged total abstinence, and even eventually agreed to join the Baptist Church.

After Houston's political career ended due to his refusal to take an oath of allegiance to the Confederacy, Margaret and Sam spent the last two years of his life in relative obscurity. Margaret worried as her eldest son, Sam Houston, Jr., joined the Confederate army and left the state for active duty. For a six month period after the Battle of Shiloh, the couple did not know if he was still alive. They eventually received news that he had been wounded and taken prisoner but were relieved when he returned home in September 1862 after a prisoner exchange. The couple continued to travel between Cedar Point and Huntsville with Margaret increasingly taking care of Houston as his health began to fail. After his death in 1863, she moved to Independence to live near her mother. However, in the fall of 1867, as she prepared to move to Georgetown to live with one of her daughters, Margaret succumbed to yellow fever. Though Houston was buried in Huntsville, her mother, Nancy Lea, arranged for Margaret to be buried in an Independence cemetery plot that she purchased for the two of them to be interred.

EDWIN WARD MOORE (1810-1865). The controversial commander of the Republic of Texas Navy, Commodore Edwin Ward Moore, was born on July 15, 1810, to a prominent Virginia family. Among many of his family members with military service, none was more influential than his grandfather Cleon Moore who served as a captain under George Washington during the Revolutionary War. Along with a young Robert E. Lee, Moore attended Alexandria Academy, co-founded by his grandfather, before entering the U.S. Navy as a midshipman at the age of 14 where he served aboard vessels stationed along the Atlantic coast and the Mediterranean Sea. In 1830, the Navy assigned him to the Norfolk Shipyard in Virginia where he acquired knowledge of ship construction, repairs, and finance.

During the mid-1830s, Moore was serving aboard the warship *Boston* patrolling the waters of the Gulf of Mexico for pirates, on one occasion saving the ship after bearing the brunt of a hurricane, when he became aware of the Republic of Texas's desire under President Mirabeau Lamar to expand its naval forces. His reputation as an intrepid and experienced naval officer, as well as his elite Virginia pedigree, impressed President Lamar and ultimately led him to appoint Moore as the commander of the Texas Navy in March 1839. He accepted the position out of a desire for a higher command and salary, increased chances for combat action with opportunities to share the profits from capturing Mexican naval vessels, and the prospect of creating and leading a new fleet from scratch.

During the summer of 1839, Moore poached some U.S. naval officers while visiting the Brooklyn Navy Yard in New York City before returning to Texas and assuming the rank of Captain. (Because he commanded a naval squadron, Moore was also granted the honorary title of Commodore.) He spent the last half of 1839 recruiting men and gathering supplies for the revamped Texas fleet, which consisted of the steamer *Zavala*, the six-gun schooners *San Bernard*, *San Antonio* and *San Jacinto*, the sixteen-gun brigs *Archer* and *Wharton*, and the large 500-ton sloop *Austin*. Moore's squadron began operations in the Gulf of Mexico in 1840, and over the course of the next three years, traveled along the Mexican coast, raiding coastal towns, attacking Mexican shipping, and allying with Mexican Federalist rebels in an attempt to convince the centralist government of Mexico to recognize Texas independence. In late 1840, the young commander led three Texas vessels to the Yucatan to clear the coast for Mexican shipping and protect rebel-held ports. Moore's force also helped to drive a centralist garrison out of San Juan Bautista in Tabasco, though when initially denied $25,000 in silver promised by federalist rebels, he ordered the town to be shelled until the funds were procured.

Moore encountered trouble with the Texas government when newly elected Sam Houston assumed the presidency. Among other Texas leaders, Houston strongly opposed the Republic's navy as an expensive extravagance and soon ordered the fleet home. After the young commodore returned to a hero's welcome in Galveston, many citizens protested when they learned that the Houston administration planned to soon sell off the ships and prevented their sale. Moore then gathered his vessels and left the port in defiance of Houston, heading back to the Yucatan coast. A year later, Moore led his fleet against a Mexican flotilla in a series of engagements from April 30 to May 16, 1843, in the Bay of Campeche. Though outgunned and facing steam-powered ironclad warships in the Mexican fleet, his wooden-hulled sailing vessels prevailed and drove off the enemy.

Despite Moore's victory at Campeche, Houston branded him a pirate, leading the commodore to return to Texas on July 14 and demand a trial to exonerate him and his crew. After court-martial proceedings, Moore and his crew were acquitted. Though he was forced to resign his commission, he successfully fought to have it restored less than a year later. Nevertheless, his days of commanding naval vessels were over. After Texas annexation, Moore lobbied Congress to convince the U.S. Navy to recognize the ranks of Texas Navy officers, leading to a compromise whereby he and his fellow officers received five years of U.S. Navy back pay. Moore's last visit to Texas occurred in 1860 when he oversaw construction of a new customhouse in Galveston. He died of a stroke in New York City on October 5, 1865 and is buried in the Ivy Hill Cemetery in Philadelphia, Pennsylvania.

Chapter 6

The 28th State in the Union, 1845-1861

Article IX of the Texas Constitution of 1845

The initial Texas state constitution, the Constitution of 1845, devotes an entire article to the issue of slavery in which the term "slave" is not avoided (as in the United States Constitution) and various protections for the institution are provided. Below is that important section of the document.

SEC. 1. The legislature shall have no power to pass laws for the emancipation of slaves without the consent of their owners, nor without paying their owners, previous to such emancipation, a full equivalent in money for the slaves so emancipated. They shall have no power to prevent emigrants to this State from bringing with them such persons as are deemed slaves by the laws of any of the United States, so long as any person of the same age or description shall be continued in slavery by the laws of this State: *Provided*, That such slave be the *bona fide* property of such emigrants: *Provided, also,* That laws shall be passed to inhibit the introduction into this State of slaves who have committed high crimes in other States or Territories. They shall have the right to pass laws to permit the owners of slaves to emancipate them, saving the rights of creditors, and preventing them from becoming a public charge. They shall have full power to pass laws which will oblige the owners of slaves to treat them with humanity; to provide for their necessary food and clothing; to abstain from all injuries to them, extending to life or limb; and, in case of their neglect or refusal to comply with the directions of such laws, to have such slave or slaves taken from such owner and sold for the benefit of such owner or owners. They may pass laws to prevent slaves from being brought into this State as merchandise only.

SEC. 2. In the prosecution of slaves for crimes of a higher grade than petit larceny, the legislature shall have no power to deprive them of an impartial trial by a petit jury.

SEC. 3. Any person who shall maliciously dismember, or deprive a slave of life, shall suffer such punishment as would be inflicted in case the like offence had been committed upon a free white person, and on the like proof, except in case of insurrection by such slave.

Source: United States, 29th Congress, *House Executive Document, No. XVI* (1845)

THOUGHT QUESTIONS:

1. What powers did the constitution grant to the Texas legislature with respect to slavery?

2. What powers with respect to slavery did the constitution deny to the legislature?

3. What provisions did the constitution include to allegedly protect the slaves from ill treatment? Considering the need for Texas to get congressional approval before statehood could take place, why do you think these provisions were added (without definite means of enforcing them)?

Anson Jones's Valedictory Speech, February 19, 1846

Following congressional approval of the Texas Constitution, Texas joined the Union when President James K. Polk signed the act of admission on December 29, 1845. On February 19, 1846, Texas President Anson Jones at a public ceremony turned over executive authority to Governor James P. Henderson. Below are excerpts from Anson Jones's remarks on this momentous day in Texas history.

The great measure of annexation, so earnestly desired by the people of Texas is happily consummated. The present occasion, so full of interest to us and all the people of this country, is an earnest of that consummation; and I am happy to greet you as their chosen representatives, and tender to you my cordial congratulations on an event the most extraordinary in the annals of the world, and one which marks a bright triumph in the history of republican institutions. A government is changed both in its officers and in its organic law—not by violence and disorder, but by the deliberate and free consent of its citizens; and amid the most perfect and universal peace and tranquility, the sovereignty of the nation is surrendered, and incorporate with that of another.

There is no precedent for this and henceforward "Annexation" is a word of new import in the political vocabulary of America, to form a subject for the speculations of the Statesman and the intellectual labors of the Sage. Nations have generally extended their dominions by conquest; their march to power involving bloodshed and ruin, and their attainment of it often following by suffering and calamity to a despairing and subjugated people. It was left for the Anglo-American inhabitants of the Western Continent, to furnish a new mode of enlarging the bounds of empire, by the more natural tendency and operation of the principles of their free government. Whatever objections may have been heretofore urged to the territorial enlargement of the Union, those objections must now be regarded as overruled and as being without practical effect. Annexation is the natural consequence resulting from congenial impulses and sympathies; and the operation and influence of like sympathies and impulses is destined, as soon as can be important or necessary, to settle all conflicts in relation to the claim of the United States to any territory now in dispute on this continent.

In accordance with the provisions of the new constitution adopted in the Convention, called by me on the fourth of July last, a State government is now perfectly and fully organized, and I, as President of the Republic, with my officers, am now present to surrender into the hands of those whom the people have chosen, the power and the authority which we have some time held. This surrender is made with the most perfect cheerfulness, and in respectful submission to the public will. For my individual part, I beg leave further to add that the only motive which has heretofore actuated me in consenting to hold high and responsible office in this my adopted and beloved country, has been to aid, by the best exertions of such abilities as I possessed, in extricating her from her difficulties and to place her in some safe and secure condition, where she might be relieved from the long pressure of the past, and repose from the toils, the sufferings and threatened dangers which have surrounded her. I have considered annexation on favorable terms, as the most secure and advantageous measure for Texas, and as affording the best prospect for the attainment of the object I had in view, and have, accordingly, in different capacities labored most assiduously to open the door in the United States, to its accomplishment. In this I succeeded. I sincerely wish the terms could have been made more advantageous, more definite and less fraught with subjects of future dispute; but as they proved entirely acceptable to a vast majority of my fellow citizens, I felt it to be my imperative duty, so soon as that fact was known, faithfully and promptly to carry into full effect the will and wishes of the people. This I have done. . . .

I am happy to congratulate you, gentlemen, upon the universally proposition condition of our country at the present time. Our foreign relations have all been closed in a manner satisfactory, I believe, to all the governments with which we have had intercourse. The frontier is quiet and secure, and the husbandman sows and reaps his field in peace. Industry and enterprise have received new guarantees and a new impulse—a market is found at home for nearly everything our citizens have to dispose of, and a large and very desirable immigration to the country now taking place. The expenses of the government since I have been in office, have all been paid in an undepreciated currency—a very considerable amount of debt incurrent by previous administrations has been paid off, and a surplus of available means sufficient to defray the expense of the government, economically administered, for the next two years, at least, is left at the disposition of the State; and I venture the belief that, without resort to taxation, the public domain, if properly husbanded and disposed of, will raise a fund sufficient to liquidate the entire national debt upon equitable principles, beside providing for the future support of the State government, a system of common schools, and other institutions for the intellectual, moral and religious improvement of the rising generation. With such a population as

Texas possesses, characterized as it is with great intelligence and enterprise, and with such elements of prosperity as she now possesses, a genial climate and a fertile soil, it will be her own fault if she does not reach an importance and a social elevation, not surpassed by any community on earth. . . .

The Lone Star of Texas, which ten years since arose amid clouds, over fields of carnage, and obscurely shone for a while, has culminated, and, following an inscrutable destiny, has passed on and become fixed forever in that glorious constellation, which all freedmen and lovers of freedom in the world, must reverence and adore—the American Union. Blending its rays with its sister stars, long may it continue to shine, and may a gracious Heaven smile upon this consummation of the wishes of the two Republics, now joined together in one. "May the Union be perpetual, and may it be the means of conferring benefits and blessings upon the people of all the States," is my ardent prayer.

The final act in this great drama is now performed: the Republic of Texas is no more.

Source: Executive Record Book, Anson Jones, Texas State Library and Archives Commission

THOUGHT QUESTIONS:

1. Why did Jones favor Texas annexation to the United States?

2. Did Jones express any minor objections or reservations about the process (as opposed to the goal of annexation)? Explain.

3. According to Jones, what was the condition of the Republic at the time of the transition to statehood?

Petition for the Emancipation of a Slave

In November 1847, a Houston slave owner and over eighty other residents signed the following petition addressed to the state legislature seeking permission to free a slave woman named Liley.

State of Texas
County of Harris

To the Honorable the Senate and House of Representatives of the State of Texas

We the undersigned present to the favorable consideration of the Representatives of the Free inhabitants of the State of Texas the colored woman Liley, who has been a resident of the City of Houston for the last five years. By her industry and good conduct she has been enabled to realize sufficient of means to purchase her freedom, and we feel interested in her case and feel that it is one of those cases that ought to receive the favorable notice of a free and generous people and as such we ask that a law may be passed emancipating her, and authorizing her to remain in Texas.

Houston Nov 1st 1847

I Cynthia Ewing lately the owner of the colored woman Liley, do certify that she is a woman of a good moral character, that she has fully paid me for her liberty—and I ask that the Legislature of Texas may pass a law to emancipate her.

[signatures]

Source: Texas State Library and Archives Commission

THOUGHT QUESTIONS:

1. What positive attributes did the petitioners ascribe to Liley?

2. Where did the petitioners wish Liley to go if she was legally emancipated? Could this request cause a minor controversy? Why?

3. Based on a reading of this document, what is implied about the degree of power that the state legislature possessed with regard to the emancipation of slaves?

A Texan's View of the Mexican War

Born in 1816, Charles DeMorse was a young, idealistic Northerner who came to Texas in 1835 to support the Texas revolt against Santa Anna, though he arrived after the Battle of San Jacinto. After a short career as a lawyer in Matagorda, he moved to Clarksville in Northeast Texas and founded the **Northern Standard** *in 1842. He served as the newspapers' longtime publisher and editor. During the Civil War he fought as a colonel in the Confederate army in Arkansas and the Indian Territory. Though he supported a quick reunion with the North after the conflict, the lifelong Democrat strongly opposed Radical Reconstruction with scathing editorials in the* **Standard**. *After Reconstruction ended, he turned his attention to the concerns of small farmers. When he died in 1887, the Texas Press and Editorial Association eulogized him as the "Father of Texas Journalism." In this piece, DeMorse uses the power of his pen to energetically support the U.S. war with Mexico.*

At last we have a real "sure enough" war on hand; something to warm the blood, and draw out the national enthusiasm. It seems that the "Magnanimous Mexican Nation" has at last come out of its chapparal [sic.] of wordy diplomacy, treachery, meanness and bombast, and concluded for a while, only a little while, to act like white people. There is at last—our pulses beat quickly with the thought—an opportunity to pay off a little of the debt of vengeance which has been accumulating since the massacre of the Alamo.

We trust that every man of our army, as he points his rifle and thrusts his bayonet, will think of his countrymen martyred at the Alamo, at Goliad, at Mier, whose blood yet cries aloud from the ground for remembrance and vengeance, and taking a little closer aim or giving a little stronger thrust, will give his blow in his country's cause and an additional "God speed."

Source: *Northern Standard* (Clarksville, Texas), May 13, 1846

THOUGHT QUESTIONS:

1. How does DeMorse characterize the Mexican people?

2. How does he evoke the past, specifically the Texas Revolution and the violence of the Republic period, to rally his readers for war?

3. What standard elements does this editorial possess that makes it similar to many common efforts to boost countrymen's enthusiasm for war at the beginning of a conflict? Can you explain a modern-day comparative example?

John H. Reagan Discusses the Possibility of Secession

During the antebellum era, public discourse on political issues often took place in the form of published exchanges of letters between noted figures in newspapers. On the eve of the 1860 presidential election, the possible secession of the southern states if the Republican candidate Abraham Lincoln won was one of the most popular topics to be openly discussed in this manner. One of these public dialogues involved John H. Reagan, an East Texas Democratic Party congressman who later became Postmaster General for the Confederate government during the Civil War. In October 1860, he replied to a series of questions posed to him by George Paschal, a prominent Unionist who supported the Constitutional Union candidate John Bell. In the excerpt shown below, Reagan answers Paschal's fourth query: "Do you think that the election of Lincoln would be, of itself, sufficient cause to dissolve the Union, or to resist his inauguration? And would you join in such attempt at secession or resistance?"

To your fourth interrogatory I answer: that Lincoln stands before the country the representative of the anti-slavery ideas and agitators of the times--that his election or defeat must rest alone upon the determination of the people of the free States to carry out those ideas and to execute the purposes of these agitators, or to repudiate those ideas and arrest that agitation. The one idea of opposition to negro slavery brought the republican party into existence, and now holds it together. His election by a purely sectional vote of the people of the free States would pledge his administration and party and section to carry out the doctrines upon which he is run and would be elected. The doctrines of his party are that negro slavery, as it exists with us, is religiously, morally, socially and politically wrong. It is proclaimed by the great leaders of that party, by its political presses, by its political conventions, by its ministers of the Gospel, and by every other means they have of giving currency and importance to the declaration, that, it is its mission to abolish slavery in the Union. Their legislation in most of the free States, and their efforts at legislation in Congress, prove that the federal Constitution presents no barrier to the accomplishment, of their purposes, where they have the power to override and disregard its provisions. They are pledged to exclude slavery from the common Territories, to abolish it in the District of Columbia, in the Forts, Dock Yards. etc., and to prevent the inter-State slave trade. They have no power over this question in the States where it exists. The Federal Constitution recognizes our right of property in slaves in the common Territories, in the District of Columbia, and in the Forts, Dock Yard, etc. The Constitution confers no power on Congress or any political body to interfere with or destroy that right of property. The successful application of the republican doctrines would violate the plain specific provisions of the Federal Constitution in several particulars. They would strike down the sovereignty and equality of the States by denying them the right to regulate and control their own domestic institutions in their own way. They would take away and destroy our right of property in negro slaves in the Territories, in the District of Columbia, etc. in violation of that provision of the Constitution which declares that no citizen shall be deprived of his property except by due process of law, and another which declares that private properly shall not be taken for public uses without just compensation. They deny the equality of the people of the slaveholding [States] with those of the non-slaveholding States, in respect of their right to go into and occupy the common Territories so long as they remain in a Territorial condition, with their negro property, recognized as such by the Constitution and declared to be such by the Supreme Court of the United States [in the Dred Scott case]. The Constitution of the United States was made by white men, the citizens and representatives of twelve slaveholding and one non-slaveholding States, and it was made for white men. It denied the right of citizenship to the negro race whether bond or free, and recognized them as property when they are held bondage. The people of the Southern States now own near five millions of these negroes, and they are worth to them near three thousand millions of dollars. They constitute an important element in society well as of the wealth of the Republic, and are the chief producers of more than two thirds of the foreign exports of the Union. They are and ever have been, under all circumstances, and probably ever will incapable of free self-government. They are now more intelligent, better fed, better clothed, and more contented and happy than any other equal number of that race in any other part of the world, whether bond or free. The success of the republican doctrines would liberate among us this large number of negroes, would strike down our agriculture and commerce. Involve us inevitably in a war of races, which would result in the murder of many of the white race of all ages and of both sexes, and in the burning of a and destruction of a large amount of property, and in the ultimate extermination of the negro race among us. The success of those doctrines would also subvert the Federal Constitution, change the character of the Federal Government, and destroy our rights in respect to slavery. And all this would be done to gratify the passions and prejudices and malice of the party of which Mr. Lincoln is the head and representative in this contest, and not because of any pretense even that they have any material or political rights involved in the question....

Looking at these facts, and others which I will not now present, I am bound to conclude that the doctrines of the republican party are unconstitutional, unjust, cruel to both races, revolutionary and destructive of the best interests of the South as well as of the Union, and that the election of Lincoln would be success of a revolution which must destroy our present constitutional Government, and with it our rights, equality and security as a people. So regarding his election, I am for resisting it, in case it should occur, by the best and most effective means which could be adopted by the States to be injured; and of adopting such recourse as will secure our rights in the Union if we can, but out of it if we must. Every instinct of self preservation demands of us to demand and insist on this security, and to obtain it peaceably if we can, and if reason and peaceful means should fail, then it is equally our duty to maintain our rights which God and Nature placed at our command.

The plan of action which I would recommend to meet such an emergency is this: that if Lincoln should be elected, as soon as that fact shall be ascertained, for the Government of all the slaveholding States to convene the legislatures at once, for the purpose of enabling them by law to provide for State Conventions. And that those State Conventions should provide for a general Convention of delegates from all the States aggrieved. And that this General Convention should submit to the free States propositions requiring a renewal of the original guarantees of the Constitution in favor of our rights, in such specific form as to settle forever the question as to the extent and character of the rights of the slave States and of the owners of slave property. One of the conditions should be that we would not continue our political connexion [sic.] with any State which would not repeal all of its laws intended to hinder the recapture of fugitive slaves; another should be to demand an equal participation in the settlement and occupation of the common territory, and a safe guarantees for the admission of future slave States into the Union; another should be the suspension of the agitation of the question about abolishing slavery in the District of Columbia, in the Forts, Dock Yards, etc. and another that the inter-[state] Slave trade should not be interfered with by Congress. If they should agree to these, we should remain in the Union, and support and cherish it as heretofore. If they would refuse these guarantees, then my judgment is, that we should form a separate confederacy of such States as would unite in the movement.

If the Southern States would adopt this course promptly, I believe the free States would renew these guarantees of the Constitution to us; and upon such an issue crush out and annihilate abolitionism, and that the Union of the States would be preserved. But if I am mistaken in this, then their refusal to do so would assure us of our fate, if we should remain in their power, and warn us of the necessity of self preservation.

I indicate this as the plan which meets my approval, but will, if the emergency shall arise, agree to such other plan, if this be not the best, as my be adopted by the people of the South, to resist the establishment of the doctrines of the Republican party. I have thought this would be the best, because it would rest on the will of the people, and be supported by the authority of State sovereignty, acting in support of their own reserved rights and powers, and maintaining the rights of their people against palpable and dangerous violations of the Constitution.

If we fail to adopt some such course, on the happening of such a contingency, and adopt the timid and foolish policy of compromising away our rights for the sake of peace, no one can doubt the early and complete abolition of slavery, and the visitation upon us of all the calamities which must follow such a result.

I fear the evil day is upon us, and believe duty and patriotism alike require us to face the danger and prepare to avert it.

I may be excused for adding, for myself, that I am one of those who have clung to every reasonable hope for the Union. That I have resisted, as I am still ready to do, every measure which I supposed would endanger it, whether proposed in the North or the South, without inquiring for the consequences to myself. I clung steadfastly to the hope that the Democratic party would maintain its nationality, and preserve the Constitution and the Union. But unbridled ambition, preferring self to country and appealing to the free-soil sentiments of the Northern wing of the party, has destroyed its unity, if not its nationality, and with it, there is but too much reason to fear, prepared the way for the separation of the States.

You will see that I have chosen not to answer this question categorically, but I have aimed to answer it fully and fairly. I know not how far my views may be sustained by the popular judgment, but the times require that this question be answered with candor and frankness.

Very respectfully,

JOHN H. REAGAN

Source: *Dallas Herald,* October 31, 1860

THOUGHT QUESTIONS:

1. In what ways does Reagan try to portray Lincoln and the Republicans as a whole as abolitionists when the Republican party platform and their candidate for president committed only to try and resist the spread of slavery into the western territories?

2. How does Reagan describe the slaves in bondage? How is that portrayal contradicted by his own vision of what would happen if the slaves were freed?

3. What was Reagan's proposed "plan of action" if Lincoln was elected?

Convention Delegates Issue a Declaration of Causes to Justify Texas Secession

After Abraham Lincoln's election in November 1860, Texas joined most of the slave states in declaring that it was "unratifying" the U.S. Constitution and, thereby, seceding from the Union. On February 1, 1861, the Texas Secession Convention adopted an ordinance of secession by a vote of 166 to 8. On the following day, the delegates approved this more lengthy declaration of causes which "impelled" Texas to secede.

A Declaration of the Causes which Impel the State of Texas to Secede from the Federal Union

The government of the United States, by certain joint resolutions, bearing date the 1st day of March, in the year A.D. 1845, proposed to the Republic of Texas, then **a free, sovereign and independent nation**, the annexation of the latter to the former, as one of the co-equal states thereof,

The people of Texas, by deputies in convention assembled, on the fourth day of July of the same year, assented to and accepted said proposals and formed a constitution for the proposed State, upon which on the 29th day of December in the same year, said State was formally admitted into the Confederated Union.

Texas abandoned her separate national existence and consented to become one of the Confederated Union to promote her welfare, insure domestic tranquility and secure more substantially the blessings of peace and liberty to her people. She was received into the confederacy with her own constitution, under the guarantee of the federal constitution and the compact of annexation, that she should enjoy these blessings. She was received as a commonwealth holding, maintaining and protecting the institution known as negro slavery-- the servitude of the African to the white race within her limits-- a relation that had existed from the first settlement of her wilderness by the white race, and which her people intended should exist in all future time. Her institutions and geographical position established the strongest ties between her and other slave-holding States of the confederacy. Those ties have been strengthened by association. But what has been the course of the government of the United States, and of the people and authorities of the non-slave-holding States, since our connection with them?

The controlling majority of the Federal Government, under various pretences and disguises, has so administered the same as to exclude the citizens of the Southern States, unless under odious and unconstitutional restrictions, from all the immense territory owned in common by all the States on the Pacific Ocean, for the avowed purpose of acquiring sufficient power in the common government to use it as a means of destroying the institutions of Texas and her sister slaveholding States.

By the disloyalty of the Northern States and their citizens and the imbecility of the Federal Government, infamous combinations of incendiaries and outlaws have been permitted in those States and the common territory of Kansas to trample upon the federal laws, to war upon the lives and property of Southern citizens in that territory, and finally, by violence and mob law, to usurp the possession of the same as exclusively the property of the Northern States.

The Federal Government, while but partially under the control of these our unnatural and sectional enemies, has for years almost entirely failed to protect the lives and property of the people of Texas against the Indian savages on our border, and more recently against the murderous forays of banditti from the neighboring territory of Mexico; and when our State government has expended large amounts for such purpose, the Federal Government has refuse reimbursement therefor, thus rendering our condition more insecure and harassing than it was during the existence of the Republic of Texas.

These and other wrongs we have patiently borne in the vain hope that a returning sense of justice and humanity would induce a different course of administration.

When we advert to the course of individual non-slave-holding States, and that a majority of their citizens, our grievances assume far greater magnitude.

The States of Maine, Vermont, New Hampshire, Connecticut, Rhode Island, Massachusetts, New York, Pennsylvania, Ohio, Wisconsin, Michigan and Iowa, by solemn legislative enactments, have deliberately, directly or indirectly violated the 3rd clause of the 2nd section of the 4th article [the fugitive slave clause] of the federal constitution, and laws passed in pursuance thereof; thereby annulling a material provision of the compact, designed by its framers to perpetuate the amity between the members of the confederacy and to secure the rights of the slave-holding States in their domestic institutions-- a provision founded in justice and wisdom, and without the enforcement of which the compact fails to accomplish the object of its creation. Some of those States have imposed high fines and degrading penalties upon any of their citizens or officers who may carry out in good faith that provision of the compact, or the federal laws enacted in accordance therewith.

In all the non-slave-holding States, in violation of that good faith and comity which should exist between entirely distinct nations, the people have formed themselves into a great sectional party, now strong enough in numbers to control the affairs of each of those States, based upon an unnatural feeling of hostility to these Southern States and their beneficent and patriarchal system of African slavery, proclaiming the debasing doctrine of equality of all men, irrespective of race or color-- a doctrine at war with nature, in opposition to the experience of mankind, and in violation of the plainest revelations of Divine Law. They demand the abolition of negro slavery throughout the confederacy, the recognition of political equality between the white and negro races, and avow their determination to press on their crusade against us, so long as a negro slave remains in these States.

For years past this abolition organization has been actively sowing the seeds of discord through the Union, and has rendered the federal congress the arena for spreading firebrands and hatred between the slave-holding and non-slave-holding States.

By consolidating their strength, they have placed the slave-holding States in a hopeless minority in the federal congress, and rendered representation of no avail in protecting Southern rights against their exactions and encroachments.

They have proclaimed, and at the ballot box sustained, the revolutionary doctrine that there is a 'higher law' than the constitution and laws of our Federal Union, and virtually that they will disregard their oaths and trample upon our rights.

They have for years past encouraged and sustained lawless organizations to steal our slaves and prevent their recapture, and have repeatedly murdered Southern citizens while lawfully seeking their rendition.

They have invaded Southern soil and murdered unoffending citizens, and through the press their leading men and a fanatical pulpit have bestowed praise upon the actors and assassins in these crimes, while the governors of several of their States have refused to deliver parties implicated and indicted for participation in such offenses, upon the legal demands of the States aggrieved.

They have, through the mails and hired emissaries, sent seditious pamphlets and papers among us to stir up servile insurrection and bring blood and carnage to our firesides.

They have sent hired emissaries among us to burn our towns and distribute arms and poison to our slaves for the same purpose.

They have impoverished the slave-holding States by unequal and partial legislation, thereby enriching themselves by draining our substance.

They have refused to vote appropriations for protecting Texas against ruthless savages, for the sole reason that she is a slave-holding State.

And, finally, by the combined sectional vote of the seventeen non-slave-holding States, they have elected as president and vice-president of the whole confederacy two men whose chief claims to such high positions are their approval of these long continued wrongs, and their pledges to continue them to the final consummation of these schemes for the ruin of the slave-holding States.

In view of these and many other facts, it is meet that our own views should be distinctly proclaimed.

We hold as undeniable truths that the governments of the various States, and of the confederacy itself, were established exclusively by the white race, for themselves and their posterity; that the African race had no agency in their establishment; that they were rightfully held and regarded as an inferior and dependent race, and in that condition only could their existence in this country be rendered beneficial or tolerable.

That in this free government **all white men are and of right ought to be entitled to equal civil and political rights**; that the servitude of the African race, as existing in these States, is mutually beneficial to both bond and free, and is abundantly authorized and justified by the experience of mankind, and the revealed will of the Almighty Creator, as recognized by all Christian nations; while the destruction of the existing relations between the two races, as advocated by our sectional enemies, would bring inevitable calamities upon both and desolation upon the fifteen slave-holding states.

By the secession of six of the slave-holding States, and the certainty that others will speedily do likewise, Texas has no alternative but to remain in an isolated connection with the North, or unite her destinies with the South.

For these and other reasons, solemnly asserting that the federal constitution has been violated and virtually abrogated by the several States named, seeing that the federal government is now passing under the control of our enemies to be diverted from the exalted objects of its creation to those of oppression and wrong, and realizing that our own State can no longer look for protection, but to God and her own sons-- We the delegates of the people of Texas, in Convention assembled, have passed an ordinance dissolving all political connection with the government of the United States of America and the people thereof and confidently appeal to the intelligence and patriotism of the freemen of Texas to ratify the same at the ballot box, on the 23rd day of the present month.

Adopted in Convention on the 2nd day of Feby, in the year of our Lord one thousand eight hundred and sixty-one and of the independence of Texas the twenty-fifth.

Source: E. W. Winkler, ed., *Journal of the Secession Convention of Texas, 1861*, (Austin, 1912), 61-65.

THOUGHT QUESTIONS:

1. How is the Republican Party portrayed in this declaration? Is this general portrayal accurate? Why or why not?

2. How is the institution of slavery (for both the slaveholders and the slaves themselves) characterized in the declaration?

3. In reviewing the total document, does this declaration specifically justify secession on the grounds of "states' rights" or the defense of slavery? Explain with examples from the text.

Quanah Parker

Quanah Parker was the son of Comanche chief Peta Nocona and the American woman Cynthia Ann Parker (biography of Cynthia Ann Parker at end of chapter). He refused to accept the provisions of the 1867 Treaty of Medicine Lodge, which confined the southern Plains Indians to a reservation. Quanah continued to raid in Texas but eventually surrendered and moved to the Kiowa-Comanche reservation in southwestern Oklahoma where he remained a powerful leader of his people.

Quanah Parker
Photo Credit: Library of Congress

THOUGHT QUESTION:

Where and when were Indian reservations established in Texas?

"The Main Plaza San Antonio as held by the Texas Volunteers under Col. Ben McCulloch on the morning of February 16, 1861."

Credit: UTSA's Institute of Texan Cultures, #101-0113,
Courtesy of Ellie Lamb

This depiction comes from a photographic print of the original "Homeograph" made from a sketch by Carl G. von Iwonski. Once Texans had approved secession, Confederates planned to seize all the national government's property in the state. Col. Ben McCulloch and his men moved on San Antonio to force the surrender of the federal property in the city. McCulloch pressured General David E. Twiggs, the seventy-two-year old commander of the Department of Texas, to turn over the federal arsenal and all other United States property in San Antonio. Even though Texas had yet to secede from the United States, it was now in open rebellion. The scene portrayed in the picture shows Texan troops in front of the Plaza Hotel, Main Plaza, preparing to depart on a mission to seize Federal posts on the frontier.

THOUGHT QUESTION:

Why did the Texans mobilize and force Twiggs to surrender his command before the people approved the referendum of secession?

BIOGRAPHIES

JUAN NEPOMUCENO CORTINA (1824-1894). Legendary Mexican folk hero Juan Cortina was born in Camargo, Tamaulipas, on May 16, 1824 to a wealthy ranching family that owned a substantial amount of land in the lower Rio Grande Valley near Brownsville. During the Mexican War, he formed an irregular cavalry unit under the command of General Mariano Arista, seeing action against American forces under General Zachary Taylor at Resaca de la Palma and Palo Alto. After the Treaty of Guadalupe Hidalgo, Cortina's family continued to hold estates in both Mexico and the United States, but, like many Mexican land owners in South Texas, they saw some of their lands north of the Rio Grande expropriated by Americans through legal chicanery and fraud.

Over the next ten years, Cortina built up a deep resentment toward the judges and lawyers in Brownsville who he held responsible for the loss of his land and the general mistreatment of Mexicans. He did not rise up against these injustices, however, until July 13, 1859, when he witnessed a Brownsville lawman using excessive force to arrest a drunken Mexican who happened to be a former employee of the family. When Cortina tried to intervene peaceably, he was met with stern words bearing a racial tint to them so disagreeable that he pulled out a pistol and shot the marshal in the shoulder before riding off with the prisoner. So began what historians often refer to as the "First Cortina War." Two months after this precipitating incident, Cortina returned to Brownsville leading a force of over fifty men for the purpose of exacting revenge against those who he felt had crossed him or his fellow countrymen in the past. While shouting "Viva Mexico!" and "Death to the Americans!" his men seized the town and killed five residents, including the town's jailer. After withdrawing to a nearby ranch, Cortina issued a bold proclamation declaring basic rights for all Tejanos and calling for retribution against all who violated those rights.

Over the next two months, tensions in the region remained high. The Anglo citizens of Brownsville organized a vigilante force to challenge Cortina. They captured Tomás Cabrera, one of his lieutenants, but unsuccessfully attacked Cortina at his mother's nearby ranch. As his reputation grew among the poorer Mexican residents living on both sides of the Rio Grande, Cortina found it easy to recruit new men for his growing army. Once enough men had joined his ranks, he ordered the leaders of Brownsville to release Cabrera and threatened to burn the town if they did not adhere to his demands. Shortly afterwards, a group of Texas Rangers arrived in the border town, disregarded Cortina's threats, and hanged Cabrera before launching a failed assault on Cortina's men. In early December 1859, a second company of Texas Rangers under the command of John S. "Rip" Ford reached Brownsville, followed by 165 U.S. Army troopers under Major Samuel P. Heintzelman. After several skirmishes, Cortina and his men fled to the safety of the Burgos Mountains in northern Mexico, remaining there for more than a year.

When Texas tried to secede from the Union in 1861, Cortina reappeared on the border, declaring war against the Confederates in the Rio Grande Valley, and initiated what some scholars refer to as the second Cortina War. In May 1861, Cortina and his men invaded Zapata County, pillaging and burning farms and stealing cattle before being forced to retreat back into Mexico when the Tejano Confederate captain Santos Benavides routed his men near the town of Carrizo. When Benito Juarez made him a general in the northern Mexican army, Cortina spent much of the remainder of the Civil War years engaged in the fight against French occupation forces in Mexico. Following the war, Cortina returned to the Lower Rio Grande Valley where a number of local residents, many of them newly arrived from the northern states including the mayor of Brownsville, signed a petition requesting that the Texas legislature issue a pardon to the middle-aged border raider. The state legislators, however, failed to give the petition serious consideration.

Cortina continued to be highly revered among many within the Tejano population of the Nueces Strip who viewed him as the embodiment of resistance to Anglo domination in the region. South Texas stockmen, however, viewed Cortina as a perpetual nuisance and wished to be rid of him. American diplomatic pressure, coupled with financial donations from the ranchers to the new Mexican leader Porfirio Díaz (who also wished to remove a potential rival), led to Cortina's eventual arrest by Mexican authorities and subsequent imprisonment without trial in Mexico City. There, Cortina languished until 1890 when he spent his final years under house arrest on a hacienda near the national capital where he died on October 30, 1894.

Historians have long debated the significance of Juan Cortina. Though most early American writers tended to dismiss him as a mere brigand and terrorist, Mexican and Chicano historians have overly praised him as a Tejano "Robin Hood" figure with noble intentions. More recent scholars have attempted to provide a more balanced view of the man. While pointing out his opportunism and the cruel violence often associated with many of his raids, they have endeavored to emphasize the context of his actions. Specifically, they note the radical transformation of south Texas following the Mexican War with the subsequent belittling of Tejanos by many Anglos that led to the countless bona fide grievances providing the strong resonance of Cortina's message among the masses of poor Mexicans in the region.

ELISHA MARSHALL PEASE (1812-1883). Texas governor Elisha Marshall Pease was born on January 3, 1812, at Enfield, Connecticut. After beginning the study of law, he moved to Texas in 1835 to seek greater opportunities but soon became involved in revolutionary activities. Although he first supported the Peace Party, Pease quickly changed his mind and fought at the Battle of Gonzales. Afterward, he served as the secretary to the General Council of the Provisional Government. He attended the convention at Washington-on-the-Brazos in March 1836 and wrote part of the Constitution of the Republic of Texas. Once Texas had secured its independence, Pease served as a clerk to the judiciary committee of the House of Representatives and played a significant role in recording the nation's criminal code. After agreeing to serve as Acting Secretary of the Treasury, he declined President Sam Houston's offer to become Postmaster General, wishing instead to continue pursuing his study of law in Brazoria. After admittance to the bar in 1837, Pease became a well-respected lawyer in the community.

After Texas annexation, Brazoria County voters elected Pease to the legislature where he authored the state's Probate Code. From 1849 to 1850, he served in the state senate, then married Lucadia Niles, a Connecticut woman with whom he had two daughters that survived childhood. In 1851, he made an unsuccessful run for the governorship but won two years later. In 1855, he won re-election to a second two-year term. As governor, Pease could point to numerous accomplishments. He supported the establishment of the first permanent state school fund, financed by $2 million in U.S. Treasury bonds that Texas received in exchange for surrendering its western territorial claims (part of the Compromise of 1850), though the legislature did not utilize the money for educational purposes until well after the Civil War. Pease also encouraged railroad construction through state loans; arranged funding for a new capitol building; made funds available for the construction of a hospital for the mentally ill, schools for the deaf and blind, and a state orphans' home; established several reservations for Native American groups; and helped to raise funds for the construction of the Governor's Mansion. His most important accomplishment, however, was the settlement of the state's debt. When Pease left office in 1857, the state achieved financial security while making measurable improvements in government services.

Throughout the secession movement, Pease aligned with Texas Unionists, though he chose to lay low in Austin once the Civil War began. During the Reconstruction era in Texas, Pease lost the gubernatorial election of 1866 to James Webb Throckmorton. Following his defeat, he traveled with Andrew Jackson Hamilton to Washington, D.C. to lobby Congress for a new Reconstruction policy based on black suffrage. As Radical Republicans argued, Pease believed that President Andrew Johnson's lenient program led to unrepentant and disloyal ex-Confederates to dominate the southern state governments. Returning home, he helped to organize the Republican Party in Texas. In 1867, General Philip Sheridan removed Governor Throckmorton from office and appointed Pease to be provisional governor. In a June 4 message to the state constitutional convention called for under the new congressional Reconstruction program, the governor stated his views when he asked delegates to declare the Texas secession ordinance null and void, to negate only those actions by the Confederate-controlled legislature that directly aided the rebellion (thus distancing himself from those who sought the total negation of all acts by the Texas legislature after secession, the so-called *ab initio* issue), to void all laws that discriminated against persons on account of their race or color, and to provide a provision of the new state constitution that would provide equal civil and political rights for all Texas citizens. Ultimately, Pease proved to be no Radical Republican. He remained governor until 1869 when he resigned his office in protest of the U.S. military's continued involvement in state and local politics in the form of district commander General Joseph J. Reynolds's practice of replacing moderate officeholders with radicals. In 1871, he served as president of the non-partisan Taxpayers' Convention, which protested the "unnecessary" increased cost of government under the Edmund J. Davis administration. The following year, he chaired the Texas delegation to the national Liberal Republican convention, a group with goals that included the end of federal government involvement in Reconstruction. Pease continued to practice law in Austin where he lived with his family until his death on August 26, 1883.

CYNTHIA ANN PARKER (c.1824-1870). Cynthia Ann Parker, the most famous Native American captive in Texas history, was born to Silas and Lucy Parker in Crawford County, Illinois in the mid-1820s. Her Scots-Irish family originally from Virginia had first headed west into Kentucky and southern Illinois before moving to eastern Texas when she was nine or ten years old. For protection, Cynthia's large extended family and fellow settlers built Fort Parker at the edge of Comanche country on the headwaters of the Navasota River near Groesbeck in current-day Limestone County. On May 19, 1836, over 500 Comanche, Kiowa, and Kichai warriors attacked the invaders' stockade, killing many of its inhabitants and carrying off five captives, including young Cynthia and her brother John. Though the other captives were eventually ransomed for their freedom, Cynthia remained with the Comanche for the next twenty-five years.

Over time, Cynthia forgot her Anglo upbringing and became completely indoctrinated to Comanche ways. Given the name Naduah ("Found One"), in her middle teens she married the war chief Peta Nocona who developed such affection for her that he never gained another wife, despite the common Comanche practice of polygamy. They had three children: the famed Comanche warrior Quanah (meaning "Scent" or "Fragrance"); a son named Pecos ("Pecan"); and a daughter named Topsannah ("Prairie Flower"). Quanah eventually would lead a large group of Comanche who chose to reject reservation life in favor of hunting the buffalo and raiding settlements until their defeat in the early 1870s.

On December 18, 1860, Texas Rangers under the command of Lawrence Sullivan Ross attacked a Comanche hunting camp at Mule Creek along the Pease River in north-central Texas. The Rangers killed Peta Nocona and other warriors in the assault and captured three individuals. Two of those taken were the blue-eyed Cynthia Parker and her infant daughter Topsannah. Because Cynthia remembered very little English at that point in her life, it took a while to determine her identity. Eventually, her uncle Colonel Isaac Parker confirmed that she was his long-lost niece.

While the life of Quanah Parker is often viewed as an interesting case of someone able to bridge the gap between the Native American and Anglo worlds (he became a wealthy and respected reservation leader), his mother never re-adapted to life among white people. The only picture that exists of Cynthia Parker, taken not long after the battle at Mule Creek, shows her stoically breast-feeding Topsanna while displaying cut hair—a Comanche sign of mourning for her dead husband. Shuffled around eastern Texas to live among various Parker siblings, she made several unsuccessful attempts to flee with her daughter back to Comanche country. In 1863 she received word that her son Pecos had died of smallpox. After Topsannah caught influenza and died from pneumonia in 1864, Cynthia fell into an irretrievable depression. She finally stopped eating and eventually died in 1870. Initially buried next to Topsannah in an Anderson County cemetery, Quanah arranged in 1910 for their removal to the Post Oak Cemetery near Cache, Oklahoma where he would be interred upon his death the following year. The remains of Cynthia, Quanah, and Topsannah have since been relocated to the Fort Sill Military Cemetery in Lawton, Oklahoma.

DAVID TWIGGS (1790-1862). The commander of U.S. troops stationed in Texas during the outbreak of the Civil War, David Emanuel Twiggs was born on February 14, 1790 on a Georgia plantation owned by his father, a militia commander during the Revolutionary War. After volunteering to serve as a captain during the War of 1812, Twiggs chose military service as his career. Promoted to major, in 1828, he commanded three companies in Wisconsin that built a major base of operations during the Black Hawk War. Eight years later he served as a colonel in Florida during the Seminole War. His largest claim to military fame, however, took place during the Mexican War. Serving with distinction under General Zachary Taylor at Palo Alto and Resaca de la Palma, Twiggs was first promoted to brigadier general, then to major general for gallantry under fire while commanding a division during the capture of Monterrey. After being transferred to General Winfield Scott's command in central Mexico, he led a division in the series of battles fought from Veracruz to Mexico City, suffering wounds during the fight at Chapultepec. After the fall of Mexico City, Twiggs was appointed military governor of Veracruz before being assigned commander of the Department of Texas, which manned a line of 20 forts throughout central Texas primarily to protect Texas settlers from Native American attacks.

When the secession movement began, Twiggs, who held pro-secessionist views, did not engage Texas rebels—similar to the inaction undertaken by other pro-secessionist U.S. Army officers holding commands located in other southern states. On January 13, 1861, he sent word to his superiors that he wished to be relieved from his command. While the general awaited a reply, on February 1, the state secession convention adopted an ordinance of secession and assigned commissioners to speak with the general at his San Antonio headquarters, demanding the surrender of his troops and military equipment under threat of attack by Confederate forces. Twiggs informed them that he was expecting the arrival of his replacement and that he would maintain his troops in their quarters until he was relieved. If the state's voters ratified its secession ordinance before that time, however, he stated that he would turn over all of the military equipment under his control. On February 15, Twiggs received the awaited order relieving him of command, naming a Unionist New York Yankee colonel in charge of federal troops in Texas. In response, over 1,000 rebel troops under Benjamin McCulloch moved on San Antonio to force his immediate capitulation but allowed Twiggs's men to leave under honorable terms after the general stated that he would die before he would permit his men to be disgraced by a surrender of their arms. Wishing to avoid a bloody confrontation, the commissioners were willing to compromise after Twiggs agreed that his troops (about 160 in San Antonio and 2,500 total in Texas) would surrender all public property, including forts, 44 cannon, 400 pistols, 2000 muskets, 500 wagons, and 1000 horses in exchange for their peaceable exit from the state with their personal arms.

While Twiggs viewed his actions as an attempt to avoid bloodshed, his unwillingness to engage Confederate rebels in Texas led to his vilification by northern politicians and the press, followed by his formal dismissal from the U.S. Army "for treachery to the flag of his country." At one point, Twiggs took such offense to James Buchanan publicly calling him a traitor that he wrote a letter threatening to visit the former president in person to "settle our little difficulty." On May 22, 1861, the general accepted a commission as a major general in the Confederate army and was placed in charge of the District of Louisiana. His advanced age and a host of infirmities, however, led him to resign before assuming formal command. Twiggs died of pneumonia near Augusta, Georgia, on July 15, 1862 and is buried on his family's plantation.

Chapter 7

Texas During the Civil War, 1861-1865

A Message for a Suspected Abolitionist from a Local "Committee of Safety"

The outbreak of the Civil War brought both exhilaration and fear among the citizenry of Texas. Though strong support existed for secession and morale was high initially among the majority of white Texans, from the beginning many Confederates feared not only an invasion of their state from federal troops but also a slew of potential internal threats in the form of Indian raiders, slave revolts, and attacks from anti-Confederate Unionists. Fear of the latter, bordering on paranoia in some cases, was especially high in those counties were Confederates were outnumbered by those who had voted against secession in the statewide referendum and were hostile to the notion of serving the Confederate cause in any way. In such areas, individuals such as the man addressed in the letter below, might be threatened with violence, or worse.

May 28th 1861
Mr. A. Newman
Sir

It has been reported to the Committee of safety of this County that you have expressed abolition sentiments before truthful and trustworthy citizens living in our midst and as the present crisis will admit of no such expressions we are authorised [sic.] to advise you to leave our Country at once, or at least within thirty days from this time. Else you will be dealt with according to Mob law. The excellency of your family against whom no one can say ought is the only reason of the above extension of time.

We sincerely hope you will not put us to the painful necessity of putting our designs into execution.

Prepare therefore and leave as you will be carefully watched and should you heedlessly disregard the above warning, your friends if you have any, will deeply regret your folly.

By order of the secret Committee of Safety

Source: Texas State Library and Archives Commission

THOUGHT QUESTIONS:

1. What was the gentleman in the letter accused of? Who levied the accusations?

2. What was the man told to do? What did the letter say would happen to him if he did not comply? Why was he supposedly given this warning?

3. What alternatives would a man receiving such a letter have in this situation?

An American Diplomat in Matamoros Reports on Confederate Trade With Mexico

---

During the Civil War, Matamoros, Mexico served as a major trading center for the Confederacy—a place to export cotton as well as import needed items. Blockading Union ships were hampered by the fact they could not legally attack ships containing Confederate cotton if the vessels flew the flag of a neutral nation. Further, the rebels in Texas could access badly needed war supplies via open trade with Mexico. In this report sent by a U.S. consul stationed in Matamoros, the diplomat discusses the state of affairs in Matamoros, comments on the Confederate trade with Mexico, and suggestions of ways in which the U.S. military could improve the situation.

Consulate of the United States Of America,
Matamoras, September 16, 1862.
Sir:

Your letter of the 12th, by Señor Zambrano [a Mexican customs official], was received on the 14th, and judging from what he said to you, and what he is doing here, it would seem that he is giving much aid to the rebels through the influence of his office. Before he came here, the rebels were obliged to pay heavy duties on everything carried across this river; for instance, the export duties here on flour going to Texas was $5 per barrel; it is now but $1.50, it being put down by the influence of said Zambrano.

As to the cotton, there is not one pound in fifty that ever belonged to a Mexican, neither is there one bale in ten that ever remained one week on Mexican soil, with the exception of a small amount that is on its way down from Monterey, but has not arrived yet.

It is true that cotton has been shipped from this port while our blockading ships were here, as it was decided that as the cotton paid an import and an export duty to Mexico, it became naturalized, and the only way to prevent it would be to prevent its crossing the frontier, which could be done by occupying Fort Brown with a small force.

In my certificate I merely certify that they declare the cotton to be legally shipped from Matamoras.

There is no doubt but that most of the trade with Matamoras is illegal.

I send down correspondence of Captain Hunter, in which you will see the course pursued by him to bring them to terms, and which had the most satisfactory results.

I am, very respectfully, your obedient servant,

L. Pierce, Jr.,

U. S. Consul.

Source: United States. Naval War Records Office. *Official Records of the Union and Confederate Navies in the War of the Rebellion.* Vol. 19 (Washington, 1905), 295.

THOUGHT QUESTIONS:

1. According to the American diplomat, in what ways were local Mexican officials aiding the Confederacy?

2. How quickly was Confederate cotton leaving Matamoros?

3. What proposed solution did the diplomat have for trying to prevent Texas cotton from reaching Matamoros?

General John B. Magruder's Plan to Defend Texas

Texas Confederates faced many difficulties in defending their state during the Civil War. In addition to internal concerns such as dealing with dissenters, the outward threats from Union forces were considerable. Confederates needed to protect a lengthy Gulf coastline in addition to being watchful for potential raids being launched from across the long border with Mexico. Soon after recapturing Galveston in January 1863, John Bankhead Magruder, the Confederate commander of the District of Texas, New Mexico, and Arizona, recommended the following detailed plan for the defense of Texas to the Confederate secretary of war.

Headquarters District Op Texas,
January 6, 1863. Hon. James A. Seddon,
Secretary of War:

Sir: I have the honor urgently to recommend to the favorable consideration of the Department the following plan for the defense of Texas, internally and externally:

There are about 12,000 men organized in this State, about 6,000 armed, and these indifferently. I wish to divide these into brigades of 3,000 men each, and to place them under good brigadier-generals, and each two brigades under a major-general.

The extent of the country is so great that an order is in most cases valueless when it reaches its destination. The extent of coast is about 400 miles, and the territory of the State extends from 800 to 1,000 miles in the interior. In this vast country the utmost confusion and disorganization prevail in the military administration from a want of control by the proper officers, who must be at a great distance from some portions of their commands.

Disaffection exists in a greater degree than has been represented to me, but will not spread if promptly put down; if not, it will increase.

Various other reasons induce me to ask the appointment, as soon as it is possible, of major-generals and brigadier-generals enough to enable me to carry out my plan, which is simply this:

1st. To hold the Rio Grande at all hazards. The command there must be unsupported and self-sustaining. I would assign it to General Bee, whose relations with the Mexican authorities and personal qualifications make this arrangement an excellent one. This I have already done, and I propose to give him command as far northeast as the Nueces.

2d. To assign a brigadier-general to the command of all the country from the Nueces to the Colorado.

3d. Another brigadier to the command of that between the Colorado and the Sabine, where there are railroads parallel to the coast.

4th. One brigadier-general to command on the western frontier from the Upper Nueces to the Clear Fork of the Brazos—the Indian reserve.

5th. One major-general to have his headquarters habitually at San Antonio; and,

6th. Another major-general to have his headquarters at Houston.

The commanding officer of the whole would be most of the time in the saddle, and might establish his headquarters wherever his services were most required. Similar districts might be laid out as conscript districts, each commanded by a major, the whole by a superintendent of conscripts, with the rank of lieutenant-colonel.

With this arrangement, and efficient staff officers, harmony and promptness of action and due responsibility would be easily attained. To carry it out I wish the general officers asked for. At present I have but one, Brigadier-General Bee, permanently, and Brigadier General Scurry temporarily, and in order to obtain those of the proper qualifications I respectfully recommend the inclosed [sic.] names to the favorable consideration of the President.

I am, sir, very respectfully, your obedient servant,

J. BANKHEAD MAGRUDER,
Major-General, Commanding, &o.

Source: United States. War Department. *The War of the Rebellion: A Compilation of the Official Records of the Union and Confederate Armies.* Vol. 15 (Washington, 1886), 932-33.

THOUGHT QUESTIONS:

1. How many men did Magruder report that he currently had to defend all of Texas? Did he feel this was sufficient? Why or why not?

2. According to Magruder, what problems did the great size of Texas cause his command?

3. Based on where Magruder assigned his generals and their men, where were his priorities in defending Texas? Where did he state his headquarters would be located? Why?

An Appeal to Allow Conscripted Soldiers to Remain in Central Texas

---

During the Civil War, both the Union and the Confederacy employed a military draft (conscription) to bolster their military forces. By 1863, the protracted conflict began to considerably reduce the male population of many Central Texas settlements, both from the mounting casualties and the resistance of Unionists, especially from the German settlements, to the Confederate draft. Below is a letter to the governor from a loyal Confederate in which the writer comments on the local situation and asks that further men not be taken from the region:

Boerne 12th July 1863
His Excellency Governor FR Lubbock, Austin
Dear Sir

As senator from this district I am daily asked, why is it that the most exposed parts of the district are subject to the draft and if the Governor knows our situation, but I am unable to give any satisfactory answer, only, that in the opinion of the Governor and Commanding General they are needed and should not in times like these complain.

Still I cannot think you are aware of the situation of this district. It is one where there are no negros to make and geather the crops, and at the present time not white men enough to do it. I know well that there has been a feeling against many parts of this district for their union sentiments in times gone by, but most of those who were considered disloyal have fled from the country, some to Mexico, some up a tree, and many even killed in the fight that took place last summer with Duffs company and a party making their way out of the country. [T]his has left but few to take care of the women & children left behind them[;] some may think they do not deserve taking care of, but they are among us and humanity demands us to do so, and that the sins of their husbands & fathers should not be visited upon innocent women & children, many of whom are now employed in helping to giather the crops in absince of men, those who even loyal have volunteered[,] freely leaving their wives & children exposed to depredations by indians to geather their crops with the assistance of the few men left, and many crops are not yet geathered being obliged to wait their turn, in consequence of which much grain has been lost by being exposed to late rains[.]

[T]o take one half of what now remain home would leave us in a very destitute condition. [N]o counties will suffer more than Gillespie & the portion of Kendall that formally [formerly] belonged to Blanco, which I understand has been included in the draft by an order from the Adj Genl. Malice may have induced some to represent the state of things different in these counties but it is just as I represent them to you. [T]here may be a few that ought to be forced into the army but they are found in every community and cannot be reached. [T]hose few should not be the means of making the whole community suffer, and force many to abandon their homes, move their familys into the interior[,] leaving the stock each may have to be stolen by those who geather in squads for the purpose.

I do not wish to be considered presumptuous in writing your excellency on this subject but mearly wish to let you know the situation of our people, and ask as much leniency as you can grant them as it would be ruin to many to be taken from their homes even into camps of instructions which would necessarily be a long way from their homes in this district.

[H]ad we negros in this district as in others to geather the crops our case would be different, but with our exposure to indians and not more men left than enough to protect the women & children in case of attack from them it is a hard case to take them away. It will be also impossible to geather the tithe that will soon be called for by the confederate Government as women cannot geather oxen and drive them to the depots[.] [T]herefore much loss will be sustained by the C.S. [Confederate States] in the loss of the tithe, greater I think than the good the few men could be that are now left if allowed to stay at home and geather their crops.

Our frontier regiment does excellent service and is a great protection to us but it is impossible for our regiment to protect a frontier of several hundred miles if we are left without a few men at home. [T]o those who live in the interior our dangers may appear imaginary, but to those who have felt and seen the depredations of Indians know how to dread them and when they know our men are taken from home their raids will be frequent and there will be little safety for life or property. If your Excellency will take these things into consideration and not take our men from home until their services cannot be well done without you will confer a favor upon the people of the frontier.

>   Very Respectfully
>   Your Obdt Servt
>   Erastus Reed

Source: Erastus Reed to Governor Francis R. Lubbock, July 12, 1863. Records of Governor Francis R. Lubbock, Texas State Library and Archives Commission

THOUGHT QUESTIONS:

1. What types of problems does Erastus Reed describe in Boerne and the surrounding area?

2. What is the writer's attitude toward the condition of the women and children of dissenting German men who had either left the district or had been killed?

3. What problems for the Confederacy did Reed state would develop if additional men were taken away?

Hardships during the War, 1863

In this letter to Colonel James E. McCord, Sergeant C. G. Wood describes the hardships of war on the home front along the Texas frontier. Like many Texas soldiers, Wood struggled with his sense of duty to the Confederate cause and his loyalty to his family. In many cases when a discharge or leave of absence could not be obtained, soldiers would desert their post.

Camp San Saba Oct 10th/63
Col J.E. McCord
Comdg Frontier Regt
My Dear Col

The helpless condition of my family—consisting of my wife and seven little children—has become a source of distress to my mind such as I have never known before. Eighteen months ago I joined this Regiment in the fond expectation that twelve months would end the war.

I was induced to go into the reorganization, because I thought with others, that the great struggle had reached its climax, and a very few months would suffice to end the work. Since that time my oldest and only son of sufficient size to be of any service to his mother joined the service, and my wife has been struggling on for months with her little ones alone. Winter is now approaching—my family are almost destitute of clothing—nearly out of bread—no meat—and every man in immediate neighbourhood has either moved or is making arrangements to do so.

If I move my family I must build them a house—if they stay where they are,, they are constantly exposed to danger from Indians and have as I said no one upon whom to depend for protection, my oldest boy at home being but nine years of age.

I am also receiving letters from my Father and mother "who are almost entirely helpless—one being seventy two and the other seventy ye[ars] of age" informing me of their situation and asking my assistance.

It is under these circumstances that I am desirous of obtaining a service. If you will doo the kindness to procure my discharge at your earliest convenience I shall take it as a special favour for which I shall hold myself under lasting obligations to my colonel.

I am very Respectfully Your Obedient Servant

C.G. Wood
3rd Sargt Co "K"
Texas Frontier Regt

Source: C.G. Wood to James E. McCord, Records of the Adjutant General, Texas State Library and Archives Commission

THOUGHT QUESTIONS:

1. When Wood enlisted, how long did he think the war would last?

2. What hardships confronted Wood's family during the war?

3. Based on the document, do you think that Wood's circumstance was commonplace among Texas soldiers? Why or why not?

Andy Anderson Recounts His Days as a Slave

During the Great Depression, the Federal Writers' Project of the Works Progress Administration (WPA) paid workers to interview over two thousand surviving slaves across the South. By allowing former bondsmen the opportunity to describe their experiences in their own words, the transcripts of these encounters have become a tremendously valuable primary source for historians and the general public. Andy J. Anderson, a ninety-four-year-old former slave residing in Fort Worth, was one such former slave interviewed by the WPA. Born on a Williamson County plantation owned by a planter named Jack Haley, Anderson was sold to another owner, W. T. House of Blanco County, soon after the Civil War began. In this excerpt from his WPA interview, Anderson gives some remembrances of his life under both masters.

I's bo'n in 1843. Dat makes me 94 yeahs ol', an' 18 yeahs ol' w'en de war stahted. Tharfo', dis nigger has seen a good deal of slave life an' some hahd 'speriences dunn' dat time an' good times too.

Marster Haley am kind to his cullud folks. In fact, him am kind to ever'body an' all de folks lak him. Whuppin's am not given 'cept w'en it am necessary an' dat am not often an' am reasonable w'en it am given. De udder w'ite folks use to call weuns de petted niggers.

De plantation have 12 fam'lies ob slaves. Thar am 'bout 30 ol' an' young workers an' 'bout 20 piccaninnies dat am too young fo' work. Dem dat am too young fo' work am took care ob by a nurse durin' de day w'ile de mammies am a workin' in de field an sich.

I's gwine to 'splain how it am managed on Marster Haley's place. Marster Haley am a good manager an' ever'one am 'signed to do certain jobs. It am diffe'nt now, dan 'twas den. A plantation am sort ob lak de small town. Ever'thing dat am used on de place am made thar. So, thar am de shoemaker. Him also am de tanner an' make de leathah f'om de hides.

Thar am 'bout 1,000 sheep on de Marster's place, so thar am de person dat 'tends to de sheep an' de wool. De sheep am sheared twice a yeah.

De wool am carded, spun an' weaved into cloth an' f'om dat cloth, all de clothes am made. Thar am 'bout 25 head ob cattle, sich p'vides de milk an' buttah, also beef meat fo' eatin'. Den thar am turkeys, chickens, hawgs an' bees.

De plantation am planted in cotton, mosly. Co'se, dere am co'n an' wheat. De con am fo' feed fo' de stock an' to make co'n meal fo' de humans. De wheat am fo' to make flouah. Mars- ter don' sell any co'n or wheat, 'less if he have extra. Cotton am w'at he raised fo' sale....

De wah stahts an' dat makes a big change on de Marster's place. De Marster j'ins de ahmy an' hires a man named Delbridge fo' overseer to he'p de Marster's son, John. Den, in 'bout three months, de soldiers come an' took Marster John to de ahmy by fo'ce. Deys put him on a hoss an' tooks him away.

Thar come pretty neah bein' some hu't niggers de day deys took Marster John away. You see, weuns don' know dey had de right to took Marster 'way, so weuns cullud folks crowded 'roun' de Marster an' warnt gwine to 'low dem to took him. De Marster tol' weuns to go 'way 'cause de soldiers have de right to took him an' weuns jus' git hu't if weuns try to stop de soldiers, so weuns dispatched.

Aftah Marster John am took away an' de overseer am lef' in whole charge, hell stahts to pop. De fust thing he does am to cut de rations. He weigh out de meat, three pounds to de person fo' de week an' he measures out a peck ob meal, 'twarnt 'nough. He ha'f starve do niggers an' demands mo' wo'k an' he stahts de whuppin's. I's guess he 'cides to edu-macate dem. I's guess Delbridge went to hell w'en he died.. .I's don' think he go dat far, though. I's don' see how de devil could stand him.

Weuns cullud folks on Marster's place am not used to sich treatment an' some run off. W'en deys am catched, thar am a whuppin' at de stake. Thar am a couple ob de runaway niggers dat am never catched.

I's 'scaped de worst ob Delbridge 'cause he sol' me. I's sol' to Marster W.T. House ob Blanco County. I's sho glad w'en I's sol', but it am sho't gladness. W.T. House am anudder man dat hell am too good fo'. I's not on dat place long, jus' a few months 'til I's sol' to his brothah, John House, who had a big plantation close by.

I's git one whuppin' while on de W.T. House place. De scahs am on my ahms, see thar, an' on my back too. Dem I's will carry to my grave. De whuppin' I's git am fo' de cause as I's will 'splain. 'Twas dis away; De overseer sent me fo' de dry fiah wood. W'en I's gits de wood loaded an' stahts to drive, de wheel hits a sho't stump, de team jerks an' dat breaks de whippletree [a crossbar, to which a harness is fastened to pull a plow]. I's tries to fix dat so dat de load could be hauled in. I's delayed quite a spell while de cook am waitin' fo' de wood. Aftah I's tries an' tries, it am necessary fo' me to walk to de bahn fo' anudder whippletree. De overseer am at de bahn wen I's gits dere. He am gittin' ready to staht aftah me. I's tell w'at am de delay. Me am poweful mad 'cause I's hit de stump an' sich.

De overseer ties me to de stake an' ever' ha'f hour, fo' fouah hours, deys lay 10 lashes on my back. Fo' de fust couple ob hours, de pain am awful. I's never fo'git it. Aftah I's stood dat fo' a couple oh hours, I's could not feel de pain so much an' w'en dey took me loose, I's jus' ha'f dead. I's could not feel de lash 'cause my body am numb, an' my mind am numb. De last thing I's 'membahs am dat I's wishin' fo' death. I's laid in de bunk fo' two days gittin' over dat whuppin'. Dat is, gittin' over it in de body but not in de heart. No Sar! I's have dat in my heart 'til dis day….

Source: Federal Writer's Project, Works Progress Administration, Manuscript Division, Library of Congress

THOUGHT QUESTIONS:

1. In what ways did Anderson describe the Haley plantation as resembling a "small town"?

2. How was Anderson directly affected by the Civil War while the conflict took place? Did life generally get better or worse for him? How?

3. How do experiences such as Anderson's convey the precariousness and uncertainty of life under slavery?

The War in Texas

Credit: UTSA'S Institute of Texas Cultures, #075-0384,
Source: Frank Leslie's Illustrated Newspaper, v. 17, Dec. 5, 1863, p. 173.

Texas's border with Mexico gave the state an advantage over the other southern states blockaded by the Union navy. Being so close to Mexico provided Texas cotton growers an opportunity to get their crop safely to the international market. Planters would cart their cotton from Brownsville to Bagdad, Mexico, on the mouth of the Rio Grande where the bales were loaded on a steamboat. From Bagdad, the cotton was taken outside the reach of the Union blockade to the international market.

THOUGHT QUESTION:

What troubles for the Union could have resulted if President Lincoln had ordered the U.S. Navy to stop the ships of nations known to be carrying cargoes of Confederate cotton?

"Confederate Barbarities in Texas"

Credit: Library of Congress
New York, c. 1864

This print depicting barbarities against Texas loyalists appeared in northern media outlets during the spring of 1864. Unionists were loyalist Southerners opposed to secession and the Confederacy. Texas, with its diverse population, had a significant number of Unionists. Much Unionist activity took place in Cooke, Grayson, Wise, and Denton counties. North Texas contained a large population of people from northern and upper south areas that tended to support the Union. Many people living on the frontier in central Texas who relied heavily on the army to protect them from Indian raids also opposed secession. Further, the Germans who settled in the Hill Country had experienced war in Europe and came to the United States to escape the horrors of warfare. Stories of killings of Unionists in Texas spread across both the North and the South, reinforcing the Union's accusations of southern barbarism.

THOUGHT QUESTION:

Though based on elements of truth, how might these depictions have been used by Northerners to generate outrage against the South and strengthen the determination to continue the war effort? How do war advocates in the present day use such atrocity stories for similar ends?

BIOGRAPHIES

RICHARD "DICK" DOWLING (1838-1867). Confederate war hero Richard William Dowling was born in Galway County, Ireland, in 1838. At the age of eight, he moved to New Orleans with his parents and six brothers and sisters. In 1853 he became an orphan when a yellow fever epidemic killed all in his family except for himself and two siblings. In the early 1850s, Dowling moved to Texas, settling in Houston where he became an entrepreneur. In October 1857, he received financial aid from Benjamin Odlum, the father of his fiancée Elizabeth Ann Odlum, to open a saloon named Shades. Three years later, he sold his shares in Shades and purchased the famous "Bank of Bacchus" saloon near the Harris County courthouse, which became one of the most popular gathering places in town.

When the Civil War erupted, Dowling became a second lieutenant in the Jefferson Davis Guards, a company largely composed of Irish dockworkers under the command of his wife's uncle, Captain Frederick Odlum. In early 1861, Odlum's men captured U.S. Army posts along the Texas-Mexico border before being reorganized as an artillery regiment charged with helping to defend the upper Texas Gulf Coast. After participating in John Magruder's recapture of Galveston on January 1, 1863, the Confederate general transferred Odlum's unit to Sabine Pass along the Texas-Louisiana border. On January 21, Dowling served as an artillery commander aboard the Confederate steamer *Josiah A. Bell*, outfitted with a rifled cannon and numerous cotton bales for insulated protection, as it took on two blockading Union vessels in a two-hour naval engagement resulting in the capture of the enemy vessels and their cargo.

Dowling's biggest claim to fame during the Civil War was his successful defense of Fort Griffin (a small earthwork located on the west bank of the Sabine River) against a large Union invasion force. On September 8, 1863, with a total of six cannon and less than fifty men, Dowling's artillerymen disabled two Union gunboats, captured 350 enemy soldiers, and compelled the remaining Union forces to retreat back to New Orleans. The victory was possible because Dowling's gunners made excellent use of the terrain, specifically, the narrow river pass that included a shallow oyster reef in the middle of the waterway. Dowling's men had spent months practicing with their guns, aiming at specific points where Union ships would have to travel while navigating the pass. The result at the Battle of Sabine Pass was an intense and highly efficient line of fire that achieved the victory that Confederate President Jefferson Davis would label as the Confederacy's "Thermopylae," (an allusion to the famous battle of the Peloponnesian War at which Spartan warriors defended a small mountain pass against a vast Persian army). Though the Greeks went down to the last man, Dowling's unit suffered no casualties.

Soon after the battle, Dowling was promoted to the rank of major and reassigned to recruiting duty for the remainder of the war as Confederate officials tried to capitalize on his celebrity status. After the war, he returned to Houston to run his saloon and engage in new business enterprises, such as real estate speculation, a construction company, a Trinity River steamboat, and oil and gas leases. Despite a promising future as a postbellum Texas businessman, a yellow fever epidemic, the very scourge that took his parents away fifteen years earlier, ended his life on September 23, 1867 at the age of twenty-nine.

SANTOS BENAVIDES (1823-1891). Santos Benavides, the South Texas merchant and rancher who became the highest-ranking Tejano in the Confederate army during the Civil War, was born in Laredo on November 1, 1823. In 1842 he married Augustina Villareal with whom he later adopted four children. Benavides profited not only from business success but also from his familial connections. His great-great grandfather, Tomás Sanchez, had founded Laredo in the mid-1700s, plus his uncle Basilio Benavides served many years as alcalde (during the Mexican period), mayor, and Texas state representative. Being local elites in a relatively isolated region, the Benavides family strongly supported the idea of decentralized political power. They were Federalists in Mexican politics and supported the Democrats after the American annexation of Texas. Before the Civil War, Benavides was elected mayor of Laredo in 1856 and also distinguished himself by leading various military campaigns against Native American groups, especially the Lipan Apache.

When Texas attempted to secede from the Union, Benavides and his brothers threw their support behind the Confederacy. Starting the war with the rank of captain in the Thirty-third Cavalry Regiment, he won praise for border patrol actions against the enemy along the Rio Grande River Valley, including driving off Juan Cortina's raid in May 1861. After promotion to the rank of colonel, Benavides further distinguished himself on March 19, 1864 when he successfully led forty-two troops in the defense of Laredo against over 200 soldiers of Col. Edmund Davis's Union First Texas Cavalry. After Union occupation of Brownsville, Benavides further contributed to the Confederate cause by escorting cotton trains through southern Texas so that they could cross the Rio Grande into northern Mexico and eventually deposit their cargo to awaiting ships in the port of Bagdad near Matamoros.

Following the Confederacy's defeat, Benavides resumed his commercial and ranching activities while maintaining involvement in state and local politics, serving three terms in the state legislature from 1879 to 1884 and twice as a Laredo alderman. Before his death in 1891, Benavides was a key player in building up Hispanic support for the Democratic Party in Webb County and surrounding areas of South Texas.

JOHN BANKHEAD MAGRUDER (1807-1871). John Magruder, Confederate defender of Texas during the Civil War, was born in Port Royal, Virginia on May 1, 1807. He began his higher education career at the University of Virginia, where he once had a meal with the school's founder, former president Thomas Jefferson. Magruder moved on to the United States Military Academy, graduating fifteenth in West Point's Class of 1830. The young officer's first military action took place during the Second Seminole War in Florida, but he first distinguished himself in combat under Winfield Scott's command during the Mexican War, most notably at the Battle of Cerro Gordo and the assault on Chapultepec. Afterwards, he served on frontier garrison duty in California and Fort Leavenworth, Kansas. Tall, handsome, and flamboyant, fellow officers and enlisted men warmed up to him because of his impressive drinking ability and his penchant to entertain himself and others by composing songs, staging concerts, and leading amateur theatrical productions in order to relieve everyone's boredom.

When the Civil War began, Magruder was serving in the artillery forces defending Washington, D.C., but resigned his commission when Virginia announced its attempt to secede. As a major general in the Confederate army, he was placed in charge of slowing down the advance of Union General George McClellan's sizeable forces after they landed on the Virginia coast, beginning what would be known as the Peninsular Campaign. He used all his amateur theatrical talents to completely convince the overly-cautious McClellan that there were larger forces ahead of them than actually existed, using such tactics as constantly rotating his units, placing fake cannons at numerous locations, and planting individuals to spread false information. The ruses succeeded in delaying McClellan's advance for weeks, but he soon fell out of favor with Confederate General Robert E. Lee when communications problems led Magruder to order a devastatingly foolhardy attack at the Battle of Malvern Hill.

Lee reassigned Magruder to lead the District of Texas, New Mexico, and Arizona. He arrived in late 1862, setting up his headquarters in Houston. The highlight of his tenure occurred on New Year's night in 1863 when joint land and naval forces under his command successfully recaptured Galveston after almost three months of Union control. After greatly strengthening the city's defenses, Galveston remained in Confederate hands for the remainder of the war. Near the war's end, he spent some time in Arkansas before returning to Texas in time to witness the surrender of Confederate forces at Galveston in June 1865.

After the war, Magruder left the country to offer his services to Emperor Maximilian of Mexico. He served as a major general, then returned to Houston in May 1867 after the defeat of the Imperial Mexican Army. He died in 1871 and is buried in Galveston, the location of his greatest triumph. Though Magruder married Esther von Kapff in May 1831, they rarely spent time together. Many who knew him for years were sometimes surprised to learn that he was married. The army—whether U.S., Confederate, or Mexican—was his life.

CAROLINE SEDBERRY (1827-1895). Born in Tennessee on August 23, 1827, Caroline Huntley Alexander would face challenges during much of her young adult life as the mother of nine children trying to hold down a Bosque County farm during the Civil War while her husband served as a member of the Texas state government and later in a Confederate army unit. She married William Rush Sedberry, a successful farmer, in Maury, Tennessee, and the couple began a large family that would have eleven children, though two died before adulthood. In 1853, the Sedberrys migrated with their six slaves to Bosque County, Texas (located to the northwest of Waco) and began farming and stock raising operations. Showing increased interest in politics, William Sedberry was elected county judge in 1858, presided over the meetings in which Bosque County voted to join the effort to secede from the Union, and was selected to represent his district in the new Texas state legislature.

While away in Austin, William and Caroline exchanged letters in which he updated his wife on government matters while giving directions on how she could best manage the farm in his absence. Surviving letters reveal her initial insecurity in taking responsibility for making important decisions such as when to plant crops. Though Caroline hoped her situation as farmstead supervisor would only be a temporary inconvenience, it became a full-time occupation after her husband and two oldest sons joined the Confederate army in early 1862. At her disposal, Caroline would have the labor of seven slaves (three of which were younger than fourteen) and her children, though the oldest child was her fourteen-year-old daughter Annette. Her oldest son at home, Rush, was only twelve.

With the passage of time, Caroline expressed more confidence in her letters to her husband, reporting favorably on crop yields and the overall operation of the farm, while still openly expressing her longing for him to return. She related her many transactions with local men, both positively and negatively, as she sought to collect debts, pay off her own debts, sell crops, negotiate purchases, and barter items (and slaves' labor) in exchange for needed work. She also took on the role of nursemaid and doctor when her children frequently fell ill and took up sewing and weaving, as many Texas women did during wartime, to save money while clothing her family. Then, in the fall of 1862, Caroline discovered that her headaches and frequent bouts with fatigue were not just due to her multiple daily tasks—in fact, she was pregnant again for the twelve time. Although William had been previously stationed close by (four counties over to the southeast, at Camp Speight near Millican in Brazos County), his regiment had since moved to a post near Little Rock, Arkansas. It was from there that news was sent by William Seberry's oldest son (then serving with his father), first to William's mother and then to Caroline, that William had succumbed to an illness on January 1, 1863.

An ordinary woman persevering in extraordinary times, she overcame her sorrow, gave birth to a daughter three months after receiving word of her husband's death, and kept her family together for the remainder of the war. After the Confederacy's defeat, she continued to raise her children while they farmed their land, helped by her second-oldest son who had lost an arm during the war. In 1871, Caroline married a local man named John Stith and lived a quiet life until her death in 1895.

Chapter 8

Reconstruction in Texas:
The Unfinished Civil War,
1865-1874

General Gordon Granger's "Juneteenth" Proclamation, June 19, 1865

In September 1862, President Abraham Lincoln issued the Emancipation Proclamation, freeing all slaves in areas still considered to be in a state of rebellion on January 1, 1863. Though this executive order legally liberated the slaves of Texas, the successful defense of Texas during the war meant that actual liberation would have to await the defeat of the Confederacy, the arrival of Union troops, and, in some cases, the use of troops to enforce the president's edict (some Union officers reported the need to free some slaves in Texas as late as 1866).

Issued on June 19th (shortened to "Juneteenth" by the African-American community), Union General Gordon Granger's third general order (shown below) informed the citizens of Texas that he would enforce the president's directive. The date soon became a revered holiday for African Americans in Texas and has been increasingly celebrated outside of the Lone Star State.

The people of Texas are informed that, in accordance with a proclamation from the Executive of the United States, all slaves are free. This involves an absolute equality of personal rights and rights of property between former masters and slaves, and the connection heretofore existing between them becomes that between employer and hired labor. The freedmen are advised to remain quietly at their present homes and work for wages. They are informed that they will not be allowed to collect at military posts and that they will not be supported in idleness either there or elsewhere.

Source: United States. War Department. *The War of the Rebellion: A Compilation of the Official Records of the Union and Confederate Armies.* Vol. 48 (Washington, 1896), 929.

THOUGHT QUESTIONS:

1. Now that slavery had ended, what did Granger think was the proper connection between the slaves and former masters?

2. What responsibilities did Granger place upon the freed slaves?

3. What feelings did this order probably elicit among former Confederates at the end of the Civil War?

Mrs. L.E. Potts's Letter to President Andrew Johnson

From the beginning of the Reconstruction Era, African Americans suffered at the hands of white Texans reluctant to give up the institution of slavery. In the letter below, Mrs. L.E. Potts, a white woman originally from Tennessee, describes the hardships that freed slaves suffered in northeast Texas near the town of Paris.

Dear Sir:

In addressing you I do not address you as the Chief Magistrate only but as the father of our beloved country, one whom we all look more or less for protection, but most especially the poor negroes. I wish that my poor pen could tell you of their persecutions here. They are now just out of slavery only a few months, and their masters are so angry to have to lose them that they are trying to persecute them back into slavery. It is not considered a crime here to kill a negro; they are often run down by bloodhounds and shot because they do not do precisely as the white man says. I have been at Nashville, Tennessee, all the winter, and I am being constantly reminded of the difference in their condition here and there. There have never been any federal troops in here, and everything savors of rebellion. I wish that we could have a few soldiers here just for a while, to let these rebels know that they have been whipped. The confederacy have ruined mine and my children's property. In 1858 I took my two children and went to California, with the hopes of restoring the health of my daughter, who was in deep decline, and in 1861 I was ready to return home, when the rebellion broke out, and fearing that my son, a youth only thirteen years of age, might be forced into the war, I remained there until peace. We left a large estate here, which they confiscated and destroyed all that they could. The land is all that is left to us. They stripped it of all the timber and destroyed my houses; had my notes and claims turned over to the confederate receiver, who has them yet. But it is not to my wrongs that I wish to call your attention, but, for humanity's sake, I implore you to send protection, in some form, to these suffering freedmen. Your good heart and wise head know best what to do. I have stated only facts; the negroes need protection here. When they work they scarcely ever get any pay; and what are they to do? I am a plain woman, from your own State, and hope this appeal may not be made in vain. I have never had the pleasure of your acquaintance, but as a Tennessee woman I am proud of you; and as

President I approve of your course, and hope that bright laurels may forever crown your brow. Nothing more at present, but subscribe myself,

Respectively yours & c.,
Mrs. L.E. Potts

Source: United States House of Representatives. "Conditions of Affairs in Texas." House *Executive Documents, Doc. No. 61*, Thirty-ninth Congress (1866)

THOUGHT QUESTIONS:

1. According to Mrs. Potts, what conditions did the freed slaves face in North Texas?

2. How does Mrs. Potts try to show President Johnson that she was a Unionist?

3. What is the main purpose of the letter? What did she wish President Johnson to do?

Excerpts from Major General George A. Custer's Testimony before the Joint Committee on Reconstruction

---

During Reconstruction, Congress created a joint committee to investigate reports of terrorist behavior in the South. As part of the investigation, the committee interviewed a number of individuals who were familiar with the conditions in the South between 1865 and 1866. Below are excerpts from a hearing in which congressmen questioned Major General George A. Custer, who commanded troops in Texas during the first months of federal occupation in the state.

Washington, March 10, 1866

Question: What proportion of the people, where you have been, are new or have been during the war, faithful to the Union?

Answer: In Texas it would hardly be possible to find a man who has been strictly faithful to the Union, and remained in the State, during the war. They forced all who were truly Union men to leave the State. Those who did not were murdered. . . .

Question: Have you any knowledge of an organization in that State [Texas], secret or otherwise, for the purpose of opposing or thwarting the action of the government of the United States?

Answer: It was reported to me frequently that such organizations did exist, and I have no doubt in my own mind that they have existed in the northern part of the State. I was so thoroughly convinced of the fact that I sent a considerable force into that section of the State to disperse them. The fact that such organizations did exist was confirmed by the statements, written and oral, of loyal men, and by the reports of officers sent there on duty.

Question: State what you know as to the operations or necessity of the Freedmen's Bureau, or some other agency of a similar nature in the State?

Answer: I have paid considerable attention to the action of the Freedmen's Bureau in various parts of the State; at least such parts as were embraced within the limits of my command, and I am firmly of the opinion that unless the present bureau or some substitute is maintained for an indefinite period, great wrongs and an immense amount of oppression would be entailed upon the freedmen. As it exists there at present, the bureau is totally unable to do all that might be done or that is required to be done.

Question: What feelings do these people, or a majority of them, evince at this time towards the freedmen?

Answer: There is a strong feeling of hostility towards the freedmen as a general thing. There are exceptions, or course, but the great mass of the people there seem to look upon the freedmen as being connected with, or as being the cause of, their present condition, and they do not hesitate to improve every opportunity to inflict injuries upon him in order, seemingly, to punish him for this. This feeling exists to a certain extent, and is often manifested in their courts. I might illustrate it by stating what I know to be true, that since the establishment of the provisional government in Texas the grand juries throughout the State have found upwards of five hundred indictments of murder against disloyal men, and yet in not a single case has there been a conviction, while in one judicial district, embracing seven counties, adjoining Travis county, the judge, in making to the governor his report of the last session of court held by him, stated that fourteen Negroes had been tried within his jurisdiction for various slight offences; that the fourteen had had all been convicted and sentenced to various terms in the State prison. And to show you the manner in which justice is meted out in their course towards the freedmen, one was tried and convicted of stealing one bushel of sweet potatoes, and sentenced to the penitentiary for two years. Another for stealing an equally small amount was sentenced for the same period. Then, to show you their hostility further, it is of weekly, if not daily, occurrences that freedmen are murdered. Their bodies are found in different parts of the country, and sometimes it is not known who the perpetrators are, but when that is known no action is taken against them. I believe a white man has never been hung for murder in Texas, although it is the law. Cases have occurred of white men meeting freedmen they never saw before, and murdering them merely from this feeling of hostility to them as a class.

Question: What are the views and feelings of the freedmen in Texas, as well as you could ascertain them, towards the government?

Answer: They are loyal without a single exception, so far as my experience goes. They were always our friends, both in time of war and since active hostilities have ceased.

Question: Have they any apprehension or understanding of the condition of things in that country?

Answer: They have, to a certain extent. They realize, as all Union men in the State do, that their only safety and protection lies in the general government; and they realize too, that if the troops are withdrawn, they will be still more exposed than they are now.

Source: United States Congress. *Report of the Joint Committee on Reconstruction at the First Session Thirty-Ninth Congress.* (1866)

THOUGHT QUESTIONS:

1. According to Custer, how were the freed slaves suffering during the early Reconstruction period?

2. How were ex-Confederates treating Unionists in the state?

3. What did Custer recommend with regard to the federal government maintaining a military presence in Texas? Why?

A Report From a Texas Freedmen's Bureau Agent

The Bureau of Refugees, Freedmen, and Abandoned Lands (The Freedman's Bureau) operated in Texas between 1865 and 1869. Bureau agents had numerous jobs to perform, but none were more important than protecting the former slaves from harm and helping them to adjust to freedom. Unfortunately, many ex-Confederate Texans who tried to maintain as much of their antebellum social order as possible made the agents' task nearly impossible to complete. Below is the report of a Bureau agent stationed in the town of Millican (near present-day College Station) on the subject of violence taking place in eastern Texas between 1865 and 1866.

Office Sub Assistant Commissioner
Bureau R. F. & A. L. State of Texas
Millican, Texas Sept. 7th, 1866

Lieutenant Maden
Acting Asst. Adj. Gen.
Galveston, Texas
Sir:

In reply to your communication dated Sept. 11th, 1866 that just reached me on yesterday. I have the honor to state that I have only been stationed at this Post since August 4th, 1866. And in all cases of murder and outrages committed upon Freedmen &c there is no official record. Hence I cannot give you the date and in some instances do not know anything officially of the circumstances warranted therewith. There have been more murders committed within this District upon the persons of Freedmen than (illegible). But the following are all that I have any official evidence of and of which I can furnish any data. December 8th, 1865 - John Echols, citizen of Burleson Co., shot and killed a freedman in his employ named "Kit." From the evidence on file it appears that the said Mr. Echols had the night previously beaten the wife of the freedman Kit and in the morning without any provocation I can see killed the boy Kit.

June 21st, 1866 - Marie Edwards, a freedwoman, was shot and killed by Court Brown, a citizen of Robertson County. Know nothing of the circumstances as at this time there has been no official investigation.

July 1866 - William Tate, a citizen of Robertson Co., shot and killed a freedman. Since then Tate has fled the County and as yet there has been no official investigation, but is said to have been a cold blooded murder.

July 1866 - Mr. Fields is a citizen of Grimes Co., shot and killed two freedmen, father and son, a cold blooded murder. An official investigation has not taken place.

September 9th, 1866 - Seaton, a freedman under contract with a Mr. Goggan of Burleson Co., while in custody of the Civil Authorities, was taken away from them by a party of armed men (citizens) during night and undoubtedly murdered, as I have been unable to learn any trace of him since.

September 15th, 1866 - At night on the Plantation of Dr. Hardy, Planter of Brazos Co., the Superintendent, Mr. Stout, struck a freedwoman on the head with a single tree, fracturing skull (and will beyond all question result in death). The occasion of it was the fact that the freedwoman above alluded to make some complaints about her rations being short. Since that Mr. Stout has left as I have used every effort to cause his arrest.

There are no known people living within my district, with the exception of a few discharged officers and soldiers, sojourning temporarily here and all of them, I think, will join me in stating (although no outrages have been committed against them as yet) that the feeling is becoming more cynical toward "Yankees" as they are termed daily. It will be dangerous to attempt to remain after troops are withdrawn from the community.

Sir you will please excuse my paper as I cannot get a whole sheet of paper from our A. Q. M. and am left to use what he sends me.

I am Very Respectfully
Your Obdt. Servt.
Sam C. Sloan
Capt. And Sub Asst. Commr

Source: "Registered Reports of Murders and Outrages, September 1866-July 1867," Bureau of Refugees, Freedmen and Abandoned Lands, National Archives

THOUGHT QUESTIONS:

1. What types of violence did some Texans use against the freedmen?

2. Why was there not more information about many of these crimes?

3. To what degree did the agent feel it was necessary to maintain the presence of federal troops?

Letter Describing the Rise of the Ku Klux Klan in Jefferson, Texas

---

Various terrorist groups emerged in Texas during the early days of Reconstruction. The Ku Klux Klan emerged as one of the most prominent and dangerous. The letter below explains the rise of the Klan in Jefferson, Texas. The K.R.S. mentioned in the letter stands for Knights of the Rising Sun, a predecessor to the KKK.

Jefferson Tuesday Aug 25

Hon. E.M. Pease
Austin

My Dear Sir --

The excitement was much higher with us last night than it has ever been before. It came very near resulting in a general riot and massacre. The K.R.S. had a meeting about 5 o'clock in the town Hall and invited Lieut Smith to be present. They had great complaints to make in regard to the negroes being armed, but not a word to say in regard to the outrages recurring here every day and night by their war party.

The negroes feel that they have been outraged and that unless they protect themselves they will be killed up by these outlaws. Threats have been made that their Church is to be burnt or torn down and they have simply armed themselves and when night comes, they go to their Church and await any attack that may be made upon it. They interfere with no one and will interfere with no one, but have determined if their Church is attacked, to die in defending it. Last night a party of Ku Kluxes went out to attack them, but through the efforts of Lieut Smith and several others, it was prevented. During the night however, the wildest excitement prevailed all over our city—horsemen from the direction of the Church were running at full speed. The Hall bell was rung 5 or six times, horns were blown in different parts of town. Yelling and shooting and all manner of things were done to alarm loyal men and freedmen. It was feared at the time that the troops would be attacked and they stood with their guns in their hands ready to resist them. But fortunately everything passed off without injury to anyone.

It is understood here that 300 of the expected troops have reached Marshall. If so, we may expect them here very soon. But when they come, will it be sufficient if the rebels will be quiet until they are withdrawn? This has been the practice heretofore, and the moment the troops are taken away they commence their devilment again. They must be hunted up and punished. They must be made to fear a violation and resistance of the authority of the U. States. Without it, all will go for nothing. Turning outlaws and assassins over to the Civil Authorities amounts to their sure release. They must be tried by Military Commissioners the moment they are caught and dealt with as they deserve.

By last mail we rec'd letters from our friends Judge Caldwell and Mr. Grigsly. I would write them, but don't know when the Convention will take recess and fear they might leave before a letter could reach them and in either event they can hear from us through you. We will write them by next mail.

Truly yours

D. Campbell

Source: Donald Campbell to Governor Elisha M. Pease, August 25, 1868, Texas State Library and Archives Commission

THOUGHT QUESTIONS:

1. According to the letter, what caused the increased activities of the Ku Klux Klan in Jefferson?

2. What types of violence did the Klan employ against the freedmen and their allies in Jefferson?

3. What did the writer suggest that the authorities do with the Ku Klux Klan?

Freedmen's Bureau Report of an Inspection of the Texas State Penitentiary at Huntsville, Walker County

Before dying in a yellow fever epidemic, James Devine, the Freedman's Bureau agent for Walker County, Texas, informed his superiors that the state prison located within his jurisdiction at Huntsville was steadily receiving a large number of former slaves convicted of minor offenses but given long sentences. In February 1867, the Bureau sent a special inspector, William Sinclair to investigate. The following is his report:

Head Comr. B. R. F. and A. L. State of Texas Galveston Feb 26th 1867
Lieut. J. F. Kirkman
AAA Genl.

I have the honor to submit the following as the result of an inspection of the Penitentiary of the State of Texas, situated at Huntsville, Walker Co., for your information and consideration.

There are confined in the Prison in all including both white and black four hundred and eleven convicts. Of these two hundred and twenty five are freed people. Fourteen of the freed people are females and two hundred and eleven are males. There are no white female convicts (so considered) in the prison though two of the females that are classed as freed people are almost as white as any caucassian [sic]. They were however, before the war and until its close, slaves.

The Superintendent of the prison is Jas. Gillespie. By his permission I first examined the prison records. From these I could obtain nothing more definite than the general charge which is generally theft.

In order to ascertain the specific act for which they were sent to prison I had no other recourse than to go among them and take their statements.

With the consent of the Superintendent of this Jail—It was not my intention at first to examine every convict but the statement of the few whom I originally only intended to first examine so impressed me and convinced me of the injustice of the treatment these unfortunate creatures had received at the hands of Justice that I felt if I performed the duty properly I must examine and record the statement of each particular case.

I am indebted to Cap[tain] Jas. C. Devine, Sub. Asst. Comr. at Huntsville for his assistance in enabling me to procure from the convicts the data on which the annexed report is based and also for his assistance in tabulating the same after we had made the personal examinations on which it is based. To their statements I respectfully invite your attention especially to the crimes committed or alleged and to the punishment inflicted.

I know the inclination of convicts to plead their innocence and assert the injustice of their imprisonment. I do not believe all the statements made to me and submitted in this report are correct and truthful. That the majority of them are I am fully convinced and any person listening to simple frank statements and looking into the black and apparently honest faces could not believe otherwise.

The crimes for which they are now undergoing punishment were in times of slavery punished with the lash and all these freed people have been convicted since the war closed. The trivial nature of the crime charged them and the severity of the punishment already inflicted upon them (even had they in every instance wilfully [sic] and maliciously committed the crime) should be and are of themselves sufficient arguments for their release and are most assuredly a strong appeal for our assistance in relieving them if such a thing be possible.

In many cases as you will observe the whole cause of the prosecution has for its foundation malice, and is followed up in a spirit of revenge by men embittered disappointed and foiled by the failure of their schemes. These convicts are the innocent and unfortunate victims of their wrath and disappointment. Guilty of little or no crime save that of having incurred the wrath of their former owners or employers their situation cannot but excite in the heart of any man who saw them as I did sympathy for their fate and a resolve to make the effort for their relief.

The convicts are well fed well clothed and kindly treated by the prison keepers. The severity of their sentences, the evidences of their innocence and their uniform good behavior secure them these. Many of them work outside the prison during the day and some of them without guards, though this is safe enough for a pack of trained dogs are kept for the purpose of catching runaways.

These freed people have on an average a little over 3 years to serve as their sentence. Many of them have been in prison over a year and when is added the fact that each of them before conviction was confined in a county jail for longer or shorter periods—in many instances six months—their fate is indeed hard and unjust.

Since these people have been sent to prison the law under which they were convicted has been modified and for such crimes as they are charged a lighter and more reasonable punishment is inflicted—is this not of itself an argument showing the injustice of their punishment and an appeal for pardon? Had they half the friends that many a greater rascal has they would not remain in prison one week. Unfortunately they have not.

I see by the report of the Asst. Comr. Of Alabama (a copy of which is hereunto annexed Maj. Genl. W. Swayne) that the penitentiary of that State became filled with freed people under almost the same circumstances as was this one and that the Gov. of the State upon having his attention called to the facts; and the circumstances under which they were arrested and convicted being properly presented to him issued an almost universal pardon. I believe that three fourths of the freed people now confined at Huntsville are proper subjects for the Executive Clemency of the Gov. of this State. I cannot think that he is aware of the actual condition of affairs else he would pardon them. This investigation has excited in their breasts hopes of pardon and release. That the matter may not end with this report is my earnest prayer for if ever people deserved the assistance of friends these do. Respectfully inviting your attention to the annexed report.

I Am Very Resp.
Your Obt. Servant
Wm. H. Sinclair
Inspector B. R. F. and A. L.

Source: Bureau of Refugees, Freedmen and Abandoned Lands, 1865–1869, National Archives

THOUGHT QUESTIONS:

1. For what types of crimes were the convicts most commonly imprisoned? Did the inspector believe that the punishments fit the alleged crimes?

2. What did the inspector say about the believability of the convicts who professed their innocence? What was his view concerning why so many seemed to be incarcerated to long terms for relatively petty offenses?

3. How might the authorities use the judicial system in Texas and other former slaveholding states to maintain rigid control over the freed slaves?

"The First Vote"

"The First Vote"
Source: Library of Congress

This wood engraving by A.R. Waud appearing in the November 16, 1867 issue of *Harper's Weekly* depicts an African-American man voting for the first time in his life. Following terms of one of the Reconstruction Acts, the U.S. Army supervised the registration of eligible voters, including adult male blacks, in 1867. African Americans in Texas first voted in elections for delegates to the state Constitutional Convention of 1868-69 (nine black men were chosen among the 90 total delegates). African-American voting rights were proscribed by the new state Constitution of 1869, and all states were barred from denying a person the right to vote solely on the basis of their race or color by the Fifteenth Amendment to the U.S. Constitution.

THOUGHT QUESTION:

Who objected to African-American voting rights in Texas during the Reconstruction period and why? Describe some of the various efforts employed to deny black voting rights during these years.

Visit of the Ku-Klux

Visit of the Ku-Klux drawn by Frank Bellew
Illus. in *Harper's Weekly*, v. 16, no 791 (1872 Feb. 24), p. 160

Well-organized terrorist groups began to emerge in response to political changes in the southern states, including the infamous Ku Klux Klan. Klansmen often stated that they were merely protecting white Southerners from incipient black uprisings or that they were fighting rampant black crime. Klan members also claimed that they disciplined black laborers for the benefit of white employers. Such activities were designed to keep blacks docile and politically impotent. The Klan also had success keeping African Americans within their defined social bounds. The terrorists often prevented them from owning and renting land, lynched black men who cohabited with white women, punished individuals who supported the idea of black social equality, and beat or killed African Americans accused of insolence toward whites.

THOUGHT QUESTION:

What tactics did the Klan use during Reconstruction that are similar to those used by terrorist groups today?

BIOGRAPHIES

MATTHEW GAINES (1840-1900). The African American Reconstruction Era state senator Matthew Gaines was born on August 4, 1840 to an unknown father and a slave mother on a plantation near Alexandria, Louisiana. He later stated to family members that he learned to read by candlelight from books smuggled to him by a white boy who lived on the plantation, perhaps his master's grandson. After working for many years as a field hand, the death of his master's widow in the mid-1850s led to the estate selling Gaines to a man who hired him out as a steamboat laborer. Within a few months, he attempted his first escape. He made it to Camden, Arkansas where he lived for six months before going to New Orleans. While residing in the Crescent City, Gaines was somehow recognized and returned to his master who then sold him to Christopher Columbus Hearne, a wealthy planter from Robertson County, Texas. In 1863, he made another escape attempt. While heading to Mexico, however, Texas Rangers captured Gaines in Menard County and took him to Fredericksburg where he remained until the end of the Civil War.

After the war, Gaines returned to the Robertson County area, settling in Burton (located in nearby Washington County) where he soon established himself as a black community leader and lay Baptist preacher. In 1867, an unordained minister performed Gaines's first wedding ceremony with a local woman named Fanny Sutton. The couple had two children but separated within two years. When a visiting religious official informed the community that lay preachers could not perform baptisms and marriages, Gaines assumed that his previous nuptials with Fanny were invalid. Without seeking a formal divorce, he married Elizabeth Harrison in 1870. They would eventually have eight children together.

In 1869, voters elected Gaines to be one of Texas's two black state senators during the Reconstruction Era. With his stated positions and use of dramatic rhetoric on the Senate floor, he gained a reputation as a vociferous, outspoken defender for African-American Texans, earning not only the ire of Democrats but also members of his own Republican Party. He strongly supported bills promoting public education for his people, leading the fight for passage of the legislature's acceptance of the provisions of the Morrill Land Grant College Act resulting not only in the creation of Texas A&M College for whites but also Prairie View A&M College for black Texans to attend. He was less successful in attempting to convince his colleagues to pass legislation promoting black immigration to Texas and to aid tenant farmers by giving them the first lien on their crops.

Gaines's political career began to unravel in late 1871 when a grand jury in La Grange indicted him on bigamy charges. In July 1873, a jury of eleven whites and one black in state district court heard the case which included testimony that Gaines had married his second wife without legally divorcing Fanny Sutton. Though the minister who performed the first ceremony and many others testified to their belief that the first marriage was invalid, the jury convicted Gaines who awaited the results of his appeal while housed at the Fayette County jail. In November, the Texas Supreme Court reversed the lower court's findings. He sought and won reelection to his senate seat in early 1874, but his Democratic opponent, Seth Sheppard, challenged the results on the grounds that Gaines was ineligible for office due to his felony conviction, even though the Supreme Court overturned the guilty verdict. With Democrats now in control of the Thirteenth Legislature, the Senate Committee on Privileges and Elections ruled against Gaines, who was not allowed legal counsel or the opportunity to testify on his behalf. A majority of the Senate agreed with the committee's recommendation, thus seating Sheppard in place of Gaines. No longer a controversial officeholder, his children later related how Gaines lived the last twenty-five years of his life as a contented family man and energetic lay preacher. He continued to speak his mind politically, as noted occasionally in local newspapers. In 1875, officials in Giddings arrested him for making boisterous civil rights speeches in town. During his weekly sermons and while participating in annual Juneteenth celebrations, he not only preached but often spoke passionately about political issues. He died in Giddings on June 11, 1900.

EDMUND JACKSON DAVIS (1827-1883). Edmund J. Davis, the Radical Republican governor of Texas during the Reconstruction Era was born in St. Augustine, Florida on October 2, 1827. His father was a land developer and attorney from South Carolina who moved his family to Galveston, Texas in January 1848 to seek new business opportunities in the growing town. While studying law, Davis worked as a postal clerk until his admission to the bar in 1849. After serving as a customs inspector and deputy collector in Laredo, he became district attorney of the Twelfth Judicial District at Brownsville. In 1856, Governor Elisha Pease appointed him Twelve District judge, a position he held until the outbreak of the Civil War. In April 1858, Davis married Anne Elizabeth Britton, the daughter of a state senator. The couple would have two sons. A supporter of the Whig Party until it dissolved in the mid-1850s, he joined the Democratic Party in 1855, largely to oppose the Know Nothing Party. Like Sam Houston, Davis opposed the secession movement in Texas following the election of 1860 and lost his government position when he refused to take an oath of loyalty to the Confederacy.

Fleeing the state in May 1862, he traveled to Washington, D.C. where he met President Abraham Lincoln and received a colonel's commission along with authorization to recruit Texas Unionists for a regiment to be designated the First Texas Cavalry. Davis barely escaped capture when Confederates under General John Magruder recaptured Galveston in early January 1863. On March 15, 1863, Confederates seized Davis while recruiting men in Matamoros, but the resulting diplomatic fallout with Mexican authorities led Confederate General Hamilton Bee to release him. In late 1863, Davis took part in General Nathaniel Banks's unsuccessful Rio Grande campaign. After promotion to brigadier general in November 1864, he commanded General Joseph J. Reynolds's cavalry in the Division of Western Mississippi for the remainder of the war. On June 2, 1865, he accepted the formal surrender of Texas Confederate forces at Galveston.

During the postwar period, Davis participated in state politics as a Radical Republican, taking positions calling for restricted political rights for ex-Confederates and expanded rights for the freed slaves. He served in the 1866 Constitutional Convention then ran unsuccessfully for a state senate seat. During the Congressional Reconstruction period, Davis presided over the Constitutional Convention of 1868-69 where he favored the theory of *ab initio*, which would have invalidated all state laws passed since secession had it not failed to achieve enough support.

In 1869, Davis ran for governor against Andrew Jackson Hamilton. Largely due to solid support from black voters, Davis received 39,838 votes to Hamilton's 39,055. The Davis administration was a controversial one as he faced open hostility from unreconstructed rebels and conservative members of his own party but boldly pushed for an activist government program calling for law and order backed by state police and militia forces, increased public school funding, and internal improvements.

Davis ran for reelection in December 1873 but was defeated by Democrat Richard Coke by a two-to-one margin. Without the presence of federal troops or the disbanded state police, African American turnout plummeted in the face of widespread threats and violence. Davis's supporters tried to forestall Coke's election by having the election declared invalid on the grounds that the legislature violated the state constitution by reducing the number of polling days from four down to one. In the case of ex parte Rodriguez, the state Supreme Court agreed with Davis's allies, thus nullifying the results of the election. Democrats pressed the governor to vacate his office and took steps to secure Coke's inauguration by force if necessary. For a while, Davis strongly considered making a stand but stepped aside when U.S. President Ulysses S. Grant informed him that he would not be sending federal troops to intervene. With the legislature already in Democratic hands, the takeover of the governor's office by the "Redeemers" marked the end of Reconstruction in Texas.

From 1875 until his death in 1883, Davis remained active in politics, heading the Republican Party in Texas as chairman of the state executive committee. In 1880, he ran for governor but lost easily to Oran Roberts. Two years later, he sought a congressional seat but was defeated once again. Davis died on February 7, 1883 and is buried in the State Cemetery in Austin alongside many of his old military and political opponents.

CULLEN MONTGOMERY BAKER (1835?-1869). The infamous Reconstruction-Era desperado Cullen Montgomery Baker was born sometime between 1835 and 1837 in Weakley County, Tennessee to plain folk parents who moved to Texas in 1839, eventually settling in Cass County. Apparently a mean-spirited rabble-rouser from a young age, Baker often drank whiskey and fought with others. Though in January 1854 he married a young woman named Mary Jane Petty who tried to reform his quarrelsome ways, Baker killed his first man less than nine months later. After an altercation took place between Baker and a young orphan boy, Baker whipped him in front of several witnesses, an offense that lead to his indictment and conviction for assault. Baker then decided to go after fifty-two year old Wesley Baily, a prominent local farmer who testified against him. An hour after the trial, Baker showed up at Baily's home and killed the father of seven children with a shotgun blast. This event no doubt changed his life, crossing over a line of demarcation that separated Baker from being a hard-drinking ruffian who occasionally caused minor trouble to becoming an impulsive killer. Fleeing Cass County to avoid retribution from Baily's son, Baker spent much of the next six years before the outbreak of the Civil War at his uncle's farm in Perry County, Arkansas. Before the war began, Mary Jane died in July 1860 and Baker soon killed another man, stabbing a husband (and also father of seven children) to death after Baker called at his house to thrash his wife with hickory switches for spreading the story of Baker's killing of Baily that she had recently heard.

Returning to Texas, Baker joined two separate Confederate cavalry regiments between November 1861 and early 1863. Confederate army records show that he deserted from one unit and received a disability discharge after suffering from an unspecified illness from another. He married Martha Foster in July 1862 and tried to settle down once again in Cass County, but she died in March 1866. Though distraught, he proposed marriage to Martha's sixteen-year old sister two months later, but she rejected him in favor of a schoolteacher named Thomas Orr, later to become Baker's nemesis.

With the arrival of the Union Army and the Freedman's Bureau, Baker began to lash out against the bureau's agents and the recently-freed black population across northeast Texas during a rampage lasting from mid-1866 until his death in early 1869. Along with other misfits that he came in contact with, Baker killed two Freedman's Bureau agents, at least four soldiers, a couple of white unionists, and perhaps a dozen black men (some estimates are higher), despite having federal troops chasing him and a sizeable reward posted. At first, he killed local blacks randomly but later targeted those who displayed economic independence or took part in elections, thus indirectly aiding the goals of the new Ku Klux Klan with whom he may have had ties.

Baker finally met his end in January 1869. After returning to Cass County in the fall of 1868 to settle old scores with certain ex-neighbors who had joined a posse looking for him, he killed one white resident and more freedmen before visiting the home of his former in-laws, the Fosters, in search of Thomas Orr who had angered Baker for marrying his dead wife's sister. To avoid harm to the family members, Orr surrendered and was taken by Baker and his gang to a local spot to be hanged, but Baker did not abide by the adage "if you hang a man, make sure he is dead." Lacking enough rope to simultaneously hang Orr and another man who had received Baker's ire, he ordered Orr to be cut down so that the other could be similarly dispatched. By either passing out or feigning death, Orr somehow survived and soon worked with local residents to kill Baker. When Baker discovered that Orr lived, he attempted to finish the task by revisiting the Foster farm with one of his gang members. Given whiskey by his ex-father-in-law (later claimed by Foster's son to have been laced with a heavy dose of strychnine), Baker and his companion napped for a while outside the house before Orr's group walked up and riddled the men with bullets, killing them both instantly. While some writers have romanticized Cullen Baker in much the same way that some have glorified Jesse James, the simple truth is that Baker was a cold-blooded killer with no redeeming qualities and his violent actions against local freedmen and their allies contributed greatly to the climate of fear that abetted all opponents of Reconstruction in Texas.

JAMES THROCKMORTON (1825-1894). The first governor of Texas to be elected after the Civil War, James Webb Throckmorton was born on February 1, 1825, in Sparta, Tennessee. When James was eleven, his father, a doctor, moved his large family of eight children and his wife to Fayetteville, Arkansas. After James's mother died in 1841, his father moved the family again, this time to the McKinney area of Collin County, Texas, before he died the following year. Throckmorton left Texas the following year to study medicine with his uncle in Tennessee but returned to Texas in 1847 after volunteering to serve in the army after the outbreak of the Mexican War. After serving as a surgeon's assistant in northern Mexico, recurring kidney problems led to his resignation. In February

1848, he married Annie Rattan and soon settled in McKinney to begin a medical practice while Annie gave birth to the first of ten children.

Throckmorton became a community leader in McKinney, promoted local education, and invested in land while gradually losing interest in medicine as a career. He began reading the law and eventually joined a legal partnership. Throckmorton also became more interested in politics. Initially elected to the Texas House of Representatives as a Whig (his father's political party) starting in 1851, he was chosen to serve in the Texas Senate as a Democrat following the Whig Party's collapse. Throckmorton traveled to Austin as a pro-union delegate to the secession convention. While strongly objecting to secession in the early months of 1861, he held to a view common among many Southerners who were not immediate secessionists that federal coercion to force states attempting to separate from the union was not constitutional. Thus, while not ideologically opposed to secession in theory, he adamantly disagreed with the proposition that Lincoln's election as president in 1860 necessitated such hasty action by the southern states.

Throckmorton and seven others were promptly voted down by the majority of 166 delegates who voted in favor of disunion. As the gallery hissed him loudly as he cast his vote, he reportedly responded by addressing the convention's presiding officer: "Mr. President. When the rabble hiss, well may patriots tremble."

Unlike other Texas unionists, most notably state judge E.J. Davis, who left the state to fight for the United States, Throckmorton remained in the Lone Star State and joined the Confederate army. A combination of political expediency and a desire to protect the frontier in the northern part of the state from Indian attacks influenced his decision, as did President Lincoln's call for volunteers to suppress the Confederate rebellion. Throckmorton organized a mounted rifle company in May 1861, which promptly captured three vacated U.S. forts in the Indian Territory (Oklahoma). After joining the Sixth Texas Cavalry Regiment as a company captain, he saw action against pro-Union Creeks in Indian Territory before taking part in the Battle of Pea Ridge in Arkansas. Though his unit was ordered into Mississippi to aid in the defense of the state against an impending invasion by U.S. forces under General Ulysses Grant, he fell violently ill (probably related to his ongoing history of kidney trouble) and was discharged in late May 1862. While convalescing in McKinney, the Gainesville Hangings of suspected Texas unionist "militants" took place. Though he justified the executions of those who he was convinced had unnecessarily stirred up trouble and threatened peace in the North Texas region, Throckmorton intervened successfully on behalf of unionists in Sherman also threatened with hanging by securing their eventual release. Elected to the State Senate in 1864, his desire to protect the frontier led to his re-enlistment in the Confederate army, eventually serving as brigadier general of the First Frontier Regiment.

After the war, Throckmorton was elected to the constitutional convention of 1866 where a coalition of delegates largely consisting of former secessionists and conservative unionists chose him to be their presiding officer. Once President Andrew Johnson accepted the constitution, he entered the governor's race and handily defeated Elisha Pease by a four-to-one margin. Governor Throckmorton faced constant opposition from radical white unionists, African Americans, and U.S. Army officers who appealed to the governor to do more to protect unionists, both black and white. In 1867, Congress passed the Military Reconstruction Act, which granted the U.S Army immense power within the former Confederate states. Throckmorton refused to act decisively when General Charles Griffin, in charge of U.S. troops in Texas, pressed the governor to do more to protect white and black Republicans from violence, leading Griffin to appeal to his superior, General Phillip Sheridan, for help. Sheridan responded by authorizing Throckmorton's removal as governor on July 30, 1867, by terms of a section within the Reconstruction Act that empowered commanders to enforce the law within their districts by any means necessary, including martial law and the removal of any office holders described as committing a "hindrance to Reconstruction." Throckmorton joined fellow conservative unionists, including former governors Andrew Jackson Hamilton and Elisha Pease, in formally attacking Governor Edmund Davis and Radical Republicans, viewing them as threats to Texas liberty.

Allowed to be eligible again for public office by terms of the 1872 General Amnesty Act, Throckmorton was elected to the U.S. House of Representatives in 1874 and 1876 where he mainly promoted public education and railroad expansion within his state. He sought the governorship in 1878 but failed to secure the Democratic Party nomination at the state convention. Nevertheless, he returned to the U.S. House in 1882, 1884, and 1886. Kidney problems forced him from running for another term in 1888, and stopped his final effort to regain the governor's office in 1892. He died in McKinney on April 22, 1894 and was buried in Pecan Grove Cemetery. In 1911, the town placed a statue of the reluctant Confederate, in civilian garb, in the town square next to the courthouse entrance. Notable for its exclusion of his war service, the plaque on its pedestal simply states: "A Tennessean by birth, a Texan by adoption. A slight tribute to the patriot and statesman, from his fellow citizens and admirers, because of his pre-eminent personal worth, and distinguished public service."

Chapter 9

Economic and Political Reforms, 1874-1890

A Call for Gun Control in Brown County, Texas

Located 125 miles west of Waco, Brown County developed slowly from its founding in the 1850s as settlers often had to contend with the threat of marauding Comanche and white bandits (most notably John Wesley Hardin's gang) until the area was pacified in the mid-1870s. Continued gun violence in areas no longer considered under distress eventually caused many Texas government officials to consider placing restrictions on carrying pistols, despite the fact that by the late 1870s the Colt revolver was as pervasive in Texas as cattle and cotton stalks, serving as the personal weapon of choice for most citizens wishing to have a gun for personal protection. In this 1876 letter to Governor Richard Coke, local law enforcement officials in Brown County request restrictions on the carrying of guns in their county.

Brownwood Texas June 3'd 1876
Hon Richard Coke

Austin, Texas

Dear Sir

Having become thoroughly satisfied that it is no longer necessary to allow the carrying of pistols in Brown County we respectfully ask a Suspension of the law which allows it in this county. Our county has settled very rapidly in the last few months and when lawless men are disarmed we will have no trouble enforcing law and order. And besides that, law abiding citizens are more liable to commit crime when allowed to carry six shooters. And with the assurance that it will work no hardship on any citizen and in our judgement will prevent the commission of crime.

We are very respectfully

B. Gandy J.P. Precinct no (1)
Wm. H. Scott Co. Judge
Henry Ford Co. Clk.
J.N. Gideon Dist Clerk
R.J. Ferguson County Atty

THOUGHT QUESTIONS:

1. What did the law enforcement officials specifically request in this letter and why?

2. What comments did the officials make about the impact of guns (specifically "six-shooters") on law-abiding citizens? Do you agree? Why or why not?

3. What comments did the officials state concerning possible burdens of a gun ban on law-abiding citizens? Do you agree? Why or why not?

The "Cleburne Demands" of the Texas Farmers' Alliance

Established during the 1870s in the rural areas of Lampasas, Wise, and Parker counties, the Farmers' Alliance sought to address common grievances of Texas farmers. In 1879, members reorganized the Alliance as a non-partisan self-help organization for people living in rural communities.

During the 1880s, the Alliance had established 3,000 lodges in the state and became more active in local and state politics. By 1886, the Texas Farmers' Alliance had begun moving from being a self-help organization to more of a political action group promoting a specific agenda and endorsing candidates that pledged support for their goals. Below is the group's platform adopted at the 1886 convention in Cleburne.

We, the delegates of the Grand State Alliance in convention assembled at Cleburne, Texas, August, 1886, do hereby recommend and demand of our State and national governments, according as the same shall come under the jurisdiction of the one or the other, or both, such legislation as shall secure to our people freedom from the onerous and shameful abuses that the industrial classes are now suffering at the hands of arrogant capitalists and powerful corporations.

We demand, first, the recognition by incorporation of trade unions, co-operative stores and such other associations as may be organized by the industrial classes to improve their financial condition or promote their general welfare.

2. We demand that all public school lands be sold in small bodies, not exceeding three hundred and twenty acres to each purchaser, for actual settlers on easy terms of payment.

3. That large bodies of land held by private individuals or corporations for speculative purposes shall be assessed for taxation at such rates as they are offered to purchasers on credit of one, two or three years in bodies of one hundred and sixty acres or less.

4.   We demand that measures be taken to prevent aliens from acquiring separate titles to land in the United States of America and to force titles already acquired by aliens to be relinquished by sale to actual settlers and citizens of the United States.

5.   That the law making powers take early action upon such measures as shall effectually prevent the dealing in futures of all agricultural products, prescribing such procedure in trial as shall secure prompt conviction, and imposing such penalty as shall secure the most perfect compliance with the law.

6.   That all lands forfeited by railroads or other corporation immediately revert to the government and be declared open for purchase by actual settlers on the same terms as other public or school lands.

7.   We demand that all fences be removed, by force if necessary, from public or school lands unlawfully fenced by cattle companies, syndicates or any other form or name of monopoly.

8.   We demand that the statute of the State of Texas be rightfully enforced by the Attorney General of the State to compel corporations to pay the taxes due the State and county.

9.   That railroad property shall be assessed to the full nominal value of the stock on which the railroad seeks to declare dividends.

10. We demand the rapid extinguishment of the public debt of the United States by operating the mints to their fullest capacity in coining silver and gold, and the tendering the same without discrimination to the public creditors of the nation according to contract.

11. We demand the substitution of legal tender treasury notes for the issues of national banks; that the Congress of the United States shall regulate the amount of such issue by giving to the country a per capita circulation that shall increase as the population and business interest of the country expand.

12. We demand the establishment of a national bureau of labor statistics, that we may arrive at a correct knowledge of the moral, intellectual, and financial condition of the laboring masses of our citizens, and further, that the commissioner of this bureau be a Cabinet officer of the United States government.

13. We demand the enactment of laws to compel corporations to pay their employees according to contract in lawful money for their services, and the giving to mechanics and laborers a first lien upon the products of their labor to the extent of their full wages.

14. We demand the passage of an interstate commercial law that shall secure the same rates of freight to all persons for the same class of merchandise, according to the distance of haul, without regard to amount of shipment; to prevent the granting of rebates; to prevent pooling freights to shut off competition, and to secure to the people the benefits of railroad transportation at reasonable cost.

15. We demand that all convicts be confined in prison walls, and the contract system abolished.

16. We recommend a call for a national conference, to which all labor organizations shall be invited to send representative men to discuss such measures as may be of interest to the laboring classes. . . .

Source: *The Dallas Morning News*, August 8, 1886

THOUGHT QUESTIONS:

1. What types of land reforms did the Farmers' Alliance propose?

2. What types of currency reform did the members of the Alliance seek?

3. Of these proposed reforms, which, if any, later became a reality?

The Great Prohibition Debate, 1887

The first campaign to amend the state constitution to allow a ban on the sale and manufacture of alcoholic beverages in Texas took place in 1887, four years after Frances Willard helped to found a Texas branch of the Women's Christian Temperance Union and one year after the Prohibition Party first ran candidates for office in the state. Though the proposed amendment went down to defeat on August 4, 1887 by a vote of 220,627 to 129,270, the pro-Prohibition "Drys" did not quit, focusing their efforts on local option municipal and county referendums while hoping for another chance at securing passage of a statewide ban. In 1908 and 1911, Texas voters would once again reject proposed Prohibition amendments, but by very narrow margins, before achieving success in 1919.

An extremely divisive issue in Texas during the late-nineteenth and early twentieth centuries, Prohibition nevertheless produced lively debate beginning with the initial campaign in 1887. Reproduced below are some examples of the arguments used both for and against Prohibition appearing in other newspapers that the editors of the Fort Worth Daily Gazette assembled for the edification of its readers.

...The state obtains $550,000 per annum from liquor dealers, the counties $275,000, and the cities and towns half as much as the counties, from the license tax alone. This is nearly $1,000,000 which the liquor traffic pays for the support of state and municipal government every year in the way of license tax, to say nothing of the tax which it pays on property. This revenue is required, and if the license tax is prohibited must be derived from the tax on property. To obtain $1,000,000 by a property tax, the rate must be increased not less than 20 cents on the $100 of property [the tax rate was 37.5 cents per $100 at the time]. The state, school and municipal taxes on property must be increased at the same rate. Those who are struggling must struggle the more to preserve their property. It is said that the rural population favors the abolition of the liquor traffic and so would shoulder this increased tax burden. This is the same year of our Lord and the Twentieth Legislature in which a bill was passed for the relief of the rural population a bill was passed postponing tax collections because it was urged money was too scarce to enable them to pay the present low assessment. This is also the same year in which it is found that the revenue for the support of the public schools is insufficient, although the allowance per

capita is reduced. Will the people so embarrassed by present taxation be able and willing to pay $1,000,000 more than they now pay? If there is any department of government that must suffer--should the people refuse to sustain the increased burden, will it not be first the public schools? The executive departments, boards and bureaus, the judicial and the legislative departments cannot be prohibited. They are here to stay, blossom and multiply. From a financial and economic standpoint, prohibition seems to threaten greater injury to the public schools and promise greater benefit to nonresidents and foreign land-grabbers than injury to liquor dealers and benefit to society. Do the homesteaders of Texas want to tackle a state [property] tax of 57 cents?
--*Dallas News*

What if the prohibition amendment carries? Will it plunge the state in ruin, fill our jails with criminals, break down our public institutions, ruin the youth of our country before they have scarcely placed their feet on the threshold of manhood, demoralize society, wreck the happiness of wives mothers and sisters, and encumber us with the galling chains and iniquitous yoke of slavery? Certainly not; the most ultra antiprohibitionists do not claim this for it. But one grand and glorious privilege will be denied the liberty loving sons of free America--that of going into a saloon to deplete their pocketbooks to cloud their minds to grieve their wives mothers and daughters and to render themselves incapable of performing their duties as citizens. If the prohibition amendment carries the revenues of the state will be considerably reduced but there will be a proportionate reduction in the cost of maintaining criminal courts for the simple reason that there will be a decrease of over 50 per cent in the number of crimes committed. Thus we will be nearer the ideal of an economically administered government.
--*Nacogdoches Star News*

Will any one explain in what consists the crime in drinking a glass of wine or beer any more than there is in drinking a glass of cider or lemonade? None of them are essential or necessary to man's existence. All of them are, in a sense, luxuries. So far as any one knows any of them is as beneficial as the others; if any difference, it is in favor of wines. A person could kill himself by an excessive use of either. It, perhaps, might take a less quantity of wine or beer to injure a man than it would require of cider or lemonade. But it also takes a less quantity of certain drugs to destroy life than it does of others, but it does not argue that the more potent drug is not as useful and necessary as the other. The expense of the temperate [moderate] use of wine or beer is not more than that of cider or lemonade, and even if it were, a man has a right to govern his own expense in the matter. If a state can dictate to a man the amount of his expenses in luxuries, it can in the necessaries of life also. In fact, it would be impossible to determine where articles of necessity and those of superfluity begin. So then the crime cannot be in the injury or expense attending the temperate use of intoxicating liquors. If any one man's taste prefers wine or beer to cider or lemonade, it is no other man's business to restrain him in indulging this taste anymore than any other taste.

It is clearly plain that the crime, if crime there be, is not in the use of these articles as beverages but in the abuses of them. Then reason, common sense, and justice would say punish the man that abuses them, but do not punish the man that commits no crime in the use of them. But this amendment proposes not only to prevent men from abusing

intoxicating liquors, but from a temperate use of all of them. The whole sum and substance of the amendment is that hereafter no man shall use intoxicating liquors as a beverage. Some will deny this, but the amendment itself shows that such will be the effect of its enforcement if carried. But if the amendment read that hereafter no man in this state shall use intoxicating liquors as a beverage, it would receive no support but from a few puritanical Pharisees that have a strange habit of looking after other people's business and habits more than they do their own, and thanking God that they are not as other men are for which fact other men ought to thank God they are not like them.
--*Wills Point Chronicle*

The prohibition that we advocate is directed solely against the liquor traffic and not against the individual's liberty to drink whatever he chooses. When the amendment is adopted and enforced, every man will have a right to drink as much whisky as he can get, provided he does not invade the rights of others. Under the guarantee of personal liberty given by our constitution, no laws can be passed to abridge this right. Laws have already been enacted against drunkenness, and they will remain the same after the prohibitive enactment. Of course, if the sale of liquor is prohibited, it will to a great extent prevent drinking; nevertheless, the traffic is what prohibition is after, not the personal right. To stop contagion or suppress a mob, it may be necessary to interfere with personal liberty or the rights of property; yet the law is aimed at the thing, not the rights of persons. If intoxicating liquors were a necessary article of food or drink, of course it could not be prohibited; but no one will essay to put it in a class with such articles and regulate it as they are regulated. License—and, in fact, all laws touching its manufacture and sale, have recognized this difference. It can be dispensed with and if the rights of the people demand [that] it should be. If by suppressing the saloons the liberties of persons will have a completer safeguard; if the interest of society and the welfare of the people will be better shielded; if our public institutions will be less exposed to corruption it is the duty of the people to stamp it out as a public nuisance.
--*Mineola Monitor*

Source: *The Fort Worth Daily Gazette*, May 4, 1887

THOUGHT QUESTIONS:

1. What economic arguments did the opponents and supporters of Prohibition bring up in the first two articles?

2. What arguments for personal liberty did the writer of the third piece make? How did the writer of the fourth article attempt to address the issue of personal liberty?

3. Regardless of which side of the issue that the writer was on, which of these four pieces contained the most convincing argument for their position? Why?

"Dear Sunny South": A Louisiana Woman Describes Her Trip to Denton County, Texas in 1887

During the late nineteenth century, people often wrote about their travel experiences in magazines and their local newspapers. Below are observations from a citizen from Natchitoches, Louisiana who traveled to Denton, Texas. Appearing in **The Sunny South,** *a weekly literary magazine published in Atlanta from 1874 to 1907, this account describes in vivid detail the state of the North Texas economy and society.*

Denton, Texas.
Texas Booming—A Bright, Pushing Little City—Schools, Churches, Banks and Business

EDITOR SUNNY SOUTH: Since I last wrote you I have made a very pleasant trip to Texas, to the thriving little city of Denton, Northwest of the Queen City of the West, Dallas. The latter place I took in on my return.

Let me here say that I have returned to Louisiana better pleased than ever with my native State. Having never been in Texas, I imagined that it was "flowing with milk and honey," and that dear old Louisiana was not a very desirable portion of this moral vineyard. I do not mean to say that Texas is not all she claims to be—oh! no; though she has plenty of room every way, but I do wish that fair Louisiana was as well advertised—then she would be on a grand boom indeed, for she has the best or as good natural resources.

Dallas I found to be on the boom, arranging for a grand fair to take this month, which promises to be a big thing, as she is making extensive preparations and will no doubt make it a success. Her city park is very nice; her business houses and hotels are all they should be. I found the Grand Winsor a rival of the St. Charles in New Orleans—in prices, if nothing else.

Denton is the county seat of Denton County, and was laid out by Col. Welch over a quarter century ago. It has a large square with a splendid Court House in the centre and large business houses fronting it. The ambitious little city puts on all the style of her more matured sisters in every respect except streetcars. She has a population of four or five thousand inhabitants, numerous churches and one of the best schools (public) in the State. They get aid from the State, and besides levy a special city tax. The school has directors, who are elected by the city to manage the same. Capt. Carmenyges, of Alabama, is Principal, and has a number of competent assistants. He is one of the finest educators in the State, and took pleasure in showing me through the different grades (nine). They use the word method of teaching, which I think is the natural one. I did not fail to tell him about our Louisiana State Normal school at this place, and how advanced we are becoming in the way of teaching since the Normal was established and the new methods introduced.

Denton boasts of two banks. The Exchange National is a model of its kind in arrangement and decoration. The polite cashier, Mr. Wm. A. Ponder, was kind in showing us
around, and even took us in the fireproof vault. He called our attention to the beautifully
painted scene (Southern) of the fleecy staple and golden grain on the ceiling of his office,
also to that in the directors office (Judge Carroll's), which was a cattle scene delineating
the long and short horns in all their glory on the rolling prairies of Texas, as "it was, is
now and ever shall be."

There are two flour mills in Denton—the last, but not lease, the Farmers' Alliance mills,
built, owned and managed by the Association. These mills, an immense brick structure,
were completed this year, and cost over $250,000. They were fortunate in getting Mr.
Grant to manage them, as he knows his business. He is very obliging, and seemed to take
real pleasure in showing us how flour is made. I had no idea that it went through so many
processes to come out so pure and white, but suppose it is like life—the more grinding,
sifting, fanning and rolling will only bring out the perfect individual. It rejoices one to see
the farmers doing so well. The Farmers' Alliance is in its infancy in this State. If it does
so well in infancy, what may we not expect from maturity? Texas is far ahead of us in co-
operation and real American push.

There are two newspapers, the Post and Chronicle, published in Denton. I suppose the
press will have a rest now, as Texas has just passed through one of the most heated and
closely contested campaigns ever engaged in. Lawyers, of course, all have plenty to do,
though. While there I read in the Dallas News "The Lawyer's Lament," in which it was
stated that there were too many of them in Texas; and one would think so, as the other
day there was a suit (a $10 one) in which four were interested, and the perch, divided
between them, only amounted to twenty-five cents each. I know that the Denton lawyers
are doing better, or they would not look so happy; besides, there are not so many as there
is in Dallas.

The dear SUNNY SOUTH is appreciated out there. How grand are the prairies! I felt
that awe and inexpressible feeling that sometimes comes over us on beholding the sublime
and beautiful in nature. Hoping my communication will not tire you, I am, as ever, an
interested reader of the ever welcome SUNNY SOUTH.

Eleanor. Natchitoches, Oct., 1887.

Source: *The Sunny South,* October 1887

THOUGHT QUESTIONS:

1. How does the author of the article describe Denton's economy?

2. How does the author describe the state of education in Denton?

3. What does the author say about the activities of the Farmers' Alliance in Denton?

Bettie Gay Writes to the *Southern Mercury*

Founded in 1884, the Southern Mercury served as the official newspaper of the Texas Farmers' Alliance (and later, the Texas People's Party), disseminating information weekly on a variety of topics for its members.　The organ also solicited letters from members, including women (who made up perhaps 25 percent of the Alliance's membership), who received a full page dedicated to their submissions and articles of interest to them.

　　*Bettie Gay, a wealthy widowed planter living near Columbus, was a frequent contributor to the **Southern Mercury**, giving words of advice and generally speaking her mind.　In this letter, apparently the third she submitted by the earliest to be published, Mrs. Gay comments on the high price of coffee, recommends good ways to economize, and promotes a local Alliance gathering.*

June 14, 1888. Columbus. B. G. [Bettie Gay]

This is the third time I have written to the *Mercury*, and if this goes the way of Uncle Snort's wagon load of letters, all right.

I see in the *Houston Post* of May 24 inst., that speculation in cotton, sugar and coffee, is checked on account of indifference of buyers. So far as sugar and coffee are concerned, it would cause a greater indifference if all the laboring people were to resolve to do without it till it could be bought at living prices. Several of the counties have passed resolutions to do without coffee till they can buy at twelve and a half cents per pound, but that will not do any good unless the whole Alliance gets into it.　We tried to get our county to adopt resolutions to the same effect, but there were many who thought they couldn't live without.　How did they do during the war without it?　Did anyone die from want of it? I am an old Texian, have been here since '39, am able to buy coffee, but for the benefit of the millions of slaves, I am willing to do without until it can be bought by everyone. When you send your delegate to the state convention in August, try and get them to get the whole state to adopt such resolutions.　If we go as a unit, we can accomplish anything.

I see a letter from a sister M. A. Crier of Kingsbury, advising the sisters to return to the spinning wheel and loom.　I am in sympathy with every economical move, but I differ from the sister, widely.　In the first place, it is killing on anyone to card and weave.　I speak from experience, for we had to do it during the war.　It will take three days to weave one yard of cloth; at twenty-five cents per day, it would cost seventy-five cents per yard to spin and weave a yard, besides the expense of the machinery, so you see there is no economy. It would be more healthful to raise a cotton patch, work in the open air and buy calico or muslin for five cents per yard.　You would have more and play half the time; besides one pound of cotton will make five yards or more of goods and you might drudge your life out and not accomplish anything unless the men will unite and vote in a solid body of men who will represent our interests.　You might spin, weave and work until you would faint by the roadside and the evil would be the same.

I saw some sister writing about dress making. Anyone can make a full skirt, with body or redingot[e], and we as farmers do not care to put on style till our independence is declared. What should we care for style? If we are not able to buy fashionable bonnets or hats, get a nice piece of gingham and make a neat bonnet. They are very becoming.

Our Exchange and manufactories are our salvation; let us work to save them and go without styles and luxuries except what we can raise at home.

. . . We are going to have a picnic on the 7th of July; everyone who has an interest in the Alliance, come and let us have good speakers and have a good lesson learned us, not all fun but business too. It is good for young people to talk of fun, but older ones have things more serious to think of. Too much rain, crops are not so good; hope to make good cotton crops so we can help in every enterprise.

Source: *Southern Mercury*

THOUGHT QUESTIONS:

1. How did Mrs. Gay wish Alliance members would react to the high price of coffee?

2. How did she respond to the idea of women going back to making cloth with the spinning wheel and loom? What habits did she promote as sensible ways for farm families to save money?

3. Comment on the tone of her letter—how does she come across? What role was she assuming—A radical reformer? An intellectual espousing economic theories? A motherly or grandmotherly adviser?

Demands of the Texas Federation of Labor

In 1889, labor representatives convened in Dallas to form the Texas Federation of Labor. Upon establishing their organization, the union issued the following statement of its goals.

- We favor eight hours as a working day, and demand the passage of a law so declaring.
- We favor a single tax, or a tax upon land values, and the repeal of all other taxes whatsoever.
- We favor the repeal of the national bank law, and all other class laws.
- The only equitable solution of the transportation question is in the Government ownership of the railways, telegraphs and telephones.
- We favor the abolition of the United States Senate and all State senators, because of the corruption practiced; the abolition of the grand jury system, because it is used by designing men to crush, ostracize, and persecute in some instances those who oppose existing systems, and the supremacy of either the Democratic or Republic factions, and to the end that our votes may be counted when cast and all corruption and the damnable boodle system be obliterated.
- We favor the Australian system of holding elections; the election of all officers by the direct vote of the people.
- We favor all that will secure a lien on the products of labor.

Source: *Appleton's Annual Cyclopedia and Register of Important Events of the Year 1889* (New York, 1863-1903), Vol. XXIX (XIV New Series; 1890, 791

THOUGHT QUESTIONS:

1. Which of these proposals would be considered radical today? Why?

2. Which of these proposals would not seem too radical today? Why?

3. Of these proposed reforms, which, if any, later became a reality?

Messenger and Newsboy

Credit: Library of Congress, November 1913.

For nine years, this sixteen-year-old boy from Fort Worth, Texas had been a newsboy and messenger for drug stores and telegraph companies. He was brought before the Judge of the Juvenile Court for incorrigibility at home. After being paroled, he began working again for the drug company when he got a job carrying grips in the Union Depot, working 6:00 A.M. to 11:00 P.M. (seventeen hours a day) for seven days a week. His mother thought he used cocaine. He said, "There ain't a house in "The Acre" (Red Light District) that I ain't been in. At the drug store, all my deliveries were down there."

THOUGHT QUESTION:

How might later reformers use the story of this boy to argue for laws dealing with child labor in Texas cities?

BIOGRAPHIES

MARGARET HEFFERNAN BORLAND (1824-1873). The matriarch of a southeast Texas ranch family and one of the first women cattle drivers, Margaret Heffernan was born in New York City to Irish immigrant parents. When she was five, her family settled near San Patricio after being recruited by the empresario John McMullen. Just as the Texas Revolution began, Indians attacked the farm of eleven-year old Margaret's uncle, killing not only the man and his entire family, but also Margaret's father who happened to be there assisting his brother in planting crops. Her mother soon moved the family to the town of San Patricio where they lived until the conclusion of the Revolution before relocating again, first to Brazoria, then to Victoria.

Happiness and tragedy continued to follow Margaret throughout her life. At age nineteen, she married Harrison Dunbar, a local man, who died in a pistol fight shortly after the birth of their daughter. The next year, she married Milton Hardy, a city council-man and local rancher. Their first daughter died soon after birth, but two more daughters born in 1848 and 1852 grew up healthy. Later in 1852, Margaret gave birth to a son, but not long afterward a cholera epidemic swept through Victoria and he died along with his father. Margaret inherited 3,000 acres of land, 1,200 head of cattle, town lots in Victoria, and four slaves, but also had three girls and a young nephew to support. In February 1856, she married Alexander Borland, one of the richest ranchers in Victoria County. The 1860 listed Borland's net worth at over $40,000 in real and personal property plus twelve slaves. Meanwhile, Margaret gave birth to three more boys and another girl before her fortieth birthday in 1864. Their marriage ended in 1867 when Borland succumbed to an unspecified lingering illness, leaving Margaret a widow for the third time.

Margaret took over management of the sizeable family business, but further trials lay ahead. Soon after burying her husband, a yellow fever epidemic arrived in Victoria, killing all the remaining children from her first two marriages and one of her sons with Alexander Borland. Resilient in the face of constant sorrow, she worked with her brother James and her nephew to supervise a crew of ten ranch hands who gathered their cattle and sold them locally for meat, hides, and tallow. Cattle prices in Texas remained low during the early 1870s, leading Margaret to decide to drive much of her herd northward to Kansas for the large money (perhaps as much profit as 25 dollars per head) that she heard could be made doing so. Neither she nor her ranch hands had ever trailed, but they felt their experience with cattle would be enough to handle the job. Though other women had taken part in cattle drives, Margaret was unique in that her role would be as a trail boss, the one responsible for the organization and success of the entire operation. In the spring of 1873, Margaret set out along the Chisholm Trail with her children in tow, six to ten hired hands, a black cook, and over 1,000 head of cattle. Traveling at a pace of about ten miles per day through unknown terrain, they first travelled up to Waco and Fort Worth, before crossing the Red River into Indian Territory (Oklahoma) and eventually arriving in Wichita, Kansas about two months after starting out. While waiting to de-cide whether to sell right away or to wait until brokers offered more favorable prices, the ultimate tragedy occurred. Margaret became sick with symptoms described as delirium, agitation, and "congestion of the brain." She died on July 5, 1873 at the age of forty-nine, probably from a form of meningitis. Arrangements were made to ship her body back to

Victoria where she was buried ending her personal story that overlapped so much with the history of Texas, from the Texas Revolution through the years of the Great Texas Cattle Trails. Margaret's surviving children inherited her estate, with her two sons choosing to work with cattle for the rest of their lives.

EDWARD "SANCHO" MOZIQUE (1849-1951). An African American "buffalo soldier" who later became a cowboy, Edward "Sancho" Mozique was born into slavery on June 10, 1849 in Columbia, South Carolina. His mother and six brothers and sisters were given by his master's widow to her nephew who was a doctor in Spartanburg. After the Civil War, Edward (nicknamed "Sancho" by his father who had been a French creole from New Orleans) returned to war-torn Columbia and worked as a carpenter. In 1875, Mozique and three friends decided to enlist in the U.S. Army. Ten years earlier, Congress had authorized the creation of African American military units—two cavalry regiments and four infantry regiments later known as "Buffalo Soldiers" by various Native American warriors they would encounter—for service on the western frontier. The Army assigned Mozique to Company E of the Tenth Cavalry. After receiving basic training at Jefferson Barracks near St. Louis, Missouri, he arrived at Fort Concho near the village of San Angelo, Texas in July 1875, finding a rundown garrison next to a town consisting of twenty-five hovels and a few small saloons. Because of his carpentry skills, the post commander, Colonel Benjamin Grierson, assigned him to work under the fort's wheelwright rather than taking part in field duty.

After five years of service, the Army honorably discharged Mozique. He remained in San Angelo, marrying a local woman named Alice Johnson, and worked as a carpenter helping to build many of the town's first sizeable buildings, including a hotel. When demand for carpentry work slowed, he became involved for the first time in ranch work and beginning his new profession as a cook. Though the need for a local carpenter had lessened, the growing town's restaurants and hotels, as well as the nearby ranches, were always looking for a good cook. Mozique had worked on his culinary skills while stationed at Fort Concho, often hunting birds, buffalo, and other game near the post when not on duty and preparing an assortment of dishes. He served as a cook and a cowboy at a number of ranches in the San Angelo area for the next fifty years, finally retiring in 1931.

Three years after his wife's death, Sancho Mozique died of pneumonia two months shy of his 102nd birthday on April 20, 1951. Seen as the Sage of San Angelo, many people sought to interview him to gain knowledge of the town's earliest days. He had seen a lot in his lifetime: though beginning life as a slave outside of the Lone Star State, he became a part of American settlement in western Texas, witnessed the birth of large-scale ranching in the region, and lived to see the growth of his beloved San Angelo into a bustling town of over 50,000 people by the middle of the twentieth century.

NORRIS WRIGHT CUNEY (1846-1898). The African-American Republican Party politician and union organizer Norris Wright Cuney was born on May 12, 1846, near Hempstead, Texas. The son of a slave mother named Adeline Stuart and her white plantation master, Philip Minor Cuney (he was the fourth of their eight children), Norris's father recognized his child and sent him to be educated at Pittsburgh, Pennsylvania's Wylie

Street School for blacks from 1859 to 1861. The coming of the Civil War disrupted plans to attend Oberlin College in Ohio. He found employment on a steamship that traveled to New Orleans, Louisiana where he would reside for the remainder of the conflict.

After the war, Cuney returned to Texas and settled in Galveston. In 1871, he married Adelina Dowdie. As the couple began a life together, eventually having two children, Cuney befriended George T. Ruby, the prominent local black Republican politician who headed the Union League in Texas and served as a state senator. Ruby guided Cuney's increasing involvement in politics at a time when Texas Republicans were seeking talented blacks to lead the party. In July 1871 he became the president of the Galveston Union League. The next year, he was appointed customs inspector for the port of Galveston (later named to the post of customs collector) and served as a delegate to the 1872 national Republican convention, an honor that he would continue to receive until 1892.

Despite his many federal government and Republican Party appointments, Cuney's efforts to achieve local and state elective office often eluded him. He lost a Galveston mayor's race in 1875, a bid for a Texas House seat in 1876, and a state Senate campaign in 1882. His only electoral triumph occurred in 1883, when he was elected to a Galveston city council seat. Nevertheless, Cuney's power continued to rise as he dispensed federal patronage in Texas and influenced the state's 100,000 blacks who voted during the 1880s and 1890s. In 1886, he became chairman of the Texas Republican Party, the most prestigious political position held by any African American during the nineteenth century.

Cuney also sought to aid black dock workers in Galveston. The port city's dominant local trade union was known as the Screwman's Benevolent Association (SBA), an organization specializing in loading cotton cargo onto ships using their strength and screwjack equipment. Since 1869, the group formally banned blacks from membership. By the early 1880s, Cuney believed that labor shortages, caused by the increased volume of cotton to be exported as well as the workload limits that the SBA demanded from cotton shippers, provided an opportunity for local black longshoremen. In 1883, after organizing African-American laborers into the "Screwman's Benevolent Association (No.2)" and personally purchasing equipment for their use, Cuney sent word to William L. Moody, president of the Galveston Cotton Exchange, that there were black men ready, willing, and able to load cotton aboard ships. Representing the shippers who tired of the SBA's frequent demands and desire for a slower work pace, Moody wrote back that he "heartily" welcomed the news. Cuney arranged stevedore contracts for the black workers, resulting in steep resistance in the form of a general strike by the SBA who opposed the arrival of black workers in their midst, not to mention the appearance of potential economic competitors. The SBA persevered with their strike for several months, but so did Cuney, who, to the delight of the shippers, arranged for additional black longshoremen to be brought in from New Orleans. Finally, the union voted by a very narrow margin to end the strike just as the busy fall season approached. The white SBA remained a powerful labor group, but their monopoly on the docks of Galveston had been broken. For his part, Cuney held the view that he was only working to seek justice for African-American workers who should be "given a fair chance with others in the struggle for bread." By the time he died on March 3, 1898, Cuney lived long enough to see the birth of combined black and white unions in Galveston, but not long enough to experience the substantial weakening of black political participation in Texas resulting from passage of the state's poll tax and white primary laws.

CHARLES GOODNIGHT (1836-1929). The legendary cattleman Charles Goodnight was born on March 5, 1836, on a small western Illinois farm. At the age of nine,
his family undertook an 800-mile move to Milam County, Texas, where Goodnight grew
up working on the family farm and laboring for pay on nearby plantations. After his
mother remarried, Goodnight made his initial foray working with cattle when he and
a stepbrother began tending over 400 head of cattle for a nearby owner in exchange for
keeping every fourth-born calf. As the men learned the ins and outs of cattle raising, they
amassed almost 200 animals and drove their herd in 1857 to Palo Pinto County, west of
Fort Worth, where they established a small ranch.

On the eve of the Civil War, Goodnight joined with some neighbors to aid Texas
Rangers deal with Native American raiders in the region. While serving as a scout, he
discovered the main encampment of Comanche leader Peta Nocona along the Pease River
and guided rangers under Lawrence Sullivan Ross to the location. The subsequent attack
led to the recapture of the captive Cynthia Ann Parker. Goodnight spent most of the
Civil War serving in the Frontier Regiment guarding Central Texas from Native American
marauders while gaining increased knowledge of the plains and prairies of western Texas
that he would later put to good use.

After the war's conclusion, Goodnight and other Texas cattlemen sought to profit
from exporting cattle to lucrative markets outside of the state. In 1866, he teamed up
with Oliver Loving, an older Palo Pinto County farmer and rancher, to drive a large herd
to army posts and Indian reservations in New Mexico where beef was in high demand.
For the trek, Goodnight personally constructed the first known chuckwagon to hold
food, supplies, and the personal effects of the twenty cowboys employed on the drive,
which took them west to the Pecos River then north to Fort Sumner where the cattle were
sold for a handsome profit. The route would soon be followed by large numbers of other
cattlemen and would come to be known as the Goodnight-Loving Trail. For the next few
years, Goodnight used the trail numerous times to drive thousands of cattle to markets in
New Mexico, then extended the route further north to channel herds to ranchers wishing
to stock ranches in Colorado and Wyoming.

Goodnight married Mary Ann (Molly) Dyer in 1870, and the couple resettled to a
new ranch they established along the Arkansas River five miles west of Pueblo, Colorado
where he invested in a bank and other local businesses while continuing his cattle driving operations. Six years later, the cattleman relocated again, this time to the Palo Duro
Canyon region of the Texas Panhandle where he partnered with investor John Adair to establish the massive JA Ranch. With Adair providing much of the working capital, Goodnight managed and expanded the ranch to encompass over 100,000 cattle on 1.3 million
acres, while frequently trailing cattle to the nearest railhead in Dodge City, Kansas. Over
the next dozen years, Goodnight also enhanced his reputation as a pioneer cattle breeder
by successfully crossing Texas longhorns with Herefords, as well as developing the "cat-
talo" by crossing Angus cattle with bison.

Goodnight finally left the JA in 1888 and began to limit his activities to a small
Panhandle ranch in Armstrong County located southeast of Amarillo near a small town
named in his honor. During his retirement years, he was interviewed often by journalists
and scholars seeking factual information about his life on the frontier and vivid stories of
life on the great cattle trails of Texas. He died on December 12, 1929 at his winter home
in Phoenix, Arizona and was buried in the Goodnight community cemetery.

Chapter 10

The Populist Movement, 1890-1900

Candidate Jim Hogg Promotes the Idea of a State Railroad Commission

A staple of nineteenth-century politics in the United States was the long-winded stump speech. In the days before radio and television, a lengthy, well-delivered oration either celebrating a greater cause or viciously denigrating an opponent served as a popular form of entertainment for Americans. On April 19, 1890, Jim Hogg launched his campaign for Texas governor with an epic three-hour speech before a crowd of 3,000 people in Rusk, which many at the time praised as a masterpiece. The following excerpts from Hogg's remarks focus on a major theme of his campaign—the railroads and the potential benefits of a state railroad commission.

I am in favor of the State regulating and controlling the rates of railway traffic having origin and destination within her limits to the end that justice may be done the public. As an instrument for this purpose, if I am elected Governor and the constitutional amendment is adopted, I shall do my part in having an effective railway commission created and clothed with all the power necessary to make, establish and maintain, under rules prescribed by law, reasonable rates of charges for the transportation of passengers and freight.

In taking this position I am not unmindful of the formidable corporate and political influence that I shall have to combat but I have faith that the power of plain truth will carry conviction against the turbulent stream of prejudice over artful sophistries and establish sound doctrines in the minds and hearts of an independent, just and patriotic people. Let facts be stated, truths told, the law explained, a decent campaign made, and a correct verdict will be rendered.

Railways are public highways. They are expressly so declared by our Constitution and the common law. The principles which control and govern them today are older than the government itself, and were in effective operation long before the great author of the Declaration of Independence was born; nor did he ever utter a word to change them or question their soundness. Public highways used to be nothing more or less than wagon roads, open to all who wished to travel over them on horseback, foot, in wagons, or by any other mode suitable to their own convenience and tastes. They were then, as some of them are now, kept in repair by the labor and at the expense of the people.

To perfect and keep these highways in good serviceable condition for the convenience and advantage of the public, contracts were made by the government with private parties associated together on stipulated conditions, privileges and rights to be performed and enjoyed by themselves. Such contracts were called charters, and the associations of people who entered into them were known as private corporations. These corporations got their pay for building and keeping up the public highways by charging people who hauled a load or traveled over them a toll therefor. The right to collect tolls or rates for the use of the roads was called a franchise conferred by the government on the corporations through the charter contract. Without the government's consent the corporation could not collect the toll, nor could it collect a higher rate than such as the government agreed to. Many of you well remember the old turnpike roads kept up by corporations in Virginia, Tennessee, and other States, and the tolls you had to pay if you traveled over them. You also recollect that the rates were posted up in plain letters at conspicuous places, so everyone had notice in advance of what he had to pay for the use of the road. Those items of charges were simple and few, but were fixed by law. This was the regulation of rates of a private corporation that owned or controlled a public highway. Simply that and nothing more. In the first instance, the government had power, which it exercised, of taxing the people to keep up the highways for public use. Instead of taxing the whole people to keep up a road through a particular section the just and equitable plan was conceived and adopted of making those pay only who used it. Subservient to that end and to relieve the government of such expense and trouble, private corporations were created and endowed with power to exercise that sovereign authority. As creatures of the government, in enjoyment of delegated prerogatives upon express and implied limitations, such corporations became and have been ever subject to reasonable public control and regulation.

Beginning with common earth roads graded and leveled, public highways changed, not in principle, but in condition and methods of use and enjoyment. Passing through many transmutations, from the plain dirt road to the gravel way, from the latter to the horse car line, and from that to the steam railway, the public highway, developed as it is now into the greatest civilizer known to civilization, indispensable to commerce and to the wants of the public, has never escaped the control of the power that gave it life. So long as they were earth or simply turnpike roads but little or no question was raised as to the right of the government to control or regulate them, but since they have become laid with wooden ties and steel rails, ballasted with sea shells, equipped with fine coaches, propelled by steam engines and controlled by millionaires, pools and combines, they are defiant of law and revolt at public control in all respects. They are now called private enterprises.

Those who write editorials, prepare interviews, make speeches and whisper into the ears of eager listeners against State regulation of their traffic rates, say it is "undemocratic" and sound the alarm of "paternalism" and "personal liberty." All of a sudden they become patriotic and solicitous and pretend to fear the "fundamental principles" so necessary to the perpetuity of our form of government will be destroyed. Some of them question the right of the State to pass such laws. Others more informed are too considerate and cautious to venture yet awhile quite so far, but are content in their effort to alarm the business classes.

In discussing the question they assume the railway company to have the same legal status as a citizen or a business firm. They try to make it appear that the principle which would permit or justify the regulation of railway charges would authorize and lead to the regulation of prices of goods, wages or the charges of hauling by individuals in their vehicles for private purposes. They know better, but make such arguments to confuse and embitter the people against the amendment. To draw a distinction furnishes an answer to all such delusive sophistry. The government is the creature of the people. It is by, of and for them. With their consent it is formed and based upon the fundamental law called the Constitution. That instrument expresses their will, which, in theory at least, is supreme. Railroad companies are the creatures of the government, and have no voice in making it. In other words, they are corporations for the public good, organized under laws passed by the Legislature. So the Legislature creates them, and the people elect and create the Legislature. Every individual qualified voter has the right to vote to make, repeal or amend the Constitution, and to elect members of the Legislature, who make laws under it. No corporation can vote or take part in making laws. Some of you say: "Well, if they cannot vote or make laws, they can have a powerful sight of it done." Possibly this is so, yet their legal rights are unchanged—they are the creatures of the government, authorized to act for the public good, and are subject to State control. The Constitution, as I have told you, expressly declares these roads "public highways," and now commands the Legislature to regulate the rates of traffic carried over them. So the principle of regulation has been settled by a democratic Constitution in furtherance of democratic doctrines. In this respect it is consistent with the common law. Nowhere does the Constitution require the regulation of private persons or their business in any way....

...Situated as Texas is, containing an area of 176,000,000 acres of land adapted to horticultural, agricultural and pastoral products and pursuits; possessing unlimited soils and mineral wealth, with all the timber, fuel and building material demanded by the extravagant wants of a proud people; having a coast of 500 miles upon the gulf way, accessible to all the competing markets of fie world over the natural and great highway of commerce, removed as she is so far away from the markets by all rail routes, she is peculiarly surrounded and situated as an independent State, capable in all things of controlling, with justice, fairness and liberality all her domestic and internal affairs, even to the regulation and control of the traffic rates of her railroads, to the end that no part or portion of her public or people shall suffer by the domination, rapacity or abuse of another. Let her see that our railroad rates are adjusted upon a basis of equality and justice, to the end that our producers, manufacturers and merchants may be placed on an equal footing with their rivals in other States, and the world may stand witness to her people entering the field of competition, where they will remain triumphant with consummate success. Justice and protection is what the people crave. Grant it to them and they will prove equal to the demands in the tempting arena where the survivor, unhampered by schemes of favoritism, receives his due reward.

Source: *Speeches and State Papers of James Stephen Hogg,* pp. 25-50, C.W. Raines, ed. The State Publishing Company (Austin, 1905).

THOUGHT QUESTIONS:

1. What comparisons to older forms of transportation and government regulation does Hogg make regarding railroads in his speech? Is this a valid comparison? Why or why not?

2. How does Hogg criticize the opponents of railroad regulation? Does he present an effective reply to their charges? Why or why not?

3. In the conclusion to this excerpt, what benefits of regulation will Texans enjoy following the creation of an effective railroad commission?

Governor James Hogg Offers John H. Reagan the Post of Railroad Commissioner

In April 1891, Governor James Hogg sent the following letter to Senator John H. Reagan, offering him a position on the Railroad Commission recently established to regulate the railroad industry in Texas. Reagan was a member of Congress at the outbreak of the Civil War. He resigned his seat and soon became the Confederate Postmaster General. While serving in Congress again after the war, Reagan chaired the Committee on Commerce, which four years earlier had helped pass the Interstate Commerce Act establishing the Interstate Commerce Commission to regulate the railroads nationally. Soon after receiving Hogg's request, Reagan accepted the position and resigned his Senate seat. He became the first chairman of the Texas Railroad Commission, serving until 1903.

April 21st 1891
Hon. John H. Reagan,
Palestine, Texas

My Dear Sir

I hereby tender to you a position on the "Railroad Commission of Texas." To accept this trust I know you must make unusual sacrifices; but considering public interests I feel impelled to ask you to do so.

Continuously for many years our Agricultural and Commercial interests have been severely depressed, for which there are three causes: 1st Bond insurance [?] and unecessary [sic] federal taxes, called the tariff; 2nd The want of more money as a circulating medium; 3rd Oppressive local freight rates. With the evils of the first two the federal Government alone can deal; the third is within the exclusive control of the State Government. The time has come for it to be handled.

For many years you have consistently, ably, labored with other Democrats, as a member of the House and then as Senator, in Congress, to reduce the tariff to the lowest rate consistent with the economical administration of the government, and to have coinage of silver for the people's relief.

This work will continue until just results shall have been attained. You are needed more at home where you can best render effective service to those who have always honored you, and who would not fail to do so at any time to the full extent of your ambition so far as it were in their power. For years the people have been trying to procure a Commission Law. They have one now, and it is possible for them to get relief from the wrongs of railway management. The law is useless and will become a farce without wise and just enforcement. Your long advocacy of such a measure and great experience in all public affairs, especially of those affecting the material interests of Commerce and Agriculture, warrant me to hope that, under the impulse of patriotism so often moving you to subordinate personal ambition and pride to the public weal, you will now act on the Commission and thereby aid in making it a consummate success. If you do so I feel confident that the people of this State will add to their gratitude their deepest and everlasting affections for you.

Awaiting an early reply, I have the honor to be your obedient servant and friend,

J S Hogg, Governor

Source: Texas State Library and Archives Commission

THOUGHT QUESTIONS:

1.   What did Governor Hogg identify as the three causes for the depressed Texas economy (i.e., the "Agricultural and Commercial interests")? Of these causes, which was something Hogg said the Texas government could directly affect?

2.   According to Hogg, why was Reagan "needed at home" more than in the U.S. Senate?

3.   Describe the general tone of Hogg's request to Reagan.

The Omaha Platform and Expression of Sentiments, July 4, 1892

The Omaha Platform and Expression of Sentiments laid out the official positions of the new People's Party at its initial national convention held in Omaha, Nebraska, on July 4, 1892. While addressing the concerns of Farmers' Alliance members of the coalition, the document also reflected the influence of the Greenback Party and endorsed many goals of the Knights of Labor.
    In 1892, the People's Party captured eleven U.S. House seats, several governorships, and three state legislatures. Its presidential nominee, former Greenbacker James B. Weaver, became

the first third-party candidate to receive over a million popular votes while winning four states for a total of 22 electoral votes. Despite its growing success, the 1892 election would represent the party's best national showing.

Platform

We declare . . .

First—That the union of the labor forces of the United States this day consummated shall be permanent and perpetual; may its spirit enter into all hearts for the salvation of the Republic and the uplifting of mankind!

Second—Wealth belongs to him who creates it, and every dollar taken from industry without an equivalent is robbery. "If any will not work, neither shall he eat." The interests of rural and civic labor are the same; their enemies are identical.

Third—We believe that the time has come when the railroad corporations will either own the people or the people must own the railroads; and, should the government enter upon the work of owning and managing all railroads, we should favor an amendment to the Constitution by which all person engaged in the government service shall be placed under a civil-service regulation of the most rigid character, so as to prevent the increase of the power of the national administration by the use of such additional government employees.

Finance.—We demand a national currency, safe, sound, and flexible, issued by the general government only, a full legal tender for all debts, public and private, and that without the use of banking corporations, a just, equitable, and efficient means of distribution direct to the people, a tax not to exceed two per cent per annum, to be provided as set forth in the sub-treasury plan of the Farmers' Alliance, or a better system; also by payments in discharge of its obligations for public improvements.

1. We demand free and unlimited coinage of silver and gold at the present legal ratio of 16 to 1.

2. We demand that the amount of circulating medium be speedily increased to not less than $50 per capita.

3. We demand a graduated income tax.

4. We believe that the money of the country should be kept as much as possible in the hands of the people, and hence we demand that all State and national revenues shall be limited to the necessary expenses of the government, economically and honestly administered.

5. We demand that postal savings banks be established by the government for the safe deposit of the earnings of the people and to facilitate exchange.

Transportation.—Transportation being a means of exchange and a public necessity, the government should own and operate the railroads in the interest of the people. The telegraph, telephone, like the post-office system, being a necessity for the transmission of news, should be owned and operated by the government in the interest of the people.

Land.—The land, including all the natural sources of wealth, is the heritage of the people, and should not be monopolized for speculative purposes, and alien ownership of land should be prohibited. All land now held by railroads and other corporations in excess of their actual needs, and all lands now owned by aliens should be reclaimed by the government and held for actual settlers only.

Expression of Sentiments

Your committee on Platform and Resolutions beg leave unanimously to report the following:

Whereas, Other questions have been presented for our consideration, we hereby submit the following, not as a part of the Platform of the People's Party, but as resolutions expressive of the sentiment of this Convention:

1. Resolved, That we demand a free ballot and a fair count in all elections, and pledge ourselves to secure it to every legal voter without federal intervention, through the adoption by the States of the unperverted Australian or secret ballot system.

2. Resolved, That the revenue derived from a graduated income tax should be applied to the reduction for the burden of taxation now levied upon the domestic industries of this country.

3. Resolved, That we pledge our support to fair and liberal pensions to ex-Union soldiers and sailors.

4. Resolved, That we condemn the fallacy of protecting American labor under the present system, which opens our ports to the pauper and criminal classes of the world, and crowds out our wage-earners; and we denounce the present ineffective laws against contract labor, and demand the further restriction of undesirable emigration.

5. Resolved, That we cordially sympathize with the efforts of organized workingmen to shorten the hours of labor, and demand a rigid enforcement of the existing eight-hour law on Government work, and ask that a penalty clause be added to the said law.

6. Resolved, That we regard the maintenance of a large standing army of mercenaries, known as the Pinkerton system, as a menace to our liberties, and we demand its abolition; and we condemn the recent invasion of the Territory of Wyoming by the hired assassins of plutocracy, assisted by federal officers.

7. Resolved, That we commend to the favorable consideration of the people and the reform press the legislative system known as the initiative and referendum.

8. Resolved, That we favor a constitutional provision limiting the office of President and Vice-President to one term, and providing for the election of Senators of the United States by a direct vote of the people.

9. Resolved, That we oppose any subsidy or national aid to any private corporation for any purpose.

10. Resolved, That this convention sympathizes with the Knights of Labor and their righteous contest with the tyrannical combine of clothing manufacturers of Rochester, and declare it to be the duty of all who hate tyranny and oppression to refuse to purchase the goods made by the said manufacturers, or to patronize any merchants who sell such goods.

Source: *National Economist* (Washington, DC), July 9, 1892

THOUGHT QUESTIONS:

1. What were the primary political concerns of the People's Party?

2. What proposals and beliefs of the People's Party would be considered radical today? Why?

3. Identify some People's Party proposals that have become a reality. What are a couple of notable proposals listed in this document that have not yet been adopted? Should they be? Why or why not?"

Female Populists Debate Woman Suffrage

*The pages of the **Southern Mercury** often served as a conduit for lively debate on important issues of the day. Woman suffrage became a frequent topic of discussion for female writers to the newspaper. Not all women, however, supported the proposed reform. In fact, a sample of letters written by female contributors reveals that only slightly more than half favored granting equal voting rights to women. The following exchange was initiated by Mary A. Raborn, a strong opponent of woman suffrage.*

January 3, 1895. Groesbeck. Mary Raborn.

The Populists elected a majority of the peace and constables, the county judge and representatives of this (Limestone) county, I am glad the *Mercury* lets the woman suffrage question take a back seat. We don't want any more ignorant voters than we have now. It is time to stop howling for woman's suffrage when not one woman in five hundred has ever read the Declaration of Independence and would not know the Constitution of the United States from a patent office report. We feel sure of sweeping the county in '96, for we will see that the elections are conducted fairly then.

January 24, 1895. [no location] Margaret L. Watson

. . . Mary Raborn of Groesbeck, Texas, goes on and abuses the women for wanting to vote; says they cannot tell the Constitution of the United States from a patent office report, then says: "We feel sure of sweeping the country in '96, for we will see that the elections are conducted fairly then." Oh, "Mary, Mary-so contrary!" What on earth have you to do with elections? Go and read your patent office report.

February 21, 1895. Groesbeck. Mary A. Raborn.

I am sorry the equal suffragists can see nothing better to fight for than female suffrage. I know there are many women who can be intelligent voters, but to offset all these, there are thousands and thousands of not only ignorant, but degraded women, both black and white, who would be as easily purchased as the ignorant voter of the male sex. What help would these be to reform? For my part I see something better, grander, and greater to be desired than the right to vote. . . . It does seem to me that the three great and principal questions now confronting us are fully set forth in the people's party platform: namely money, land and transportation. Let us all work (if we don't and can't vote) for a wise solution of those questions first. Then it will be time to take up minor issues. I never like to be criticized, but suppose I can bear it, however, I would like to say to Margaret Watson that I did not "abuse the women for wanting to vote." I only accused the mass, i.e., the majority, of ignorance. Yes, Margaret, I'll have a hand in helping hold the next election. I have a husband, three sons and two sons-in-law, all Pops [Populists], who will be there. Later on two more sons will added. Don't you think I'll quote just a "leetle bit"? As for reading my patent office reports, you forget I am a subscriber to the *Mercury*, consequently am not forced to such dry stuff for literature. To be serious with my dear Margaret, what is the platform or principles of the equal suffragists? I have never read it. Perhaps if I understood what they are doing, I would be an equal suffragist too. You ought to try to convert me if you think I am wrong.

Source: *Southern Mercury*

THOUGHT QUESTIONS:

1. What are Mrs. Raborn's main arguments against woman suffrage?

2. What was more important to Raborn than giving women the right to vote? Why?

3. Describe Raborn's response to Mrs. Watson's comment that she had no say in elections.

Bettie Gay Argues for Woman Suffrage

In addition to supporting the Farmers' Alliance and the People's Party, Bettie Gay was a devout woman suffragist. Below is a strong pro-suffrage letter she wrote to the **Southern Mercury** *and the editorial that prompted her response.*

On January 3, 1895, the *Mercury* carried the following editorial:

The women who are crying like John the Baptist in the wilderness of their desolation for equal rights should define the measures they propose to champion when they secure equal rights. The enfranchisement of several hundred thousand voters in Texas is an important proceeding. This vote would have the balance of power, and might be wielded for good or evil. In Colorado it was wielded for evil. The populists at least desire to know whether the women of Texas are going to vote for reform or not before that party helps lift the yoke of bondage from the necks of down-trodden female humanity.

January 17, 1895. Columbus. Mrs. Bettie Gay.

The *Mercury* Jan. 3 asked that the women of Texas define the measure[s] they propose to champion should they secure the right to vote. John the Baptist lived in the wilderness till he came forth to herald the time of the coming of the Savior. The women have been in the wilderness for one hundred years. According to the prophecy of John, it is time for them to come out of the wilderness[,] for John says: "And all flesh shall see the salvation of God." There may be those in the People's Party who, like Herod, would be willing to behead them, but the wise women of Texas will yet lead the men out of darkness, as they (the men) have been a failure in the management of governmental affairs. We propose to have a say in the laws that govern us, as intelligent beings, and not as idiots and criminals. We propose to elect representatives, not debauchees. We are the natural guardians of our children, and we want laws that the most innocent can understand. No party will give women her rights till she demands them. The time is not distant when she will demand, and not ask, any party to recognize her. All that is needed is the proper education, and that is going on faster than any party is aware of.

I am surprised at any intelligent editor laying the cause of defeat of the Populists in Colorado to women voters, when the democrats and republicans fused there to beat the Populists, and spent piles of money to buy up the floating population. All the fraud that is perpetrated hereafter in Colorado will be laid upon the women. I suppose they can stand it for they have been the burden-bearers time out of mind: but they propose to share the burdens hereafter with the would-be lords of creation. Light is dawning and humanity will soon assert its rights.

To fully define our position would take too long an article for a newspaper. If all the women were like myself they would not ask man for any rights. What more rights have they than we? Ignorance on the part of woman has kept her in slavery.

Source: *Southern Mercury*

THOUGHT QUESTIONS:

1. What is Mrs. Gay's general opinion of government controlled solely by men?

2. How does she reply to the accusation that allowing women to vote in Colorado had hurt the cause of the Populists in a recent election there?

3. What does she predict will happen when women get properly "educated" on the subject of woman suffrage?

Populist Leader John B. Rayner
on Courting the Black Vote in the 1896 Election

The People's Party in Texas had no stronger ally among the African American community than John B. Rayner, whose speaking and organizational skills proved to be a valuable asset for the Populists as they tried to spread their message across the state. In the June 25, 1896 edition of the Southern Mercury, an audience member who witnessed one of Rayner's recent speeches touted his oratorical powers, proclaiming: "What crowds of people, what throngs of people by fours, by dozens, on foot; on horses, in buggies, in wagons above the roars of applause and clapping of hands, you hear the sweet music of the illustrious Rayner. Now like a wild tornado, now like a summer evening breeze, pointed, logical, sincere, yet soft and gentle, the spirit of God is plainly mirrored from his heart, carrying conviction' at every breath." Later in the same edition of the newspaper, Rayner (profiled in a biographical sketch appearing later in this chapter) showed that he had a gifted pen as well. He wrote numerous essays during the 1890s promoting the Populist cause, including this one excerpted below in which he gave advice on how the People's Party should court the black vote in the upcoming presidential election.

…Now, what must be our methods in the present campaign?

In the main, we must never deceive our fellow men with Utopian promises, nor hold up before their expectant an ignus fatuus light [a light that often appears at night time over marshes caused by the igniting of gas released from decomposed organic matter] to get them to vote our ticket, but we must give them facts and instruction, and hold up before them an empyrean [heavenly] arc light whose power-house is God's eternal truth. In our maneuvering we must extend to the free silver democrats an "entente cordial" [peace agreement], and this can be accomplished without making a political re-approachment [sic] or the loss of any of our political prestige.

We must maneuver to get our recruits from the negro race, and how to do this should tax our power of research and political ingenuity.

First, the white populists must understand negro idiosyncrasies.

We negroes believe in a great deal of noise and ostentation, and we admire only the southern white man who is full of push, dash and southern chivalry.

It is said that the negro is a natural republican. This is a mistake; the negro has no political proclivities, his love or dislike is his politics; that is he votes for the men he knows and loves, and votes against the men whom he dislikes.

Now, if you want the negro to vote a straight people's party ticket you must put men on the precinct and county tickets whom he (the negro) likes. Kind words and just treatment go further with the negro than money or promises.

Never try to get the negro's vote and influence with money or bribes, because if you do you will fail, because when he (the negro) gets away from you he will soliloquize thus: "If it is right for me to vote this ticket, it is wrong for that white man to pay me to do so, and I am going to take his money ad vote against him."

Give the negro reform papers and reform literature and send negro speakers among them, and in the election they will vote a straight populist ticket.

Our political finessing must be just, honorable and patriotic, and not trickery on our part, but to parry the tricks of the two old parties and keep them from deceiving the people.

At every voting box we should have a campaign committee sufficient in numbers, zeal and intellect to see that the election is righteously conducted and the tickets are justly counted.

Let us conduct the campaign on righteous principles, so God can help us, and let the battle cry be: "The sword of Jehovah and the people's rights," and then the disembodied spirits of Washington, Jefferson, Madison, and Lincoln will lead the plebians [sic] to victory.

After the proud, greedy and wicked shall have been driven from our legislative, judicial and executive chambers, then God will turn the big end of his cornucopia toward us, and then will commence the human development, which will continue to evolve until humanity is made perfect.

Source: *Southern Mercury,* June 25, 1896

THOUGHT QUESTIONS:

1. What tactics did Rayner believe would work most effectively to court the black vote in Texas? Why?

2. Which tactics did he believe definitely would not work to secure the allegiance of black voters? Why?

3. Comment on Rayner's overall style of writing, including his overall tone, his use of words to paint images in the readers' minds, etc.

Bohemian Farm Family in Texas

Credit: Library of Congress

Pictured are members of the Sulak family, frugal Bohemian farmers who owned an eighty acre farm in Central Texas.

THOUGHT QUESTION:

How does this picture depict the role of children within the family?

BIOGRAPHIES

CHARLES WILLIAM MACUNE (1851-1940). Texas Farmers' Alliance leader Charles W. Macune was born on May 20, 1851 in Kenosha, Wisconsin. His father was a black-smith and Methodist minister originally from upstate New York who moved his family to the Iowa frontier in 1843. They relocated again to Freeport, Illinois where Macune spent most of his childhood. In 1852 his father traveled west to take part in the California Gold Rush, but he died of cholera along the way, leaving Macune's mother to raise the one-year old boy and his older sister. In Freeport, he received a basic public school education and worked for a nearby German farmer. His most memorable childhood experience occurred when a lawyer friend of the family introduced young Charles to Stephen Douglas and Abraham Lincoln at a reception before their famous debate in town. Macune remembers Lincoln lifting the boy on one knee and talking with him briefly in a "kind, fatherly way."

At the age of fifteen, Macune began an apprenticeship with a local pharmacist, but by the end of his teen years he started a series of restless wanderings, moving about from place to place in an attempt to find his true calling. In 1869, he went to California with his sister and her husband to labor on their recently acquired ranch but left the next year and worked for a time in a Kansas circus. In the summer of 1871, he moved to North Texas to begin a new job as a cattle driver between Texas and Kansas. By the spring of 1874, Macune had moved to Burnet, initially painting houses to support himself. From September 1874 through the spring of 1875, he entered the journalism trade when he served as editor of the Burnet *Bulletin*, a weekly Democratic newspaper. A well-read but largely self-educated man, his personal and political views on many issues of the day surfaced in many of his editorials. Calling himself a Jeffersonian Democrat who promised to be "independent in everything, neutral in nothing," he vigorously criticized the Republican Party's Reconstruction policies. Greenbackism also influenced his views of monetary theory. Like many nineteenth century frontier editors, he also emerged as a boisterous local booster. In June 1875, his standing in the community led to his election as secretary of Burnet County's Democratic Party executive committee. In the fall of 1875, he married Kentucky-born Sallie Vickrey with whom he fathered six children. Moving again, this time to San Saba, he continued painting houses while studying medicine with a local physician. In 1879, though lacking a medical school diploma, a state medical examiner in Junction City followed accepted procedure and certified him to practice medicine. After serving the Junction City and Fredericksburg communities, Macune set up a practice in 1881 in Cameron, where five years later he and another physician purchased and operated the Cameron *Herald*.

In 1886, Macune energetically joined the local chapter of the Texas Farmers' Alliance and soon became one of the group's leaders. While serving as a delegate at the state convention in Cleburne, the assembly elected him to the chairmanship of the state executive committee. Seeking unity, Macune proposed that the organization set aside what divided them and to focus instead on two main objectives: establishing a statewide cooperative enterprise for farmers to purchase and market their crops and expanding the Alliance into the West and across the entire cotton-growing South. In September 1887, the Farmers' Alliance Exchange of Texas opened in Dallas under Macune's management. With the decline of the Alliance's local cooperatives, he was hopeful that the Exchange could provide members with higher prices for their crops while offering lower prices for needed supplies than could be purchased from local merchants. By the fall of 1889, however, the undercapitalized Exchange failed. Macune's efforts to expand the Alliance beyond Texas fared much better. By the summer of 1890, the Alliance boasted more than one million members. Macune served as president until December 1889. By then, he had already borrowed money to establish the *National Economist* in Washington, D.C., which became the official newspaper for the now-christened National Farmers' Alliance and Industrial Union.

Deeply concerned with the farmers' credit problem, Macune was most responsible for creation of the Alliance's controversial subtreasury plan. Accepted by the organization at their December 1890 meeting in Ocala, Florida, the proposal called for the federal government to aid farmers in bypassing local merchants (and therefore escaping the crop-lien system) by creating warehouses to store nonperishable agricultural commodities such as cotton. Farmers who deposited their crops would borrow U.S. Treasury notes up to 80 percent of the market value from the federal government at a very low rate of interest and a minimal handling charge. After the Democrats refused to support the subtreasury plan, more radical Alliance members, much to Macune's chagrin, sought to abandon the party and chart an independent political course. Though initially supporting the new People's Party, he eventually returned to the Democrats, resigned his position on the national executive committee, ended the *National Economist,* and like many others who could not convince themselves to support the third party effort, left the movement.

After his Farmers' Alliance work, he returned to Texas and began a new series of occupations. In 1895 he founded a failed newspaper in Cameron before he began a brief attempt at the legal profession. After receiving a license to practice law in Texas, he opened a legal office in Beaumont. In 1900, however, he moved his family back to Central Texas after his daughter developed tuberculosis. He practiced medicine for about a year in Center, Texas, before beginning his final career as a Methodist minister. During the next sixteen years he preached in a number of small Central Texas communities before getting involved in missionary work with his youngest son (also a minister) in Piedras Negras, Mexico. In 1920, he completed a history of the Farmers' Alliance, donating the manuscript to the University of Texas library. Three years later, he retired to Fort Worth where he lived until his death on November 3, 1940.

JOHN B. RAYNER (1850-1918). John Baptis Rayner, the Texas People's Party's most prominent black spokesman, was born a mixed-race slave in Raleigh, North Carolina. Raised by his slave mother's grandparents, he worked on the plantation of his father, Kenneth Rayner, a Whig congressman and leader of the Know Nothing Party who acknowledged the paternity of his son. After the Civil War, the elder Rayner arranged for John's education at Shaw University and St. Augustine's Normal and Collegiate Institute, both colleges serving the freedmen in Raleigh. In the early 1870s, John Rayner moved to Tarboro, North Carolina to teach and soon engaged in local Republican Party politics, serving as a constable, magistrate, and sheriff's deputy. He married Susan Clark Staten in 1874 and began to raise two children with her. Seven years later, Rayner served as a labor recruiter for Brazos Valley planters eager to expand their cotton-growing operations and led a sizeable migration of Carolina freedmen to Robertson County, Texas. He bought a modest frame house in the black section of Calvert, but his wife died soon after their arrival. Rayner later married Clarissa Clark and raised three children with her. Meanwhile, he taught school and kept up with political matters in his new state.

Rayner took his first active role in Texas politics when he became involved in the 1887 statewide prohibition campaign. His estrangement from the Republican Party took place soon thereafter as a response to the efforts of the party's so-called "lily-white" faction, which sought to cull support from white businessmen by distancing themselves from the concerns of African Americans. Upset with the perception that Republicans were using his people as political pawns and taking their votes for granted, Rayner joined the growing People's Party in 1892. Not only did he believe that the solutions proposed by the Populists would benefit the state's black farmers, Rayner also viewed the People's Party as the best political means for African Americans to exert political clout within Texas politics. He understood that blacks did not hold much statewide political muscle as long as whites remained united within the Democratic Party, but Rayner also correctly surmised (as did many whites) that if African Americans could vote as a solid bloc they could provide the difference in elections if the rising People's Party continued to rally support from increasing numbers of white Texas voters.

Knowing the necessity of black votes for their cause, and realizing as one white Populist said that "they are in the ditch just like we are," the People's Party boldly sought inroads into the state's African-American community. They named two blacks to their state executive committee and recruited local leaders such as John Rayner into their fold. For the next six years of his life, Rayner threw himself into the Populist cause, organizing and speaking on its behalf during exhausting tour schedules across the state. He gained a reputation as the movement's leading African-American orator speaking to huge crowds and slowly building up the People's Party's support among blacks in east Texas. His work was well appreciated by white People's Party officials. As party leader H.S.P. "Stump" Ashby noted: "The work I want Rayner to do, no white man could do." At the 1894 state convention in Waco, Rayner was elevated to state party leadership when the delegates elected him to positions on the state executive committee and the platform committee. In addition to his demeanor, historian Gregg Cantrell has noted that Rayner's light complexion also "gave him a decided advantage when dealing with white people," even allowing him the rare opportunity for a black man at the time: permission to speak before white audiences.

The demise of the People's Party led to Rayner's retirement from politics and general disillusionment with the state of African-American affairs in Texas at the turn of the twentieth century. He decided to put his Populist past behind him (symbolized by the absence of any reference to the People's Party in any of his surviving personal papers housed at the Briscoe Center for American History at UT Austin) and dedicated himself to writing noncontroversial newspaper essays and fundraising for two black vocational schools in Texas—Conroe College and the Farmers' Improvement Society School—before dying at his Calvert home on July 14, 1918.

BETTIE GAY (1836-1921). Farmers' Alliance advocate Bettie Gay was born on Christmas Eve 1836 in Monroe County, Alabama. While still a toddler, her parents moved the family to Texas. Only fifteen years old, she married slaveholding planter Rufus King Gay. She spent her antebellum years on the plantation studying such topics as philosophy and science until the Civil War forced her to direct farm activities while her husband fought in the conflict. Like many Texas women after the war, Gay took to the fields to help her husband bring in a crop in addition to performing all necessary household chores and raising her son. When her husband died in 1880, she acquired the mortgage to the couple's 1,700-acre tract and managed the farm successfully enough to eventually pay off her debts.

Turning her attention to political matters that greatly interested her, Bettie Gay gravitated toward the fledgling Farmers' Alliance. With her sizeable wealth in comparison to most within the movement, she proved to be a most uncharacteristic Populist given that most male and female members came from the middling farmer class. Nevertheless, she sympathized with the movement, also viewing it as a means of promoting her other interests—woman suffrage and prohibition. In 1888 she wrote her first letter to the Southern Mercury, the official newspaper of the Texas Alliance urging members to boycott overly-priced coffee. The next year, when Nelson Dunning compiled his Farmers' Alliance History and Agricultural Digest, Gay contributed a chapter entitled "The Influence of Women in the Alliance" that gained her national notoriety within the movement. In the piece, Gay celebrated what she saw as the benefits that women gained from membership in the organization (such as recognition of female usefulness to the movement and a reduced "prejudice against woman's progress") along with the positive impact of women on the Alliance (especially the supposed calming tempering influence of women and their ability to "control the strong tempers of many of the [male] members.")

In 1892, Gay agreed to serve as a delegate from Texas to the national Farmers' Alliance meeting in St. Louis, her only official position within the Alliance. Over the next few years, she contributed ubiquitously to the Southern Mercury, providing thoughtful letters and articles on numerous topics of interest to farmers and women, including woman suffrage and prohibition. By the time of the People's Party's decline after the 1896 presidential election, Gay was in her sixties. Retiring to quieter pursuits, she lived another twenty years until her death in 1921.

JAMES HARVEY "CYCLONE" DAVIS (1854-1940). The fiery Populist orator James "Cyclone" Davis was born near Walhalla, South Carolina on December 24, 1854. His family moved to Texas in 1857, settling near Winnsboro. Though growing up on a poor Northeast Texas farm provided Davis with only a common-school education, he studied hard at night when his chores were done with the help of local attorney John D. Templeton and eventually received a state teaching certificate. In 1878, he married a distant cousin named Belle Barton and was elected to a county judgeship as a Democrat. The following year, he passed the state bar exam and opened a law practice in nearby Mount Vernon, Texas. In 1882, Davis first used his developing oratorical skills to political uses when he campaigned for John Templeton during his mentor's successful bid for state attorney general. Soon thereafter, Davis purchased the *Franklin Herald* newspaper and in 1886 served as president of the Teas Press Association.

The rise of James Davis as a famous orator came when he became a lecturer for the growing Texas Farmers' Alliance. Though the Alliance utilized the print media, the lecture circuit was a more popular and financially more efficient way for the organization to get its message out to the countryside during the late 1800s. Speakers such as Davis fanned out to the rural areas and engaged audiences at churches, schools, and town halls where the crowds gathered to cheer, hiss, stomp their feet, and pose serious questions to the lecturers. In assuming the role of part-educator, part-entertainer, Davis soon gained a reputation as one of the best. Wearing a large black hat, alligator boots, and a Prince Albert coat, the 6'3" Texan would stride into a gathering and mesmerize the crowd for hours, not only with his words, but also with the manner in which he said them, mastering over time the use of voice inflections and choreographed body movements as he attacked what he identified as the enemies of the people—usually bankers, railroad titans, and Wall Street corporate executives.

After President Grover Cleveland blamed his reelection in 1888 on his party's support for the coinage of silver, Davis left the party, though he campaigned for James Hogg, the Democratic nominee for Texas governor in 1890, after the Alliance formally endorsed his candidacy. Two years later, Davis became a Populist leader, serving on the executive and platform committees at the 1892 inaugural convention of the People's Party in Cincinnati, Ohio. For the next four years, Davis helped to energize the Populist movement by giving over a thousand speeches across the South. He received the nickname "Cyclone" after an 1894 debate in Kentucky with the state's Democratic attorney general, Watt Hardin, when an Associated Press reporter who witnessed the proceedings stated that Davis, who he described as the "Texas Cyclone," had so destroyed his opponent that there was no need for them to continue with future rounds of debates that had been planned. Davis was twice chosen by his party to run for political office. In 1892, he finished third in the race for state attorney general. He came closer to victory two years later when he narrowly lost a U.S. House race to a Democratic incumbent. At the 1896 People's Party national convention, Davis worked successfully for a fusion ticket with the Democrats after the nomination of William Jennings Bryan, an unpopular position among most Texas Populists.

After the demise of the Populists, Davis returned to the Democratic Party to support Progressive candidates for office, such as Thomas Campbell's bid for governor in 1906 and Woodrow Wilson's 1912 run for the presidency. In 1914, Texas voters elected Davis to an at-large seat to the U.S. House of Representatives where he supported a variety of Wilson administration measures to aid farmers and industrial laborers. He opposed U.S. entry into World War I, but was narrowly defeated for reelection in November of 1916 and therefore not in Congress when Wilson asked Congress for a declaration of war against Germany five months later. Mostly active in the prohibition movement after his time in Congress, he briefly emerged from political retirement to challenge Joseph W. Bailey, Jr.'s bid for an at-large U.S. House seat in the 1932 Democratic primary, mainly because Bailey's father had been such a strident opponent of Populism back in the 1890s. Davis's long career in politics finally ended when he lost to the younger Bailey in a primary runoff. He died in Kaufman, Texas on January 31, 1940 and was buried in Sulphur Springs.

Chapter 11

Society and Culture,
1874-1900

A Reward for Sam Bass and Fellow Outlaws

In the spring of 1878, Sam Bass and his gang held up four trains within twenty-five miles of Dallas. In April, Governor Richard Coke charged 2nd Lt. Junius W. Peak of the Frontier Battalion with raising a special Texas Ranger detachment to track down Bass and his gang. With the aid of local posses, Peak and his men harassed Bass for several months, driving him from North Texas.

After being betrayed by one of his own men, Bass fought the Rangers in a gun battle in Round Rock on July 19, 1878. The wounded Bass was captured outside of town the next morning. He died on July 2. The following is a reward announcement issued by the Union Pacific Railroad Company for Bass and his associates.

REWARD: Sam Bass and other outlaws
$10,000 Reward

Omaha Train Robbers
Description

William Heffridge alias Bill Heffery: 5 feet 8 or 9 inches high 145 or 150 [pounds] 28 to 30 years old light Brown hair light Beard and mustach[e] front tooth gone Tattoo on hand and dancing girl Tattooed on arm.

Sam Bass: 5 feet 7 or 8 inches high 140 or 150 pounds 23 to 25 years old described as quite young and boyish looking dark complexion Hair black and cut short. mustach[e] cut short Beard black, thin and not very stiff has very white teeth shows his front teeth when laughing is slow talker and don't talk much drinks very little does not use Tobacco is called a Texas man

Jack Davis: 5 feet 11 inches high some think 6 feet 190 pounds 30 years old large heavy Broad shouldered man brown eyes dark hair and beard mustache not very heavy slow in his walk and has habit of walking with his hands behind his back Talks and drinks a great deal Rode a dunn colored horse with a glass eye

James Berry: 5 feet 9 inches high 180 pounds 30 or 35 years old Sandy or Red hair with a little gray in it Sandy Beard and mustache chin Beard quite long Red or Florid complexion Blue eyes full round face which gets very red when he has been drinking Talks a great deal

Tom Nixon: 5 feet 8 inches high 140 to 150 pounds 25 years old Light Hair and Beard not very long or heavy Blue eyes was riding a horse with a W and heart Brand

> E.M. Morsman
> Superintendent, Union Pacific Rail Road

Source: Texas State Library and Archives Commission

THOUGHT QUESTIONS:

1. What characteristics did the railroad official use to describe the outlaws?

2. How are the descriptions of these men similar to those used by law enforcement trying to alert the public of dangerous criminals today? How are they different?

3. What explains the similarities and differences between then and now?

Account of Engagement with Comanche Indians, February 16, 1875

Southwest Texas near Uvalde had been home to the Comanches, Tonkawas, and Lipan Apaches. Since the days of Spanish occupation, battles between Native Americans and white settlers were a common feature of life in the area. Though nominally protected by Fort Inge since 1849, Indian raiding and outlaws hampered development until the 1880s. This document provides an account of one such engagement between whites and Comanches

Uvalde Feby 16th 1875
San Antonio Herald

Upon a recent visit to Frio Cañon, situated in the Northern portion of this County, where Messrs Patterson: Watkins: and Smith, have some six hundred acres of well irrigated land under cultivation, and many more susceptible of like improvements, (surrounded by beautiful Mountains,) and had the pleasure of meeting Messrs Humphry: Green: Avant:

Patterson: Sawyer: Blackburn: Goodman: and Wells, who had just returned from an "Indian Scout" of fifteen days duration—

The Indians, came to Frio Cañon on the 25th of January 1875, stealing five horses from Sawyer & Shores; proceeded down the Blanco to its confluence with the Sabinal, where they Killed a Mexican by shooting him in the back with an arrow and mutilating him in a horrible manner—

They moved then, in the direction of Frio City, capturing thirty-nine horses from Messrs Brown, Allen, Gray: and Honeycut: turned Northward, passing with their stock along the "divide" of the Nueces and Dry Frio, crossing the Nueces at Camp Wood; and upon reaching the "divide" of the Frio, Sabinal, Llano, and Devil Rivers, they encamped in a dense thicket, near Beaver Lake—The scouting party above referred to as having been formed, started two days after the Indians passed Frio Cañon in hot pursuit; keeping on their trail, until the Indian Camp was reached—The attention of the Scouting Party was first attracted by a few loose horses, and upon riding around the thicket in which the Indians had their Camp they discovered one in the act of bridling a horse, when Humphry, Avant and Sawyer gave him several shots, as he drew back into the thick brush—This seemed to startle them; and another making his appearance in a different quarter, Humphry and Sawyer drove him to cover, with his hands placed upon his side, "minus" the saddle, shield and bridle which he brought with him—Wells and Goodman were not asleep on their post for as the Indians emerged from the woods, they gave them Winchester Music to retreat by, while Patterson Wells and Green were speeding across the plain to "cut-off" a party of Indians coming to Camp, with pack mules, loaded with Buffalo meat—The Indians abandoning the mules took to their horses and escaped into the woods—

Patterson had succeeded in cutting off one Indian from the woods, and was charging him, when his horse fell, giving him a severe fall, from which he did not recover in time to avail himself of his previous advantage—

The "boys" now determined to enter the brush and capture or drive the Indians from their Camp—Leaving four men to guard their horses, four entered the copse and moved in the direction of the smoke, which "so gracefully curled" above the trees, until they reached the Camp, which they found deserted—They, then began firing through the thicket with the hope of discovering the whereabouts of the Indians or of driving them from Cover, but without success—

The day was now "far Spent" and the men being worn-out with fatigue and hunger, (having had no food for several days) concluded that, they had best recapture all the stock and retire to some point for the night where they could protect themselves & animals—In accordance with this view, the Party "gathered" the stock, consisting of thirty five horses; two Spanish mules; one pony; and commenced their home-ward march arriving safe and sound at Frio Cañon on the 13th February—They captured out of the Camp four shields, several head-dresses, one "Marine Glass" and numerous trinkets.

Between the covers of one of the shields (to which hung a woman's scalp, with light hair) was found the photograph of a beautiful white woman and the following certificate–

Office Kiowa and Comanche Agency, I.T. 3 No 28" 1874

To Mochecut, alias Black Beard, A-quo-ha-da Comanche Chief, has been for some time using his influence for good and promises to continue at Peace and friendship towards the White people—I ask for him kind treatment at the hands of all with whom he comes in contact, as long as he continues to conduct himself in a proper manner

J.M. Haworth, U.S. Ind Agt—

. . . This paper, with the above recital, contains a lesson of hatred, treachery, and maudlin imbecility, that an Indian only on the side and a Grant on the other can teach— "Let us have peace" means peace to the Indian and oppression to the South; the quiet of the grave and the peace of the charnel-house—

Texans must suffer every wrong and outrage, at the hands of savage Indians; be insulted through their Governor, by a "landelan" [?] Attorney General but if a fish is caught (even during Lent) by a British subject, from the waters of the ocean, that wash the shores of Massachusetts; Ben Butler goes junketing to Canada at an enormous expense to the Government and demands indemnity for the Past and Security for the Future—If a horse is stollen [sic.] from Michigan by a Canadian, "old Zac Chandler" swears like a pirate; makes belligerent speeches in the Senate and calls upon the Government to investigate the outrage—We must protect ourselves, and if all the frontier people will show the pluck and determination of our Scouting Party, "Indian raids" will soon be a thing of the past– Texas–

Since writing we have ascertained beyond a doubt that two Indians were Killed

Source: Texas State Library and Archives Commission

THOUGHT QUESTIONS:

1. How are the Comanche portrayed in this document?

2. What overall tone toward the Comanche does the writer utilize?

3. What was the writer's opinion of President Grant's "peace policy" designed to create improved relations between Americans and native groups in the West?

Texas State Prison Inmate Fred Stone's Testimony to Investigators (1875)

Operating on low budgets after the Civil War, Texas and other southern states eventually responded to the pressure to maintain their prison systems through convict leasing, whereby a private company took over management of the state prison at Huntsville and agreed to cover the costs of housing, feeding, and guarding prisoners. In 1872, the Texas state government accepted *a competitive bid from Ward, Dewey, and Company of Galveston and awarded the firm a 15-year lease of the prison in exchange for $325,000. The prison was overseen by a three-man board and a state inspector who reported monthly to the governor's office.*

While Ward, Dewey, and Company reportedly made some improvements to the Hunstville facility's aging buildings, by the mid-1870s the state prison became known for its horrible living conditions and brutal punishment of prisoners, leading the Legislature in 1875 to order a public investigation which determined that a sizeable number of convicts had indeed suffered cruel treatment, died of minor maladies, or had been shot trying to escape. The following is the transcript of an interview conducted by state investigators with Fred Stone, an inmate serving a ten-year sentence for counterfeiting, who was promised immunity from retribution in return for his testimony.

Fred Stone.
Examined in private by the Assistant Attorney General on his visit to the penitentiary April 15, said:

I am a convict and will tell you all I know, relying on your assurance that I shall not be punished for it. One man died in his cell last night. Two others died a few days ago. They do not take them into the hospital until they are ready to be buried. We have worked in this room (chair bottoming room) all winter without fire and with the door open. I am in for ten years and shall die here. The character of punishment is just what[ever] the guards like to inflict. The "horse" was used here up to three or four weeks ago [a classic military punishment in which a prisoner is made to sit on a wooden "horse" with his arms bound behind his back and weights tied to his legs for an extended period of time]. There is no appeal from the guards. I was an inmate of the penitentiary for two months before conviction; was sent here for safe keeping. I had been here but three weeks when I was taken out of my bed and put in the "stocks" and left there for thirty or forty minutes. He also whipped me. They said I was in a plot to get out all the prisoners. I lay in the "blind cell" for about a week. The captain was then satisfied there was nothing in it at all.

The only reason I can assign for such punishment is that I objected to coming here. I came here last July. Have never been punished but once since then. While being punished the Captain said he did it "to keep things straight." [I] am here for counterfeiting. [I] was sent from Austin, Travis County. There are some here who will tell you everything, but they are afraid. That man there has his back so injured by punishment that he cannot work at all. His brother was taken out to work on the railroad and was shot and killed. I shall be punished for telling you this; they say I am a desperado.

When visitors are here we get from 15 to 20 minutes to our meals; when no one is here we are hurried through them. We get plenty of food such as it is. We have had bacon three times in twelve months. We had bacon when the Governor was here and at Christmas. Potatoes we have had two or three times since I have been here. When a guard falls asleep men run away and then they are brought back and punished. This is on the outside. The last time I saw a man punished on the horse was three or four weeks ago; am sure it has not been more than six weeks since. When the man was taken off he could not walk. I never was horsed. It affects the back. I have known persons die in the stocks. I did not see it but I know it. There was a man stocked and taken to his cell. It was Cell no. 7. The next morning I saw his bed in the back alley and it was full of blood.

Source: Testimony of Fred Stone, April 15, 1875. Investigations, Records Relating to the Penitentiary, Archives and Information Services Division, Texas State Library and Archives Commission.

THOUGHT QUESTIONS:

1. What types of punishment did Stone personally experience? Why did he think he was treated this way?

2. What other types of punishment did Stone witness at the prison?

3. Why do you think Stone agreed to speak with the investigators? What direct reasons does he give for speaking out and what does he subtly imply about his situation that led to his willingness to testify?

A Monthly Prison Inspection Report Shows Little Change

As a result of the 1875 investigation into conditions at the Huntsville State Prison, the Legislature authorized the construction of another state penitentiary at Rusk (completed in 1883). Ward, Dewey, and Company was allowed the chance to improve conditions but in Huntsville, but further negative reports such as the one below submitted by inspector J.K.P. Campbell in September 1875 eventually led to the company's lease to be terminated in 1877.

A new firm, Cunningham and Ellis, signed a five-year-lease to take over management of prison operations in January 1878. The work of convicts on cotton or sugar plantations, railroad projects, and the construction of the new prison at Rusk led to the system's first profits, but continued reports of brutality toward inmates led to the termination of Cunningham and Ellis's contract in 1882 along with several new contracts being drawn up with other companies.

The leasing system in Texas eventually collapsed when a newspaper exposed the bribery of legislators involving the awarding of the new agreements. In the aftermath of the scandal, all leases were terminated. Nevertheless, state officials still refused to raise taxes to build more prisons, preferring simply to hire out inmate labor to private individuals and companies.

I regret to say that the Rules & By laws adopted by the Board of Directors July 16th 1875 and approved by you July 22nd 1875 have not been complied with by the Lessees. The ration prescribed is not issued to the Convicts or the number of meals given. For breakfast the ration issued is corn bread and beef—occasionally bacon—and corn meal coffee without sugar. [The dinner ration is] corn bread and beef—occasionally bacon—and when the men go to their cells at night they get a piece of cold corn bread. No pure coffee is issued, except to the sick in Hospital and they have no sugar to put in it. A small quantity of rice, sugar, & molasses were furnished the Hospital yesterday which is the only articles of the kind furnished this month. This is sumptuous fare for sick men! The convicts get from 1 to 1 ½ oz of Tobacco weekly instead of ¼ pound as directed by the Rules and By laws.

The convicts within the walls are clothed well enough for Summer. I also regret to say that the dispensary is allmost [sic] destitute of all kinds of medicines and how the Physician can treat the 49 Sick convicts without medicines I am at a loss to understand. The attention of the Board of Directors has been called to this matter by me frequently both by letter, and verbally. The Hospital accommodation and food for the sick are not what they should be. Owing to the fact that 144 convicts have been sent out on plantations &c. this month quite a number of the cells are destitute of suitable bedding—which I am assured will be supplied as soon as cloth can be woven to make new mattresses.

On the morning of the 18th inst on reaching the Prison about 7 o'clock to my surprise I found a stillness and quietness as if it were Sunday. The convicts all locked up in their cells & the guards collected about in groups & idle; upon inquiry I found that the guards had refused to do duty on account of having nothing to eat. Enough however were prevailed upon to take charge of the shops, & about 8 o'clock the men went to work. The Convicts had nothing to eat for breakfast that day but cold corn bread. I regret to say we had quite a number of visitors who saw this Sumptuous Meal.

The outlaw I. cell building is in very bad condition and has been so for 10 or 11 months – a portion of the roof was blown off by a storm, and the great concussion caused by the explosion of the boiler of the saw mill last fall which opened the joints of the tin roof—it leaks very badly, and when we have continued rain the whole building becomes very wet, and the cells are not in a condition to be occupied yet the men sleep in them. The Cabinet shop just south of this building leaks equally as much. The Paint shop leaks very badly also—in fact every roof about the entire prison needs repairing. The contract between the Lessees and the state expressly provides that the buildings shall be kept in good repair.

The Lessees have promised me again and again that they would put the buildings in good repair, but they do not do it. I have called the attention of the Director to this matter very often. The new cell building which we were assured would be completed during 1874 is not yet half done and for the past two months very little work has been done on this building. To judge the future by the past it will be a long time before it is completed. You will see that we have 621 convicts within the walls, and only 278 cells making 2 27/100 men for each cell. If we had the 137 cells which the new building would give us it would be a great relief to the convicts.

The punishment of convicts now is as seldom as it was frequent when I first entered on duty as Inspector and I am glad to say that only a few men have been put in the stocks this month, and two or three put in the dark cell for a short time. I consider this as doing well when you take into consideration that many of the men are idle in the shops owing to the want of material….

Source: Records Relating to the Penitentiary, Archives and Information Services Division, Texas State Library and Archives Commission.

THOUGHT QUESTIONS:

1. Describe the different types of inadequate prisoner care that Inspector Campbell relates in his report. What are some of the extreme punishments the inspector mentions being used at the prison?

2. How did the inspector describe the physical condition of the prison's buildings?

3. Though this late-19th century effort at "privatization" failed at many levels, the idea of private companies taking over public services and running them efficiently (and profitably) continues to this day. What are some public services that you think would be best left to the state or federal governments to handle? Which public services could (or should) be contracted out to private companies? Why?

A Public Appeal against Lynching, 1893

Originating out of efforts by citizens during the antebellum period to organize against criminals when local law enforcement proved inadequate to the task, the practice of lynching evolved during the post-Civil War era as a means of instilling terror upon blacks in order to keep African Americans in a second-class status. Often more than just a simple hanging in a backwoods area, as time went on, the instances of large mobs acting in open public view increased, as did the perpetrators' brutality. Torturing the victim beforehand, as well as dismembering the corpse to pass out pieces to the witnessing crowd as souvenirs, became more commonplace. To the extent that any pattern can be discerned from such medieval practices, many historians have noted that lynchings usually involved a black man accused of committing a black-on-white crime or an African American crossing the societal color barrier in some way deemed egregious, such as socializing openly with whites or disrespecting white people. Blacks who assaulted, raped, or killed other blacks would not be the victim of a lynching. Further, though whites were still occasionally hanged by local citizens in rural areas for crimes such as cattle rustling and horse thievery, they did not receive the barbaric treatment before, during, and after their executions—that was reserved for African Americans alone. Those acts were done to deliver a ghastly punishment to the accused perpetrator as well as to send a terrifying message to the local black community at large that such offenses would not be tolerated.

Not all supported the growing vigilante actions of revenge-seeking crowds, as evidenced by this editorial appearing in an 1893 issue of the **Waco Morning News**. *Nevertheless, despite such calls, the practice only increased in frequency into the early decades of the twentieth century, with over 500 taking place in Texas between 1880 and 1930. In 1916, downtown Waco would become the scene of one of the most infamous lynchings in southern history when a crowd of over 15,000 witnessed the torture-killing of Jesse Washington, a mentally-challenged teenager recently convicted by a jury for the rape and murder of his white employer's wife.*

MOB LAW.

No matter how atrocious may be the crime, there is no lynch law in France, Germany, Holland, Belgium, England and Scotland. The law is relied upon for punishing criminals, and it does punish them with certainty. Why should we resort to lynch law in Texas any more than the Europeans do? That is the way to look at the subject. In Birmingham, Ala., a man who had murdered his wife and child was arrested and put in jail. A mob attacked the jail for the purpose of lynching this man, but were repulsed [by] the fire of the sheriff and his posse. The murderer was subsequently tried, convicted and hung by due process of law. That was far better. It was regular and legal. Justice presided. Passion, fury and vengeance preside at a lynching. Texas has laws to punish every crime, and courts to administer and enforce those laws, so there is no occasion for resorting to lynch law, which demoralizes and hardens those who participate in the lynching. Lynch law does not repress crime half as much as does the punishment by the arm of justice and of law. Rape is not stopped by lynching rapists. The terror inspired is of short duration. But the demoralizing [sic.] effect of lynching is lasting. Men should reflect on these things and let the courts mete out the punishment of crime. Formerly in Italy, the crime of highway robbery was punished with death, and every robber killed his victim to silence him and prevent identification. The certainty, and not the severity of punishment, is that which makes "the law a terror to evil doers." Every public officer should use to the utmost his power and influence to prevent a resort to lynching. Gray-haired men and it is well that this is the case, and these fathers and grandfathers, should use their influence against lynching. They could, nine times out of ten, maintain the supremacy of the law. The trouble is, that lynching becomes chronic and infectious--"appetite grows by what it feeds on," and contempt for law and order also becomes chronic and contagious. Boys grow to manhood with the idea, ingrained in them that lynch law is right and proper, and worthy of applause, and they follow the example set them by their fathers. The [Waco Evening] News is not unmindful of the fact, that its views will be disrelished, if not condemned [sic], by some of its readers, yet it is satisfied the disuse of lynch la[w] would be a gain to Texas in various respects, and feels it to do its duty to express these views.

Source: *Waco Morning News*, February 16, 1893

THOUGHT QUESTIONS:

1. What did the writer say about the use of lynching as a possible deterrent to crime? What evidence did he provide to support his point of view?

2. What did the writer say about the effect of lynching on public attitudes toward due process and law and order?

3. Did the writer believe the views he expressed would be popular among his readers? Why might some civic boosters among the business community of towns, such as newspaper owners, not support the publicity generated by a lynching?

Lt. Henry O. Flipper Seeks Vindication

A native of Georgia born into slavery in 1856, Henry Ossian Flipper received an appointment to the U.S. Military Academy at West Point, New York in 1873. During his four-year stay, he overcame harassment and ostracism to become the academy's first African American graduate and the first African American commissioned officer in the regular U.S. Army. After a stint at Fort Sill, Oklahoma, the Army stationed Second Lieutenant Flipper at Forts Elliott, Concho, Quitman in Texas where he worked as a signal officer, supervised the installation of telegraph lines and road construction, and took part in the campaign against the Apache chief Victorio. At Fort Davis in West Texas, he served as the post quartermaster in charge of the base's supplies and equipment. In 1881, when he discovered $3,791.77 of post fund missing, Flipper attempted to conceal the loss until he could find or replace the money. Upon learning of the missing funds, Flipper's commanding officer, Col. William R. Shafter, immediately filed embezzlement charges against him in an effort to force him from the army. A court-martial found him not guilty of the theft charges, but convicted him of "conduct unbecoming an officer and a gentlemen" and ordered him dismissed from the Army.

After his service career abruptly ended, he worked as a civil engineer, surveyor, and legal assistant in Texas, northern Mexico, and Venezuela. For the remainder of his life, Flipper contested the charges, sought to clear his name, and regain his commission. In 1898, a bill reinstating him into the Army and restoring his rank was introduced in Congress on his behalf. To bolster his case, he sent the letter shown below along with a brief supporting his case to Congressman John A. T. Hull of Iowa, chairman of the House Committee on Military Affairs. Congress ultimately ignored the bill and several later ones, and Flipper died in 1940 without vindication. In 1976, the Army granted him an honorable discharge. Twenty-three years later, President Bill Clinton issued him a full pardon:

Santa Fe, New Mexico, October 23, 1898

Hon. John A. T. Hull,
Des Moines, Iowa

Dear Sir:

I send you, in this mail and under separate cover, a printed copy of the Brief I have prepared in my case under Bill, H.R. 9849, which was so kindly introduced in the House for me by the Hon. Michael Griffin, at the last session of Congress.

In May last I submitted to you and to the members of the Sub-Committee a type-written copy of a Brief I had hastily prepared in Washington. I have carefully rewritten and revised that Brief and now send you a copy for your perusal and consideration.

In coming to Congress with my case, I do so because there is no individual or other tribunal to which I can go, no official or other official body with power to review the case and grant or refuse my petition. In coming to you, to the Committee and to Congress, I do not ask that aught to be done for me from motives of mere sympathy and yet I cannot help feeling that all of us can and do sympathize with those who have been wronged. I am sure that, after reading my Brief through, you will understand and appreciate the struggle I made to rise above the station to which I was born, how I won my way through West Point and how I made as honorable a record in the Army as any officer in it, in spite of the isolation, lack of social association, ostracism and what not to which I was subjected by the great majority of my brother officers. You will recognize also the almost barbarous treatment to which I was subjected at the time I was accused and tried.

It will not be possible, I apprehend, for you or any member of the Committee to wade through the 1000 or more pages of the record, nor is it necessary, but, if you should do so, you will readily be convinced that the crime of being a Negro was, in my case, far more heinous than deceiving the commanding officer.

My utter helplessness and conviction then arose from that cause and without the generous assistance of yourself and the other gentlemen of the Committee, in Committee and on the floor of the House, I shall be equally helpless now.

I believe my case is a strong one as well as a meritorious one and one that will commend itself to you for approval and will enlist your sympathy and support.

I ask nothing because I am a Negro, yet that fact must press itself upon your consideration as a strong motive for the wrong done me as well as a powerful reason for righting that wrong.

I ask only what Congress has seen fit to grant to others similarly situated. I ask only that justice which every American citizen has the right to ask and which Congress alone has the power to grant.

In my Brief I offer for your consideration two cases, one occurring before my trial and of which I should have had the benefit as a precedent, and the other occurring after my trial. They will show how white officers of long years of experience and high rank have been treated for the same offense as that for which I was tried and dismissed. I also present six precedents in which Congress has granted to dismissed officers precisely what I am asking.

I do not believe Congress ever had before it a case as deserving of favorable action as my case, and for that reason I do not hesitate to appeal to you and to ask you to champion it for me and to see that both the Committee and the House take speedy and favorable action and pass the bill just as Mr. Griffin introduced it without amendment of any character. You will have my gratitude and that of my entire race, as well as the satisfaction of having righted a great wrong done to a member of a harmless but despised and friendless race.

Relying upon you, as I do, I have the honor to be,
Very truly yours,
Henry O. Flipper

Source: Library of Congress

THOUGHT QUESTIONS:

1. According to Flipper, why was he seeking help from Congress? On what grounds did he seek vindication?

2. In his letter, what "crime" did Flipper state he was subjected that was far more of an issue than concealing from his commanding officer that some funds were missing?

3. What evidence did Flipper wish to introduce in order to show that white officers in similar circumstances were treated much differently than he had by the Army?

Uncle Tom's Cabin—As It Will Have to be Played If Johnson Wins

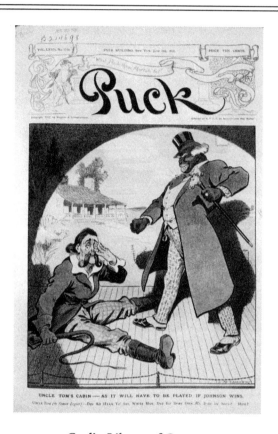

Credit: Library of Congress

This cover illustration in *Puck*, June 22, 1910, is a caricature of Jack Johnson (biography at the end of the chapter) as a large, wealthy man having knocked down Simon Legree. Racial animosity among whites ran deep and many called out for a "Great White Hope" to take the title away from Johnson. Former heavyweight champion James J. Jeffries came out of retirement for the sole purpose of defeating Johnson, but Johnson proved stronger than Jeffries. The outcome of the fight triggered race riots across the United States. (Biography at the end of chapter.)

THOUGHT QUESTION:

Why was there so much hatred toward Jack Johnson? What do you think he represented?"

Virginia K. Johnson Home

Credit: Library of Congress
October 1913

Virginia K. Johnson was born in Lynchburg, Virginia, in 1843. During the Civil War she was arrested and imprisoned as a Confederate sympathizer. In 1872, she married William Hudson Johnson and the couple moved to Brownwood, Texas, and later to Dallas. After her husband's death, Virginia became active as a member of the First Methodist Church and president of the Central Circle of the missionary society, the King's Daughters. In 1893, Virginia Johnson opened a home called Sheltering Arms, a haven for women in danger of resorting to prostitution for lack of other means of support. In 1897 Sheltering Arms expanded, offering refuge to unwed mothers. A large proportion of the girls came from farms, their lives stunted by the monotonous work of cotton picking.

THOUGHT QUESTION:

Describe the limited opportunities that existed for urban women living at the turn of the twentieth century.

BIOGRAPHIES

JACK JOHNSON (1878-1946). Boxing legend Jack Johnson, the first African American to win the world heavyweight boxing championship, was born in Galveston on March 31, 1878. He left school in the fifth grade to help support his parents, both former slaves, and their nine children. He swept out a barbershop, worked as a porter in a gambling house, and later labored as a dockworker. Johnson began his boxing career as a sparring partner and participant in "battle royals," where several black youths would fight each other at the same time with the winner receiving money thrown to him from the white spectators. He started fighting in private clubs in the Galveston area, finally becoming a professional prizefighter in 1897.

Johnson left Galveston in 1899 and did not return. He spent his time traveling the country, fighting, and gaining increasing recognition. By 1902 he won over 50 fights against white and black opponents. In 1903 he won the Negro heavyweight championship, but the reigning white heavyweight champion, Jim Jeffries, refused the challenge to fight him. Johnson had to wait until after Jeffries's retirement for his opportunity. In 1908, he defeated the Canadian world champion Tommy Burns in Australia. The boxing community did not recognize Johnson as the actual champion until 1910 when Jim Jeffries came out of retirement to fight Johnson in Reno, Nevada, but was soundly defeated. Race riots broke out in many parts of the country, including Texas, as a result of Johnson's triumph.

Jim Jeffries was the first of many recruited "great white hopes" charged with the task of defeating Johnson, who infuriated the majority of whites because of his color, his taunting and trash-talking of opponents, and his non-conformist behavior, especially scandalous public relationships with white women. He was easily the most famous (and in many circles the most hated) African American in the country. Johnson's propensity for white women (usually, but not always prostitutes) made him a constant target for authorities. In 1913 he fled a conviction for violation of the Mann Act, a federal law designed to combat prostitution by forbidding the transportation of women across interstate lines for "immoral purposes." In practice, authorities during the Progressive Era often used the law as a weapon to prosecute individuals engaging in premarital, extramarital, or (as in the case with Johnson) interracial relationships. Facing a fine and prison time if he remained in the country, Johnson left the United States for an extended tour in Europe, Mexico, and Canada.

Johnson finally lost the heavyweight championship to a white man, Jess Willard, in Havana, Cuba in 1915. Despite his age (he was 37 by then) and the extreme tropical heat, he was not knocked out until the 26th round. In 1920, Johnson returned to the United States and was arrested for his Mann Act conviction and served over a year in Leavenworth Prison. Upon his release, he returned to boxing, but he was well past his prime. He gave up professional fighting in 1938. During the last decade of his life he promoted fights, refereed bouts, and occasionally managed and trained boxers. Johnson's raucous life ended the way he lived it—in a high-speed car crash near Raleigh, North Carolina in 1946.

WILLIAM SYDNEY PORTER [pseudonym for O. Henry] (1862-1910). The writer William Sydney Porter was born on September 11, 1862 in Greensboro, North Carolina. His aunt, a schoolteacher, was largely responsible for his deep love for literature, developing the child into a voracious reader. Until the age of fifteen he received his only formal schooling at her small schoolhouse. He started working at his uncle's drug store and received his pharmacist license in 1881. The next year, however, Porter joined a close family friend, Dr. James Hall, on a trip to visit Hall's four sons who managed a La Salle County ranch in South Texas. The doctor had been concerned because Porter had developed a persistent cough and believed the Texas climate and rigorous ranch life might help him. Porter continued reading while working on the ranch for two years, gaining an intimate knowledge of ranch life that he later integrated into many of his short stories. In 1884 Porter moved to Austin. During the next three years he worked many jobs while starting to write as a journalist. His first known use of his pseudonym appeared during these years, apparently coming from his habit of calling "Oh, Henry" to his cat.

He met and courted his future wife, seventeen-year old Athol Estes with whom he eloped in 1887 because her family objected to their courtship because she was ill at the time with tuberculosis. A son was born to the young couple, but he died soon after birth. In 1889, a daughter, Margaret Worth Porter, was born.

Porter worked as a draftsman in the General Land Office, headed by Dr. James Hall's son Richard, who had become land commissioner, while continuing to contribute to newspapers and magazines. He resigned when Hall's term expired in 1891 and became a teller and bookkeeper at the First National Bank of Austin. Disliking the job, he attempted to start a humorous weekly journal, the *Rolling Stone,* but it failed within a year. Nevertheless, his writings caught the attention of the editor of the *Houston Post.* Porter and his family then moved to Houston and from October 1895 to June 1896 he wrote a column for *Post* often based on his observations while hanging out in local hotel lobbies listening and talking to people. During this time, federal auditors examined the books of the First National Bank and discovered many discrepancies with the methods that Porter used to keep track of accounts. These irregularities led to his indictment on embezzlement charges. Porter denied any wrongdoing and returned to Austin, but fled before his trial, first to New Orleans and later to Honduras, leaving his wife and child behind. In January 1897 he returned to Texas after receiving word of Athol's renewed health problems and surrendered to the court. Six months later, his wife died. In February 1898 Porter was declared guilty of embezzlement and sent to serve five years in a federal penitentiary in Ohio.

At age thirty-five, he entered the penitentiary and the lowest point in his life having lost his job, his home, his wife, and his freedom. He served three years of his sentence, largely working in the prison hospital before being released early for good behavior. He emerged from the prison reborn, consistently using the pseudonym O. Henry to conceal his identity. During his prison years, he wrote at least twelve stories and sought to have many of them published. *McClure's Magazine* had already published one of his stories, "The Miracle of Lava Canyon," in 1897. Upon his release, Porter moved to New York City. In 1903 he signed a contract with the New York *Sunday World* to write a weekly feature story. In 1904, he published his first book, *Cabbages and Kings*, which included stories from his Central American experiences. In the book, Porter coined the phrase "banana republic," which has since been used to describe all small unstable nations in

Central America. In 1906 *The Four Million*, a collection of New York stories appeared. In *The Heart of the West* (1907) O. Henry published many of his Texas stories, including "The Reformation of Calliope," "The Caballero's Way," and "The Hiding of Black Bill." His years in Texas enabled him to write about cowboys, Texas Rangers, Mexicans, and pioneers with authenticity, depicting the life and times of Texas as he later depicted New York City life. He eventually published more than 300 stories and gained fame as one of America's favorite short-story writers.

In 1907 he married a childhood sweetheart, but after months of poor health he died three years later at the age of forty-eight on June 5, 1910. Upon his death, he was praised as a master of the modern short story. His stories are especially noted for their unexpected endings and for their sympathetic portrayal of the hopes and dreams of common people. Not a bad legacy for an ex-convict who, nevertheless, made the most out of his exceptional abilities.

ELISABET NEY (1833-1907). One of Texas's first professional sculptors, Elisabet Ney was born in Münster, Germany on January 26, 1833, to a stone-carver and his wife. Allowed by her father to work with clay and handle his instruments, she developed an aptitude and interest in sculpting at an early age. She enrolled at the Munich Academy of Art in 1852 and, after graduating with highest honors, moved to Berlin to study under Christian Daniel Rauch, the most famous sculptor in Europe at the time. Under Rauch's teaching, Ney combined classical traditions with realism and accuracy to scale—a style for which Rauch was known. Through Rauch, she became acquainted with Germany's artistic and intellectual elite. During the late 1850s and 1860s, as her reputation spread, she traveled around Europe to complete portraits of such luminaries as the philosopher Arthur Schopenhauer, Italian patriot Giuseppi Garibaldi, German Chancellor Otto von Bismarck, and King Ludwig II of Bavaria.

In 1863, Ney married Edmund D. Montgomery, a Scottish physician and scientist. Wishing to start a family in a peaceful environment away from crowded cities and the tumult of German politics, the couple left Europe in 1871 to settle briefly in Thomasville, Georgia, where a young German friend had moved after marrying an American girl. Though two sons were born to the couple there, Ney and her husband sought better surroundings. In 1873 Ney traveled alone to Galveston where she contacted the German consulate seeking advice about a suitable place to settle in Texas. When Ney visited the Liendo Plantation near Hempstead in Waller County, she instantly fell in love with the dilapidated historic Greek-Revival home on the premises. Supposedly, she immediately announced "Here I will live. And here I will die!" For over twenty years, while Montgomery continued his scientific work, she gave up sculpting to run the plantation and sought to make Liendo the quiet serene place that she and her husband desired. Life at Liendo, however, did not fulfill her hopes. One son died not very long after arriving at the plantation, the other proved to be extremely disobedient and independent, and the efforts to raise cotton, cattle, and a dairy operation resulted in repeated financial losses. While her husband thrived in the isolation, publishing many noted works, Ney came to look upon Liendo as a "lovely cursed retreat."

After visiting Austin at the invitation of Governor Oran M. Roberts, Ney decided to resume her career in sculpting. In 1892, she built a studio in the Hyde Park area of

Austin and began lobbying wealthy citizens and the state legislature for commissions. During the next fifteen years she completed a number of portrait busts as well as statues of Stephen F. Austin and Sam Houston, currently located in the state Capitol, and a memorial to Albert Sidney Johnston at his gravesite in the State Cemetery. In addition to her sculpting, Ney took an active role in Austin civic activities, promoting the arts and welcoming visitors to her studio. She died on June 29, 1907 and is buried next to her husband at the Liendo Plantation. Four years after her death, many of her supporters founded the Texas Fine Arts Association in her honor and established her Austin studio as the Elisabet Ney Museum to preserve her memory and legacy. The museum has been modernized and reconstructed to retain its original look and displays most of her famous works with free admission to the general public.

HENRY OSSIAN FLIPPER (1856-1940). Henry O. Flipper, the first black graduate of the United States Military Academy (USMA) at West Point, was born a slave in Thomasville, Georgia on March 21, 1856. His family moved to Texas in 1857, settling near Winnsboro. Though his parents had separate owners, Flipper's father was able to give money to his master earned from side jobs as a shoemaker to allow the purchase of his mother before a planned move to Atlanta, thus keeping the family intact. After the Civil War, Flipper was educated at local American Missionary Association schools and spent a year at Atlanta University before ambitiously asking the new Republican congressman for his district, James Freeman, for an appointment to West Point, which was granted. Flipper joined four other black cadets who were ostracized from the majority white cadets. In 1878, a year after he became the first African American to graduate from the USMA, he published a book about his experience entitled *The Colored Cadet at West Point.*

Upon graduation, he was commissioned a second lieutenant and assigned to the all-black Tenth Cavalry Regiment and became the first African-American officer to lead the so-called "Buffalo Soldiers," who had previously only served under white officers. While deployed in Oklahoma and Texas, Flipper was involved in overseeing engineering projects such as draining ditches, building wagon roads, and installing telegraph lines before engaging in combat against the Apache chief Victorio in 1880, during which he received a commendation. With Victorio's defeat, Flipper was sent to Fort Davis in West Texas to serve as the post quartermaster and commissary officer. His troubles there began after Colonel William Shafter assumed command in March 1881. Though he accepted Buffalo Soldiers as enlisted men, he despised the thought of black officers serving in the U.S. Army. Shafter worked to undermine Flipper, first by removing him as quartermaster without cause soon after arriving, though the colonel told him that he wanted the quartermaster's safe to remain in Flipper's quarters. In July 1881, the young lieutenant discovered that over $2,000 was missing from the safe. Knowing that any reported loss in post funds might be grounds for his removal from the army and fearing a set-up, Flipper made an unsuccessful attempt to cover the discrepancy. Shafter promptly ordered Flipper's arrest and charged him with embezzlement of government funds, leading to court martial proceedings. In December 1881, the court acquitted Flipper of the main charge, but found him guilty of "conduct unbecoming an officer and gentleman" for giving false statements about the alleged theft when confronted, leading to his dismissal from the army.

Flipper fought for his exoneration and the restoration of his officer's commission for the remainder of his life while endeavoring to make a living in the private sector. He remained in Texas for a couple of years, finding employment in El Paso as an engineer for a survey company. Flipper worked for a variety of land companies in New Mexico, Arizona, and northern Mexico while seeking an act of Congress to restore his status in the army, but such efforts came to naught, even with the military's manpower needs following the outbreak of the Spanish-American War in 1898. Flipper joined an American mining company in northern Mexico in 1901, eventually impressing Albert Fall after the future U.S. Senator from New Mexico purchased the company. Fall later called Flipper to Washington to work on his subcommittee on foreign relations as a translator and advisor on Mexican politics. In 1921, after Fall became Secretary of the Interior he hired Flipper to act as a special assistant with the Alaska Engineering Commission, which had been organized to create a rail system for the Alaska Territory. Two years later, he accepted employment as an engineer with an American petroleum company operating in Venezuela until his retirement in 1930. Flipper lived with his brother, a bishop of the African Methodist Episcopal Church, at his home in Atlanta until his death as a result of a heart attack on May 3, 1940.

Decades after his death, family descendants allied with scholarly researchers began a campaign to clear Henry Flipper's name. In 1976, the U.S. Army revisited the lieutenant's case. While reaffirming his innocence on the embezzlement charge, the review board determined that in spite of his definite guilt in falsifying reports and lying to his commanding officer, his dismissal from the service was an unduly harsh punishment and recommended instead its substitution with an honorable discharge. Later that year, the USMA unveiled a bust of Flipper in his honor at West Point's library, and since 1977, has presented the annual Henry Ossian Flipper Award to a graduate demonstrating "the highest qualities of leadership, self-discipline and perseverance in the face of unusual difficulties while a cadet."

Chapter 12

The Progressive Era and WWI, 1900-1919

A Heated Anti-Ferguson Letter

Elijah L. Shettles was born in Mississippi in 1852. Growing up, he traveled the Southwest and lived a wild, hard-drinking gambler until he was "saved" by a revival preacher and called to the Methodist ministry. He worked as a preacher, editor, and church administrator for the next 30 years. In this letter to fellow prohibitionist Dr. Alexander Dienst, Shettles chides the dentist for coming out in favor of James E. Ferguson for governor.

Navasota Texas July 18th 1914

Dear Doctor: I have read and reread your "Jim Ferguson the Citizen and Philanthropist." I was deeply pained too when I read that stuff. I thought I saw signs of hydrophobia at the time I visited you June 12th, and if I remember correctly I cautioned you to be careful lest you should do your then-friend Shuler [R.D. Schuler, pastor of University Methodist Church in Austin] harm. I do not know if you can recall just what happened or passed between us, maybe you can after you get sober, if you ever do again, for you were drunk on the blood of Tom Ball's [Thomas H. Ball, the prohibitionist politician and former mayor of Huntsville who was defeated for the Democratic nomination for governor in 1914 by Ferguson] character, when you wrote . . . .

Now Doctor if you wanted to vote for your man, and you told me the reason for it was not what he had contributed to the charities of this country but because you had been playing billiards with him, I [would have had] no objection, but the thing I resent is not that you are making a fight to save the dirtiest business this side of hell, but that you will bolster up or undertake to do it with the fact that you are a member of the Methodist church, a steward in it. I would have suffered my right arm paralyzed, my tongue to cleave to the roof of my mouth, before I would have done this dirty work for the business that your man stands for. [To] Align yourself against the 1100 Methodist preacher[s] in Texas—some of whom have been with you in sorrow, and bereavement, many of whom have loved and admired you . . . [for] your man and what he stands for . . . is simply incomprehensible to me—I do not understand it on any other hypothesis than that you are drunk as I stated in the [beginning]. . . .

I have been trying to live a religious life nearly twenty four years, I have had some sore trials, and severe temptations—it was not to return to my old habits it was not to return to the gang you have taken up with; but it has been when men like you have done just as you have done this time, members of the church who will turn from their friends and stab them in the vestibule of the house of my Lord. You know that 90 percent of the good people of this state will support Mr. Ball – I mean the church people, outside of the catholics and the one other wiskey- [sic] loving bunch; you know that all we have been working for in the way of moral reform will be set back for several years if your man is elected, and you lined up with that gang. . . .

Now just a word about what you said about Mr. Ball and Doctor Rankin [George C. Rankin, editor of the *Texas Christian Advocate*], and you have the permission of this writer to say it about him if you care [to]: I know Mr. Ball, I know Mr. Rankin, I knew Mr. Ball's habits before he became a candidate, I have known him for several years, he is a gentleman, a scholar, an angel, or anything else you care to put in beside the character assassins led by your jim who have sneaked into his social home and come out and sneaked around among the poor uninformed people and lied like midnight murderers would do, and you my once-friend will endorse it, eh. . . .

Source: Texas State Library and Archives Commission

THOUGHT QUESTIONS:

1. What is Shettles's primary objection to Ferguson's candidacy? What did he believe a Ferguson victory do for the cause of "moral reform" within the state?

2. What did Shettles state was wrong with Dienst, leading the doctor to endorse Ferguson?

3. What effect did Dienst's endorsement of Ferguson have on their friendship? How does this letter show the potential divisions that the Prohibition issue could have on fellow members of the Democratic Party in Texas during these years?

Governor William P. Hobby on Prohibition

Prohibition was a divisive issue during the Progressive Era. During the 1918 special session of the Texas state legislature, lawmakers introduced numerous measures to curtail alcohol use within the state, ranging from proposed bans on the sale of alcohol within a ten-mile radius of military bases (which would have affected every major Texas city) to a drive for so-called "statutory prohibition" that would ban the sale of alcohol within the state without the necessity for a constitutional amendment.

In this letter, Hobby asks political advice on the prohibition question from progressive attorney Martin M. Crane, who had previously served as lieutenant governor and attorney general. Ultimately, the legislature ratified the federal Prohibition amendment in 1918 and Texas voters approved a Prohibition amendment to the Texas constitution in 1919.

February 9, 1918
Gen. M. M. Crane
Commonwealth Bldg., Dallas, Texas

My Dear General Crane:

I have held up an answer to your letter a few days because I have been thinking so seriously about this difficult problem. I do not intend in these times to say positively that I will or will not pursue a given course, because the emergencies of the situation may cause me to do tomorrow what I would not do today.

Do you think that I can justify statutory prohibition on the grounds that it is a war measure when the President does not hesitate to take over the railroads of the country or the coal mines of the country, yet does not adopt prohibition, which could be done by a proclamation; and does not even ask the states to adopt statutory prohibition. Again, would not my position be weakened and Ferguson's strengthened, if I approved statutory prohibition and the court should nullify the act; and it would remain that way during the next year? Please think over these phases of the question; and then would it inconvenience you to come down here some time next week and confer with me at length with respect to the situation. If I should go to Dallas, it would be necessary for me to meet so many people that I would scarcely have an opportunity to talk with you much in one day.

I am extremely anxious to do something, but I do not want to do the wrong thing. I would appreciate your assistance in this matter, because the end I want to accomplish is the same end you have in mind, even though we should differ about the best means to accomplish that end. The political situation in Texas now, in my judgment, requires that no mistake be made; and I will go into this at length with you more thoroughly when I see you, which I hope will be in the next few days. I thank you for your interest.

Yours sincerely,
Wm Hobby, Governor of Texas

Source: Texas State Library and Archives Commission

THOUGHT QUESTIONS:

1. On what grounds was Governor Hobby considering the use of statutory prohibition?

2. What concerns did Hobby bring up concerning the employment of this method of bringing about prohibition in Texas?

3. What do Hobby's concerns say about the delicacy of the matter in Texas politics at that time?

Governor Hobby on Woman Suffrage

An organized woman suffrage movement in Texas began with the organization of women's clubs promoting the reform in Austin and San Antonio. In 1913, women from several Texas cities formed what would become the Texas Equal Suffrage Association for the purpose of overcoming opposition from men (and many women) who wished to continue the custom of denying the direct role of women in the sometimes crude world of politics. A tactic often employed by suffragists was to demonstrate through their advocacy of better schools, playgrounds, parks, sanitation, and workplace safety that women could play a major role in bringing much needed reforms while at the same time upholding their traditional roles as protectors of the family. Strong opposition to suffrage came from Governor Ferguson, who received the ire of suffragists. Consequently, they actively supported the movement to impeach Ferguson, correctly believing that Lieutenant Governor Hobby favored their cause. In March 1918, a special session of the legislature gave women the right to vote in primary elections in Texas. In the July 1918 primary elections, Texas women helped Hobby achieve a tremendous victory and elected Annie Webb Blanton the first female statewide officeholder as state superintendent of public instruction. Texas women won the right to vote in all elections when the nation ratified the Nineteenth Amendment to the U.S. Constitution in June 1919.

In 1915, Governor Hobby married Willie Cooper. After her death in 1929, Hobby would marry Oveta Culp, who went on to lead the Women's Army Corps during World War II and serve in the cabinet of President Eisenhower. In this letter to his father-in-law, former state legislator and congressman Samuel Bronson Cooper, Hobby ponders the passage of the women's suffrage bill.

March 25, 1918

Judge S.B. Cooper
641 Washington Street
c/o Customs Court of Appeals
New York City.

Dear Mr. Cooper:

The session of the legislature now drawing to a close has been a busy and eventful one, and there has been so much to do in connection with it that I have not tried to write you, because of lack of time, and because I preferred to wait until most of the work was over to write you. Now, as it is almost at an end, I write to tell you, in my judgment, it has been the most successful special session of the legislature in the history of the State. Indeed if the satisfaction and gratification of the people is any evidence, it surpasses in this respect.

I am confident that the people, and a very vast majority, want state-wide prohibition and woman suffrage. I am confident that prohibition should be adopted in time of war just the same as when the sale of liquor is prohibited and when the saloons are closed up when there are unusual conditions or some strained situation in a community in time of peace.

I have been in favor of woman suffrage for several years because I have considered it an inevitable development in the course and progress of events. I have felt that women would soon come to take just the place in the political life of the country as they have come to take in the last twenty-five years in the commercial life of the country. Hardly a business establishment, or office of a professional man, or shop, or factory, or bank, or store, or industrial concern of any kind is in existence today where women do not take an essential part in the operation of same. Not as responsible a part as men take, but a place that makes them part and parcel of the commercial life of the country, and under these conditions women will continue to be a more important factor in business affairs. Taking this position in the business activities of the country and a more conspicuous place in the civic and even the military affairs of the country, I consider that their becoming a factor in the political affairs of the country is inevitable.

The last National Democratic platform committed the party to woman suffrage. The President of the United States has become a champion of it. The House of Representatives and the Senate at Washington have each by a two-thirds vote have gone on record in favor of it, and it has been adopted by practically a two-thirds vote in the House and Senate of Texas. Therefore, I would consider it an unwise and unjustified act to veto the measure passed by the Texas Legislature. But over and above all things else, I am convinced that the people of Texas have thoroughly, and carefully, and deliberately considered the question of prohibition and woman suffrage, and a majority thereof are in favor of it; and, therefore, the Governor of the State – the agent of all the people – should approve what he thinks is the will of the people, unless it conflicts with his conscience, and in that event, he should resign.

The political news I get from over the State is most encouraging and after the legislature is over I will have to begin an active campaign I presume.

Willie is very well indeed, and we are hoping to have you visit us before long.

> Affectionately your son,
> Wm Hobby

Source: Texas State Library and Archives Commission

THOUGHT QUESTIONS:

1. What was the governor's stated position on the adoption of alcohol prohibition in wartime?

2. How did Hobby explain his support for woman suffrage?

3. What was Hobby's view concerning what a governor should do if he vetoed an act of the state legislature that had the support of a large percentage of the state's population?

An Article Linking Prohibition & Suffrage

Erminia Folsom graduated from the University of Texas in 1907 and taught school for a while before embarking on a lecturing and writing career promoting various reform movements during the Progressive Era. She was actively involved in the Texas Equal Suffrage Association, the Texas Prison Association, and Texas Woman's Christian Temperance Union. Eben L. Dohoney was a former state legislator who long supported woman suffrage and prohibition. He authored the local-option clause in the Constitution of 1876 giving localities the ability to ban the sale of alcohol and was the Prohibition Party's candidate for governor in 1886. As Dohoney writes in the note attached to the bottom of this draft of a proposed newspaper article linking the two reforms of Prohibition and woman suffrage, he wished to enlist her support in a combined effort to facilitate the passage of both reforms.

SUFFRAGE AND PROHIBITION

The State-wide prohibitionists have the cart before the horse. If they would help the suffragists to secure equal citizen suffrage; the vote of the women would enable us to carry prohibition easily. The male voters will not be able to carry prohibition for years to come; for two reasons; or rather two existing conditions. First, at least 1/10 of the prohibitionists, will vote liquor out of the county, but not out of the state. Whatever may be the reason for this; it is a fact, which must be recognized.

Second, Texas is such a fine liquor market, that the millionaire brewers and distillers will not lose its trade, without a tremendous struggle. They act on the Jesuistic principle "that the end will justify the means." And they will have sufficient illegal votes cast in the principal cities to defeat prohibition. The election officers in these cities being favorable to the traffic, will allow this to be done. So we will be compelled to rely on local option, for years to come, unless we let the women vote. Their vote added to the male prohibitionists, will make the majority so large that it could not be overcome by illegal votes.

We therefore suggest, that the suffragists and prohibitionists make a combined effert (sic) to have a Constitutional amendment submitted to a vote of the people for equal citizen suffrage; and that such an amendment for prohibition, be postponed until the women can vote. The combined vote of the suffragists and the prohibitionists can easily adopt a suffrage amendment; and with the ballot extended to the women a prohibition amendment can be adopted later.

Many voters like myself, are life-long suffragists, and also life-long prohibitionists; but there are some suffragists who are not for prohibition; and many prohibitionists who have not yet declared for suffrage. When it must be evident that both these reforms must stand or fall together, every good citizen should be ready to pool these issues; and support both reforms. With a view to this, we suggest a conference of suffragists and prohibition-ists to be held at an early date to counsel together.

Both reforms are purely non-partisan; and both are entirely just and humane, and we trust that every good citizen, no matter what his or her party relations may be, will unite in this laudable movement to secure the liberty; and protect the lives and property of the people of Texas.

I hope there will be a ready response through the columns of the News to this sugges-tion; and if favorable, that the conference will be called soon.

As it is important to get the matter before the legislature, before it is engrossed in other legislation; and as that body assembles early in January, 1915, ---- we should be ready to urge the adoption of a constitutional amendment to be submitted to a vote of the people for equal citizen suffrage. And thereby secure not only freedom for the women; but the power to crush the liquor traffic.

E.L. Dohoney

Dec 20th 1914
Paris Texas

Dear friend—I send you this carbon copy of the original, which I have mailed to the *Dallas News* for publication.

Do this to give you notice of the campaign I will soon inaugurate; and also in the hope that you may be able to get an Austin paper to publish the article.

Yours for Liberty and Justice
    E.L.D.

Source: Texas State Library and Archives Commission

THOUGHT QUESTIONS:

1. Which reform did Dohoney believe should come first—woman suffrage or prohibi-tion? Why? (i.e., What link did Dohoney make between woman suffrage and prohibi-tion?)

2. In Dohoney's view, what would the continued denial of woman suffrage mean for the prohibition movement in Texas?

3. What did Dohoney propose should be done to bring suffragists and prohibitionists together to organize for their mutual benefit?

A Link between Woman Suffrage and Race

Choice B. Randell served as a city attorney in Denison before being elected to the U.S. House of Representatives in 1901. He became unpopular with his colleagues when he began to call for measures to prevent members of Congress from receiving gifts from corporations or individuals with an interest in pending legislation. Randell was defeated in a bid for the Senate in 1912 and returned home to practice law in Sherman. In this letter to Erminia Folsom, Randell highlights a common argument employed by suffrage opponents in the South -- the race issue.

Sherman, Texas, Nov. 25, 1910
Erminia T. Folsom,
University Station, Austin, Texas,

Dear Madam:

 Business of a pressing nature, and sickness in my family have prevented an earlier reply to your letter of the 2nd inst.

 I do not favor the agitation of woman suffrage at this time. There are to be considered many complications, one of which is the race question. What effect do you think the right of women to vote would have in sections of the country where there is a large negro population? Do you think we can afford to have woman suffrage so long as the negro is a citizen and a voter?

 Would not the presence of negro women as voters very much complicate conditions about the polls during an election?

 Are those in favor of woman suffrage in favor of negro women being allowed th[e] vote? I ask these questions not in any spirit of criticism, but as suggestions and a desire to know what is your position and that of your associates.

Very respectively,
C.B. Randell

Source: Texas State Library and Archives Commission

THOUGHT QUESTIONS:

1. Did Congressman Randell completely rule out ever supporting woman suffrage? Why or why not?

2. What "complications" did Randell believe race brought to the woman suffrage issue?

3. What underlying concerns and fears do you think might have motivated those Southerners opposed to suffrage who used racial arguments to justify their opposition?

An El Paso Musician Laments the Popularity of Jazz

Though existing for many years in African American communities, jazz music gained main-stream popularity across the country during the 1910s and 1920s when white Americans discovered the art form. Many younger Americans went crazy over the music, attracted to its liveliness, syncopated rhythms, and improvisational nature. Predictably, there was a large backlash against jazz, especially among the older generations, as exhibited in the responses given by a musician when interviewed about the subject by a curious local newspaper reporter in El Paso.

"It is sad. Indeed, that the atmosphere of El Paso that once charmed the ears of the tourist with the entrancing strains of the Mexican serenade; whose plazas sent forth the sweet concord of sounds that made it talked of in all corners of the country has at last been polluted with that thunderous jazz racket that echoes from the underworld." …

"Can anyone doubt the evil effects of a music so coarse and sensual?

"Most business musicians, when asked if they like jazz, will answer in the negative, but will say they play it because the public demands it. I do not believe the general public wants it: but only a small per cent consisting mostly of the rounders and sports of the town, who have enough money and social influence to force the managers of amusement places to cater to their whims. Consequently, the skilled musician is displaced by the jazz player who is usually a fakir but who fills the bill to the satisfaction of this racket loving element.

"I think it time that the musicians and music loving people were organizing a crusade to fight the noise demon and recover the lost art of music.

"What is the popular song of today? The lyrics consist of a lot of silly, foolish twaddle that would not be tolerated anywhere but in a song or the insane asylum; or of vulgar suggestions that are only understood in the underworld. Yet the innocent young music student buys it, takes it home and drums at it until she learns this perfectly lovely jazz melody; then she goes to the dance hall and there swings to its degrading rhythm in the arms of some young man who labors under the delusion that Orpheus and Terpsichore have collaborated to give him the latest artistic creation--the classic jazz fox trot.

"I am rearing two daughters and, from my own observations as a dance player, they shall never enter the dance hall so long as the present popular jazz style of dancing prevails. I have been a professional violinist for 20 years and many times I have thanked the good Lord that he bestowed a bit of the divine art on me, for both artistic and business reasons, until the recent jazz innovations, and now I feel like smashing my violin to pieces and crying out for the wash board or sewing machine, the hum of which would be a relief to the loathsome jazz racket."

Source: *El Paso Herald*, Jan. 28, 1919

THOUGHT QUESTIONS:

1. What criticisms of jazz music did this musician offer?

2. What were her objections to the lyrics of jazz songs and the accompanying dance moves?

3. What similarities do you see between this woman's criticism of jazz and later generations' criticism of rock and roll, hip-hop, and other forms of music popular among the nation's youth?

Camp Cotton, El Paso, Texas

**Credit: UTSA's Institute of Texan Cultures,
#075-0784, Source: Philip Goodrich, Jr.**

This photograph shows a tent center set up for National Guard units assigned to Fort Bliss during the 1916 Punitive Expedition against Pancho Villa. Involved in a long and brutal war in Europe (in which the U.S. was initially neutral), Germany wanted to provoke a war between Mexico and the United States in an effort to keep the American military preoccupied. To achieve their goal, Germany encouraged internal divisions in the Mexican government, primarily between President Venustiano Carranza, General Victoriano Huerta, and Pancho Villa. In March 1916, the United States was forced to send military personnel to the border when Pancho Villa's men raided the small town of Columbus, New Mexico. President Woodrow Wilson sent General John J. Pershing in charge of what became known as the "Punitive Expedition" into northern Mexico to capture Villa, but the American forces were unsuccessful.

THOUGHT QUESTION:

If the United States simultaneously went to war against Mexico and Germany in 1917, where would the bulk of the initial American military forces be deployed? Why?

BIOGRAPHIES

GEORGE SHERMAN CONNER (1864-1939). George S. Conner, prominent African-American physician of Waco during the early twentieth century, was born on April 6, 1864. The youngest of seven children, Conner's parents were free blacks residing in Blount County in eastern Tennessee. After his father died in 1866, his mother relocated the family from their farm to the town of Louisville in Blount County. The 1870 census shows five-year old George attending a local school. In 1876, he graduated from the Freedman's Normal Institute in Maryville and moved to Knoxville with his family. His mother continued to stress education for her children and enrolled George in Knoxville College, a Presbyterian school established to aid the blacks after the Civil War. In the early 1880s, the family began to go their separate ways. After graduation, Conner moved to Lewisville, Arkansas to teach school for two years. By 1885, he resided in Paris, Texas where he taught school, became a principal, and helped to organize black schools in the area. In 1887, Conner met and married Mattie Jackson, a teacher from Nashville, Tennessee.

After teaching for a few more years, Conner decided that he wanted to become a doctor. He applied and was admitted to Flint Medical College in New Orleans, Louisiana. In 1894, Conner became one of the 120 students to graduate from the small school during its twenty-two year existence. Admired and respected by administrators and fellow classmates, he was chosen to be class valedictorian. After graduation, he made a trip to Waco to visit a friend and soon chose the town as the site for his medical practice. The needs of the city's growing African-American population certainly contributed to his decision—Waco only had one black doctor at the time—but Conner must also have sensed the opportunity to become a leading member of the rising black middle class in the community.

By successfully becoming a physician, Conner was certainly in elite company. The 1900 census shows that Texas only had 136 black doctors in the entire state. (By contrast, there were close to 5,700 white doctors in Texas in 1900.) Nevertheless, he still had many obstacles to overcome: he was unknown to the people of Waco when he arrived; many blacks were reluctant to believe that any African-American doctor was qualified to treat their maladies; he had no automobile to service the community; and, due to his race, he was denied hospital privileges. Despite these realities, he built and maintained a solid practice and also prospered as a church and civic leader over the next four decades. For forty-four years, he served as the musical director for the choir and orchestra of the New Hope Baptist Church, in addition to providing guidance as a deacon and trustee. Conner also served as Grand Secretary of the local Masonic lodge and Treasurer of the United Brothers of Friendship fraternal club. As a sign of his prominence within the local black community, the doctor had the honor of hosting the African-American opera singer Marian Anderson in his home after she gave a concert at Baylor in 1939 just a few months before his death.

Conner never fathered any children but came to view the greater community as his extended family. After his first wife Mattie died in 1922, he spent a year in mourning before marrying Jeffie Obrea Allen, McLennan County's home demonstration agent for the Extension Service. While his wife was often away providing aid to local rural folk, Conner continued to prosper financially as a medical practitioner and emotionally by giving back to his community in a myriad of ways as a local leader. When he died on February 14, 1939, Conner left his wife an estate valued over $40,000. His life story demonstrates the potential for some African Americans to carve out a comfortable existence within the confines of the Jim Crow Era in Texas but also the strong need for education to often make such possibilities a reality.

MINNIE FISHER CUNNINGHAM (1882-1964). Prominent woman suffrage leader and long-time liberal activist Minnie Fisher Cunningham was born to a wealthy planter family on March 19, 1882 on Fisher Farms, near New Waverly, Texas. Her father, Horatio Fisher, was a prominent planter who served a term in the House of Representatives (1857-58). He introduced Minnie to politics by taking her with him to political meetings in nearby Huntsville. Educated at home by her mother, Minnie passed a state test to earn a teaching certificate when she was only sixteen. She taught for a year before enrolling in the University of Texas Medical Branch at Galveston, eventually becoming one of the first women to receive a degree in pharmacy in Texas. She worked at a Huntsville pharmacy for a year but grew unhappy at the large inequity in pay when compared to male pharmacists.

In 1902 she married Bill Cunningham, a lawyer and insurance executive who soon ran successfully for county attorney, providing Minnie with her first exposure to campaigning. The couple moved to Galveston in 1907, but their marriage was an unhappy one, due to her increasing political interests and his constant drinking. She began her political activities by joining the Women's Health Protective Association in Galveston, which centered on sanitization and beautification efforts after the massive 1901 hurricane, which devastated the city. In 1910 she was elected president of the Galveston Equal Suffrage Association and began touring the state for the woman suffrage cause. In 1915 she was elected to her first of four annual terms as president of the Texas Woman Suffrage Association (later known as the Texas Equal Suffrage Association). During her first year as president, the number of local chapters in Texas quadrupled. In 1917 she moved to Austin, opened state suffrage headquarters near the Capitol, and launched the campaign that resulted in legislative approval for woman suffrage in state primary elections. Cunningham and other suffragist leaders were able to garner success by carefully walking the line between assertiveness and deference when dealing with male politicians. They were able to convince many progressive-minded men that women could aid them in their reform efforts through the vote while still maintaining the traditional image of women as protectors of the home.

In 1919, Carrie Chapman Catt, president of the National American Woman Suffrage Association, persuaded Cunningham to lobby Congress for passage of the Nineteenth Amendment. When Congress obliged and sent the amendment to the states for ratification, Cunningham met with governors and a host of state politicians to urge ratification. She also helped to organize the National League of Women Voters and became its executive secretary.

In 1928, she became the first Texas woman to run for the United States Senate, challenging incumbent Earle Mayfield with a pro-prohibition and anti-Klan platform. She finished fifth of six candidates in the Democratic primary, then campaigned for the eventual winner Tom Connally. During the Great Depression she worked in College Station as an editor for the Texas A&M Extension Service and an information specialist for the Women's Division of the Agricultural Adjustment Administration.

She returned to Texas politics in 1944 when anti-Roosevelt forces (the so-called "Texas Regulars") at the Democratic Party state convention elected "uninstructed" delegates to the national convention. Outraged Roosevelt supporters responded by electing their own slate of delegates. Angered that the incumbent governor Coke Stevenson did not take a public stand on the split within the party, Cunningham, among other candidates, rose to challenge him. Though Stevenson won the primary by a large margin, Cunningham managed to finish second in a field of nine candidates.

In 1946 she retired to Fisher Farms in New Waverly to raise cattle and pecans, but she continued to support the Democratic Party and liberal causes for two more decades. When the University of Texas Board of Regents fired the school's president, Homer Rainey, she denounced the move and actively supported his unsuccessful bid for the governorship. After the U.S. Supreme Court's *Brown vs. Board of Education* decision, Cunningham supported desegregation at her local school board. In 1952 she campaigned for Adlai Stevenson's presidential bid and Ralph Yarborough's campaign for governor. Mortgaging her farm in order to ensure the maintenance of a liberal mouthpiece in Texas politics and society, Cunningham helped found the *Texas Observer* in 1954. Remaining politically active to the end, at the age of seventy-eight, she managed the local New Waverly campaign headquarters for John F. Kennedy 1960 presidential campaign. She died on December 9, 1964, and was buried in New Waverly.

PATTILLO HIGGINS (1863-1955). Pattillo Higgins, the initial driving force behind the vast discovery of oil under Spindletop Hill outside Beaumont, was born on December 5, 1863, in Sabine Pass, Texas. At the age of six, his family moved to Beaumont, where he attended school until the fourth grade when he began apprenticing with his father, a gunsmith. As a teenager, Higgins developed into a local troublemaker. When he was 17, his errant ways caught up with him as he became involved in a dispute with a sheriff deputy preventing Higgins from harassing a local black minister. When the deputy fired a warning shot over Higgins' head to show his earnestness, Higgins shot the deputy and killed him, but not before the deputy managed to shoot Higgins in the left arm. The wound later became infected, necessitating its amputation. At Higgins's trial, the wayward youth was able to convince the jury that he had fired in self-defense, so they acquitted him.

After the incident he went to work in various lumber camps along the Texas-Louisiana border. In 1885, Higgins attended a Baptist revival meeting that convinced him to abandon his raucous behavior and settle down in Beaumont as a respectable businessman. Having saved up some cash while working in the lumber camps, he established himself as a real estate broker. In 1886 he diversified by forming a brick manufacturing company. Higgins became interested in studying oil and gas because of their necessity to burn bricks evenly in his kiln. After a trip to Pennsylvania to learn about these fuels, he started to read everything he could about geology. The more he read, the more he became convinced that there very well could be oil and gas resources under Spindletop Hill, a salt-dome formation located on the outskirts of Beaumont. With the financial help of George Carroll, Higgins purchased about half of Spindletop, and they reached an agreement with George

Washington O'Brien who owned the other half. In August 1892 the men incorporated the Gladys City Oil, Gas and Manufacturing Company (named after Higgins's favorite Sunday School student) with Higgins serving as treasurer and general manager. The company drilled unsuccessfully for seven years, and the Gladys City directors doubted that they would ever recover their investments. Refusing to quit, Higgins started to place ads in newspapers and trade journals, seeking an engineer interested in developing the tract. Anthony Francis Lucas, a Croatian immigrant who had experience with salt-dome formations, responded and negotiated a lease in 1899 with Gladys City to drill on Spindletop.

After initial drilling failed and money ran low, Lucas ventured to Pittsburgh for financing. He entered into an agreement with Guffey and Galey, who had successfully developed Texas's first commercial oil field in Corsicana. They agreed to provide funds for more exploration, but the agreement heavily favored the creditors if any oil was discovered. In September 1900 Lucas signed a new twenty-year lease with Gladys City. On January 10, 1901, Lucas hit pay dirt when his crew punctured a hole in a massive deposit of oil about 1,000 feet below the surface—an estimated oil production of 100,000 barrels a day flowed from the well for nine days until capped.

After the gusher, Higgins sued Lucas and Gladys City Oil, Gas and Manufacturing Company for royalties (he had since left the company after a dispute with the other directors, but maintained an interest in the Spindletop venture). The parties settled out of court, followed by Higgins's formation of the Higgins Oil and Fuel Company centered on a 33-acre lease he maintained in the center of Spindletop Hill. His wells on the site would eventually produce twice the amount of oil as the original gusher. In 1902, East Texas lumber magnate John Henry Kirby was able to arrange a successful hostile takeover of Higgins's company, with Higgins selling out to Kirby for $3 million.

Higgins then created the Higgins Standard Oil Company, which explored other Texas Gulf Coast salt-dome fields. Over the next forty years, Higgins continued to engage in wildcatting. Though sometimes making small new discoveries, he was never able to duplicate his Spindletop success. He earned a reputation as a maverick, not only in the oil and gas community, but also in his personal life. Among other eccentricities, Higgins developed a habit of adopting orphaned girls and made one of them, Annie Johns, the sole heir to his fortune in 1905. A bachelor until he reached the age of forty-five, he married Annie in 1908 when she was eighteen. They eventually had three children. He died in San Antonio on June 5, 1955 at the age of ninety-two.

JOSÉ DE LA LUZ SÁENZ (1888–1953). The esteemed Tejano educator, World War I veteran, and civil rights activist José de la Luz Sáenz was born on May 17, 1888, in the rural South Texas community of Realitos. Following the death of her husband, his grandmother had brought the family to Texas from the Mexican border village of Mier during the 1870s. Sáenz's father performed ranch work while his mother tended to their home and six kids until she died in 1896. His father remarried four years later and moved the family to the nearby town of Alice for improved educational opportunities for his children. Sáenz attended segregated Mexican schools until his graduation from Alice High School in 1905. He then joined his father at a railroad work site and began his long career as an educator teaching the laborers' children during the day and the adult workers at night. After moving to San Antonio, he taught in segregated Mexican schools and obtained a full-time teaching certificate, which enabled him to teach and serve as principal in numerous South Texas school districts over the next several years. In 1915, Sáenz married María C. Múzquiz, but after she died within a year, he married his brother's widow, María Petra Esparza and began a family that would eventually have nine children.

Upon America's entry into World War I, Sáenz wanted to show his patriotism by volunteering for the United States military. He joined the U.S. Army in February 1918 and served as a private in the Intelligence Section, which allowed him the opportunity to use his language skills in English, Spanish, and French to process many of the documents coming through army headquarters. In 1933, Sáenz published *Los Mexico-Americanos en La Gran Guerra y Su Contingente en Pro de la Democracia, la Humanidad y La Justicia: Mi Diario Particular*, the only known Tejano World War I veteran diary ever to be published. Consisting of daily entries from his enlistment, service in France, and discharge in June 1919, Sáenz made a conscious effort to document without embellishment the common and unique experiences of the Mexican- and U.S.-born Hispanic soldiers that he encountered in order to note their contributions to the war effort and promote the call for equal rights at home after the war's conclusion. (In 2014, historian Emilio Zamora published an edited and translated version of the diary for Texas A&M University Press).

After the war, Saénz became an activist leader, working to create a statewide civil rights organization to overturn discrimination in the Lone Star State, an effort that bore fruit with the creation of the League of United Latin American Citizens (LULAC) in 1929. Sáenz authored the inaugural LULAC constitution and served on the federation's first board of trustees. Throughout the remainder of his life, Saénz publicized LULAC's efforts with countless articles in English and Spanish-language newspapers across the state. After his retirement from teaching, he received a bachelor's degree from Sul Ross State Teachers College. An elementary school in Alice, Texas, was named in honor for work as an educator and civil rights activist. He died in Corpus Christi on April 12, 1953 and is buried in the National Cemetery at Fort Sam Houston in San Antonio.

Chapter 13

The Rise of Urbanization, Expanding Opportunities, and the Invisible Empire, 1920-1929

A Texas Citizen Questions the Klan's Methods

During the 1920s, a second incarnation of the Ku Klux Klan appeared in Texas. In the Reconstruction Era, the Klan used violence to further its efforts to maintain white supremacy and overthrow the Republican state government. The new Klan of the early twentieth century emerged as an extreme reaction to modernity—seeking to prevent (by threats and violence if deemed necessary) societal acceptance of looser sexual morals, new risqué modes of dress, and the teachings of science over the preaching of Christian orthodoxy, not to mention interracial interaction and ideas of racial equality. While a large number of Texans joined the Klan in the first half of the 1920s, a majority balked at joining such a group, though as this anti-Klan letter to a Lubbock newspaper indicates, the organization's methods may have turned them off but their overall goals had many citizens' sympathies.

Other Side of K.K.K.

So much has been said from press and rostrum on the Ku Klux Klan, mostly excusing and encouraging them, that I feel it a citizen's duty to say something on the other side, especially to let the world know that at least one good citizen of Slaton does not endorse the K. K. K. methods. Deep, sober thinking forces the conclusion that if the K. K. K. with their past nature and methods continue to grow in popularity, our free democracy in all but name will end. For all elections, court actions, and most preaching will be subject to the will of the "Invisible Empire."

Yet, I am not greatly alarmed, as I see in the Ku Klux Klan, so far only an eruption on the body politic, caused by impurities and bad functioning which I think will soon be counteracted by better thinking. Thought, like the white corpuscles, some of us may have to make the supreme sacrifice.

The hope is that the cure comes before the Klan goes the way of corruption that all human empires go whether visible or invisible, whether German or Holy Roman, in spite of all declared righteous principles.

In opposition to the idea of empire, our government was born and bred, embodying the principles of liberty and equality of all men in law and the right of fair court trials which the Klan sets at naught. For the Klan to deny that they have dealt with citizens contrary to law in the face of scores of well known incidents like the Carrell killing in Oklahoma and the Peeler Clayton killing at Austin is absurd. And if they do nothing illegal their whole masquerading regalia is absurdly useless.

The only occasion there could have been for the Ku Klux Klan was when a large number of newly made citizens were turned loose on us who were too ignorant to appreciate a free government but superstitious enough to be ruled by crooks and goblins. With our intelligent citizens, among whom are the most dangerous criminals, such methods as that of the Ku Klux Klan will only engender resentments and resolves to meet force with force and cunning with cunning and devilment will be increased. Might, terror and intimidation never did and never will make right.

It is indeed hard for a reasoning mind to harmonize the idea of an "Invisible Empire" ruled by "Supreme Kleagles," and "Grand Goblins," and other royal spooks with 100 per cent Americanism. And the idea that our government needs the partnership or assistance of that "Empire" in its administrations would have been shocking to an American patriot.

I fear the Klan movement will weaken faith in our government. We could put out of business in a few hours the strongest bank in our town by starting agitation movements purporting to be necessary to make that bank efficient. The same psychology will apply in government. The Klan will suplant [sic] the government in the hearts of all who regard it as necessary to a proper rule.

All good citizens heartily endorse most of the principles publicly advocated by the Klan but many of us can reason to no other conclusion than that its nature and methods will tend exactly opposite to its purposes. There cannot be serious doubt that public sentiment so favorable to such deeds as the tar and feathering at Slaton tended to encourage the mob that shed blood at Wilson. And to doubt that such deeds will increase as the activities of the Ku Klux Klun increase is unnatural.

If the same citizens that compose the Ku Klux Klan would spend the same time and money and thought in combining and co-operating as American citizens in helping our government to be more efficient as they do as members of the "invisible empire" the results would be much better. Our government provides for secrecy in ferreting out wrongdoing and makes it the duty of every citizen to help enforce the law.

The excuse usually made in justification of [the] Ku Klux Klan is that our courts and juries are too lenient but the best that can be said of the Ku Klux is that they are the same material, or the same grade of material, that compose our juries and officials. Then why can't they deal with criminals the same law that they would in disguise and darkness. If the law will not permit proper action then correct the law. The answer is lack of moral courage. We are afraid if we boldly enforce the law we will be hurt in business or influence. Therefore we go under mask to do what we ought to do openly and thereby cultivate our cowardice. No race can maintain or gain supremacy except by building constitutional character which is done by performance of duty and that must not be done with supremacy as a purpose. To foster our cowardice with disguises will tend toward race inferiority instead of supremacy.

Can anyone conceive of Jesus Christ as being a Ku Klux Klan or acting behind a mask? But he did openly and boldly take the law in his own hand one time and whipped the gamblers out of the temple.

I claim that citizens even now should do likewise in certain circumstances.

If these suggestion for enforcing law and order be followed it will not be necessary to profanely ill divert the cross of Christ from being an emblem of meek and lowly sacrifice to a flaming emblem of terror and intimidation as did Constantine of another empire.

And likewise, the American Flag. With best feeling toward all Ku Klux Klan members.

W. P. FLORENCE

Source: *Lubbock Avalanche*, June 20, 1922

THOUGHT QUESTIONS:

1. What are the main objections that Mr. Florence has against the Klan's methods? To what did he believe that they would lead?

2. How did he use an example of the old, discredited version of Reconstruction to justify the existence of the original Klan during the 1860s and 1870s?

3. What are some ways that Mr. Florence expressed sympathy for the Klan even while condemning their methods?

Governor Pat Neff's Message to the 38th Legislature on the Establishment of a State Parks System

Governor Pat Neff considered the establishment of the State Parks Board to be one of his most important achievements. At its inception, the board received no appropriations from the legislature to purchase land; it could only solicit land through donations. By the 1930s, some land was added to the system in this manner, but much of the land remained idle until New Deal agencies such as the National Youth Administration, the Work Progress Administration, and especially the Civilian Conservation Corps began developing the parks within the system during the Great Depression. In this message, the governor called on the legislature to establish a state parks system for the benefit of the state.

May 1, 1923

TO THE MEMBERS OF THE THIRTY-EIGTH LEGISLATURE
SECOND CALLED SESSION

GENTLEMEN:

In the train of consequences following the development of the automobile and its wide and varied use, as the concurrent result of improved highways, is the response by all classes of our people to the "back to nature" call. Nothing is more conducive to the happiness and contentment of a people, a State's most valued asset, than for them to go "back to nature," where the bees hum, the birds sing, the brooks ripple, the breezes blow, and the flowers bloom. Here, spending their hours of recreation on blue-bonneted hills and daisy-decked meadows, in an atmosphere sweet with the perfume of flowers of a thousand hues, the old grow young, the sick regains health, and the weary enjoy a quiet rest. The health, welfare, and happiness of the people of Texas is largely enhanced by the number of places within her borders where the people in vacation and leisure periods can go for rest, recreation, and relaxation. Texas, by nature, is rich and radiant in scenic beauty spots peculiarly adapted in climate and environment to out-door life. These primeval and picturesque places of nature charm and characteristic beauty are rapidly disappearing before the onward march of cold, consuming commercialism. These places particularly suited for park and picnicking purposes should be preserved not only for the present, but for posterity. These camping and outing places, these rest and recreation resorts, these breathing spots for humanity where the weak, the weary, and the worn are nursed, in the lap of nature, back to health, wealth, and happiness, should be established along our highways, and scattered throughout the State wherever trees grow and water runs.

By the establishment of a system of parks and camping places throughout the State, we will make of Texas the mecca for automobile-tourists, and bequeath to posterity a most valuable legacy.

In keeping, therefore, with the foregoing thought, I recommend that there be created by this Legislature, a state parks committee, composed of six members to serve without compensation, said committee to be charged with the duty of soliciting donations of land in tracts large or small to be converted by said committee into public parks, said committee to be also charged with the duty of investigating and locating tracts of land, large or small, suited for public park purposes, and reporting said findings and all data concerning said tracts of land to each regular session of the Legislature to the end that Texas, by either donations of land, or acquisition by purchase of same, may establish, before it is too late to do so, a system of state parks where the rank and file of the people of Texas and elsewhere may go and forget the anxieties, the strife, and vexations of life's daily business grind.

Respectfully submitted,
PAT NEFF
Governor

Source: Texas State Library and Archives Commission

THOUGHT QUESTIONS:

1. What specific benefits did Governor Neff see for Texas if the Legislature created a system of state parks for its citizens?

2. What connections did Neff make between the recent availability of the automobile for many Texans and a new state parks system?

3. How is the tone of Neff's often lofty rhetoric revealed in this address?

The President of the Texas League of Women Voters Supports Miriam Ferguson in the 1924 Democratic Primary for Governor

The 1924 Democratic gubernatorial primary heavily divided the party. After the initial primary, a runoff ensued between the Ku Klux Klan's choice, Felix Robertson, and Miriam Ferguson, the wife of the impeached and resigned former governor who many correctly suspected was merely using his wife's name on the ballot to make a bid to return to power. The choice between a Klansman and a Ferguson gave many Democrats, including Jesse Daniel Ames, the President of the Texas League of Women Voters, much to think about. Eventually, many Democrats like Ames threw their support toward Ferguson (the winner) largely as a vote of the lesser of two evils. In this excerpt from her response to Northwestern University Political Science professor Perley O. Ray's letter seeking her views on the party's choices, Ames explains her reluctant position.

Georgetown, Texas
August 30, 1924

My Dear Mr. Ray:

Your letter has been sitting on my desk since Monday, unanswered but not forgotten. I have been in doubt about our question and even now I answer only from my desires bolstered up possibly, by some foundation in fact I supported Mrs. Ferguson in the second primary even to the extent of speaking for her. I was not at all sure that the University might not be damaged, but the chances seemed slight and besides I felt there was something else in the state in addition to the University. The opposition, Mr. Robertson, was bad in every way besides that of being the candidate of the Ku Klux. And he was brought out by the Klan.

. . . Mr. Robertson was never heard of except as favorable to the Breweries in 1905, until the Klan of Dallas County made him police judge of Dallas. Then later they elected him District Judge. His personal character lacked much of being good. The Klan had taken over the Democratic Party in Texas, which means of course the state of Texas. The appointive power of the Governor is immense. In four years he would have appointed six of nine Regents of the University and the same number of all other state institutions. Following the tactics of the Klan in the past, no one but Klansmen would be appointed and no one but Klansmen would be permitted on the faculty. You may recall that our last legislature passed a law requiring a certain affirmation of religious faith for all faculty members and did something or other about the theory of evolution in the curriculum. The judiciary and both judges and District attorneys are filled by appointment of the Governor. Since the Klan has been in control of Dallas County, there has not been a single arrest of a Klansman if he were known to be one, and no convictions when such an accident occurred. The Klan would have been in power for twenty years at least.

The Fergusons announce that it is for one term only. If they proposed damaging the schools, they could not do so for only a third of the regents would be their appointees.

Besides Mrs. Ferguson has clearly indicated, I am enclosing an article for your consideration, that she intends no fight on the schools. She is seeking vindication, not vengeance, this she has said repeatedly in the press. Vindication means that she must make a record for herself as a good governor. It is the only way that they can prove that they have been under a cloud unfairly. It is possible that she will seek to restore Jim's status. It is only natural to assume that she will and only natural that she should want to. It is my opinion that she intends now to give us as good an administration that we have had in years. But we must pull to-gether and not fight what may happen. We must wait until it happens, since in a way it is all we can do. Mrs. Ferguson will be our next Governor, or rather, Jim will through her. We cannot avoid that. But if the best people will get behind them and help and advise until it is no longer possible to do so, then I believe it will come to be the people's government. Mr. Ferguson proposes some drastic cuts in the machinery of the state. Some of them I regret exceedingly because they aim to injure the public health work. One, if he carries it out, will put our Sheppard-Towner [a federal law passed in 1921 which provided for federally financed instruction in maternal and infant health care and gave 50-50 matching funds to individual states to build clinics to assist women with pre-natal care] health out of commission. This you know, I hate. But it is and was a question in my mind, as to the greater ill—the Klan or Ferguson. Then there are many things the Fergusons will do that will be held against them because they are the Fergusons. That will be unfair and unjust. . . .

Finally, I have called on Mrs. Ferguson. She is devoted to her husband. She will be largely if not entirely influenced by him at first, and possibly all the way through. She is a bit vindictive and somewhat bitter, which is natural, but Mr. Ferguson does not seem to be. I think our opportunity to help unobtrusively and without hope of reward, is very great. We who helped impeach Mr. Ferguson and later have talked about him all over the state, can expect to do nothing more than that, but that will be much.

Sincerely yours,
Jessie Daniel Ames

Source: Texas State Library and Archives Commission

THOUGHT QUESTIONS:

1. What fears did Ames relate if Felix Robertson were elected governor in 1924?

2. In what ways did Ames try to explain away the many doubts that many individuals (including Dr. Ray) had about Ferguson's candidacy?

3. To what extent did Ames believe that Miriam Ferguson's administration would be influenced by her husband?

A Supporter Writes Governor Miriam Ferguson
Concerning Her Pardoning Policies

From the beginning of her term in office, Governor Miriam Ferguson pledged to adopt a liberal pardoning policy, citing the reduced cost to taxpayers among other reasons. The governor had the power to grant convicted felons several types of clemency, including pardons, paroles, and furloughs. On average, Ma Ferguson pardoned an average of 100 convicts a month, for a total of over 2000 during her first term. As this letter from a mercantile company worker indicates, even many Ferguson supporters were alarmed by the number of pardons issued to violent criminals, especially with unproven allegations in the media and elsewhere that the governor and her husband Jim were accepting bribes in return for grants of clemency.

April 17, [19]25
Mrs. M.A. Furgerson, Gov.

Dear Gov'.

While I have all along, been an ardent Furgerson Suporter, yet I have never had an inclination to meddle and this is not my mishion now but solely to flash the red light as a signal of danger, many of your surporters every where under the laod of the prison reckord you have been making for the past two or three months and the opposition are keeping quiet but saying "I told you so." While I have no desire to stand in the way of any ones freedom but don't you think you are going too strong on this line for the good of good government, the only way we can answer is with a dry grin, it looks to me as though its putting clubs in the hands of the Ku-Klux and others who oppose and if a riot starts many of you ardent supporters will be at a disadvantage to do any real good. While I think Jim was right in his university shuffle but this is a far different kind of issue from the above, be carefull else we loose all and give the high Collars an excuse to say that persons of our rank incabble of being in such high places.

Now if you could get a hustle on the board of control and get them to release the victoms in the asylams who cant get out, you would certainly be going in the right direction that no one could dispute. I have just a statement in the Star-Telagram of the 14th that the Head man of the Rockafelow instutute, saying the Profeshion knew but very little more about the working of the mind and the nervious system than they did in the middle ages, this is the stand I [have] taken when I fought the Sychopathic instutions of Dallas and Galvestion.

Yours Truly,
A.G. Love

Source: Texas State Library and Archives Commission

THOUGHT QUESTIONS:

1. What reasons does this Ferguson supporter cite to explain his concern with the governor's liberal pardoning policy?

2. What were his opinions about the government maintaining state mental institutions? Why do you think he held that view?

3. Given the attitude of the Fergusons toward Prohibition, explain how the governor's pardoning policy helped to undermine enforcement of that law.

A Citizen Writes Dan Moody about the Governor's Prohibition Stand

In 1928, Houston publisher Jesse Jones persuaded the Democratic Party to hold their national convention in Houston, the first time since the Civil War that a major party convention had been held in the South. The party entered the convention deeply divided between their rural southern Protestant wing strongly supportive of Prohibition and the emerging urban, Catholic, and anti-Prohibition faction. The Governor of New York, Al Smith, a Catholic who was rabidly anti-Prohibition won the nomination, much to the chagrin of most Texas Democrats. Governor Dan Moody led an effort to put a "bone-dry" Prohibition plank in the party's official platform. Moody became known across the country when the meeting of the platform committee was broadcast nationally over the radio, though he lost the fight when the party instead adopted a plank pledging merely "honest enforcement" of the Constitution.

Moody found himself in a tight spot. Campaigning for Smith would jeopardize his pro-Prohibition credentials. If he refused to help Smith, many Democrats would accuse the young governor of betraying his party. Eventually, Moody took a neutral stance by neither campaigning for Smith nor repudiating him. In the end, Smith's opponent Herbert Hoover took advantage of the divided Democrats by carrying Texas, the first Republican ever to do so. The following letter to Moody comes from a California citizen who heard Moody's efforts over the radio.

Huntington Park, Calif.
2424 E. Live Oak St.

July 3, 1928

Gov. Dan Moody,
Austin, Tex.

Dear Governor:
    Heard you twice via radio at the Houston convention. From the political aspect of the question it seemed at the moment that you did right not to bring in a minority report

on Prohibition. I believe, however, that Gov. Smith's injecting the question into his reply upon the nomination at the hands of the convention has given another aspect to the question.

This morning's paper infers that you are going to stick with Smith. I have admired your record and shall regret it, if that is true. A man in politics has as much right to bolt a candidate, as the candidate has to bolt the platform.

Gov. Smith has been a "nullificationist" in New York, of the 18th Amendment. It has become a trite saying to speak of America as consisting of the United States and New York.

For over twenty years I have voted the Democratic ticket, but it will be necessary for me to "part company" this fall. Tennessee is my home and Cordell Hull is a friend of mine. Gov. McMillan, Harvey, and others have rendered valued service for democracy. But there is a determined effort to have a "Prohibition fight" and I think it is well that it has come this year instead of at a later date.

As I see it, the campaign this fall is to be one of great moral upheaval. America has set its face to better days, and will not turn back. There is a feeling among some of our leaders that one is at liberty to obey the laws he likes, and disobey the one he does not. That is not democratic and it is not American.

I have confidence that you will move in the right direction during this campaign.

Sincerely,
T.M. Burgess

Source: Texas State Library and Archives Commission

THOUGHT QUESTIONS:

1. What are the writer's attitudes toward Governor Moody upon reading a newspaper report that Moody was going to stick with the nominee Al Smith?

2. What are the writer's general attitudes toward Smith?

3. How does this letter show the divisiveness of the Prohibition issue for the Democratic Party during the 1920s?

Legendary Texas Ranger Frank Hamer Reports to Governor Moody on the Sherman Race Riot

The Sherman Riot of 1930 was one of the major outbreaks of racial violence in the United States and brought international notoriety to Texas race relations. The crisis began with an accusation of rape of a white woman by an African American male. The accused, a farmhand named George Hughes, was arrested and scheduled for trial within a week of the incident. Meanwhile, a mob gathered each night outside the jail.

On May 9, 1930, Texas Ranger Frank Hamer (later to become famous for ambushing the famous killers Bonnie and Clyde) escorted Hughes to trial at the county courthouse. A huge crowd packed the courthouse building and surrounding grounds. When District Judge R.M. Carter attempted to start the trial, the crowd forced open the courtroom doors to get at the prisoner before being turned back by the Rangers.

The Rangers were flushed out when someone threw a can of gasoline into a broken window and the courthouse caught fire. Fearful for his life, Hughes demanded to remain locked in the courthouse vault where he was being held. The mob held back firemen and cut their hoses. Within an hour, the building was gutted, with only the walls and the vault remaining. The mob tried to break open the vault and skirmished with National Guardsmen who had been sent to Sherman by Governor Dan Moody. Just before midnight, they succeeded in breaking open the vault and removing Hughes's body. The crazed crowd, now numbering over 5000, dragged his body behind a car, hanged it from a tree, and set it on fire. The mob then burned down black businesses, preventing the fire department from putting out the flames.

When the violence continued after Moody dispatched more National Guard units, the governor declared martial law in Sherman for the next two weeks. Fourteen men were eventually indicted for crimes connected to the riot, but only two were convicted and sentenced to two-year terms. The riot attracted international publicity and condemnation. In the following letter sent to Governor Moody, Frank Hamer reports on the beginning of the troubles and his attempt to protect the prisoner from the mob.

May 13, 1930
Hon Dan Moody, Governor, State of Texas.

In compliance with your request, I am herewith furnishing you with a statement in regards to the trouble at Sherman, as per your order. On May 7th, Sgt. Wheatley, Rangers J.E. McCoy, J.W. Aldrich and myself left Austin at 4:25 P.M., for Sherman, Texas to report to the District Judge for duty, to be on hand in District Court in which George Hughes, negro, was to be tried for assault on a white woman in Grayson County, a few days before. On the morning of the 9th of May the negro was brought into the court room, the jury was empanelled, the trial proceeded to get under way. It was while the first State witness was on the stand testifying, that the crowd made a rush on the District Court room to get the prisoner and in their attempt to do so, two double doors opening into a hallway near the District Court room were broken down. The District Judge ordered the prisoner locked up in the District Attorney's vault and then we immediately proceeded to disperse the mob which we did by the use of our guns, without firing, and tear gas bombs. The District Judge and other officials then decided that a change of venue should be ordered in the case. The crowd made two other attempts to rush the court room on the second floor and was beaten back each time.

I instructed my men that the next time they rushed the court-house that I would fire on the mob, but for them to hold their fire until I gave orders to shoot. In a few minutes the mob attempted to rush the court room again, coming up the stairway and I fired a shot-gun loaded with buckshot, wounding two men, so it was reported to us, this stopped the mob. I had heard a number of them say prior to the time that I fired on them, that "you can't shoot us." It never occurred to me what they meant until a newspaper man came up stairs and showed me a message that he said he had received over the A.P. wires reading as from the Governor, "protect the negro if possible, but do not shoot anybody." I informed him that I had received no such message, however, at this time, this report seemed to have been well circulated among the crowd.

I saw the District Judge and told him about the report and informed him that I didn't believe the Governor would issue such orders, because we probably could not hold the prisoner if such order was issued. One of the agitators walked to the foot of the stairway and asked me if I was going to give the prisoner up to them, I told him we were not, he says "well we are coming up to get him," I said "any time you feel lucky, come on, but when you start up the stairway once more, there is going to be many funerals in Sherman." For twenty or thirty minutes, things were quiet.

They started brakeing [sic] out windows down stairs, the sheriff and deputies had previously gone down stairs, leaving myself and men to guard the negro and the stairways, then all at once the flames from the lower story of the courthouse swept up the stairways and on up to the ceiling over our heads to the second floor and myself and men barely escaped the burning building. The flames cut us off from the vault and we could not have opened the vault if we could have gotten to it, as we did not know the combination, so we came out and down into the crowd. Flames from the burning building was pushing everybody off the square.

Among the crowd were many women and children. We stood around a few minutes. I thought it necessary for me to communicate with you, as I heard the troops were on their way. Not caring to discuss this with you from Sherman, we were talking to a man and I asked him if he had a car, he said he did, I asked him to drive us to Howe, from which point I called you. While waiting there for a second message from you, I heard the operator say to someone over the phone, "I am glad they burned the courthouse." Thinking probably that you might have something to say over the phone, not for the public, we drove down to McKinney and waited there for further communication. At no time did

I tell anyone that I had received a message from you ordering me not to shoot anybody and when I fired on the crowd in their last attempt to rush the courtroom, we had them whipped off and they could not have taken the prisoner from us in any way only by burning the courthouse as they did and we never dreamed of the gang doing that until the building was enveloped in flames.

The man that advised me as to the message coming over the wires, I do not know his name but it will be no trouble to learn his identity.

Respectfully submitted,
Frank A. Hamer
Captain, State Rangers

Source: Statement from Frank Hamer, May 13, 1930, Records of Dan Moody, Texas Office of the Governor, Archives and Information Services Division, Texas State Library and Archives Commission.

THOUGHT QUESTIONS:

1. According to his report, to what lengths did Hamer go to protect the prisoner?

2. Why did the mob believe that Hamer would not open fire upon them if he felt compelled to do so?

3. Did Hamer have any idea that the mob would go to the extent of burning down their own courthouse to get to the prisoner? Why or why not?

Looking Backward

Credit: Library of Congress, Laura E. Foster, artist
Illustration in *Life* magazine, August 22, 1912.

This cartoon shows a woman at the top of a staircase with steps labeled "Loneliness," "Anxiety," "Suffrage" and "Career," approaching a stand labeled "Fame," as she looks back at children holding out flowers standing on lower steps labeled "Home," "Children," "Marriage," and "Love."

THOUGHT QUESTION:

What is the message of this cartoon?

BIOGRAPHIES

ANNIE WEBB BLANTON (1870-1945). An educator, woman suffragist, and the first woman in Texas elected to statewide office, Annie Webb Blanton was born on August 19, 1870, in Houston. One of her brothers, Thomas Lindsay Blanton, represented a district in central West Texas in the U.S. House of Representatives from 1917 to 1936. After graduating from La Grange High School in 1886, she taught in Fayette County before moving to Austin to teach elementary and secondary schools after her father's death in 1888. Teaching provided her with necessary income as she studied at the University of Texas. From 1901 to 1918, Blanton taught English at North Texas State Normal College (now the University of North Texas) in Denton. As a member of the faculty, she published a series of grammar textbooks while writing forcefully in favor of equal rights for women.

After women obtained the right to vote in Texas primaries, Texas suffragists asked Annie Blanton to run for state superintendent of public instruction, and she accepted. The campaign proved to be quite harsh, with accusations that Blanton was everything from an atheist to the puppet of special interests. She responded by lumping the incumbent with the former resigned governor, James Ferguson. In the July 1918 primary, the first in which Texas women exercised their voting rights, Blanton defeated the incumbent and another rival by a large margin. Her general election triumph in November made her the first woman in Texas elected to a statewide office.

During her tenure as state superintendent, Blanton established a system of free textbooks, received a revision of teacher certification laws, raised teacher salaries, and made efforts to improve rural education. She was reelected in 1920 and served as state superintendent through 1922. Instead of seeking a third term, she ran unsuccessfully for a congressional seat. Blanton returned to the University of Texas to receive her master's degree, taught in the UT education department until 1926, then left to earn her Ph.D. from Cornell University. She returned to the University of Texas in 1927 and remained a highly-regarded education professor there until her death on October 2, 1945.

MORRIS SHEPPARD (1875-1941). John Morris Sheppard, United States senator and sponsor of the Eighteenth (Prohibition) Amendment, was born near Wheatville in Morris County, Texas, on May 28, 1875. His father served many years as a district attorney and district judge before being elected to two terms in the U.S. House of Representatives. Morris was named after an ancestor of his mother's, Robert Morris, a signer of the Declaration of Independence and the Constitution. In 1891 Sheppard enrolled at the University of Texas where he excelled as a student. After earning his bachelor's degree in 1895 he began attending the university law school. Upon graduation he attended Yale University, earned a master of law degree, and began practicing law in his father's firm.

In 1902 Sheppard ran for Congress and won the seat once held by father who had recently passed away. By 1912 he acquired the reputation of a skilled and entertaining orator on the House floor and on the stump for fellow Democrats and many Progressive issues around the country. In 1913 Sheppard won election to the U.S. Senate. Highly supportive of Woodrow Wilson, Sheppard actively worked for the new president's policies on tariff reduction, war preparedness, and, after World War I, the League of Nations. He also supported other popular Progressive reforms, such as rural credit programs, child labor laws, antitrust regulations, and woman suffrage.

Prohibition of alcoholic beverages increasingly became Sheppard's highest priority. As far back as 1913, he had supported a constitutional amendment to ban the sale of liquor. In March 1917 he authored a law abolishing the sale of liquor in the District of Columbia. On April 4, 1917, the day Congress declared war on Germany, Sheppard introduced the Senate resolution for the prohibition amendment. By the end of 1917 the measure passed the House, and by 1919 the Eighteenth Amendment gained the required three-fourths approval of the states necessary for ratification. Sheppard also helped to write the Volstead Act, which outlined details concerning the enforcement of the eighteenth Amendment.

Sheppard remained politically active throughout the 1920s and 1930s. Among his more noteworthy achievements, in 1921 he co-authored the Sheppard-Towner Act, which provided federal funding for maternity and child care clinics on a matching basis with the states. Although the law lapsed in 1929, some of the ideas within the legislation found their way into the Social Security Act of 1935. By 1929, Sheppard rose high enough in the leadership to become Senate Democratic whip. During the Great Depression, he strongly supported most of Franklin Roosevelt's early New Deal initiatives (except, of course, the repeal of prohibition which took place with the ratification of the Twenty-First Amendment.) In 1934, Sheppard became the most senior member of Congress and authored the Federal Credit Union Act, which established the nation's non-profit cooperative credit union system. Sheppard furthered his pro-Roosevelt credentials when he supported the president's so-called "court packing" efforts to reform the U.S. Supreme Court.

During his last term, Sheppard became increasingly involved in foreign affairs. As chairman of the Military Affairs Committee, he worked on increasing defense spending, supported veteran aid bills, and fought for passage of the Selective Service and Lend-Lease Acts. On April 9, 1941, Sheppard died from a brain hemorrhage. In a lively special election campaign, Governor Wilbert Lee "Pappy" O'Daniel defeated Lyndon B. Johnson before winning a full term the next year. Nevertheless, O'Daniel's subsequent lackluster performance as senator stood in marked contrast to Morris Sheppard's long-standing record of achievement.

LAWRENCE A. NIXON (1884-1966). Lawrence Aaron Nixon, an African-American physician and voting-rights advocate, was born in Marshall, Texas. He graduated from Wiley College in Marshall and received his M.D. degree in 1906 from Meharry Medical College in Nashville, Tennessee. He began to practice medicine to the black community of Cameron in Milam County. In 1909 ten black men were lynched in Texas. One of these murders occurred in Cameron and compelled Nixon to become involved in civil rights issues. The month after the lynching, he moved to El Paso with his wife and infant son. There he began a successful medical practice, helped to found the Myrtle Avenue Methodist Church, and helped to establish the local chapter of the National Association for the Advancement of Colored People (NAACP).

In 1923 the Texas legislature passed a law prohibiting blacks from voting in Democratic primaries. In July 1924, with the help of the NAACP, Nixon took his poll-tax receipt to a Democratic primary polling place and was refused a ballot. This rejection formed the basis of his first legal challenge against the state's white primary law. In the Supreme Court's 1927 *Nixon v. Herndon* decision, all of the justices concurred that the state of Texas had unlawfully deprived Nixon of his rights under the Fourteenth Amendment to the U.S. Constitution. When the legislature wrote a new law giving a political party's executive committee the power to determine party membership and eligibility to participate in its primaries, Nixon sued again and triumphed again in the *Nixon v. Condon* decision.

Though Nixon's cases rocked the boat, his efforts did not sink the system. Ultimately the Court allowed (in *Grovey v. Townshend*) the Texas state legislature to pass a law allowing the Democratic Party's state convention to adopt a resolution excluding black from voting in its primaries. Nevertheless, Nixon's efforts laid the groundwork for subsequent legal challenges that finally culminated in a new Supreme Court to outlaw white primaries entirely in the 1944 *Smith v. Allwright* decision. On July 22, 1944, Dr. Nixon calmly entered the same El Paso voting place where years earlier he had been denied admittance and voted in a Democratic Party primary.

In l955, Nixon became a member of the previously all-white Texas State Medical Association and the El Paso County Medical Society. He retired in l963 and died from injuries sustained in an automobile accident on March 6, 1966, just as the dramatic changes of the Civil Rights Movement were beginning to become realized.

JANE MCCALLUM (1877–1957). Woman suffragist leader, reform lobbyist, and two-time Texas secretary of state Jane Yelvington McCallum was born on December 30, 1877, in La Vernia, Texas. Her father, a Wilson County sheriff, sent her to local public schools before arranging her attendance at a woman's college in Mississippi. In 1896, she married Arthur McCallum, a teacher recently arrived from North Carolina then serving as school superintendent in La Vernia. She moved with him to a few posts in South Texas before they achieved stability in 1903, when he began serving as the city's school superintendent for the next four decades. The couple had a daughter and four sons, but family life did not stifle her growing interest in politics.

McCallum began her political activities by campaigning locally for prohibition and woman suffrage. In October 1915, she was elected president of the Austin Women's Suffrage Association and began working for Minnie Fisher Cunningham, the president of the Texas Equal Suffrage Association, to coordinate a statewide suffrage campaign by serving as both the publicity manager for the proposed Texas state constitutional amendment on full suffrage and the chair of the ratification committee for the parallel federal amendment effort. To promote woman suffrage, McCallum delivered numerous speeches and wrote a recurring column supporting full suffrage in the Austin *American* newspaper.

After the suffrage movement achieved its success, McCallum began to focus her energies on a variety of social and political reforms. After state superintendent Annie Webb Blanton organized a "Better Schools" Amendment to the state constitution to repeal existing taxation limits and thus allow localities to potentially improve funding for public schools through increased levies, McCallum agreed to serve as publicity chairman. Patterned after World War I loan drives, the effort utilized county organizations, lecturers, posters, newspaper advertisements, and automobile stickers to spread the word to the public. Voters approved the measure by almost a two-to-one margin in November 1920. From 1923 to 1925, she served as executive secretary of the Women's Joint Legislative Council, an alliance of six women's groups lobbying for prison and educational reform bills, stricter prohibition enforcement, state funding for maternal and child health care, and the end of child labor. Though not always successful, the efforts of the "Petticoat Lobby" of female activists, as opponents dubbed them, were nevertheless an influential force for enduring progressive reform during the 1920s. McCallum campaigned for Dan Moody's 1926 run for governor against Miriam Ferguson. Moody appointed her to be the state's first female secretary of state in January 1927, a position that she continued to hold under Governor Ross Sterling from 1931 to 1933. Shortly after assuming office in 1927, during an audit of state government holdings, she discovered an original copy of the Texas Declaration of Independence in a vault of the state Capitol and soon endeavored to restore the document for public display. Her collection of biographical sketches of early American leaders, *Women Pioneers*, was published in 1929.

McCallum remained active in civic affairs throughout her life. During the 1940s, she was appointed to the first Austin city planning commission, led a protest against the firing of University of Texas president Homer P. Rainey, and continued to write a weekly column on women's issues every Sunday for the Austin *American-Statesman*. She died on August 14, 1957, and was buried in Oakwood Cemetery in Austin. Three years before her death, McCallum took part in breaking another gender barrier. After Texas voters approved a state constitutional amendment in 1954 allowing females on juries, she agreed to serve as the first woman grand jury commissioner for Travis County.

Chapter 14

The Great Depression and the New Deal, 1929-1940

Louisiana Governor Huey Long Invites Texas Governor Ross Sterling to the New Orleans Cotton Conference to Discuss the Cotton Holiday Plan

With the onset of the Great Depression, politicians and private citizens offered countless plans to counter the economic downturn. In 1931, Governor Huey Long of Louisiana led the "Cotton Holiday" movement to deal with plummeting cotton prices. Long stipulated that the plan would not go into effect until 75 percent of the South cotton-growing acreage was taken out of production, thus all eyes pointed to Texas. If the Lone Star State did not adopt the law then there would be no Cotton Holiday for the South because Texas produced one-third of the nation's cotton crop. Governor Ross Sterling opposed the proposal, as did a majority of the Texas Legislature, so the Long Plan was never attempted. The downward slide in cotton prices would continue for two more years until the Agricultural Adjustment Administration was created in the first year of Franklin Roosevelt's presidency.

In this telegram to the Texas governor, Long invites Sterling to New Orleans to discuss the Cotton Holiday Plan with representatives from other cotton-growing states. Sterling eventually sent the state's agricultural commissioner James E. McDonald to go in his place.

August 17, 1931
Hon. Ross S. Sterling:

We can restore the prosperity of the South and materially the balance of the world within less than two weeks time if the cotton-producing states have governors and other officials who have the courage to act now and decisively.

The only way that this can be done is to prohibit by law at once the raising of a single bale of cotton in all cotton growing states during the year 1932. The farmers yet have their cotton and if action is immediately taken along this line they will get the benefit of the price that will result from this move. If such action be taken by all the states immediately the farmers will get more money for this year's crop alone than they will get for this and the next two cotton crops they raise. A condition of near bankruptcy to a large part of our population and industries can be avoided if the officials of the southern states are willing to act now. . . .

I am issuing this call to ask all the governors, lieutenant governors, congressmen and senators of the cotton growing states to meet here in New Orleans on this Friday the twenty first of August to organize for immediate steps to avoid cotton raising in America next year. Meeting at the Roosevelt Hotel at 10 o'clock in the morning.

With this year's crop we will have a surplus to carry over 15,000,000 bales for next year. With this condition we are going to have no market at all. If we will stop the cotton raising altogether we will afford a market for what we now have and next year we will still have all that the world can use. The Lord told us to lay off raising these crops one year out of seven to let people have time to consume them.

Louisiana will pass this law if other states will join us. Wire me at once that you will attend.

I think I am lawyer enough to tell you that the laws I have in mind are valid and sound and will do the work that will save your state. Will you not come here and let's get to work on something that actually settles the cotton trouble?

Please issue notice to your farmers to gather their cotton and sell none of it until the result of this meeting is accomplished, because we want the benefit to go to the farmer. When that is accomplished all business prospers.

Huey P. Long
Governor and U.S. Senator-Elect

Source: Texas State Library and Archives Commission

THOUGHT QUESTIONS:

1. According to Long, how would farmers benefit from his plan if they were not to raise any cotton in 1932?

2. According to Long, how soon would it take for the cotton holiday's benefits to begin to be seen by farmers?

3. What did Long say about the legal ability for states to pass legislation along these lines?

A Protest Against the Imposition of Martial Law by Governor Ross Sterling

On the same today he received Huey Long's invitation to attend the New Orleans Cotton Conference, Governor Ross Sterling announced the declaration of martial law in the East Texas Oil Field and ordered over 1,000 National Guardsmen and Texas Rangers into the region. In addition to establishing general control over the area, the troops and law enforcement officers were expected to reduce the distribution of so-called "hot oil" – or oil produced above the strict quotas established by the Texas Railroad Commission. On February 2, 1932, the Texas Supreme Court ended martial law in the East Texas Oil Field when it declared that the governor's actions were illegal. While some had applauded the governor's action, others opposed it, including the writer of the following letter, R. M. Farrar, the president of Union National Bank in Houston.

August 19, 1931

My Dear Governor:

If I read correctly the history of Texas, excepting on in the RECONSTRUCTION ERA is there recorded such extreme usurpation of power by the Governor as is involved in your recent declaration of martial law.

To me, as a citizen, the reasons assigned, namely, "RIOT, INSURRECTION, REBELLION, TUMULT," are even more amazing.

Every man, woman and child in the State is probably of the opinion that the real purpose is to increase the price of oil, and if our Government is henceforth to concern itself with such subjects it will have, indeed, immeasurably enlarged the complications and scope of Government – and in the experiences of mankind through the ages on down to the present, all such attempts have ended in disaster, I believe, without a single exception.

When I read of your action I recalled the headlines of the story on Hidalgo County in "Collier's" [Magazine] a year or two ago – "HIGH HANDED AND HELL BENT" – and I am wondering if the large majority of citizens do not, in fact, feel likewise.

You have certainly gone far afield with an innovation which may plague us all for a generation – yourself included.

If our Governor may appropriately use the military forces of the State in behalf of the producers of oil, he may, in the opinion of most of us, do likewise in the interest of other producers – from corn, cotton, cattle and lumber to chewing gum, automobiles, sewing machines and mules.

Yours very truly,
R. M. Farrar

Source: Texas State Library and Archives Commission

THOUGHT QUESTIONS:

1. According to Farrar, how often had governors declared martial law within the state? Did he imply that this was something done too often or very rarely?

2. What did the banker state was the governor's "real purpose" being the declaration of martial law?

3. In the end, why did Farrar oppose the governor's actions?

A Citizen Writes Governor James Allred to Oppose the Appointment of Sarah Hughes to a State District Court Judgeship

Sarah Tilghman Hughes was born in Baltimore, Maryland. After a stint as a science teacher, she attended George Washington University Law School, earning a law degree while working on the Washington, D.C., police force. She married a classmate, George Hughes from Palestine, Texas, and moved to Dallas to begin a private law practice. Hughes became one of the first women elected to the Texas House of Representatives. In 1935, Governor Allred appointed her to a vacancy on the Fourteenth District Court in Dallas, making her the first woman state district judge in Texas. In 1936, she was elected to the position and continued to serve as district judge until 1961, when President John F. Kennedy named her to the federal bench. Judge Hughes became a national figure on November 22, 1963, when she administered the oath of office to Lyndon Johnson on Air Force One following the assassination in Dallas of President Kennedy.

Though coming fifteen years after the passage of the 19th Amendment, Allred's appointment of Hughes to the state district court was, nevertheless, controversial. While many male and female Texans supported the move, others, such as State Senator Claud Westerfeld of Dallas (who said that Hughes as a married woman "ought to be home washing dishes") and the writer of the following letter, strongly opposed it.

Frijole, Culberson County, Texas,
Feb. 5th, 1935.

Hon. James V. Allred
Governor of Texas,
Austin, Texas.

Dear Sir:

The papers are telling of your appointing a woman to a Judgeship in Dallas and I take the liberty, which I consider is the privilege of any tax payer in our state, to urge you to not continue the practice of appointing women to high positions in the state. I had a mother whose memory I revere, I have a wife whom I loved to the extent of living with her for over 28 years and we raised three fine daughters now grown to womanhood, so I have had some experience with women, intimately. And I tell you now, Governor, that when you have lived another score years you will learn that a woman is always a woman first and Governor or Judge or this or that next. This Dallas woman may know the Law, she may have unusual ability, but she or no other woman is fit to sit on the bench and judge her fellow man. Her personal dislikes will enter into the case before her, frequently, and you know, from your experiences as an attorney that that is not the desired conditions in our Courts. Justice, you know, is supposed to be blind.

Our good president, Mr. Roosevelt, whom I greatly admire and whom I consider a real blessing to the United States at this time, has made the mistake too many times of appointing a woman to a place of high authority. A woman on the Cabinet! Unprecedented. He probably, and you, too, are looking for the womens' vote in 1936, but if you make us a real Governor, which, by the way, Texas has not had for some time, you will be reelected without throwing this sop to the women. My wife, who is some years your senior, was as disappointed as I when we read of your appointment to the bench of a woman.

Do you ever read Kipling? If so you will remember "The Colonel's lady and Judy O'Grady are sisters under the Skin."

I hope you won't think me presumptious [sic.]. When you go to the Carlsbad Caverns over the line in New Mexico, stop by and eat fried chicken with us.

Yours very truly,
W.R. Hegler

P.S. I do not expect an answer to this, there is no reason why you should take the time to do so, but I do hope it will make you think.

Source: Texas State Library and Archives Commission

THOUGHT QUESTIONS:

1. What was the nature of the "experience" that the writer claimed to have with women leading him to conclude that he was qualified to comment on the notion of appointing women to government positions?

2. Why did the writer believe that Hughes, or any other woman, was unqualified to "judge her fellow man"?

3. What reason did the writer speculate was the true reason why President Franklin Roosevelt and Governor Allred would ever appoint women to high positions in the state and federal governments?

Emma Tenayuca Discusses Early Influences

During the Great Depression, Emma Tenayuca made a name for herself as a young fiery activist for San Antonio's downtrodden. Though only in her late-teens and early twenties, Tenayuca helped organize highly-publicized strikes among the city's cigar makers and pecan shellers. Eventually, the inability to find work and threats against her life forced her to leave San Antonio for over two decades. In this excerpt from an oral interview, she discusses the multiple influences that compelled her to get involved in labor activism.

Tenayuca: . . . There was one place here where I used to go, particularly with my grandfather, and I went with my father quite a few times, and that was La Plaza de Zacate. That was the square, Milam Square, right in front of the Santa Rosa Hospital. . . . You could go to one corner of the plaza and listen to someone preaching or reading the Bible; you could go to another place, and you could see a group of people, one person reading the newspaper to other workers—the latest news from Mexico. . . .

Interviewer: Mostly Mexican people, or different kinds of people?

Tenayuca: Mostly Mexicans, yes, yes. It was the center of activity. San Antonio was more or less the center where all of these people came. . . . San Antonio has always had a large Spanish-speaking population. But after World War I, or even before World War I, the development of agriculture brought lots of peasants. They had a reason to come. I mean, great heavens, Mexico didn't have one president who stayed in power in that time. They left office; they were assassinated . . .

Interviewer: So, what was happening in Mexico had very, very much influence on the people here?

Tenayuca: Oh, it had a tremendous effect here. This was the first place where they came, you see. . . .

Interviewer: How is it that you became involved in labor ideas?

Tenayuca: Remember, we didn't have radios; we didn't have this; we didn't have that; we didn't have a lot of things. So, this going to the plaza and just listening, you see, was our source of information. . . . Grandpa would buy us a cone of ice cream, and we'd lick it. Then we'd go around and look. This place was always crowded on Saturdays and particularly Sundays. Where else could people have gone—these Magónistas or the others— where they could speak to a crowd; they already had a crowd.

Interviewer: Would you say that those were the motivating factors that got you involved in labor organizing? Or, what was it that got you going in that direction?

Tenayuca: Remember when we went to the plaza what we would see. Did a man come there alone, by himself, on Sundays? No, he brought his family. How were these kids dressed? You'd see them with overalls; sometimes they had shoes, and sometimes they were barefooted. I would just go barefooted when I was a kid. So, they were different; they were different from us. And then, you began to notice those things. . . .

Interviewer: Was your grandfather interested in labor issues as well?

Tenayuca: He was very interested; he was certainly interested in civil rights, as far as Catholics were concerned. And he knew that we were, at that time, I guess, a minority and certainly a minority here.

Interviewer: What did he do? What was his occupation?

Tenayuca: My grandfather was a carpenter. He worked in his old age, and he worked quite a few years. He worked in a lumberyard. He had his home; he was a very hard-working man. He read the paper, went to Mass, went to communion, confession once a year—my grandmother couldn't get him to go more. We would all get together; my cousins would say, "Grandpa's getting ready to unload."

Interviewer: (Laughter) Well, tell me about your first labor activities and how you actually got involved in them.

Tenayuca: Well, there were many things that happened here that contributed to the development of my ideas. I think it would have been very hard for me to look at the situation here in San Antonio, and with the background that I had, not to have had the feelings; and then I loved my grandfather very, very much. In 1929 Wall Street crashed; in 1932, the closing of all the banks. My grandfather lost some money in one of them, but he didn't tell anybody but me. He came over to me and said, "I've lost everything I have." And he was already about, I guess, sixty-five or close to seventy. So, I don't know, I felt that had an awful effect on me. . . .

Source: Institute of Texas Cultures

THOUGHT QUESTIONS:

1. How did the political activities at La Plaza de Zacate influence young Emma?

2. Which family member seems to have had the most influence on Emma's activism and how?

3. What circumstances and other factors beyond family and the Plaza contributed to young Emma's desire to help others through labor activism?

Two Displaced Texas Sharecroppers Write to the Secretary of Agriculture

---

In response to the collapse in farm prices caused by the combination of chronic overproduction and the great drop in consumer demand due to the Great Depression, Congress passed the Agricultural Adjustment Act in 1933 creating a new agency – the Agricultural Adjustment Administration (AAA) – to oversee the government's plans to adjust the supply of seven major farm commodities to existing demand. By encouraging farmers to produce less through the inducement of subsidies (payments), the AAA hoped to infuse farmers with cash while taking surpluses out of the market in an effort to raise the prices of the crops that they did raise and sell in the marketplace. Despite the program proving to be a lifesaver for farm owners everywhere, the reduction of land for production purposes hurt southern sharecroppers particularly hard because of the reduced need for farm labor. Though the AAA cotton contract stipulated that landowners were expected to reduce production without upsetting the number of workers on their land "as much as possible," in practice, hundreds of thousands of sharecroppers, mostly involved in cotton production, were simply thrown out of work across the South. In Texas, the number of croppers was reduced from 105,122 in 1930 to 39,821 by 1940, a 62 percent reduction.

Though their lives were often characterized by immense poverty, living off the land by raising a cotton crop was the only lifestyle large numbers of sharecroppers ever knew. Though some were able to find work on another farm, large numbers were set adrift, unable to find steady work, forcing many of them into small towns and cities to seek employment or relief on the government dole. Thousands of southern sharecroppers wrote government officials to explain their situation. The anxiety felt by these people is clearly revealed in these two letters written by desperate Texas croppers to the Secretary of Agriculture Henry A. Wallace.

W.A. Harrick (Floyd County sharecropper) to Secretary of Agriculture Henry Wallace, dated January 10, 1935

I am writing you a few lines in regards to the farm that I am renting. I work the place last year on the halves. The landlord never said any thing about me not staying here this year until yesterday the 9th. That he wanted the place to handle him self. That he was going to have it work different this year. They would not let me sind up for eny of the cotton reduction. . .

So I am forced to move to a town and get on the relief, something I have never in all my life had to do, unless the goverment help a little farmer. I have a wife and six children age 18 to 2 years old. We want to stay on the land but how can we, with such landlords?

G.H. Summers to Secretary of Agriculture Henry Wallace, Hale Center, TX (no date, c. 1937)

in reguard to the triple A Plan I cant say I am against it. But Will Say this. It has Put more Families on the relief than any one thing Because the man that has got the land wont let a man have any of it Because he wants all of those checks that he gets from the goverment to run his Big Auto. Then in the fall he gets a Big Bunch of Mexicans to gather the cotton and wont hardly hire a white Family. It wood Bea all right if a man could get some land to work. I am with my wife and three groan girls and cant get no land to work. Some men work in 2 or 3 Sections and wont let a man have any of it on the account of them checks he gets from the Goverment. So you See that puts lots of Families on the releaf. I have farmed all my life But cant get any land now. But I aint the only one. There are thousands in the same Fix I am in now. Mr Wallace you study this over and see what you think about it.

Source: AAA Records, National Archives II, College Park, Maryland.

Thought Questions:

1. What did these two sharecroppers desire most? Who did the sharecroppers most blame for their predicament?

2. Describe the croppers' feelings toward receiving government relief. Did they accept it grudgingly? Willingly?

3. Leaving aside spelling and grammar issues, how well did the croppers articulate their plight?

Lasca Fortassain Discusses San Antonio Mayor Maury Maverick and the La Villita Restoration Project

---

Located in downtown San Antonio, the La Villita Restoration Project was undertaken in the midst of the Great Depression by workers from the National Youth Administration (NYA) – a New Deal work agency that employed youth from relief families. Though the NYA provided work-study jobs for students still enrolled in high schools and colleges, it also developed skills-training programs for out-of-school youth, such as the 1,800 who constructed La Villita. The purpose of the project was to restore the old Spanish district to its old architectural flavor while paying the unemployed workers much-needed skills in the process. It still exists today as an historic arts village with shops and entertainment near the Riverwalk.

Lasca Fortassain organized and supervised a stenographic bureau for the City of San Antonio during the term of Mayor Maury Maverick from August 1939 to February 1941. In this excerpt from an oral interview, Fortassain describes the mayor's passion for the La Villita Project.

Interviewer: How did [Maverick] feel about the La Villita Project? I've read in some newspaper articles that he went out on a moonlit night and just had a vision of this or something, you know, and that's how it came to him. Do you think that might be credible or is that part of the legend of Maury Maverick.you know, put out by Maury Maverick?

Fortassain: I have never heard him testify to a vision, but he was a man of vision. He was always envisioning things that would be good for the city, and he was very concerned about the people. So, the Villita Project, in a way, was sort of an intertwining of his interests in what would be good for the city and what was good for the people. He saw it as a people place and also a place that would bring money to the city.

We were beginning to have conventions, so we needed to have a lot more [places to go]. He saw that we needed to have an open-air place to take advantage of the beautiful weather in San Antonio. There needed to be an open-air place where people, convention groups, and other groups could meet. He also was extremely interested in good neighbor relations with Mexico and had a great interest in the whole cause of liberty. . . .

Interviewer: I do know he was determined that the houses, as they were restored, should be named after South American liberators.

Fortassain: Yes, the whole cause of freedom was so important to him that he sort of put everything together: his interest in the freedom of man and the freedom of peoples, his interest in the Latin American countries, and his interest in improving the economic situation in San Antonio. But, as far as this legendary vision is concerned, it was my understanding that the restoration of that area was something that had long been a dream of the women in the Conservation Society. Whether Maury had the dream independently or whether this was something that, because he knew those ladies and it had come up in discussions and started him thinking about it, I don't know. My own interpretation has always been that they were all interested in the same things.

But the Conservation Society women did not know the ropes, and Maury did, having just been in Washington and having just gone through for the past several years the business of helping to get legislation written, as a result of which we were able to get a WPA [Works Progress Administration] project [the Riverwalk] to clean up the river and make the river banks a place of enjoyment. He knew where the money was, in what piece of legislation, and what it was possible to do with the appropriations. He knew about the National Youth Administration.

All of these, of course, were "depression children"—government depression children, but the money was for useful purposes. The projects would never have been set up had not there been such unique unemployment all over the country. The river was a WPA [project]. La Villita was a National Youth Administration project. . . .

Interviewer: How about opposition to this? Surely in America there was opposition. You know there must have been.

Fortassain: I suspect there was opposition, perhaps not so much to the project as to Maury, because there was a strong political faction working against him, of course. He defeated them at the election, but they didn't lose any time attacking him during the course of his turn at the wheel.

Interviewer: Did he only serve one term?

Fortassain: Yes, that's right.

Interviewer: So they did succeed in getting him?

Fortassain: They succeeded in getting him out of office, but not before he started so many things that have meant so much to San Antonio. In the years since I have been back in San Antonio, since 1962, I have heard any number of the people who fought him say, "Well, old Maury was a kook, but he did some good things." The people who opposed him based their opposition on the idea that Maury was a radical and even a Communist. A lot of people's sniping at him was done from that point of view.

But, at the time the Villita project was mounted, there were all sorts of opposition, all sorts of comments. "Well, crazy Maury, just sitting there figuring up ways for the city to waste money." Because the city did, I suspect, have to put in a piece of the money. I think that was a part of all of those projects. I don't think they were one hundred percent funded, although I might be wrong in my recollection.

Interviewer: Well, then he was so politically adept that he just kind of moved over them or went around them or...?

Fortassain: Well, they couldn't keep him from making an application to NYA, as that was a project that would employ San Antonio youth. And the project was not to be a one-time thing; it wasn't just rebuilding, restoring Villita. Inherent in it was the codicil that they teach, they re-teach particularly the Mexican-American youth, the arts and crafts of their forefathers, which were rapidly going into disuse. There was no market for them. The older people who did these things were, I suspect, getting less and less work. They weren't teaching their children. Many of them had learned their crafts in Mexico, and, when they came here, it was a different ambience completely.

There was the same sort of thing there [Villita] that had been in a small community in Mexico out in the country where everybody taught his sons and the women passed on to the daughters the things that they knew. So, there were classes in copperwork, and there were classes in weaving. The tiles that were originally the paving in La Villita were made by these young people; the curtains, original curtains, I remember, in the office, had been woven by students from the project.

Another stipulation in the proposal was that these places be rented; there'd be shops, but, where there was a shop selling something, they also had to be making something. They didn't have to be making everything they sold, but they were supposed to be making some things that they sold. I think that is honored more in its absence now than it is in the presence.

When they started out, it was to be that way, and it likely would have continued that way had we not gone to war because all of these young people either volunteered or were drafted. The young people who had been working for the project became involved in the war. I suspect it was some defense industry for a great many of them because they were of draft age or of the age to volunteer, and they went into military service.

Interviewer: Was the project completed . . . in 1941?

Fortassain: Yes. I left in 1941 in February, and, by the time I came back in August of 1942, La Villita was a jumping joint. There was something going on at La Villita every night, in two or three places. The Cos House was available for rent, and there were things going on in Juárez Plaza and entertainment of the very top type. . . .

Source: Institute of Texas Cultures

THOUGHT QUESTIONS:

1. According to Fortassain, what were some of the reasons for Maverick's support for La Villita?

2. Was there any opposition to Maverick and/or the project? Why?

3. What else did Fortassain mention was an important underlying purpose for the restoration project beyond the basic construction work involved?

Cotton Spinner

Credit: Library of Congress

This picture shows a fourteen year old cotton spinner in a Brazos Valley Cotton Mill. The overproduction of cotton did not hurt millers, ginners, and shippers but could ruin growers because of low prices.

THOUGHT QUESTION:

How did the New Deal's Agricultural Adjustment Administration propose to deal with the overproduction problem? Who benefited and who were hurt by the government's policies?

BIOGRAPHIES

JOHN NANCE GARNER (1868-1967). Vice President of the United States for two terms during the Franklin Roosevelt Administration, John Nance Garner was born to farming parents near Detroit, Texas (Red River County) on November 22, 1868. At age eighteen he attended Vanderbilt University in Nashville, Tennessee for one semester before dropping out. He moved to Clarksville, Texas, read law, and was admitted to the bar in 1890. Garner moved to Uvalde in South Texas hoping that an arid climate would help him deal with respiratory problems. There he joined a law firm and was appointed to fill a county judge vacancy. When he ran for the regular term, Garner defeated a local rancher's daughter, Mariette Rheiner, who he married two years later.

Garner was elected to the state legislature in 1898 and served for four years. In 1903 he helped create a new Fifteenth Congressional District and succeeded in being elected the district's representative, a position he would hold for the next thirty years. During his initial terms, Garner was content listening and examining the legislative process. He did not make his first speech on the House floor until 1911. It has been said that during his early years in Congress, he clung to the number-one rule for political success: get elected, stay there, and gain influence through seniority. In 1909 Garner became the Democratic Party whip. During the First World War, he acted as an important liaison between President Woodrow Wilson and the House of Representatives.

In 1931, when the Democrats gained a majority in the House of Representatives, his colleagues elected him to the position of Speaker. Garner soon became a potential 1932 presidential candidate. Although he did not pursue the nomination vigorously, he gained moderate support leading up to the Chicago convention. After he released his delegates to Franklin D. Roosevelt, the New York governor offered Garner the vice-presidential nomination, which he accepted. On November 8, 1932, he and Roosevelt were elected.

In the early years of Roosevelt's administration, Vice President Garner's role was crucial in getting congressional support for numerous New Deal measures. His experience, political knowledge, plus his personal relationships and influence with members of Congress, aided Roosevelt immensely. His role as a congressional liaison between the White House and Capitol Hill with Congress was crucial to Roosevelt's early success. Garner became the most powerful vice president in the nation's history up to that time.

Though not supportive of all New Deal initiatives, Garner continued to support Roosevelt until the spring of 1937 when his more conservative philosophy led him to start vigorously opposing the president's pro-union policies, expanded social programs, deficit spending, and his so-called "Court Packing Plan" by which Roosevelt sought to reform the Supreme Court by adding additional members if its elderly members refused to resign. Along with many other Democrats, Garner vehemently opposed the plan on the grounds that it would disrupt the government's separation of powers and worked hard to successfully defeat the proposal. By 1938 Garner led a group of conservative Democrats and Republicans in Congress who worked to stifle further New Deal reforms. As the 1940 presidential campaign season rolled around, Texas Democratic Party politicians came out for Garner. Polls showed Garner to be the favorite if Roosevelt chose not to run again, but Roosevelt did run for an unprecedented third term and won.

In 1941, at the age of seventy-two, Garner returned to private life. Much of the details of Garner's inner workings as vice president will never be known because he inexplicably burned his public and private papers after his retirement. He spent the rest of his years quietly in Uvalde, managing his land holdings, fishing, and informally advising Democratic politicians. On the morning of Garner's 95th birthday on November 22, 1963, President John Kennedy telephoned Garner from Fort Worth to offer him birthday wishes a few hours before he was assassinated. Garner died on November 7, 1967, a few days before his ninety-ninth birthday.

SAM RAYBURN (1882-1961). Samuel Taliaferro Rayburn, Texas state legislator, congressman, and longtime Speaker of the United States House of Representatives, was born in eastern Tennessee, on January 6, 1882. In 1887 the family moved to a forty-acre cotton farm in Fannin County, Texas. At the age of eighteen he entered East Texas Normal College (now Texas A&M—Commerce), completing the three-year normal-school course load leading to the B.S. degree in just two years. He taught school for two years before pursuing his desire to become a lawyer and legislator. In 1906 Rayburn won a seat in the Texas House of Representatives. In between sessions, he attended the University of Texas law school and was admitted to the State Bar of Texas in 1908. He was twice reelected to the state legislature. During his third term he served as Speaker. In 1912 he was elected to Congress as a Democrat representing the Fourth Texas District.

Beginning in 1913 he served his district as congressman for forty-eight consecutive years, the longest record of service in the House up until the time of his death in 1961 (John Dingell of Michigan has since surpassed this record, having served 54 years as of 2009). He would be a participant in the passage of most of the significant legislation of the first half of the twentieth century, though he only served on one House committee—the Interstate and Foreign Commerce Committee.

Rayburn was a close personal friend and ally of John Nance Garner, serving as Garner's 1932 campaign manager in his 1932 bid for the Democratic presidential nomination. Rayburn's negotiations led to the formation of the Roosevelt-Garner ticket. He became a leading supporter of the New Deal. As chairman of the Interstate and Foreign Commerce Committee from 1931-37, Rayburn was responsible for ushering through Congress legislation of lasting importance, such as the Truth in Securities Act, the bills establishing the Securities and Exchange Commission and the Federal Communications Commission, the Public Utilities Holding Company Act, and the Rural Electrification Act.

House Democrats elected Rayburn to become Majority Leader in 1937. Three years later, they chose him to be Speaker. Rayburn served as Speaker of the House in every Democratic-controlled Congress from the Seventy-sixth through the Eighty-seventh (from 1940 to 1961). During two brief periods of Republican House majorities (1947-49 and 1953-55), he served as Minority Leader. As Majority Leader and then Speaker, Rayburn guided the final New Deal measures through the House. During World War II, he arranged financial support for the war effort, and in the postwar years he opposed efforts by conservative Democrats and Republicans to repeal many New Deal measures. During Dwight Eisenhower's Republican administration, Rayburn worked closely with Lyndon Johnson who was serving as Senate Majority Leader. Later, Rayburn supported

Johnson's 1960 presidential run, eventually working to have Johnson chosen to be John Kennedy's vice president.

Throughout his congressional career, Rayburn's reputation for honesty was unimpeachable. He accepted no money from lobbyists and rarely traveled on the public expense. Within his district, Rayburn was an immensely popular politician admired for his approachability and his desire to aid them with their problems and arrange funding for noteworthy local projects, including rural electrification, farm-to-market roads, hospitals, air fields, and lake construction.

Politics was his life. In 1927 he married Metze Jones, the sister of his friend, fellow congressman Marvin Jones, but the marriage lasted only three months. He remained unmarried thereafter. Rayburn died of cancer at age seventy-nine on November 16, 1961 and is buried in Bonham, the location of his beloved Sam Rayburn Library. Completed in 1957, the library housed Rayburn's public and private papers for many years until they were moved to the Center for American History at the University of Texas at Austin.

EMMA TENAYUCA (1916-1999). The Depression Era labor organizer Emma Tenayuca was born in San Antonio on December 21, 1916. Her first exposure to the struggles of working people came as a child when she visited La Plaza de Zacate, a place where socialists and anarchists in San Antonio would speak and listen to workers' grievances. She became a labor activist before finishing high school. In 1933 police arrested her for joining protests against the Finck Cigar Company. During the Depression she lobbied the mayor of San Antonio to improve the distribution of federal relief, founded two local chapters of the International Ladies' Garment Workers Union, and organized protests against the beating of migrant workers by U.S. Border Patrol agents. Like some other activists concerned about labor issues during the Depression, Tenayuca joined the Communist Party in 1937. She was briefly married to party organizer Homer Brooks.

In 1938, Tenayuca became known across Texas for her efforts leading a highly-publicized strike against San Antonio's leading industry—the Southern Pecan Shelling Company. She convinced 12,000 mostly Hispanic pecan shellers to walk off the job in protest against a proposed 50 percent wage reduction. On multiple occasions police fired tear gas on the picketers and arrested Tenayuca and over a thousand strikers, but they pressed on with their demands. The walkout ended when the operators agreed to arbitration. After Congress passed the National Labor Relations Act, the new national minimum wage raised the workers' wages to twenty-five cents an hour, but thousands lost their jobs the following year when operators decided to start mechanizing their shelling plants to counter the rising labor costs. In 1939 Tenayuca became chairperson of the Texas Communist Party. That year when she and other speakers planned to hold a Communist Party gathering at San Antonio's Municipal Auditorium, rioters violently broke up the meeting.

The ubiquitous death threats against her, coupled with being blacklisted by numerous local employers, convinced Tenayuca to leave San Antonio by the end of the 1930s. After briefly relocating to Houston, she moved to San Francisco, California. Eventually pursuing a degree in education, she received her teaching certification from San Francisco State College in 1952. Though she never remarried, she had a son while living in California. Tenayuca returned to San Antonio in the late 1960s, earning a master's degree in education from Our Lady of the Lake University in 1974. She worked for the Harlandale School District until her retirement in 1982 and lived in San Antonio until her death in 1999.

JAMES FRANK DOBIE (1888–1964). Descended from settlers who moved to Texas from Virginia in 1834, the renowned folklorist J. Frank Dobie was born on a South Texas ranch in Live Oak County on September 26, 1888. His ranching background heavily influenced his character, personality, and writings, though over time he shed the racial prejudices of his upbringing. His early interest in literature spawned from his fundamentalist father reading the Bible to Frank and his siblings while his mother read them classic English novels. In 1906, he attended Southwestern University in Georgetown, where he met his future wife Bertha McKee. Upon graduating, he worked as a reporter for San Antonio and Galveston newspapers before getting his first teaching job at Alpine High School. Returning to Georgetown in 1911 to teach English classes at the Southwestern University preparatory school, he moved to New York City in 1913 to pursue a master's degree at Columbia University.

Dobie joined the University of Texas as a faculty member in 1914, but left to serve in an artillery unit after U.S. entry in World War I. His battalion arrived in France just as the war ended, and he was discharged from the service in 1919. Dobie resigned his position to spend a year managing his uncle's sprawling 250,000-acre South Texas ranch, but resumed teaching at UT in 1921, determined to describe the old-time ranching life and culture of Texas through his own publications and by invigorating the young-but-stagnant Texas Folklore Society. After failing to receive a promotion because he lacked a doctorate, he served as chair of the English department at Oklahoma A&M (now Oklahoma State) until 1925 when allies on the University of Texas campus orchestrated his return.

Dobie began writing a series of articles on aspects of Texas history, culture, and folklore for magazines while working on his first book, *A Vaquero of the Brush Country.* Published in 1929, the work based on interviews and the autobiographical notes of aged open-range cowboy John Young established Dobie as a lively chronicler of Southwestern culture. He presented the material in narrative form as a device to describe the lives of late-19th century cattlemen and Southwest cattle culture in realistic terms, counter to the popular images derived from the Wild West shows, Hollywood western movies, and dime novels that he disregarded as the work of mere "sensation mongers and sentimentalists." Dobie became a nationally known literary figure with the release of his next work, *Coronado's Children*, in 1931. Though not characterizing himself as a scientific folklorist, Dobie nevertheless traced his collection of richly-detailed fortune-seeker tales of lost mines and buried treasure set in the Southwest back to their origins and described how they were embellished over time. Published in the midst of the Great Depression, the book appealed to many Texans and Americans who not only longed for the nostalgia of rural worlds lost, but also hoped to strike it rich during a time of economic despair. His follow-up books on past Texas rural life and folklore that appeared during the Depression, *On the Open Range* (1931), *Tales of the Mustang* (1936), *The Flavor of Texas* (1936), *Apache Gold and Yaqui Silver* (1939), and *The Longhorns* (1941) further solidified his status as the leading Texas literary figure of his day.

During World War II, Dobie was invited to teach American literature at Cambridge University, an eye-opening experience that he credited with greatly broadening his perspectives on many aspects of life in a chronicle he later published entitled *A Texan in England*. After he began to disagree vehemently with the far right members of the UT board of regents for maintaining racial segregation on campus and their frequent attacks on academic freedom by criticizing liberal professors and firing president Homer P. Rainey, the board dismissed him when he requested an extended leave after his overseas teaching tour ended in 1947.

After his discharge, Dobie focused his energies on writing, leading to the publication *The Voice of the Coyote* (1949), *The Ben Lilly Legend* (1950), *The Mustangs* (1952), *Tales of Old Time Texas* (1955), *Up the Trail From Texas* (1955), *I'll Tell You a Tale* (1960), *Cow People* (1964) and almost finished *Rattlesnakes*, which his wife edited and published in 1965. He also continued to write a popular Sunday newspaper column where he earned the reputation of being a humorist and outspoken critic of Texas politicians, popular trends of the day, architecture that he despised, and most social, cultural, and religious restraints on individual liberty. He died on September 18, 1964, four days after receiving the Medal of Freedom from his friend, President Lyndon B. Johnson, and was buried in the State Cemetery in Austin. His gravestone proudly states: "I have come to value liberated minds as the supreme good of life on Earth."

Chapter 15

World War II and Texas,
1941-1945

**An Excerpt from a Library of Congress "Man on the Street" Interview
Conducted in Austin, Texas after the Japanese Attack on
Pearl Harbor (December 9, 1941)**

*On December 8, 1941, Alan Lomax, head of the Library of Congress's Archive of American
Folk Song (now the Archive of Folk Culture), sent a telegram to fieldworkers in ten different
localities across the United States, asking them to collect "man-on-the-street" reactions of ordinary Americans to the Japanese attack on Pearl Harbor and the subsequent declaration of war
by the United States. Twelve hours of opinions recorded in the days and months following the
attack from more than two hundred individuals in cities and towns across the United States,
including Texas. They feature a wide diversity of opinion concerning the war and various
social and political issues of the day. Interviewees understood that their responses might be used
in a radio broadcast on the Mutual Broadcasting System.*

*The questioner in the following excerpt from one of these interviews was John Henry
Faulk, soon to become a well-known author and radio humorist originally from Austin, Texas.
He would later become embroiled in Cold War blacklisting after being falsely labeled a communist by McCarthy-Era extremists. Faulk had entered the University of Texas in 1932, and
under the guidance of J. Frank Dobie, Walter P. Webb, and Roy Bedichek he developed into an
adept collector of folklore. At the time he conducted his "man-on-the-street" interviews, Faulk
was teaching English in Austin at his alma mater.*

John Henry Faulk: Well, Mr. Brodie when did you first hear about Japan attacking the
United States?
J. C. Brodie: Sunday evening.
John Henry Faulk: Well, what do you think about it? What was your reaction to it?

J. C. Brodie: I think it was an outrage.

John Henry Faulk: Do you think they had any right in the world to do it?

J. C. Brodie: I do not. We were trying to make peace with them at the time, our president was.

John Henry Faulk: And they jumped. Why do you reckon they jumped us?

J. C. Brodie: Well, I think that Germany was the cause of them jumping us if you want to know what I think about it.

John Henry Faulk: What chance you reckon we've got of winning?

J. C. Brodie: I think that's a cinch that we'll win.

John Henry Faulk: How come?

J. C. Brodie: We're the strongest nation on earth. We've got more resources than any nation on earth. And we're the out fightin-ist people on earth [interviewer laughs]. And don't mind doing it when the time comes.

John Henry Faulk: Well, that's good, but they tell me that Germany's been putting up a considerable battle too. So has Japan's been fighting [and practicing (?)] a long time in China.

J. C. Brodie: Well the Japs are fighting little nations. But they haven't enough resources, to my opinion, to fight the United States.

John Henry Faulk: I think that's true too. And it seems like they spread out a long ways too.

J. C. Brodie: They've got too much territory to cover and my information, they haven't enough navy to take care of it and their navy is too weak to fight the United States.

John Henry Faulk: How are they in the air, you reckon?

J. C. Brodie: That, I couldn't answer the question "how good they are in the air." But I'll venture to say one thing, that they won't be a match to the American people. . . .

John Henry Faulk: You don't reckon Russia's going to help her do you?

J. C. Brodie: I do not. Russia, I think, will stand straight by the United States.

John Henry Faulk: I believe that too.

J. C. Brodie: [inaudible]

John Henry Faulk: Well, do you got any ideas on just why we got down to ever having this war? I mean why Japan would ever start a war with us?

J. C. Brodie: Well, the United States, the way I understand it, demanded them to abandon their fight on China. They're aggressive nation and the idea was with them they wanted half of China and all of it. And when they had to give it up, they'd fight before they'd give it up.

John Henry Faulk: And they just realized the United States wasn't taking more foolishness.

J. C. Brodie: They talked peace so long until they seen there's no room for peace. It was either fight or back up.

John Henry Faulk: Do you reckon they'll try to attack us here at the United States? Reckon that they'll try to get on the mainland?

J. C. Brodie: I don't think so.

John Henry Faulk: You know I listened to the radio last night late, and they said that there were war ships over in San Francisco, in the area, but I don't believe that. You don't believe the United States is any danger of attack?

J. C. Brodie: I do not. Not from Japan

John Henry Faulk: What about Germany? Reckon she'll . . . do you reckon she's going to get in this war? Or do you reckon she's just going to let Japan fight it out?

J. C. Brodie: Well, according to their pact, Italy and Japan and Germany is already at war with the United States.

John Henry Faulk: I didn't know they would fight with Japan just --

J. C. Brodie: Well, they make an agreement that if one was attacked the other would be a partner. That's what they've already --

John Henry Faulk: Yeah, but Japan hasn't been attacked, Japan did the attack against us.

J. C. Brodie: I understand she did the attacking, but didn't you listen last night on the radio, that they had one of the big German airplane men over there conducting their air raids for her?

John Henry Faulk: No, I didn't hear that. Did you hear that?

J. C. Brodie: Yeah, they're doing that. . . .

John Henry Faulk: Oh well, that's bad then. . . .

J. C. Brodie: And all of Hitler's countries that he's attacked and taken was attacked on a Sunday morning. And Germany, in my opinion, has ram-rodded this thing all the way through and attacked it on a Sunday morning when they knew it would be a quiet morning. And lots of the men out at church or off looking around or something at the time.

John Henry Faulk: Weren't expecting it.

J. C. Brodie: Wasn't expecting attack.

John Henry Faulk: In other words, that was German, Germany had a hand in them this?

J. C. Brodie: Germany, I think was in the [thick (?)] of it.

John Henry Faulk: Well, do you . . . ready to see the United States through, huh? Ready to see her fight it to the last Jap?

J. C. Brodie: Yes. I'm sixty-seven years old and if they need me I'll go up front.

John Henry Faulk: Good, well that's the way to talk. I believe most of America feels that way now since the United States has been attacked.

J. C. Brodie: I believe that ninety percent of the people in the United States are whole-hearted to win the war. That's what I think.

John Henry Faulk: And I believe we've got the foodstuff and the ammunition and everything else it's going to take.

J. C. Brodie: We can produce anything we need for [inaudible] . . . As far as food's concerned, fighting's concerned, wool's concerned, and manufacturers is concerned, and the United States has ample of everything.

John Henry Faulk: Yeah, I don't believe that they can . . . I don't know what Japan can do about holding out against us in the face of all that. They're cut off from most of their supplies.

J. C. Brodie: Well, I wouldn't imagine that China or Japan or any of her allies have anything to send her in the way of needing.

John Henry Faulk: . . . I don't know what she's going to do about oil now.

Unidentified woman: [unintelligible question]

John Henry Faulk: Yeah, we've been supplying them with oil.

J. C. Brodie: Mexico has too.

John Henry Faulk: She's quit.

J. C. Brodie: She's quit, she's an ally of the United States. If they can't capture oil in some other region over there to draw from I don't know where it could come from. . . .

Unidentified woman: [unintelligible question]

John Henry Faulk: Mr. Brodie, how long do you reckon this war is going to last? How long are you looking for it to last?

J. C. Brodie: Six months.

John Henry Faulk: And by that time we'll have—

J. C. Brodie: — have Japan whipped.

John Henry Faulk: Well, do you reckon it's just a matter of whipping Japan though? Seems like to me Germany and Italy are going to have to be subdued.

J. C. Brodie: Well, I think that too. I think that Japan and Italy will be the whip. It may take longer then if we have to fight them to do it, but just Japan by herself, I think we'd whip her in six months.

John Henry Faulk: Yeah, I believe that too.

J. C. Brodie: If they can get a hold of Japan's navy and destroy it, they're through. And if the United States will fight like Hitler does and Mussolini and bomb Japan, their manufacturers and set them afire, they're made out of flimsy materials and if they ever start fires in them why they'll burn her off the face of the earth. . . . And I understand their manufacturing outfit don't cover much more than a hundred acres of land and it's all right together. And if they hit their railroad that runs through the center, as small as Japan is, and tear it up they have no way of transportation.

John Henry Faulk: That's right.

J. C. Brodie: And so much of the population lives out on the edges of the water and not even land to live on.

John Henry Faulk: Well, you reckon Japan has her rights, I mean her demands, you know she says the reason she's got it spread out is to have some place for the population to live. You reckon that's true?

J. C. Brodie: That is true.

John Henry Faulk: Well, then what do you reckon is the solution for that is? Reckon, we ought to give her land?

J. C. Brodie: Well, the way I understand them, they're a people that don't believe in religion. They're atheists and the best thing to do with them is to take them off the face of the earth.

John Henry Faulk: Just obliterate them.

J. C. Brodie: That's what I think.

John Henry Faulk: Well, I was going to ask you, what do you think ought to be done at the end of the war? I mean what kind of peace do you think ought to be written? Do you think they ought to give the Japanese, the Italians, and the Germans any rights at all?

J. C. Brodie: Well, the Germans, the only way to keep out of war with Germany is to do away with Germany entirely and put them under other governments and have no Germany at all. As long as there's a Germany there'll be wars. Twenty-three or four years ago we whipped Germany, she threw up the sponge and they're right back worse than ever.

John Henry Faulk: Do you remember that last war very well?

J. C. Brodie: I guess I do.

John Henry Faulk: Well, what do you, do you think we're as well-prepared for it as are for this one?

J. C. Brodie: We're better prepared for this one than we was for the other.

John Henry Faulk: Do you think we're fighting this one with any more justification than we did the last one?

J. C. Brodie: Yes I do.

John Henry Faulk: In other words, we were really attacked this time.

J. C. Brodie: We were really attacked this time. It's our duty as a nation to defend it and whip the aggressors.

John Henry Faulk: That's right. And of course like you mentioned, many of those when they were over here those Kurusu and that other fellow, the ambassador over here making overtures of peace.

J. C. Brodie: All they were doing was just stalling for time and lying. That is the end of it.

John Henry Faulk: I wonder if Roosevelt was fooled by any of this, you reckon?

J. C. Brodie: I think not.

John Henry Faulk: They realized it?

J. C. Brodie: Yeah.

John Henry Faulk: Did the war come as much of a surprise to you, did you—

J. C. Brodie: Not at all. They did just what I thought they would do, attacked without any—

John Henry Faulk: Any warning.

J. C. Brodie: —any warning whatever. . . . People as a whole are behind the president a hundred percent.

John Henry Faulk: That's what it seems to me. I think Roosevelt did the right thing.

J. C. Brodie: I do. I think we have a wonderful president and a wonderful mind and a wonderful foresight. I think we have the right man in the right place at the right time. . . .

Source: American Folklife Center, Library of Congress

THOUGHT QUESTIONS:

1. According to the man interviewed, why did the Japanese bomb Pearl Harbor?

2. How did he feel the U.S. would do in the war? How long did he think the war would take?

3. What did the man feel should be done with Japan and Germany after the war? What reasons did he give?

General Henry H. "Hap" Arnold Celebrates the Work of the WASPs at Their Final Graduation Ceremony Sweetwater, Texas (December 7, 1944)

During the summer of 1941, before U.S. entry into World War II, famous female pilots Jacqueline Cochran and Nancy Harkness Love submitted proposals for the use of women pilots in non-combat missions to the U.S. Army Air Forces (USAAF). General Henry H. "Hap" Arnold, commander of the USAAF, eventually allowed creation of the Women's Airforce Service

Pilots (WASPs), with the female pilots to be trained to fly "the Army way" at Avenger Field in Sweetwater, Texas, though they were to retain civilian status. More than 25,000 women applied for WASP service, less than 1,900 were accepted, and 1,078 completed their training to become the first women to fly American military aircraft. During the war, WASPs performed vital support role, including ferrying aircraft from factories to military bases, towing aerial targets, and training male pilots.

In this commencement speech delivered at Avenger Field, General Arnold salutes the contribution of the WASPs to the war effort.

I am glad to be here today and talk with you young women who have been making aviation history. You and all WASPs have been pioneers in a new field of wartime service, and I sincerely appreciate the splendid job you have done for the AAF [Army Air Forces].

You, and more than nine hundred of your sisters, have shown that you can fly wingtip to wingtip with your brothers. If ever there was a doubt in anyone's mind that women can become skillful pilots, the WASP have dispelled that doubt.

The possibility of using women to pilot military aircraft was first considered in the summer of 1941. We anticipated then that global war would require all our qualified men and many of our women. We did not know how many of our young men could qualify to pilot the thousands of aircraft which American industry could produce. There was also the problem of finding sufficient highly capable young men to satisfy the demands of the Navy, the Ground Forces, the Service Forces, and the Merchant Marines. England and Russia had been forced to use women to fly trainers and combat-type aircraft. Russian women were being used in combat.

In that emergency I called in Jacqueline Cochran, who had herself flown almost everything with wings and several times had won air races from men who now are general officers of the Air Forces. I asked her to draw a plan for the training and the use of American women pilots. She presented such a plan in late 1941 and it formed the basis for the Air Forces' use of the WASP.

Frankly, I didn't know in 1941 whether a slip of a young girl could fight the controls of a B-17 in the heavy weather they would naturally encounter in operational flying. Those of us who had been flying for twenty or thirty years knew that flying an airplane was something you do not learn overnight.

But Miss Cochran said that carefully selected young women could be trained to fly our combat-type planes. So, it was only right that we take advantage of every skill which we, as a nation, possessed.

My objective in forming the WASP were, as you know, three:
1. To see if women could serve as military pilots, and, if so, to form the nucleus of an organization which could be rapidly expanded.
2. To release male pilots for combat.
3. To decrease the Air Forces' total demands for the cream of the manpower pool.

Well, now in 1944, more than two years since WASP first started flying with the Air Forces, we can come to only one conclusion – the entire operation has been a success. It is on the record that women can fly as well as men. In training, in safety, in operations, your showing is comparable to the overall record of the AAF flying within the continental United States. That was what you were called upon to do – continental flying. If the need had developed to fly aircraft overseas, I feel certain that the WASP would have performed that job equally well.

Certainly we haven't been able to build a plane you can't handle. From AT-6s to B-29s, you have flown them around like veterans. One of the WASP has even test-flown our new jet plane.

You have worked hard at your jobs. Commendations from the generals to whose commands you have been assigned are constantly coming across my desk. These commendations record how you have buckled down to the monotonous, the routine jobs which are not much desired by our hot-shot young men headed toward combat or just back from an overseas tour. In some of your jobs I think they like you better than men.

I want to stress how valuable I believe this whole WASP program has been for the country. If another national emergency arises – let us hope it does not, but let us this time face the possibility – if it does, we will not again look upon a women's flying organization as experimental. We will know that they can handle our fastest fighters, our heaviest bombers; we will know that they are capable of activities which you have proved you can do.

This is valuable knowledge for the air age into which we are now entering.

But please understand that I do not look upon the WASP and the job they have done in this war as a project or an experiment. A pioneering venture, yes. Solely an experiment, no. The WASP are an accomplishment.

We are winning this war – we still have a long way to go – but we are winning it. Every WASP who has contributed to the training and operation of the Air Forces has filled a vital and necessary place in the jigsaw pattern of victory. Some of you are discouraged sometimes, all of us are, but be assured you have filled a necessary place in the overall picture of the Air Forces.

The WASPs have completed their mission. Their job has been successful. But, as is usual in war, it has not been without cost. Thirty-seven WASPs have died while helping their country move toward the moment of final victory. The Air Forces will long remember their service and their final sacrifice.

So, on this last graduation day, I salute you and all WASPs. We of the AAF are proud of you; we will never forget our debt to you.

Source: Dwight D. Eisenhower Presidential Library

THOUGHT QUESTIONS:

1. How does Arnold describe the origins of the WASPs?

2. What did Arnold say the objectives were in forming the WASPs?

3. What did Arnold say the WASP program showed about the capability of women as pilots?

A WASP Remembers Her Basic Training at Avenger Field in Sweetwater, Texas

In recent years, a renewed interest in the WASPs had led many scholars to track down as many surviving female pilots as possible to collect their thoughts and memories about their wartime experiences. Most of the women fondly remember their time as a WASP. In the following oral history excerpt from the large collection of interviews housed at Texas Women's University, Jean Cole describes her entry in to the WASP program and some memorable aspects of her basic training.

. . . I heard about the WASPs. I joined, and I went over to Dayton, I think it was, Ohio, to take my physical, and Marge Gilbert also lived in Richmond, Indiana, and we both joined the WASPs together. We went down together, as I remember, on the train, and I can remember the train had open windows, and I'd never seen desert country before.

I was just amazed at Texas, going through Texas. We got to Sweetwater, and I don't quite remember how we got [to Avenger Field], it seems to me we got picked up in the cattle car right at the railroad station, but that could be wrong. I remember the first night I was out there, I could hear these airplanes flying. Oh, it seems though they were flying all night. They would fly right over our barracks and everything just shook, it was the most exciting thing I can imagine. Every night, in fact, from then on, early in the game, at least, I can remember those airplanes flying over the barracks shaking everything.

We had to wear zoot suits, I remember those, and sometimes, first we wore hairnets, they couldn't quite figure out what to do with our hair. Then the hairnets, they didn't like that, so then they decided that we would wear turbans, and we really looked ridiculous, we all had white turbans, and we wore them for a long time. On Saturdays we always had an inspection, and three or four people would come, some from the Army, and we were always trying to hide our booze. And they would find it. We tried all sorts of places, but they would always find it, and take it away from us. Finally we all settled on burying it outside between the barracks so, I think somebody else has already told this story, but we all had a little stick sticking up to mark the place where we had our bottles buried. . . .

What we liked best was the AT-6. I don't know anybody who didn't like the AT-6. It was just a fun airplane . . . One experience I had in the AT-6 was, I think it was sort of a short night crosscountry, or we were somehow, I had to go away from the area, at night, in the AT-6. When I came back, you always had to fly, there were people flying in quadrants over the airport, and they would be flying at different elevations so that they wouldn't run into each other, and all the cross-country people had to come in under them, at 3,000 feet.

So, I can remember, when I got away, I could not get my radio to work, and the only thing I could hear on that radio was Mexican music. So I came in on my Mexican music and came underneath, and I said, three cheers, here's a chance to buzz the tower, because I don't have any radio, so how am I going to get a light to land? It was very windy that night, and I came in and buzzed the tower. That was a lot of fun, and then I went up, circled around, and headed in to land, so they would know that I was the one who buzzed and I wanted to come in. Well, I got a red light, flash, red light, flash, so I went around again. I couldn't see anything wrong, I couldn't see any reason why they were giving me a red light, everything looked fine on the ground, but I came around again and they gave me another red light. I couldn't figure it out, I said maybe they don't know who I am, and I buzzed them again. Then I went around for the third time, and I'm coming in just right, and I got another red light. I said this is nonsense, I've gotta come in, I can't stay up here all night, and I can't talk to them.

So I came heading on in, and landing, and as I got near the ground I sort of noticed that I was going real fast. I put on more flaps, and more flaps, and the more flaps I put on, the faster I went. Well, I was bound I was going to land that airplane anyway, so on about the last third of the runway, which is a no-no, I got the wheels down, but it was still going like a son-of-a-gun. I went right up to the lights at the end of the runway, and had to swing left real fast and almost ground looped to get that thing stopped. The minute I hit the ground, the radio came back on again, and I heard them saying, make your approach to land 180 degrees due south, and I had just landed zero degrees to the north, which is the way I took off. It never occurred to me that the wind would switch 180 degrees in that short time! But then I quick looked over and I saw the tee, there was a lighted tee, so that if you can't hear any radio, you can look at the tee to see which way to land. Which I hadn't even thought of doing. But they didn't know that, and the tee was still pointing north. So they must have just changed it not but a very short time ago, because they hadn't gotten around to switching the tee.

Of course there was an ambulance rushing along as I came in, and there was a fire engine rushing along when I came in, and the guy who was head of the post was there. I got out of the airplane because they were all gathered around, and he said, you know, you just landed downwind. I said, I didn't have any radio, and the tee is pointing north, what was I supposed to do? He said you kept getting red lights, you got three red lights and you came in and landed anyway. I said, I was tired, and I wanted to go to bed. This was about three o'clock in the morning. I looked at him, and he looked at me, and he laughed. I sort of knew I was in, at that point, and he knew that they had made a mistake by having the tee not turned around, so I never got in any trouble for that. I have a feeling that they always liked the girls to be unafraid, they wanted you to be gung-ho and ready to do anything, sort of, so they knew you wouldn't get scared and chicken out on anything. I had always said that one of my little goals, was to land that darned AT-6 downwind. Apparently that had got around, and so he thought I had done that on purpose, and he thought that was sort of neat. Well, I hadn't done it on purpose, and I was scared to death, but since he didn't know that everything went okay. And I didn't have any problems with that. . . .

Source: Women Airforce Service Pilots Oral History Project, The Woman's Collection, Texas Woman's University

THOUGHT QUESTIONS:

1. What were Cole's first impressions of Texas? How did she describe her arrival and initial experiences at Avenger Field?

2. What were Cole and the other WASPs trying to hide from Army inspectors? How did they finally succeed in keeping them hidden?

3. Regarding the AT-6 incident mentioned, why did Cole "buzz the tower"? How did the head of the post react when she told him why she did it? In Cole's opinion, why did he react that way?

Brigadier General Lillian Dunlap Reflects on the Beginning of Her Career in the Army Nurse Corps during World War II

Brigadier General Lillian Dunlap was born in Mission, Texas and grew up in San Antonio. She entered Santa Rosa Hospital School of Nursing in 1939. Following the Japanese attack on Pearl Harbor, she entered the Army Nurse Corps as a second lieutenant at Brooke General Hospital and served for thirty-three years, eventually becoming a brigadier general stationed in Washington, D.C. In a lengthy oral interview conducted in 1990, she traced the development of the Army Nursing Corps through her life in the military. In this excerpt from that interview, General Dunlap described the beginning of her long career as an army nurse during World War II.

Interviewer: Will you please tell us about your military career? It must have been very interesting.

Dunlap: . . . I entered the Army Nurse Corps, November 16, 1942, here at Brooke General Hospital as a second lieutenant, because at that time the Chief of the Army Nurse Corps was a major; the chief nurse at Brooke General Hospital had twenty years' service, and she was a captain. Her assistant was a first lieutenant, the operating room supervisor was a first lieutenant, and everybody else was a second lieutenant.

So when I entered the Army Nurse Corps, my goal was to get to be a first lieutenant. I thought I would have reached the top at that point. At Brooke General Hospital, units were being organized for shipping overseas. In February of 1943, I was assigned to the Fifty-ninth Station Hospital. Twenty-three nurses from Brooke General Hospital left by troop train to go to Camp Young, California. We didn't know we were going there. Our orders read an APO number, and we thought it said India, so we thought we were headed to India. We got to Indio, California, and were offloaded there onto ambulances and taken to Camp Young, California, which no longer exists. It was out in the desert between Indio and Desert Center. This was a large training area where the tanks were maneuvering in preparation for shipping overseas. . . .

We actually were on maneuvers in the desert, taking care of the patients out there for six months. Then our unit went by troop train back across the country to Camp Chaffee, Arkansas, and we had jungle maneuvers there, working half time in the hospital and then on jungle maneuvers-jungle training-for four months. Then we went back across the country on a troop train to Camp Stoneman, California. On Thanksgiving Day, 1943, we shipped out on the West Point for the Pacific. . . .

We were headed for Australia, but three days out of Australia the ship was diverted to Milne Bay, New Guinea. They needed the amphibious engineer troops aboard the ship, right quick-like, up in New Guinea. So we went to Milne Bay. They offloaded those troops, and, in addition, there were two of us hospital units on the ship so they offloaded us also.

It was interesting; they weren't expecting us-these women-so some of the men, the male officers, moved out of their area, which was thatched huts in a coconut grove, and they moved us into those facilities. Of course, they put guards around the perimeter to protect us. We did not function as a unit there. We stayed there until January, and then we went by an army hospital ship along the coast of New Guinea up to Oro Bay and inland to a thousand-bed hospital at Dobadura. I was at Dobadura for one year.

. . . We had a thousand beds in ten wards of one hundred patients each. Now, the wards were in the shape of a cross. They poured a concrete slab in the shape of a cross. They put tarpaper siding up about waist-high, then it was open to the top with corrugated metal roofing for the top.

We had ten wards in a semicircle; the operating room, the headquarters, and X-ray and things like that were in enclosed buildings, but the wards were not. Our nurses' quarters were kind of like I think you see horse stalls now at the stables. Two of us lived in a tiny little cubicle, again with a concrete slab flooring and tarpaper waist-high. We did have screens in there and under the metal roof. They look like the stables at a racetrack now.

This was my first experience taking care of war casualties. Or taking care of any kind of casualties because, remember, I came right out of nurses' training. When I was in nurses' training, nurses could not start intravenous; they couldn't do major dressing. You would get the dressing tray and assist the physician while he changed the dressing. You couldn't insert nasogastric tubes or do anything like that. Well, it was a rude awakening, to find yourself in the situation where you were expected to do all of those things because, of course, in a situation like that, your physicians are spending most of their time in the operating room as the casualties come in.

We had a large number of surgical patients--the trauma patients--but we had a still larger number of medical patients because of the environment and the disease in the tropics. We had a lot of malaria, hepatitis, jungle rot (a terrible dermatitis that they had no cure for, and still don't), scrub typhus, dengue fever, all of those different tropical diseases that the troops encountered in the jungles. . . .

The care of these patients, although under primitive conditions, truly, in comparison to today, was good care. They got the best care. Of course, that's evidenced by the few who died in the situation. We didn't have the evacuation of our patients in the Pacific Theater as they had in Europe because any of the vessels being used over in the Pacific were for troops and supplies. We just didn't have them. So patients who were in the jungle down there in Dobadura could be spinal injuries, amputees, anything that should go back to a general hospital, stayed with us in our primitive jungle hospitals for months. Then they would be evacuated by ship or plane to Australia, where we had larger hospitals. . . .

Source: Institute of Texan Cultures

THOUGHT QUESTIONS:

1. How much training did Dunlap have before shipping out to the Pacific Theater?

2. How did Dunlap describe the working conditions for the nurses and doctors at Dobadura? What kind of patients did she encounter?

3. Did Dunlap feel that she was adequately prepared for what she and the other nurses were asked to do? Why or why not?

A Texas Tank Commander Recalls Saipan and Iwo Jima

The Veterans History Project of the Library of Congress's American Folklore has been gathering firsthand soldier (and noncombatant) accounts of their military experiences since 2000. Interviews with veterans of the First World War (and conflicts as recent as the fighting in Iraq and Afghanistan) are included in the collection, many of which are available online. Large numbers of Texas veterans of World War II have been interviewed for the project, including Canara G. Carruth, who served as a tank commander in the Marine Corps's Second Armored Amphibious Battalion. Hailing from the small town of Pampa in the Texas Panhandle, Carruth enlisted in 1943, serving in the Northern Marianas Campaign (Battles of Saipan and Tinian) and taking part in heavy combat on Iwo Jima. After the war, Carruth returned to Pampa, got married, and eventually worked as a furniture store salesman until his retirement in 1994. Below are excerpts from the transcript of his interesting 2010 oral interview.

Interviewer: Why did you join?

Carruth: I had a reason to join. My -- one of my uncles, which was my mother's brother, was in the Bataan March. And he was taken prisoner and shipped up to Japan. And I later found out that when he finally passed away -- he was as big a man as I am -- and he weighed less than 100 pounds. So he, more or less, starved. I just figure, I can get even for Uncle Rusty. In other words, I just wanted to go do my part because they treated him so bad, you know....

Interviewer: Was there anything special you did for good luck?

Carruth: Well, I don't know about that. I was -- something that really bothers me, even to this day, and it -- every now and then they show it on television, but as we went around the island of Saipan on the north end, there was some extreme cliffs there. And these people were jumping off this cliff and killing theirselves [sic.]. The Japanese had told them that we were so mean that we would kill their babies and eat them and all of this kind of stuff... Bozart [his tank gun loader, a Texan from Lockhart] and I, after the island was secured, we decided to go up the incline there, which they call a mountain, but it was about 7- or 800 feet above sea level, and get some bananas. Because they weren't shot up like they were down on the beach, you know. So he and I go up there one afternoon, and we found some beautiful bananas, got bananas and everything. I had one on each shoulders with a board behind me. I heard him hollering, "You bring a weapon?" And I said, "No. Why?" He said, "I'm looking at Japanese" -- only he didn't call them a Japanese -- "right straight in the eyes." And I said, "Let's get out of here." So we started down that hill just as hard as we could run. And that Jap was shooting at us, and the dirt was just flying everywhere, but he never did get us. And when we got back to camp, we dared anybody to eat the bananas besides us....

Interviewer: Were you awarded any medals or citations?

Carruth: Yeah, but I don't remember what they are. I've got them out there at the house, but I don't know what they were. I --

Interviewer: Do you remember how you got them, what you got them for?

Carruth: Most of them was just issued things. Now, I need to explain a little about -- I was in D -- A, B, C, D company, my battalion, and I was the last platoon in the battalion, I was. I was in it. Well, by the time all the ranks and medals and what have you come down, there wasn't none left for people in the third platoon. So we got gypped out of a few medals, but I don't care about them. I mean, so what. One time -- one time I got out and pushed a round out of 75 in hung fire, and I should have got a medal for that, but I didn't.

Interviewer: Do you want to tell me the story about it?

Carruth: Well, it was when we was going to Iwo, and it was real, real crazy about Iwo. We didn't receive any fire whatsoever going into the island. And of course we were shooting at gun emplacements up on top of Mount Suribachi [a volcanic uplift on the island made famous by Joe Rosenthal's Pulitzer Prize-winning photograph of the flag raising atop the summit after its capture]. Well, this -- this dud, that's what it was, it didn't fire. And the only way we could get it out is get out there and push it out with a rod. So I climbed out of my turret, went around and pushed the stinker out, and throwed it in the ocean. So that's -- that's how come I should have got a star for that, but I didn't.

In a sense, we was in enemy territory for sure. But we weren't receiving any fire. We received it after we got on the beach. That's when we started getting all that fire. But my tank was one of the first tanks that even got on the beach. We were right below Mount Suribachi, and we did make it up. My driver, he was a very excellent driver. He got us up there, and we started firing into Mount Suribachi. By the time that we got up and got set up, why, all the Japanese cut loose with everything they had. I mean, boy, there was iron flying everywhere. Well, a beach patrol had come ashore. And he said, "Get that thing off the beach because you're drawing too much fire." So I told Steve, I said, "Get going, Steve." Well, he was already turning because he was listening to the radio, too. So we went back out into water. And my crew, we would float around the volcano, and we would fire into what we thought was gun emplacements or anything. And we'd get some fire back every now and then. But for five days, we floated around out there, seven of us in a tank.

Well, before we got off the beach, we got hit, too, and it tore the top off of my engine and knocked the turret in right in the middle of my back about that far, about three inches. And it was that thick. And it just shook the old tank like a baby rattle when it hit us. It just shook all over. Well, we got out there. And on the fifth day, the old engine just give up. So a sailor come by in a Higgins boat and wanted to know if he could help us. I said, "We're going to shore." So we went to Iwo Jima after five days. But in this five days, we had a lot of things happen. We were there when the flag was raised and everything, and the horns honking and all of this kind of stuff. But that was the fifth day also.

But one afternoon, we were water soaked out there in the water. I mean, your skin wrought up and everything. Well, we talked the LST [short for "landing ship tank" – a landing craft designed to carry vehicles, cargo, and troops ashore during amphibious operations] fellow into letting us come ashore -- I mean, come aboard, and he fed us. Because we had been eating rations all this time. Well, I told my crew, I said, "He is going to have to throw us off this ship." I said, "We're not going off here." Well, he made his word stick, so we had to get off the ship. And, of course, there weren't some very nice words said about that fellow. But anyway we had to get back in the tank, and we started back around the volcano, and it is dark. All at once the sirens was going off. And here come a Japanese airplane. And, boy, ammunition, every other -- every fifth bullet was a tracer. You'd see it. The sky was just full of red tracers. And he picked the ship to hit. Guess what? He got that LST we got kicked off of. The next morning, the whole front of it was burned up. We never did see him. But we kind of apologized to that fellow. I never did see him, but in our mind we apologized for what we called him, you know....

Interviewer: Would you like to say anything about how your service and experience has affected your life?

Carruth: ... it makes a man out of a kid, that's for sure. And, you know, it does some things, really -- in other words, you know, to kill a person, that kind of gets under your skin and all of that kind of stuff; but you know if you don't kill him, he will kill you. See, so you don't have a lot of choice. That bothers me because that's quite what it amounted to. But, truthfully, I never had any just hand-to-hand fighting the whole time I was there because I was in this tank all the time, see. And if we killed somebody, why, I didn't know it. I mean, it is very possible we did and all of that. But we didn't have it like the infantry has it. In fact, on this trip, my wife and I went to back to the Marianas, there was a guy from California. And he said he hit the beach on Saipan that morning and jumped in a hole, and there was two live Japs. And he said, "I'm still here." In other words, that's assuming he had to kill two people, see....

Source: Veterans History Project, American Folklife Center, Library of Congress

THOUGHT QUESTIONS:

1. Why did Sergeant Carruth volunteer for military service—for patriotic or personal reasons? Explain.

2. A common theme in many interviews with combat veterans is the luck they sometimes experienced to explain how they survived the war. How do the excerpts from Carruth's story follow that theme?

3. Though a veteran of heavy combat, how did Carruth explain that he was partially insulated from the most brutal aspects of warfare by serving in a tank?

A Texas POW in Europe Discusses His Incarceration

Aside from serving on a German U-Boat during the second half of the conflict, being a member of an American or British bomber crew in Europe was the most dangerous job to have during World War II. The Library of Congress Veterans History Project has performed a large number of oral interviews with Texas bomber pilots and crew members who survived the war, some of whom were shot down and taken prisoner. One riveting example, excerpted below, was given by John R. Lemons, Jr. of Dallas who was downed over Germany and taken prisoner on his eighth mission.

Interviewer:
Were you ever a prisoner of war?

John R. Lemons, Jr.:
Yes, I was. Mission number eight--I call it seven and a half. You know why I say that? I got half way there and didn't get half way back. Anyway, my eighth mission was to Kassel, Germany, and our Bomb Group was leading 300 airplanes. So, our 445th Group was leading [50 to] 60 planes behind us and for some reason we made a deviation on approach to the target, and made a turn and everybody was supposed to follow us, but [it] turns out we were wrong and they were right. They refused to go, and we went on and within five minutes we dropped our bombs and all along no fighter escorts, nothing, ... and all of a sudden the sky was full of planes, not ours. 125 [to] 150 ME 109s [and] FW 190s [German fighter planes] attacked us. We had 35 planes, [in] three minutes we lost 25 planes just like that, and I was one of those and we were on fire, [the] plane was burning....I bailed out at 235 [23,500 feet]. Plane on fire, I knew it was going to blow up any minute, it did blow up a little later on when I was out, and I didn't know whether anybody ever survived, but I pulled my rip cord at 235, and I'm right in the battle, I mean, the fighters are shooting at everybody, and shooting planes are still burning and on fire, and here I am within five feet of the fighter and of course I passed out because I've been out of oxygen a few minutes I'm sure, for a minute or two at least, and when I came to, I was still above

the cloud, the solid cloud cover. We were at 235, as I said and at 12,000, I probably came to and I could see the clouds beneath me and when I broke through the clouds I could see the ground and, of course, then I was trying to figure out how can I miss those trees, I didn't want to land on those trees....

I was able to get my 'chute to let me clear the trees from here to that ball out there. And so I missed that and as soon as I hit the ground I folded up my 'chute, and before I could say boo, two German farmers had me with pitchforks. They asked me and I said, "Americans, Americans," and they were after me and two young soldiers about 16 years old, which were Wehrmachts [German regular army soldiers] came to my aid and they took me away from those two farmers, and probably saved my life, because they were probably going to kill me. So, they marched me to town and, of course, it was a lot of problem getting to town and finally [I] was put in a basement in City Hall. It turned out it was a Wehrmacht barracks, I didn't know that at the time, and we had by that time 25 or 30 airmen like me who had been in my Bomb Group and had been shot down and captured, some with wounds, and lots of burns and all kinds of problems and we had no, no medical help at all. So, the next morning they asked us all that could walk to take and literally carry all those that couldn't and put them on the train. And so I was able to walk with a litter to get one airman on the train. And of course they took me to [an] interrogation camp from there...

Interviewer:
Do you know where they took you?

John R. Lemons, Jr.:
Yes, Weslar, Germany, it's close to the town of Frankfurt, if you know where Frankfurt is. And there you go through interrogation, you know it's like the Air Force had a training film that shows you, if you should be shot down or captured what you're supposed to do and what to expect. Of course, you know that, so it was just like sitting in the movie. Like me sitting in a movie watching what I've already seen. Of course, they threatened you that they were going to turn you over to Gestapo and all that kind of stuff. After three or four days, they finally turn you loose and put you on a train, and I wound up going to [a] prison camp in Old Poland. You know where Poland is now? It's on the Baltic Sea; we were about three miles from the Baltic Sea, in old Poland, real east of Berlin. And we stayed there until certain things happened and that was from September the 27th [1944], which was the day I was shot down. I got there on October the 5th, and by December we could hear artillery fire. We knew what it was, the Russians were coming...We were told that we would be marched out....January the 31st, about two o'clock in the morning... we marched for a while and they put us on a train, and that went on for about six or seven days. [We] went through Berlin, dodging air raids and all that kind of stuff, until we got to another camp which is called Nuremberg....When we got to that camp it was an Old Italian prisoner of war camp. The Germans, you know, got mixed with them. So we were in there and that was a lice-infected place. You had no place to sleep, no room for you, and again something was happening....We got BBC every day, if you think we didn't have means of knowing what was going on, we did. So we knew that the Americans and British were about to roll on this camp, so the Germans did the same thing again. They said we're out with you and out you went. They took out 2,500 of us again and [we were] marched

for 13 days to go to Lewisburg, which is near Munich. Across the dam you know down to the [Isar] River and that's where I was when General George S. Patton, kept coming, and sure enough on the 29th day of April. He ran through the camp, ran over all the barbed wire with all of the tanks, and we were free....

Interviewer:
What was the food like that you got, maybe you should go with not your prisoner of war food, but the other food?

John R. Lemons, Jr.:
Well, you go for prisoner of war food [or] you had no food. The thing you may have heard of, maybe you haven't heard of, I don't know, is the American Red Cross is supposed to send to prisoners of war what they call a food parcel....It's kind of like a ten-in-one, if you heard of [what] the military called a ten-in-one pack. It's a little box that would be about that big and about that thick and had enough food in there to last you one week, for one man, you had 1,000 calories a day. And they would have cigarettes and pipe, cards, soap, wash rag, and canned goods, cheese, powdered milk, stuff that could actually go for a week, but Germans never gave you that. What, they would do, in my first camp, they were able to give me what they call [a] two-men-on-one parcel, except that they robbed half of it, so they gave you half of a ration and divided by two; so, it was nothing. So we had the German food which was usually black bread, a little margarine, and sometimes a piece of baughslaughter [horsemeat], a bucket of [what] we called "green hell," which was a bucket of grass with water in it, and a gallon bucket. We had 25 men to a room and we had one loaf of bread about that big and the thing you had to do there was after you make everybody happy with that [loaf] of bread in 25 pieces and make them the biggest piece they got, I want that one, so, we had a system, you know a card system, so that's what you'd do. Put your card down and that's what you got and that was it. So that's what we did for everything....Food was always a constant problem and the only way to get food is either you could trade for it, if you could find a German soldier or guard who would take one of your cigarettes, if you had some. I saved all mine, I didn't smoke, so that was like money. You could trade a cigarette for a loaf of bread. One cigarette gets you the whole bread.

Interviewer:
Wow.

John R. Lemons, Jr.:
So, of course, if you're marching on the road, you know, we slept in barns and slept on in the woods, anywhere they could park us. Every night, we marched 13 days from Nuremberg to Lewisburg, see, so we learned how to find potatoes buried in the farmer's yard and we even got a few chickens. Potatoes were easy to find, turnips were easy to find...The guards couldn't watch us, the farmer couldn't watch, they had three, four hundred guys in a barn, he couldn't watch us all if he had to, one guard couldn't watch, so we were pretty much loose.

Interviewer:
Did you ever feel any pressure or stress?

John R. Lemons, Jr.:
Oh, I probably did, but I always knew that I was going to get to go home soon. I didn't know when, but I knew the war was going to be over. Of course, when I was shot down, you know, that's the first thing that guys already captured would [ask] you—you're brand new, you just flew in yesterday and got shot down, you know. Well, I know the war is over at Christmas, we come in optimistic, the war will be over before Christmas and we'll all be home for Christmas, and [then] Christmas came and went and we still weren't home. So that's the next guy behind me, we asked the same thing. They were optimistic too, but it didn't work as fast as we thought.

Interviewer:
How did the soldiers entertain themselves?

John R. Lemons, Jr.:
…Walk around all day. Of course, you had barbed wire and they had towers with guns up there that if you wanted to cross that line they would shoot you anyway. But you didn't dare get over the warning wire like if you're playing with a football or a baseball and the ball fell over there in the wrong spot, you get somebody to get him to let you know. We didn't want to go get the ball because we knew he had his hand on his gun. So that's the only, you didn't dare go by the wire is what I'm trying to say, but we had the deck of cards [that] came in those parcels and we would play cards, we would play drinking games, anything you could think of.…

Interviewer:
Do you recall any particularly humorous or unusual events?

John R. Lemons, Jr.:
They had sometimes they had what they called entertainment over at the mess hall, and put on a show and guys would play dancing girls, or something like that you know, dress up. I didn't participate in that but it was entertainment watching them.…

Source: Veterans History Project, American Folklife Center, Library of Congress

THOUGHT QUESTIONS:

1. How did Lemons say he was captured? What were the general locations of the prison camps in which he was held by the Germans?

2. What did the prisoners eat and how did Lemons and the others scrounge for food or trade to supplement their diet?

3. What did the prisoners do to relieve their boredom? What did Lemons say they had to be careful not to do?

Crystal City Internment Camp

Credit: UTSA's Institute of Texan Cultures, (top #098-1011, Courtesy of Betty Fly) Housing units in the Crystal City Internment Camp, Texas, 1943-1945, (bottom left #079-0385 and right #079-0386, Courtesy of Mona Baskin) Looking down the road with a guard tower in the background of the Japanese internment camp and a guard on horseback riding along the wire fence.

Japanese American civilians in FBI custody were held at this site during World War II as well as German and Japanese Latin Americans and at least one Italian Latin American family. Several types of housing were provided. One room shelters were provided for couples and those with children. Internees were issued "coupon checks," to purchase food or clothing items at a general store. A Surveillance Division patrolled the fence line and provided the armed guards for the towers, while an Internal Security Division operated a small police force inside the compound. In the winter, mud was everywhere and in the summer, the heat was intense with frequent dust storms. The Crystal City camp inducted 4,751 internees, including 153 births. The facility closed in February 1948.

THOUGHT QUESTION:

Why did the federal government establish these camps?

BIOGRAPHIES

OVETA CULP HOBBY (1905-1995). Oveta Culp Hobby, commanding officer of the Women's Army Corps, the first Secretary of the Department of Health, Education and Welfare, and Chairman of the Board of the *Houston Post* was born in Killeen, Texas on January 19, 1905. The daughter of a state legislator, Oveta Culp attended public schools, graduated from Temple High School, and studied at Mary Hardin Baylor College in Belton.

In 1925, the speaker of the Texas House of Representatives asked Oveta to serve as legislative parliamentarian, which she performed until 1931 while continuing her education at the University of Texas. She became a clerk for the Banking Commission, codifying the banking laws of the state. Later she became a clerk for the legislature's judiciary committee. In 1928 she helped organize the Democratic Party Convention held in Houston and worked in Tom Connally's campaign for United States senator against Earle Mayfield. After working with a successful Houston candidate's mayoral campaign, Oveta agreed to serve as assistant to the city attorney. In 1930 she ran her only campaign for elective office when she unsuccessfully sought a seat in the legislature from Houston.

Oveta Culp knew former governor, then editor and publisher of the *Houston Post*, William Hobby, through her father. They resumed their friendship when she was the Houston city attorney's assistant. Though she was only twenty-six and he was fifty-three, they married in 1931. The couple eventually had two children. In 1931 Oveta Culp Hobby began to learn the newspaper publishing business. She reviewed books for the *Houston Post*, edited copy, wrote editorials, and acted as assistant to her husband. She also performed a myriad of civic obligations, including serving as a board member for Houston's Museum of Fine Arts, a member of the Houston Symphony Orchestra Committee, and a citizens' committee to plan a flood-control program for the city. In the summer of 1936 the Hobbys both survived a private plane crash in a cotton patch on a flight from Dallas to Houston when a fire developed in the oil line. Unharmed, Mrs. Hobby pulled her unconscious husband from the burning wreckage.

In June 1941 the Army contacted Oveta about possibly serving as organizer of the women's activities. The War Department was receiving numerous requests from women after Congress passed the Selective Service Act asking how they could do their part to serve their country. She refused, citing her work load and family obligations, but agreed to create an organizational chart with recommendations on ways women could serve. She was eventually convinced to come to Washington and implement her plan, heading the Women's Interest Section of the War Department's Bureau of Public Relations. At General George Marshall's request, she studied the role of women in the British and French armies and prepared a plan by which the United States could learn from their experiences.

Hobby was heading home to Houston when she learned of the Japanese attack on Pearl Harbor. She returned to Washington, where General Marshall placed her in charge of the new Women's Army Auxiliary Corps (WAAC). Because Congress had been unwilling to make the WAACs an integral part of the army, the corps served an ambiguous role in the War Department that required forceful action by Hobby and others if they were not to be ignored. Though never a militant feminist, she perfectly understood the numerous barriers to women that existed at the time. Hobby worked diligently to ensure proper treatment in every imaginable situation from salary issues to uniform design to basic respect from career military officers who despised the thought of women soldiers in the army. All volunteers, the WAACs soon proved their value to the military, performing vital support functions from secretarial work and PBX operations to kitchen patrol and parachute folding. When the corps was first organized, Congress reluctantly agreed to allow women to perform fifty-four army jobs. Hobby (who attained the rank of colonel) eventually arranged for the number of responsibilities for women be increased to 239. Exhausted from her duties, she resigned in July 1945. Six months earlier she received the Distinguished Service Medal for outstanding service.

Hobby resumed her career as director of the family-owned KPRC radio and TV stations as well as executive vice president of the *Houston Post*. Though Democrats, the Hobbys were supportive of General Dwight D. Eisenhower's successful 1952 presidential campaign. In 1953 she became the first Secretary of the new Department of Health, Education, and Welfare. In 1955 Mrs. Hobby resumed her position with the *Houston Post* as president and editor. Continuing her lifelong commitment to public service, she served on numerous boards, including the American Red Cross and the American Cancer Society, and special committees for the remainder of her life. In 1984 Hobby was named to the Texas Women's Hall of Fame. She died on August 16, 1995 and was buried at Glenwood Cemetery in Houston.

CHESTER NIMITZ (1885-1966). Chester William Nimitz, commander of the U.S. Pacific Fleet during World War II, was born in Fredericksburg, Texas, on February 24, 1885. With his father having died before he was born, his grandfather, Charles H. Nimitz, a German immigrant and owner of the Nimitz Hotel, served as his influential father figure. Nimitz sought an appointment to the United States Military Academy primarily because he had little chance otherwise of affording a college education. Upon learning that he would not receive an appointment there, he applied for admission to the United States Naval Academy. After receiving a nomination there, he excelled and graduated seventh in his class in 1905.

He served two years as a midshipman aboard the *U.S.S. Ohio* before being commissioned and given command of the gunboat *Panay* in the Philippines. After transfer to the command of the destroyer *Decatur*, the ship ran aground and Nimitz was court-martialed. He received a stern reprimand and assigned to submarine duty where he gained valuable expertise on the use of submarines in naval warfare. Shortly after his marriage to Catherine Vance Freeman in 1913, Nimitz left for Europe to study diesel engines in Germany. He returned to Brooklyn Navy Yard to supervise the installation of the first diesel engines to power U.S. Navy vessels.

During World War I he served as chief of staff to Adm. Samuel S. Robison, commander of the Atlantic Submarine Force, then as executive officer of the battleship *South Carolina*. After the war, Nimitz went to Pearl Harbor to build the submarine base and command the Submarine Division. He then attended the Navy War College where he developed a plan for a theoretical Pacific war against Japan that he eventually applied during World War II. In 1926, the Navy assigned Nimitz to the University of California at Berkeley to develop the prototype for the Naval Reserve Officers Training Corps. The ROTC model he produced would be duplicated in colleges and universities across the country. Nimitz left Berkeley in 1929 with the rank of captain and held numerous commands before being promoted to rear admiral. In 1939 he became chief of the Bureau of

Navigation, a position he held when the Japanese attacked Pearl Harbor. When Admiral Husband E. Kimmel was relieved as commander-in-chief of the Pacific Fleet after the raid, Nimitz was chosen to replace him.

With the rank of fleet admiral, Nimitz sought to exploit Japan's mistakes and the positive aspects of the American position, especially the fact the submarine base at Pearl Harbor remained intact and no aircraft carriers were destroyed due to their absence from Hawaii when the Japanese attacked. From his headquarters, Nimitz directed the initial defense maneuvers, culminating in the successful engagements in the Coral Sea and at Midway Island. He then coordinated the counterattack against the overextended Japanese via the "island hopping" strategy whereby American forces attacked only important selected islands and bypassed others to quickly approach the Japanese home islands. Nimitz signed the peace treaty for the United States aboard the battleship *Missouri* in Tokyo Bay on September 2, 1945.

With the return of peace, Nimitz succeeded Admiral Ernest King as commander-in-chief of the United States Fleet for two years before being assigned to general "duty as directed by the Secretary of the Navy." He then served as a United Nations roving ambassador and regent of the University of California. He died on February 20, 1966, and was buried in Golden Gate National Cemetery, San Bruno, California.

MACARIO GARCÍA (1920-1972). Recipient of the Congressional Medal of Honor during World War II, Macario García was born into a farm worker family on January 2, 1920 in Villa de Castaño, Mexico. In 1923 the family moved to Texas, settling in Sugar Land near Houston. With his siblings, he helped to support his family by picking crops.

García was drafted into the army in late 1942. Wounded during the Normandy invasion, he recovered and rejoined his unit in the Fourth Infantry Division. On November 27, 1944, he bravely distinguished himself in battle in western Germany when he singlehandedly assaulted two enemy machine-gun emplacements blocking his company's advance. Though wounded in the shoulder and foot, he crawled ahead towards the machine-gun nests and destroyed the position with grenades, killing six German soldiers and capturing four others. President Harry S Truman personally awarded García the Medal of Honor at a White House ceremony on August 23, 1945. García also received the Purple Heart, the Bronze Star, and the Combat Infantryman's Badge. The government of Mexico awarded him the Mérito Militar, the Mexican equivalent of the Medal of Honor. García received an honorable discharge from the army with the rank of sergeant. He returned to Texas with great fanfare as a war hero and was often asked to speak at meetings and banquets.

Despite his elevated status, García attracted media attention in September 1945 when he was involved in a fracas at the Oasis Café, a popular restaurant in Fort Bend County near Sugar Land. While the proprietor later stated that García and his party were told to leave because of his supposed drunkenness and belligerency, the veteran denied such claims and asserted that they were refused service because they were Hispanic. Upset over being treated as a second-class citizen despite his military service, García's quarrel with the café owner and staff escalated to the point that dishware and punches were thrown, culminating with the veteran receiving a blow to the back by someone wielding a baseball bat. After the police were called, García was arrested and spent the night in jail. His case immediately became a symbolic rallying point for the Tejano community after John J. Herrera, the vice president of the League of United Latin American Citizens, sent copies of local coverage of the incident to national journalist Walter Winchell, who accepted García's version of events and publicly shamed Richmond, Texas during his nationally syndicated radio broadcast for what had transpired. At that point, Fort Bend County prosecutors formally charged García with assault to justify the actions that local law enforcement had previously taken and thus further reinforced the narrative that the police had tried to shield the allegedly drunken war hero from embarrassment, but now authorities had no choice but to press charges. As LULAC and other groups organized fundraisers for García's defense, enabling the hiring of quality lawyers including former governor James V. Allred, news organizations from across the state began requesting space in the county courthouse to witness and report on the proceedings of the coming trial. Such publicity inevitably contributed to a series of postponements into the following year, followed by a formal dismissal of the case.

On June 25, 1947, García became an American citizen. In 1951, he earned his high school diploma. The next year he married Alicia Reyes, with whom he raised three children. Like other soldiers in the postwar years, he found difficulties finding steady work. The Veterans Administration (VA) eventually hired him to be a counselor. García stayed at the VA for twenty-five years until dying in a car crash on Christmas Eve, 1972. He was buried in the National Cemetery in Houston with full military honors. In 1981, the Houston City Council honored him by officially changing the name of Sixty-ninth Street, running through the heart of the city's Mexican American neighborhood, to Macario García Drive.

AUDIE MURPHY (1925–1971). Audie Leon Murphy, the most decorated American combat soldier of World War II, was born into a poor sharecropper family in Hunt County, Texas. After his father abandoned his wife and twelve children, Audie, the seventh oldest, dropped out of school in fifth grade and found a cotton-picking job to add to the family's meager income. He also learned how to use a rifle to hunt small game to supplement the family diet. When his mother died in 1941, he worked at various jobs in Greenville while county authorities placed his three youngest siblings in a local orphanage.

After the Japanese attack on Pearl Harbor in December 1941, he sought to enlist in the Marines as an army paratrooper, but the five-foot-five-inch Texan was turned down due to his size and youth. He entered the U.S. Army as an infantryman in June 1942, aided by his eldest sister who signed an affidavit falsely claiming that he was a year older than his 17 years. After basic training at Camp Wolters, he was sent to Fort Meade, Maryland for advanced infantry training. Murphy was shipped to North Africa in early 1943 and assigned to the 3rd Infantry Division, promoted to corporal, and saw his first action during the invasion of Sicily. He participated in the September 1943 landing at Salerno in southern Italy and was promoted to platoon sergeant after a series of engagements through February 1944. He received the Bronze Star for single-handedly taking out a German tank, which threatened his platoon in early March, before taking part in the June 4, 1944 liberation of Rome. During the Allied invasion of southern France, Murphy received the Distinguished Service Cross for actions taken on August 15, 1944, when he charged and eliminated a German position after his best friend was killed by enemy troops pretending to surrender. He received his first Purple Heart after receiving a heel wound from mortar fire in September 1944 in northeastern France. His first Silver Star came after leading a daring attack on a German machine gun position holding a commanding position blocking his unit's advance. After being promoted to second lieutenant in October 1944, Murphy was shot in the hip by a German sniper, taking him out of action for four months.

Rejoining his platoon in January 1945, Murphy led a defense against a German armor attack with significant infantry support. Ordering his men into nearby woods for cover, Lieutenant Murphy called in artillery support from a field radio while firing from the .50 caliber machine gun mounted atop a disabled tank. Though wounded in the leg, he was able to repel the advancing Germans for over an hour, killing or wounding 50 enemy soldiers in the process. For his actions, Murphy received the Congressional Medal of Honor, the Legion of Merit medal from the French government, promotion to the rank of first lieutenant, and removal from the front lines for the remainder of the war. The Texan's fame had reached a point that the U.S. military would not risk the blow to national morale should his luck run out on the battlefield.

After the war, actor James Cagney brought Murphy to Hollywood and convinced him to pursue a career in film. Though he admitted to lacking any natural acting talent, Cagney signed the veteran to his production company believing that his boyish good looks and his war hero status, helped with acting lessons and voice training, could lead to a profitable career. After appearing in a few bit parts, Murphy's first leading role was as a youthful delinquent on the run from the law in 1949's *Bad Boy*. Universal Studios then offered him a seven-year contract, soon earning accolades for his portrayal of Billy the Kid in *The Kid from Texas* and the youth in a remake of *The Red Badge of Courage*. In 1955, he reached his highest fame as an actor when he portrayed himself in *To Hell and Back*. Based on his best-selling autobiographical book, the film became the biggest success to date for Universal Studios. He continued to appear in films, mostly subpar westerns, through the 1960s.

Murphy suffered from bouts of insomnia and nightmares since his military service ended, and reportedly slept with a loaded pistol under his pillow. He self-medicated with sleeping pills to help prevent nightmares, but his frequent episodes of stress continued and alarmed his friends and colleagues. His first wife, the actress Wanda Hendrix, claimed he once pointed his pistol at her during a moment of extreme agitation. Murphy talked openly about his troubles (now identified as posttraumatic stress disorder, or PTSD) and lobbied for the government to study and provide relief for veterans dealing with mental health issues after their service. His perceived need for thrill-seeking action led to, among other vices, a gambling habit that cost him the fortune that he earned through movies (he made over $4 million appearing in over 40 films during his 20-year career) and he and his second wife declared bankruptcy in 1968.

Murphy began to rebound in the early 1970s when he assumed the directorship of an investment company. On May 28, 1971, however, the veteran of numerous near-death encounters on the battlefields of Europe died when the small, twin-engine plane in which he was travelling on a business trip crashed into a mountain near Catawba, Virginia during inclement weather. A week later, he was buried with full military honors at Arlington National Cemetery. Murphy's final resting place located near the Tomb of the Unknown Soldier is the cemetery's second most-visited gravesite, after that of President John F. Kennedy.

Chapter 16

On the Threshold of Modernization, 1945-1959

Thurgood Marshall received his law degree from Howard University School of Law in 1933. He served as Special Counsel for the National Association for the Advancement of Colored People (NAACP) from 1938 to 1950 and Director and Counsel for the NAACP's Defense and Educational Fund from 1940 to 1961. Among other cases, Marshall successfully argued the landmark **Smith v. Allwright, Sweatt v. Painter,** *and* **Brown v. Board of Education** *cases before the U.S. Supreme Court. He served as a U.S. Circuit Judge and U.S. Solicitor General before President Lyndon Johnson nominated him to be the first African-American Supreme Court Justice in 1967. In this excerpt from an oral interview, Marshall describes the early attitudes of NAACP leaders toward Lyndon Johnson in the years before he became president.*

Interviewer: . . . Did you have any knowledge of Mr. Johnson back when he was a congressman or senator?

Marshall: I knew of him when he was a congressman, and I knew of him directly through Aubrey Williams and people like that in the [National] Youth Administration. The first I became interested was when he ran for the Senate.

Interviewer: Was this in the '48—?

Marshall: Yes, in Texas. I was in Texas working on the primary cases, and all of our people of the NAACP in that area were enthusiastically behind him.

Interviewer: Excuse me, sir, this must have been in '41 then, when Mr. Johnson first ran for the Senate and didn't get elected.

Marshall: It was '41 when he first ran. It was '41, because that's when the primary cases started. If I remember correctly, in the runoff the labor support dwindled away but the Negro support stuck with him. But when he became a senator, he was not among the liberals.

Interviewer: I was going to ask you about that. You said that the NAACP people in Texas were favorably inclined toward Mr. Johnson in those days?

Marshall: Solidly. So was the national office.

Interviewer: Did they have any real basis for this?

Marshall: Yes. Well, they knew him. The Negroes down there, they know each other pretty well. They were a pretty hard bunch. We followed their judgment. I didn't know him. But we couldn't engage in politics. All we could do was to talk about it. But Walter White, the head of the NAACP, did meet with him, as I remember, and did say that he was all right.

Interviewer: Did Mr. Johnson have any direct connection with what became the primary cases?

Marshall: No, none at all. He had no connection with them one way or the other. I never saw him, so he could not have had any connection. I ran the case and I didn't—

Interviewer: You certainly would have seen him.

Marshall: I would have known it, yes.

Interviewer: Then after 1948—after he became a senator—was there any change in this feeling?

Marshall: Well, Walter White, who handled the legislative matters in Congress, got very angry with him and stayed angry until he died, as a matter of fact.

Interviewer: On what basis?

Marshall: He just wouldn't support any of the legislation the NAACP was after. Walter White chalked it up to his great admiration for Sam Rayburn. He thought Sam Rayburn was calling the turn. Now whether that's true or not I don't know. But on our records he was not a liberal senator.

Interviewer: Incidentally, did Mr. Johnson have any connection with your other Texas case in the '50's?

Marshall: None.

Interviewer: *Sweatt versus Painter* at the University—?

Marshall: None. Not one way or the other. . . .

Interviewer: How about, I guess what is <u>the</u> case, the school integration case—*Brown versus the Board of Education*?

Marshall: Nothing. He had nothing to do with it at all.

Interviewer: This attitude you mentioned that Walter White had—did Mr. Johnson's activity in connection with the '57 civil rights bill change that any?

Marshall: Walter was dead in '57; Walter died in '55.

Interviewer: That's right. Roy Wilkins—

Marshall: Roy Wilkins took over then. No. Roy did not have the same opinion of him. Roy had a better opinion of him. He felt that he was the type of man in the Senate who could get things done, but he didn't. But he could have. He just chalked it up to politics. But he didn't have any—. As a matter of fact, Roy had very good thoughts about him. I know that as then and as of now.

Interviewer: What was the general opinion among civil rights leaders like yourself, of the '57 bill? Did you feel it was progress?

Marshall: Nothing. It wasn't doing any good. It was just barely progress because it had been a hundred years—eighty years—since we'd had one. The smallest slice was good rather than the whole loaf of bread. But it was understandable in my book because it was a strictly political move of getting something done. But when we'd been fighting since 1909 for something, it was good. Then when we looked at it, we had a different feeling.

Interviewer: Mostly I guess because of the elimination of Part 3 divisions?

Marshall: Sure. Oh, yes, we fought to the bitter end on that. Yet as you look back, it was great progress, it seems to me, to get them to move at all. I don't know, and I guess nobody would know, just what was sold in there and how it was sold. Whether we could have gotten more or not I don't know. Nobody will know except—well, Lyndon Johnson would know and those people that were running that inner corps of the Senate in those days. You see, as I looked at him as a senator and leader, they always said he was a great compromiser, but I've always thought that he had the compromise in his pocket when the thing started each time. He just waited for the right time to take it out.

Interviewer: You mean he had already figured out what was going to happen?

Marshall: Sure. He always won. Well, that all changed when he became President, anyhow.

Interviewer: In those years before Mr. Johnson left the Senate, did you ever talk to him about this problem of compliance with the '54 decision?

Marshall: I never talked to him. I don't remember having ever talked to him until I came down as Solicitor General; I don't believe. I might have, but I don't remember. . . .

Interviewer: To get back to Mr. Johnson, was there any dismay among civil rights leaders like yourself when he showed up on the '60 ticket for the Democratic party?

Marshall: It wasn't dismay; it was great surprise! If I remember correctly, some of them were dismayed. I was not. I have a funny feeling of giving the people a chance. And I remember before Averell Harriman went to the convention, in his house he talked to me about Johnson being Vice President and was positive he was going to be, and asked me what was my impression.

Interviewer: This was before the convention?

Marshall: Before the convention.

Interviewer: Harriman must have been one of the very few people who was seriously considering that.

Marshall: Before the convention. I told him I thought there was no problem at all. I said, "Because in my book Texas is not South; it's Southwest," and that his record wasn't that bad. But I do remember that other people in NAACP hit the ceiling.

Interviewer: Surely not Mr. Wilkins himself?

Marshall: Yeah, oh he did hit the ceiling! He bounced off the ceiling.

Interviewer: But I believe he calmed down or endorsed—

Marshall: Very shortly thereafter—it wasn't long.

Interviewer: Did anyone have to talk to him to—?

Marshall: At that stage they were all talking to the Kennedys. I don't know how many times Roy must have been in there with the Kennedys. Once I talked to Bobby—that's all—just once. Roy ran the show, I mean. Being in Legal Defense I had to stay out of anything that looked like politics, so I did. But once I talked to--I had a very unsatisfactory conference with Bobby about the civil rights movement.

Interviewer: When was that?

Marshall: Shortly after they took over—about the first of the year, I guess.

Interviewer: After President Kennedy was inaugurated?

Marshall: Yes.

Interviewer: It was an unsatisfactory conference?

Marshall: Yes.

Interviewer: In what way?

Marshall: He spent all this time telling us what we should do.

Interviewer: What sort of suggestions did he have for you?

Marshall: Well, that we ought to concentrate on this and concentrate on that and what have you. I told him that so far as I was concerned we had been in the civil rights business since 1909, and he'd been in the President business a year. Well, I mean, that's the way--. But Roy used to have many conferences with the President, very rewarding ones.

Interviewer: People have said that the intensity of the civil rights movement kind of caught the Kennedy Administration by surprise when they came in.

Marshall: [It] should have. I don't know. I did have a conference with the President about three months before he announced his candidacy, when he was a senator, about just what was cooking. I'm sure I didn't pull any punches with him. I don't remember. It was a lunch and we spent about two hours together. But he got the story. He knew what it was. But I don't think the President realized the urgency of it.

Interviewer: You're referring to President Kennedy now?

Marshall: Yes. I don't think he realized.

Interviewer: Apparently, the activity in the South—Dr. King's activities and others—pushed the Kennedy Administration.

Marshall: Somebody pushed them. . . .

Source: Lyndon B. Johnson Presidential Library

THOUGHT QUESTIONS:

1. According to Marshall, how inclined were black Texans to support Johnson during his runs for the Senate in 1941 and 1948? How did the national NAACP leaders feel about Johnson at this time?

2. How did NAACP leaders feel about Johnson after he was elected in 1948? How did they feel about Johnson being chosen to be John Kennedy's running mate in 1960?

3. Discuss Marshall's comments about John Kennedy's approach to civil rights issues as he entered office.

===

House Concurrent Resolution No. 48 Creating the Gilmer-Aikin Committee (August, 1947)

===

The passage of the Gilmer-Aikin Laws (named for Representative Claud Gilmer and Senator A.M. Aikin, Jr.) became the most lasting achievement of the 51st Legislature and Governor Beauford Jester's governorship. This House Concurrent Resolution created the committee charged with studying public education reform. The committee's work led to three bills that overhauled the administration and financing of the Texas public school system by consolidating school districts, providing more equal funding between prosperous and poor districts, making district funding contingent on attendance, raising teacher salaries, and supplementing school staffs with education specialists. It remains the basis for the state's public school system today.

WHEREAS, Over a period of many years unequal educational opportunities have existed throughout the State of Texas between the several schools comprising the public school system of Texas; and

WHEREAS, There are many factors entering into and complicating this situation; and

WHEREAS, Leading educators and educational authorities, both in and outside the teaching profession, agree that the educational inequalities, above mentioned are increasing rather than decreasing, so that in spite of the foresight and evident intentions of the founders of our State and the framers of our State Constitution to provide equal educational advantages for all, Texas continues to lag further and farther behind educationally; and

WHEREAS, It is imperative that a long range public educational program be formulated for the State of Texas; now, therefore, be it

RESOLVED, by the House of Representatives, the Senate concurring, That a Committee composed of eighteen (18) members be immediately constituted to study same and all other questions relating to improvement of the public school system of Texas, and particularly with a view to effecting school district reorganization; obtaining uniform and adequate local support in the financing of an adequate, improved, and uniform school program for Texas; that necessary and suitable steps be taken to obtain the desired attendance in the schools by the children of Texas, and at least to an extent comparable with other States; that the School Laws of Texas be revised and recodified; that the methods, systems, and policies of other States of the United States, upon like subjects, be studied and recommended, where deemed applicable to Texas; and that unnecessary divisions and differences among school organizations, interests, and groups be ascertained and determined to the end that the best educational advantages may be obtained for the greatest number as promptly as possible; and, be it further

RESOLVED, that the Speaker of the House of Representatives shall appoint three (3) Members of the House of Representatives and three (3) additional members of said Committee: the Lieutenant Governor shall appoint three (3) Members of the Senate and three (3) additional members of said committee; and the Governor shall appoint six (6) members of said Committee; and, be it further

RESOLVED, That there is hereby appropriated out of the Contingent Fund of the Fiftieth Legislature the sum of Twenty-five Thousand Dollars ($25,000), or as much thereof as may be necessary,

Source: Texas State Library and Archives Commission

THOUGHT QUESTIONS:

1. What problems were identified at the beginning of the resolution leading to the need for the creation of the committee?

2. What were supposed to be the major goals of the committee?

3. Who were to serve on the committee tasked with this important work?

The U.S. Supreme Court's *Sweatt v. Painter* Decision

U.S. Supreme Court

SWEATT v. PAINTER, 339 U.S. 629 (1950)
SWEATT v. PAINTER ET AL.
CERTIORARI TO THE SUPREME COURT OF TEXAS.
No. 44.
Argued April 4, 1950.
Decided June 5, 1950.

W. J. Durham and Thurgood Marshall argued the cause for petitioner. . . .
MR. CHIEF JUSTICE VINSON delivered the opinion of the Court.

This case and *McLaurin v. Oklahoma State Regents* . . . present different aspects of this general question: To what extent does the Equal Protection Clause of the Fourteenth Amendment limit the power of a state to distinguish between students of different races in professional and graduate education in a state university? Broader issues have been urged for our consideration, but we adhere to the principle of deciding constitutional questions only in the context of the particular case before the Court. . . .

In the instant case, petitioner filed an application for admission to the University of Texas Law School for the February, 1946 term. His application was rejected solely because he is a Negro. Petitioner thereupon brought this suit for mandamus against the appropriate school officials, respondents here, to compel his admission. At that time, there was no law school in Texas which admitted Negroes.

The state trial court recognized that the action of the State in denying petitioner the opportunity to gain a legal education while granting it to others deprived him of the equal protection of the laws guaranteed by the Fourteenth Amendment. The court did not grant the relief requested, however, but continued the case for six months to allow the State to supply substantially equal facilities. At the expiration of the six months, in December, 1946, the court denied the writ on the showing that the authorized university officials had adopted an order calling for the opening of a law school for Negroes the following February. While petitioner's appeal was pending, such a school was made available, but petitioner refused to register therein. The Texas Court of Civil Appeals set aside the trial court's judgment and ordered the cause "remanded generally to the trial court for further proceedings without prejudice to the rights of any party to this suit."

On remand, a hearing was held on the issue of the equality of the educational facilities at the newly established school as compared with the University of Texas Law School.

Finding that the new school offered petitioner "privileges, advantages, and opportunities for the study of law substantially equivalent to those offered by the State to white students at the University of Texas," the trial court denied mandamus. The Court of Civil Appeals affirmed. Petitioner's application for a writ of error was denied by the Texas Supreme Court. We granted certiorari, because of the manifest importance of the constitutional issues involved.

The University of Texas Law School, from which petitioner was excluded, was staffed by a faculty of sixteen full-time and three part-time professors, some of whom are nationally recognized authorities in their field. Its student body numbered 850. The library contained over 65,000 volumes. Among the other facilities available to the students were a law review, moot court facilities, scholarship funds, and Order of the Coif affiliation. The school's alumni occupy the most distinguished positions in the private practice of the law and in the public life of the State. It may properly be considered one of the nation's ranking law schools.

The law school for Negroes which was to have opened in February, 1947, would have had no independent faculty or library. The teaching was to be carried on by four members of the University of Texas Law School faculty, who were to maintain their offices at the University of Texas while teaching at both institutions. Few of the 10,000 volumes ordered for the library had arrived; nor was there any full-time librarian. The school lacked accreditation.

Since the trial of this case, respondents report the opening of a law school at the Texas State University for Negroes. It is apparently on the road to full accreditation. It has a faculty of five full-time professors; a student body of 23; a library of some 16,500 volumes serviced by a full-time staff; a practice court and legal aid association; and one alumnus who has become a member of the Texas Bar.

Whether the University of Texas Law School is compared with the original or the new law school for Negroes, we cannot find substantial equality in the educational opportunities offered white and Negro law students by the State. In terms of number of the faculty, variety of courses and opportunity for specialization, size of the student body, scope of the library, availability of law review and similar activities, the University of Texas Law School is superior. What is more important, the University of Texas Law School possesses to a far greater degree those qualities which are incapable of objective measurement but which make for greatness in a law school. Such qualities, to name but a few, include reputation of the faculty, experience of the administration, position and influence of the alumni, standing in the community, traditions and prestige. It is difficult to believe that one who had a free choice between these law schools would consider the question close. Moreover, although the law is a highly learned profession, we are well aware that it is an intensely practical one. The law school, the proving ground for legal learning and practice, cannot be effective in isolation from the individuals and institutions with which the law interacts. Few students and no one who has practiced law would choose to study in an academic vacuum, removed from the interplay of ideas and the exchange of views with which the law is concerned. The law school to which Texas is willing to admit petitioner excludes from its student body members of the racial groups which number 85% of the population of the State and include most of the lawyers, witnesses, jurors, judges and other officials with whom petitioner will inevitably be dealing when he becomes a member of the Texas Bar. With such a substantial and significant segment of society excluded, we cannot conclude that the education offered petitioner is substantially equal to that which he would receive if admitted to the University of Texas Law School.

It may be argued that excluding petitioner from that school is no different from excluding white students from the new law school. This contention overlooks realities. It is unlikely that a member of a group so decisively in the majority, attending a school with rich traditions and   prestige which only a history of consistently maintained excellence could command, would claim that the opportunities afforded him for legal education were unequal to those held open to petitioner. That such a claim, if made, would be dishonored by the State, is no answer. "Equal protection of the laws is not achieved through indiscriminate imposition of inequalities." *Shelley v. Kraemer* (1948).

It is fundamental that these cases concern rights which are personal and present. This Court has stated unanimously that "The State must provide [legal education] for [petitioner] in conformity with the equal protection clause of the Fourteenth Amendment and provide it as soon as it does for applicants of any other group." *Sipuel v. Board of Regents* (1948). That case "did not present the issue whether a state might not satisfy the equal protection clause of the Fourteenth Amendment by establishing a separate law school for Negroes." *Fisher v. Hurst* (1948). In *Missouri ex rel. Gaines v. Canada* (1938), the Court, speaking through Chief Justice Hughes, declared that "petitioner's right was a personal one. It was as an individual that he was entitled to the equal protection of the laws, and the State was bound to furnish him within its borders facilities for legal education substantially equal to those which the State there afforded for persons of the white race, whether or not other negroes sought the same opportunity." These are the only cases in this Court which present the issue of the constitutional validity of race distinctions in state-supported graduate and professional education.

In accordance with these cases, petitioner may claim his full constitutional right: legal education equivalent to that offered by the State to students of other races. Such education is not available to him in a separate law school as offered by the State. We cannot, therefore, agree with respondents that the doctrine of *Plessy v. Ferguson* (1896), requires affirmance of the judgment below. Nor need we reach petitioner's contention that *Plessy v. Ferguson* should be reexamined in the light of contemporary knowledge respecting the purposes of the Fourteenth Amendment and the effects of racial segregation.

We hold that the Equal Protection Clause of the Fourteenth Amendment requires that petitioner be admitted to the University of Texas Law School. The judgment is reversed and the cause is remanded for proceedings not inconsistent with this opinion.

THOUGHT QUESTIONS:

1. What overall constitutional issue did the Justice Vinson state was involved in this case?

2. Why did the Supreme Court believe that the State of Texas failed to develop a law school for blacks that was comparable to the University of Texas Law School?

3. What did Justice Vinson mean when he wrote: "The law school, the proving ground for legal learning and practice, cannot be effective in isolation from the individuals and institutions with which the law interacts"?

A Shivers Supporter Praises the Governor

The 1952 presidential election marked a turning point in the evolution of the conservative wing of the Democratic Party in Texas into the beginnings of a revitalized Republican Party. After becoming governor, Allan Shivers took control of the Democratic Party executive commit-tee and filled it with his supporters. He also arranged changes in state election laws allowing for candidates to run in both the Democratic and Republican Party primaries. Conservative Democrats, nicknamed "Shivercrats," were able to run as candidates for both parties, giving Shivers effective control of both parties while compelling many voters to cast votes for Republicans for the first time. The "Tidelands Controversy" also weakened Texans' allegiance to the Democratic Party as the furor against President Truman and 1952 Democratic Party nominee Adlai Stevenson resulted in Shivers' endorsement of Republican candidate Dwight D. Eisenhower for president (Eisenhower eventually carried the state.)

The power struggle during the 1950s and 1960s among conservatives such as Shivers, moderates such as LBJ and Sam Rayburn, and liberals such as Ralph Yarborough greatly weak-ened the Texas Democratic Party's hold on state politics. The internal dissension began to subside in the 1970s only after many conservative Democrats left the party to join the Republicans.

This letter to Governor Shivers from a supporter refers to several issues (including segregation) and personalities (such as Lyndon Johnson) that divided the party during the 1950s

May 10, 1956

Honorable Allan Shivers
Governor of Texas
Austin, Texas

Dear Governor Shivers:

Thanks for your thoughtful expressions in regard to your visit with us as a most en-joyable part of our Centennial Celebration.

I hope that you have noticed that Kerr County went for States Rights, Interposition and Allan Shivers. We regret that others have not the foresight that we believe is ours, and your many friends here (as all over Texas) will remember you even as those yet unborn will read about you as one of the greatest Governors Texas ever had.

It has been suggested by ACE REID (a noted cow-boy cartoonist widely known and who lives here now) that one of us should stand up in the Dallas Convention and nominate our Pedernales river "ranchman" [Lyndon Johnson] as the Leader of the Texas Delagation [sic.] AND George Parr [the South Texas political boss] as Texas' Favorite Son. He said if one of us would, he'd guarantee through his connections to have a cartoon in almost every newspaper in the USA about it.

Thanks Governor, for your clean, richly blessed life and the good that you have done by both precept and example. Those who know you best, like Capt. Clint Peeples and others who analyze you when you are not aware of it, love you for the true Christian character which is yours, for your family life and the wonderful examples you set for others in your daily life.

I might run on and on, but you have other things to do than read what I might write, so with a closing GOD BLESS YOU and may all the good things in life be yours, I am

Sincerely,
J. Lovic Bullard

Source: Texas State Library and Archives Commission

THOUGHT QUESTIONS:

1. Based on Bullard's comments about "states' rights" and "interposition," what was his stand on maintaining segregation? How did Shivers use such sentiments to maintain political support during the 1950s?

2. Based on the phrases that he used, what are Bullard's attitudes toward Lyndon Johnson?

3. What overly praising comments did Bullard make about the governor? In his opinion, what made Shivers a great governor?

Excerpt from an Interview with Dr. Isidore J. Lamothe on Segregation in the Medical Field

Isadore Lamothe grew up in Louisiana and attended Howard University Medical School in Washington, D.C. before moving to Marshall, Texas after World War II. Lamothe participated in Marshall's civil rights struggle during the 1950s and 1960s, and for decades has served as a general practitioner for African American families in the Harrison County area of Northeast Texas. In this excerpt from an oral interview, Dr. Lamothe describes one of the lesser-known aspects of racial discrimination, namely, segregated medicine.

Lamothe:
. . . I was not allowed to practice in the hospital here. There were a couple of little private hospitals in the area—one in Jefferson that was owned by a Dr. Raymond Douglas, seven or eight beds, something like that. Accreditation wasn't nearly as stringent, and it probably wasn't even required or mandated at that time to operate a clinic or hospital like that. Then there was another one in Longview that was owned by an oil corporation or something. Dr. O.J. Moore operated that one. We could deliver babies in those [hospitals] from people who were able to afford it; insurance played a little part in those days. Didn't play a real great big part because a delivery in that day and time was thirty-five dollars.

So, if you had the money, it would be all right. If you didn't, we'd go on and do it anyway.

Memorial Hospital would have no part of us whatsoever. For fifteen years I practiced here, doing hospital medicine in the home. There were times when I was giving IV fluids and nailing a nail upon the wall and hanging the bottle from the nail and starting...

Interviewer:
So, there weren't black doctors; there weren't blacks going into these hospitals? Right?

Lamothe:
Black patients were going into the hospital, sure, but they were segregated; they were on the bottom floor. Talking about deliveries—the deliveries were being done, and they were put in these little rooms, and their babies were put in the dresser drawer. No cribs or nothing like that, no special facilities for babies at all, no pediatric unit or anything like that. No incubators, no anything for the black kids. And I understand that a number of them just didn't survive.

We got to the place where we could call a white doctor if we wanted to or if we knew that a patient needed to be admitted. Refer that patient to the white doctor, and he would admit the patient. Now, when the patient got better, he could either keep the patient if he wanted to, or he could refer back. Well, some of them kept the patients, and we had no control over that.

Interviewer:
The patient didn't have any control over it?

Lamothe:
Well, this has been a kind of a community where people, particularly blacks, have been made afraid of the system. They didn't contest anything. If somebody white said, "You do this," you do it, because you have some kind of an innate fear that something is going to happen to you—impending doom. Many times it had to do with jobs; other times it had to do with being able to get loans, maybe, the little bitty loans that they got, because they didn't get but a pittance. No black folk could get any big loans whatsoever.

But, in any event, they had that unfounded fear. Consequently, when the white doctor says, "Okay, you come back to see me next week, or the next week" after they get out of the hospital, they come back. And I don't see 'em anymore. And there were a few who would not accept our patients at all.

All of them had segregated waiting facilities, and I say waiting facilities, not necessarily waiting rooms. Because I know of one who had his office in this building, and the black waiting facility was on the back porch. The back porch had no heat, so that when wintertime came it was cold back there, and people would go back and sit on that back porch and wait for this guy. They'd see all of the white patients first, and then, if the evening came along and there was still some time, they would open the back door and say, "Come on in, Susie or John" or whoever. And, if they got to the point where they were tired and didn't want to do any more, they'd tell the rest of them to come back tomorrow, sick or no sick. It didn't make any difference. But that was the kind of system we were in. . . . .

Source: Institute of Texan Cultures

THOUGHT QUESTIONS:

1. Was Dr. Lamothe allowed to practice medicine at the local hospital? Why or why not?

2. How were black patients generally treated at the local segregated hospitals?

3. How did segregated hospitals impact Dr. Lamothe's practice of medicine?

A Texas Corporal Survives Pork Chop Hill during the Korean War

Often referred to as "The Forgotten War," the Korean War began in June 1950 when North Korean forces invaded South Korea. President Harry Truman soon assembled a coalition of United Nations (U.N.) members who sent troops to drive out the invaders and liberate South Korea. For the next three years, heavy fighting ensued between the North Koreans and their communist Chinese allies versus the South Koreans and U.N. forces (primarily American troops). Though the brutal conflict had entered a period of long stalemate, both sides continued to exchange attacks across the mountainous central portion of the country while peace talks dragged on. In April and July of 1953, just before an armistice agreement ending the war was signed, a couple of intense battles erupted around a location that came to be known by the Americans as "Pork Chop Hill." The Americans suffered over 1,000 casualties in both fights, but inflicted over 5,000 casualties on their Chinese attackers. Among the participants was Corporal Lino P. Juarez of Rio Hondo, Texas who related what he remembered about the combat for the Library of Congress's Veterans History Project.

Lino P. Juarez:
...Pork Chop was really -- I'm a survivor. I consider myself a survivor of Pork Chop. Pork Chop was a very, very ugly situation, very, very ugly, and we fought there about 12 days. I say "we." The Seventh Infantry Division was assigned to defend Pork Chop. Now, a division is composed of about approximately 17,000 or 20,000 men ... and they were assigned to defend Pork Chop. They would put in a battalion and then another one and another one, you know, and they were eating us up....It came our turn, and we were going in trucks to the objective, and I made a remark -- we were about 20 guys to a truck, we were in a convoy -- and I told one of my buddies who is a medic, I said, "You know, after we get through with this -- with this assignment they should send us home. This is going to be a very tough, tough thing." And the guy says, "Yeah, Juarez. They are going to send us home all right, in boxes."....

Anyway, on my way there I said -- I said a prayer. I had a prayer. I said, "God, I know where I'm going. I know a lot of men have died there already. And I know there is some on this truck that are going with me [who] are not going to make it. But I ask for -- I ask from you to give me what it takes, the courage to do what I have to do, and to come out alive, and I promise that I will serve you the rest of my life if you allow me to come home."....

When we reached the objective, my squad leader said, "Juarez, you go."... I didn't ask questions. But go where? Go where? I didn't ask. So I says, "Okay, Lino, what are you going to do?" I knew that it was bad. So I said, "Okay, Lino," talking to myself, "you get up and you do not allow -- don't make yourself a target. You get up and you jump down immediately and you go wherever you have to go, but move, move." So I got up and I jumped down, you know, and I ran toward the mountain. And they had a little road, dirt road, going around the mountain. So I said -- When I got here, I just blend myself against the wall to protect myself from the enemy, the enemy fire. So I said, "Okay. Where do I go from here?" I had no briefing whatsoever. None. None, my friend...

Interviewer:
Were you under gunfire?

Lino P. Juarez:
Well, we didn't know where the -- I didn't know where the enemy was. I know that they were there, but I didn't know where. Well, and I blend myself right against the wall of the -- of the mountain so I could be protected. It would be very hard for them to hit me because I was again blend against it. I was just lying like that....I knew I had to move because if you stand still they are going to get you. You've got to -- You've got to move, you know. So I kept moving and never looking back. So I went to the first bunker....And I came to it. I see the door. And it was full of wounded and dead people....There was a clearing station where they treat you and patch you up a little bit and then put you out. And at the entrance there was a young soldier that was bleeding from the knees down, bleeding bad, and you would -- the blood was like you were pouring water on him. It was just all red, all red below the knees, and he was -- he was dying, you know. He was going like this, his feet were. And I said, "Well, you know, this is not the place for me to be for sure," so I kept on going.

Well, I finally got to my destination what I -- that I found by just the guidance of God and that was the right location. I got in and it was dark. It was very dark because we were underground. And it smelled bad. The stench was unbearable. So I said, "Well, this is -- this is the spot." And I walked in and then I knelt....I made myself a target. I did not know there was an opening ... on the trench, and there was a [Chinese] sniper assigned to that opening, and anyone that would pass by there or make a target, he would -- he would kill them. The sniper, that's all he was doing. Well, I didn't know. And there was a very nice breeze. It was very hot. It was July. So I put myself there not knowing. And a guy, another veteran that was there that we went to relieve, yelled at me. He says, "Hey, get away from there, Soldier," and I jumped. You know, I jumped. And I says, "Why?" He says, "I don't know. I don't understand." "You don't understand what?" "Why you didn't get killed. I don't understand." He said, "You were there long enough for that guy to pump not one, but three bullets into you." "Oh, man, well, thank you for saving my life."...

Our assignment was to defend Pork Chop for 36 hours....And don't ask me, I don't remember eating, I only had water, no food at noontime. We didn't eat nothing, no supper, no breakfast, very little sleep. And I don't know how we -- I don't know how I kept my composure. But about two or three o'clock in the morning, there was a big group of

Chinese coming toward us and we got word of it and so we requested artillery....I said, "Okay. Send it in." "Where?" "Right on top of us. Send it in." We had to stop the damn Chinese from coming in, you know, because we were only a few guys. So there it comes, boom. And I was -- We were in dirt. We would just fall. I could feel the dirt falling over me, you know, but we were able to survive the barrage....There were certain stretches of time....It was one round per second, boom, boom, boom, boom. Never in the history of the United States Army had there been such heavy concentration of firepower in a small area like in Pork Chop, never up to that point.

The following day...I was assigned...the highest point...which is always the most dif-ficult one....At about two or three o'clock in the morning, I couldn't help it, man, I just -- I was sitting down or standing up, and I just dozed off for a little bit, and my gunners opened up....They got three, three guys, three Chinese. The following day we went to check in the morning. Three Chinese tried to get in. Because...the trench was open, we [had] put some lumber, whatever we could find, buckets, whatever we found to make a noise if the Chinese would come. And sure enough, they hit the stuff and the guy woke up and opened fire...

The next day...the biggest part of the company was pulled out, but since I -- since we held the highest point...we moved back some, which was a mistake. And then we could -- we could hear them. I mean, I could hear Chinese at night. They were walking over me. I could hear them. I could hear them talk, you know. And then they started throwing grenades and I opened fire on them. And I don't know if I hit anybody or not, but they stopped firing -- they stopped throwing grenades. What they do is they throw a grenade, and if you don't respond, then they come, they charge, you know. But if you respond, "Hey, these guys are still alive," so they pull back.

And thank God, you know, that that was -- My men, as we waited -- Believe me. Believe me that man can only take so much and they "run out of gas" and they freeze. And I told the guys to get ready because it looked like we were going to get hit again. And I told the ... gunner, machine gunner, "Set up the machine gun and get it ready." And the gunner told me, "I can't. I can't do it." "What do you mean you can't?" "I can't." So a young -- a young fellow says, he told me, "I can do it. I can do it, Juarez." "Well, get it on." So he mounted the machine gun and got it ready, put the belt on, and put it in action. And my men were -- were gone. I mean, they were exhausted, no nerve left on them, no nothing, nothing. So I said, "Okay." And at that moment I said, "Well, this is it for us. This is it for me. Here I'm going to say. Here I'm going to -- This will be my last day." And I was -- I started a cold sweat. My sweat started sweating and I could feel it was cold coming down and my throat ran dry, went dry, I mean, just dry as it could be. And I drank a little water and it didn't quench my thirst. You know, it was terrible. So we waited and waited and waited. And all of our sergeants and only one guy, one Negro, a first -- second lieutenant, stayed with us. He was calling in by radio to come and pick us up because he says, "They haven't picked us up." And the personnel carriers to pick us up didn't want to get to us because we were the furthest, los que estaban mas lejos, the furthest out. They picked up the guys that were closer to them--esos los sacaron.

Interviewer:
They left you there?

Lino P. Juarez:
Yeah. Those son of a guns. So this guy, the colored guy, kept on trying and trying and trying and he finally got through, and he told them, "Send in the personnel carrier. We have a bunch of wounded, a lot of wounded guys." They were all dead. There were no wounded. You know, we lost over half of the company. But he had to tell them something to send the darn things in. So finally, man, about three o'clock, and I knew -- I knew that if we didn't get out that night we would have been -- we would be goners. I knew. There was only a few left. But thank God that we were able to pull out. For some reason or another, you know, after it looked like we were lost, lost the whole damn thing, including ourselves, for some reason the Chinese decided to withdraw.

And it -- it was just a coincidence at that moment the personnel carriers arrived. And I was the first in my company to go in and I was -- I was supposed to have been the last one also. But there was a big dude in front of me, a Gringo, a big Anglo boy in front of me. He weighed about 250; six, six, something like that; a big husky guy. And I -- I was behind him, you know. I said, "Okay, now, what's going to happen, Juarez?" I was think-ing -- I was always thinking ahead, "How are you going to get out?" Well, I know that the tank can't get very close to us, so I know I have to run to get to the tank. So I tapped him on the shoulder. I talked to him because I was -- I was -- you know, I was -- I had -- I had a lot of authority. I said, "You bring the rear," but with a -- with a very strong voice and -- you know. "Okay. Okay." So my mentality was this. If I would -- If I were to get hit as I was running toward the tank, I only weighed 129 pounds, I know that guy could pick me up from my belt and drag me anyplace because I knew he was a big dude.... It's kind of funny, you know. But if you are to survive when you are -- You never underestimate the enemy. You know that they -- that they got weapons. You know they are after you. And you have got to be on the ball at all times, be prepared and be ready, and be ready to die with no fear. My theory is, if you doubt, if you doubt, fear develops and fear will destroy you. That's my mentality. So I did not allow for doubt and fear to set on me. That's why I'm here today.

Source: Veterans History Project, American Folklife Center, Library of Congress

THOUGHT QUESTIONS:

1. How prepared did Juarez say that he and his men were when they arrived at the battle site?

2. How well did Juarez convey how nerve-wracking and stressful the situation was for he and his men?

3. What did he believe their chances of survival were if the relief did not come when it did? How did Juarez and the men finally get the personal carriers to come and pick them up?

LBJ and the U.S. Astronauts

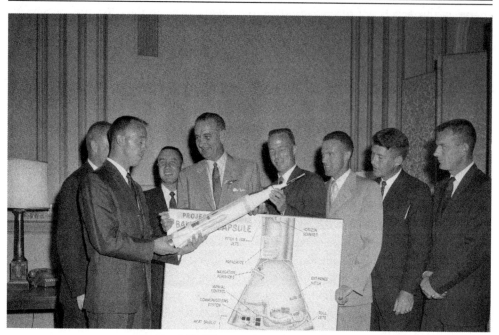

Credit: LBJ Library photo by Frank Muto
May 28, 1959

The Lyndon B. Johnson Space Center in Houston serves as the headquarters for the National Aeronautics and Space Administration's (NASA) manned spaceflight operations, training the astronauts and coordinating all human spaceflights from the Mission Control Center. Initially called the Manned Spacecraft Center (MSC), the complex originated from legislation shepherded through Congress in 1958 by then-Senate Majority Leader Lyndon Johnson. In September 1961, NASA chose Houston as the site for its MSC. Within two years, the facility was operational.

In this photograph taken on May 28, 1959, Senator Johnson poses with U.S. astronauts. (From left to right): Alan Shepard, John Glenn (behind Shepard), Gus Grissom, Lyndon Johnson, Scott Carpenter, Gordon Cooper, Walter Schirra, Deke Slayton.

THOUGHT QUESTION:

How has the Johnson Center aided the Texas economy as well as contributed to the modern-day image of the Lone Star State?

BIOGRAPHIES

JACK KILBY (1923-2005). The inventor of the monolithic integrated circuit while working as an engineer with Texas Instruments (TI), Jack St. Clair Kilby was born on November 8, 1923 in Jefferson City, Missouri. Exposed early in his life to the world of engineers through his father who ran the local electric utility company in Great Bend, Kansas, he decided in high school that he wanted to become an electrical engineer. He applied to the prestigious Massachusetts Institute of Technology but fell slightly short in his score on the entrance exam. A few months later he joined the Army who assigned him to a radio repair shop at an outpost on a tea plantation in northeast India during World War II. After the war, he used funding through the G.I. Bill of Rights to attend college, receiving a B.S. degree in Electrical Engineering from the University of Illinois and his M.S. in the same field from the University of Wisconsin. In 1947, Kilby began his engineering career with the Centralab Division of Globe Union in Milwaukee, developing ceramic-base, silk-screen circuits for consumer electronic products.

In 1958, Kilby joined TI in Dallas. That same year while working with borrowed and improvised equipment, he designed and constructed the first electronic circuit in which all components were fabricated in a single piece of semiconductor material. It was half the size of a paper clip. The successful demonstration of that first simple microchip made history as a revolutionary breakthrough that made possible the high-speed, large-capacity, and increasingly compact computers of today.

Kilby continued to pioneer military and commercial applications of microchip technology, leading teams that built the first computers incorporating integrated circuits. He later co-invented the first hand-held calculator and the first thermal printer used in portable data terminals.

In 1970, Kilby took a leave of absence from TI to work as an independent inventor, exploring the use of silicon technology for generating electrical power from sunlight. From 1978 to 1984 he held the position of Distinguished Professor of Electrical Engineering at Texas A&M University. He officially retired from TI in the 1980s but maintained close ties to the company.

Before passing away in Dallas on June 20, 2005, Kilby received the nation's most prestigious science awards—the National Medal of Science, the National Medal of Technology, and induction into the National Inventors Hall of Fame—in addition to receiving the Nobel Prize in Physics in 2000.

GUS GARCIA (1915-1964). Mexican American civil rights attorney Gustavo C. Garcia was born in Laredo on July 27, 1915. He attended public and Catholic schools while growing up in San Antonio. In 1932 Garcia graduated as the first valedictorian from Thomas Jefferson High and received an academic scholarship to attend the University of Texas where he received a B.A. degree in 1936 and an LL.B. in 1938.

After passing the state bar exam, Garcia served as assistant to Bexar County district attorney John Schook and later to assistant city attorney Victor Keller before being drafted for service in World War II. He became a first lieutenant in the Army and was stationed in Japan with the Judge Advocate General's Corps. Returning to San Antonio after the war, he joined the office of the Mexican Consulate General. In 1947 he filed suit against Cuero school authorities in an effort to force closure of the Mexican school there. After the *Mendez v. Westminster ISD* case ended *de jure* segregation of Hispanic children in California, Garcia and other lawyers filed a similar suit in Texas. The resulting *Delgado v. Bastrop ISD* (1948) case made segregation of Tejano children illegal in Texas.

In 1949 he aided the family of Felix Longoria in their efforts to secure justice when a local funeral home director in Three Rivers refused to let them hold a wake for the deceased soldier (because he was Hispanic) when the military shipped his body home from the Philippines. The affair outraged and aroused the Tejano community and caught the attention of Senator Lyndon Johnson who arranged for Longoria's eventual burial at Arlington National Cemetery.

From 1951 to 1952 García served as legal advisor to the American G.I. Forum. He worked to pass a general antidiscrimination bill in Texas. As an attorney in the case of *Hernandez v. State of Texas,* he filed a writ of certiorari with the United States Supreme Court to seek review of the conviction of Pete Hernandez who was convicted of killing a Tejano laborer by an all-white jury in Edna, Texas near Victoria. García petitioned the conviction on the grounds of Tejano exclusion from jury selection, pointing out that Hernandez failed the opportunity to be tried by a jury of his peers since no Hispanic had served on a jury in the county for over twenty-five years. The Supreme Court voted unanimously in favor of overturning Hernandez's conviction. The ruling legally ended the common practice of excluding Mexican Americans from Texas juries solely on grounds of ethnicity.

In 1955 Garcia's struggle with alcohol led to several hospital stays and the number of his public appearances waned. For a while he ran a law firm in Kingsville, but after he passed several bad checks a complaint was filed against him seeking disbarment. The state suspended García's law license from August 1961 until August 1963. Upon the resumption of his law practice, he died of a seizure on June 3, 1964 and was buried with full military honors at Fort Sam Houston National Cemetery at San Antonio. The League of United Latin American Citizens arranged his services and later established the Gus C. Garcia Memorial Fund in his honor.

BUDDY HOLLY (1936-1959). A legendary rock-and-roll pioneer, Charles Hardin Holley (known to the world by his professional name "Buddy Holly") was born on September 7, 1936, in Lubbock, Texas. Though not from a family with deep musical roots, his tailor father and his wife encouraged their children's musical talents. Always known to his family as "Buddy," he made his musical debut at the age of five, appearing with his brothers in a talent show in nearby County Line. During his childhood he took piano lessons, briefly studied the steel guitar, and taught himself how to play the acoustic guitar. At Hutchinson Junior High School he befriended Bob Montgomery and the two formed the "Buddy and Bob" duo that performed a variety of bluegrass music and early rockabilly music at local clubs and high school talents shows. In 1953 they joined bass player Larry Welborn and earned a regular spot on a Lubbock radio station's Sunday program. While attending Lubbock High School, Holly never doubted that he would pursue a career as a professional musician.

In 1954 and 1955 the groups made some demo recordings in Wichita Falls, hoping to land a recording contract, but in 1956 Decca Records (a well-known country-and-western label) offered Holly a solo contract. Decca tried unsuccessfully to fit Holly into the country mold and ended their relationship after releasing two unsuccessful singles.

Nevertheless, he returned to Lubbock determined to make it big in the music business. In February 1957 he and three other musicians traveled to independent producer Norman Petty's studio in Clovis, New Mexico, and adopted the name "The Crickets." From that point on, Holly's career took off.

Brunswick Records signed the Crickets, while Holly signed a solo contract with Brunswick's Coral subsidiary. His records included Holly's unmistakable vocal style, incorporating yoddling, hiccup-like sounds, nonsensical syllables, and abrupt changes of pitch along with the classic mixture of western rockabilly and African American rhythm-and-blues that helped characterize the early rock-and-roll sound. The first Crickets single, "That'll Be the Day," was released in May 1957. It reached number three on the pop charts and number two on the rhythm-and-blues charts. At first many listeners assumed that Holly and his bandmates were African Americans. On their first eastern tour in July 1957, the Crickets discovered that they had been booked along with several black artists. During the next few months, they appeared on television's "American Bandstand," "The Arthur Murray Dance Party," and "The Ed Sullivan Show" and Holly released the wildly popular "Peggy Sue" (as a solo effort), "Oh Boy!" and "Maybe Baby" (with the Crickets).

In the summer of 1958 Holly met Maria Elena Santiago, a Puerto Rican native who worked as a receptionist at Peer–Southern Music when Holly and the Crickets stopped in for a business meeting. Holly asked her out for dinner that night and then impulsively asked her to marry him. She accepted and they were married at Holly's home in Lubbock.

When his next group of singles failed to capture his earlier success, Holly reluctantly agreed to the breakup of the Crickets and carry on as a solo artist. He began to experiment with songs utilizing strings and orchestral backing. In January 1959 he agreed to go on the "Winter Dance Party" tour with young Ritchie Valens and J. P. (the Big Bopper) Richardson. They traveled by bus for much of the midwestern winter, but after a February 2 show in Clear Lake, Iowa, but Holly decided instead to charter a plane to fly him and his band to Fargo, North Dakota, just across the Red River from their intended destination in Moorhead, Minnesota. When the other performers heard of his plans, they wanted to come, too, and two of Holly's band members, Waylon Jennings and Tommy Allsup ended up giving up their seats to Richardson and Valens. The plane crashed soon upon takeoff in light snowy conditions at about 1:50 a.m. on the morning of February 3, 1959. There were no survivors.

Though he died at a very young age at the height of his popularity, Holly's influence on rock-and-roll music is immeasurable. Countless rock musicians copied various elements of Holly's style, showmanship, and instrumentation, including the Beatles, the Rolling Stones, Bob Dylan, the Grateful Dead, Bruce Springsteen, and Elvis Costello. In 1971 songwriter Don McLean commemorated February 3, 1959 as "the day the music died" in his hit single, "American Pie." In 1986, Holly was among the first class of inductees admitted to the new Rock and Roll Hall of Fame.

The city of Lubbock finally realized the potential of tourist dollars after 1978 release of the movie The Buddy Holly Story led to renewed interest in the life of the city's most famous son. In 1979 the city helped raise money for an 8 ½-foot high statue honoring Holly, now located near the Lubbock Memorial Civic Center. In 1983 the city converted the area around the statue into a "Walk of Fame" honoring West Texas musicians. The annual Buddy Holly Music Festival, held each Labor Day weekend, began in 1995. In September 1999 the city opened the Buddy Holly Center to honor the musician's legacy.

LULU B. WHITE (1907–1957). The civil rights activist Lulu Belle Madison White was born in 1907, the tenth of twelve children of former slave parents, in the small town of Elmo near Dallas. She attended segregated public schools in Elmo before enrolling at Butler College, a black coeducational junior college institution located in Tyler, with the desire of becoming a teacher. After one year at Butler, she transferred to Prairie View College after meeting Julius White, then a prominent black businessman in Houston. She received good grades while at Prairie View and was socially active, holding many leadership positions in a variety of social clubs. Upon graduating *magna cum laude* with a bachelor's degree in English, she married Julius White and embarked on a teaching career. Unable to secure employment with the Houston Independent School District, she accepted a full-time position in Lufkin located 120 miles to the north of Houston. For a salary of forty dollars per month, she remained in Lufkin during the week and returned to Houston over the weekends. In 1935, she secured a job at a black elementary school in Houston and taught for two years before she resigned to dedicate her energies to civil rights activism.

White's husband had been an active member of the Houston chapter of National Association for the Advancement of Colored People (NAACP) for many years, serving as the plaintiff in several white primary cases. She now joined the organization full-time, becoming a major fundraiser and organizer of a large number of new chapters throughout the state. In 1939, she became the president of the Houston chapter and within four years the group had the largest membership of any chapter in the South. Upon the Supreme Court's 1944 *Smith v. Allwright* decision outlawing the white primary, White undertook a major campaign to educate blacks who were able to pay their poll taxes to vote. When the NAACP looked for a case that would integrate the University of Texas in 1945, White lobbied for Heman Sweatt to be the plaintiff and worked with the NAACP Legal Division to press the case to its successful conclusion in 1950. Sweatt later credited her leadership for maintaining his resolve during the uncertainty of the prolonged litigation. She continued to organize local protests for change, most notably against segregated local department stores in Houston and in favor of equal pay for black and white public school teachers. White resigned as leader of the Houston chapter in 1949 to become the NAACP's state director. Though her premature death from heart failure on July 6, 1957, just as the grass-roots civil rights movement was gaining impetus in the South, deprived her of long-term recognition compared to other activists, her colleagues understood and appreciated her vital role in laying the foundation for the significant breakthroughs soon to come.

Chapter 17

The Turbulent Decade: Reform and Reaction, 1960-1972

Republican Senator John Tower Reflects on his Historic 1961 Victory

In 1961, John Tower became the first Republican to win a statewide office in Texas since Reconstruction when he defeated William Blakley in a runoff of a special election for a U.S. Senate seat vacated by Lyndon Johnson who had been elected Vice President of the United States. An assistant professor of government at Midwestern State College in Wichita Falls, Tower had recently lost the 1960 Senate race to Johnson, who was allowed by state law to run for both the U.S. Senate and the vice presidency in the same election. Aided by name recognition, a divided Democratic Party, and low voter turnout, Tower stunned the political world with a narrow upset victory. He went on to serve four terms in the U.S. Senate, and later chaired the Tower Commission investigation of the Reagan Administration's dealings during the Iran-Contra Affair before dying in the crash of Atlantic Southeast Airlines Flight 2311 on April 5, 1991 in Brunswick, Georgia. In this excerpt from his 1971 oral interview with Professor Joe Frantz at the Lyndon B. Johnson Presidential Library, Senator Tower discusses the factors that he believed contributed to his triumph.

TOWER: The one advantage I had is that I could count on the support of all the Republicans, of course, and of a pretty good sizeable conservative following that I had developed during the course of my Johnson campaign.

DR. FRANTZ: You were just fresh off of advertising too.

TOWER: Right. It occurred to me that I was really a favorite for a run-off spot anyway, whether I ran first or second. And of course the Democrats' strength was diluted by the fact that there were five major Democrat candidates and only one Republican candidate, so that made it an almost certainty that I would get into the runoff. And as it turned out, I ran first, with about 35-percent of the vote; Blakley came in second with around 20 percent (these are rough figures); and behind him was Jim Wright, and then Will Wilson, and then I believe Henry Gonzalez and Maury Maverick in that order. Then that put me in the run off with Blakley.

DR. FRANTZ: Did you have any preference of whom you faced in the runoff?

TOWER: It occurred to me that Blakley would be the best one I could run off against, because I had then figured to pick up the dissident liberal Democrat votes. I thought I would probably pick up most of the Maverick, Gonzalez votes, and probably a sizeable portion of the Wright votes.

DR. FRANTZ: Did you ever feel the hand of Johnson at all in this campaign?

TOWER: No, I didn't. And I don't think Lyndon really realized that I was the threat that I was. I think had he known it, that perhaps a little bit more would have been done for Blakley, but I think they went too much on the assumption that in a runoff situation, a straight fight with a Democrat, I wouldn't make it.

DR. FRANTZ: You had gotten 35 percent. That was just about your top.

TOWER: Yes. Under the old plurality system, of course I would have been elected right off the bat.

DR. FRANTZ: Hands down.

TOWER: Too, Blakley, whom I think a very fine gentlemen, but he had no political acumen whatsoever--absolutely none! He was not a good candidate, he didn't like crowds, he was not a particularly good speaker. So he had his problems. He was adequately funded, and again I had to really scrap for money. But too I think my political judgment was a lot better than Blakley's. Lynn Landrum(?) of the Dallas News used to refer to me as the "li'l perfessor" in a somewhat contemptuous way, but the fact of the matter was the "li'l professor" had been teaching political science for some years and knew more about it than Bill Blakley did.

DR. FRANTZ: Well you made sense, and Blakley seemed kind of lost.

TOWER: I exploited the divisions in the Democratic party too. The dissident Democrats voted for me.

DR. FRANTZ: Were you ever actually approached personally by the liberal wing to talk about ways and means, what they would like to do?

TOWER: I certainly had communication with them. I guess Maury Maverick and I were about as friendly opponents as we could have been during the campaign. So I had some liaison.

DR. FRANTZ: Has that ever caused you any problem since, the fact that you did have this support from the liberal wings--?

TOWER: No, because I never had to promise them anything, you see, I never had to commit myself on a position to them. As a matter of fact, they regarded me as a Neanderthal conservative, but they also felt I was an honest one because I wore the Republican label. And their mentality was that the conservative Democrats are not really Democrats, and of course still that's their view. So in effect they put it this way--"If we're going to have a Republican senator, let's have one that calls himself a Republican." That was their rationale.

DR. FRANTZ: Were you surprised at how well you ran in the race?

TOWER: Well I just barely won it by a margin of about 10,000 votes--about 51-percent or a little less. Of course it was a low turnout. In a high turnout situation--

DR. FRANTZ: What do you do to make people come out in a case like that?

TOWER: In this particular instance we had a superior means of getting our voters out, because the Republican organization organized in the urban areas using a page right out of the COPE handbook on political organization, the Peter O'Donnell's of this state who knew how to get people out to canvass precincts and do that kind of thing. This is what we did. We produced our vote and the other side didn't. There was not much interest in the race, and so in that particular instance we could wield an influence out of proportion to our numbers.

DR. FRANTZ: I always felt that if you were just grading an organization in this case, that the Republican organization got the A in this instance for hard work.

TOWER: Right. The Republican organization performed and the Democratic organization didn't perform. The Democrats always used to fight in battles at primaries centered around courthouse cliques, whereas the Republicans started the fighting in general elections. Still the Democrats are not as good at fighting general elections as the Republicans are, although they beat us pretty regularly, but that's just by virtue of sheer numbers. Again, we polled a percentage of votes 'way out of proportion to the people that identified themselves as Republicans....

DR. FRANTZ: ...You went to Washington, and of course you're immediately catapulted into a national figure because you're the first Republican senator from this state since Lord knows when.

TOWER: Since Reconstruction.

DR. FRANTZ: And of course you've also taken Lyndon Johnson's seat, which gives you a double exposure there. Now then, what was the reaction in the Republican circles--the Republicans have just lost a national election and are a little gloomy, although it has been a squeaker and they can take some comfort in that, but they have lost the White House anyhow? But here comes a new fresh ray of hope out of the man's backyard.

TOWER: I was something of a unique figure, of course, and I think that my election did, after having lost the Nixon campaign in '60. I think my election did give the party a little shot in the arm. And of course the Republicans paraded me around Washington for days. I was in instant demand as a speaker for Republican affairs over the country, and so very early got to be a national politician really, and not just confined to state politics, and something of a national Republican figure--maybe not from the standpoint of the general public, but from the standpoint of the party rank and file.

Source: Lyndon B. Johnson Presidential Library

THOUGHT QUESTIONS:

1. Which factors did Tower say contributed most to his victory?

2. What opinions did Tower have about his runoff opponent William Blakley?

3. As the only Republican member of the U.S. Senate from the South (until South Carolina's Strom Thurmond switched parties and became a Republican in 1964), how was Tower treated by fellow Republicans in Washington? Can you think of any current politicians who receive similar treatment because of their ability to win office in a place where the opposition party dominates the political landscape?

Excerpts from Remarks Intended for Delivery by President John F. Kennedy to the Texas Democratic State Committee, Austin Municipal Auditorium (November 22, 1963)

President John F. Kennedy came to Texas in late-1963 to prepare for his 1964 re-election effort. Knowing that his endorsement for the introduced civil rights bill (later to be known as the Civil Rights Act of 1964) outlawing segregation in public accommodations was very unpopular among many southern Democrats (including many Texas Democrats), Kennedy's staff arranged for a two-day publicity tour of major Texas cities to culminate with a speech before the Texas Democratic State Committee in Austin. Lee Harvey Oswald's assassination of the president prevented the delivery of a speech, excerpts from which are included below, which the president hoped would unite Texas Democrats for the impending campaign.

One hundred and eighteen years ago last March, President John Tyler signed the Joint Resolution of Congress providing statehood for Texas. And 118 years ago this month, President James Polk declared that Texas was a part of the Union. Both Tyler and Polk were Democratic Presidents. And from that day to this, Texas and the Democratic Party have been linked in an indestructible alliance—an alliance for the promotion of prosperity, growth, and greatness for Texas and for America. Next year that alliance will sweep this State and Nation.

The historic bonds which link Texas and the Democratic Party are no temporary union of convenience. They are deeply embedded in the history and purpose of this State and party. For the Democratic Party is not a collection of diverse interests brought together only to win elections. We are united instead by a common history and heritage—by a respect for the deeds of the past and a recognition of the needs of the future. Never satisfied with today, we have always staked our fortunes on tomorrow. That is the kind of State which Texas has always been—that is the kind of vision and vitality which Texans have always possessed—and that is the reason why Texas will always be basically Democratic.

For 118 years, Texas and the Democratic Party have contributed to each other's success. This State's rise to prosperity and wealth came primarily from the policies and programs of Woodrow Wilson, Franklin Roosevelt, and Harry Truman. Those policies were shaped and enacted with the help of such men as the late Sam Rayburn and a host of other key Congressmen—by the former Texas Congressman and Senator who serves now as my strong right arm, Vice President Lyndon B. Johnson—by your present United States Senator, Ralph Yarborough—and by an overwhelming proportion of Democratic leadership at the State and county level, led by your distinguished Governor, John Connally.

It was the policies and programs of the Democratic Party which helped bring income to your farmers, industries to your cities, employment to your workers, and the promotion and preservation of your natural resources. No one who remembers the days of 5-cent cotton and 30-cent oil will forget the ties between the success of this State and the success of our party.

Three years ago this fall I toured this State with Lyndon Johnson, Sam Rayburn, and Ralph Yarborough as your party's candidate for President. We pledged to increase America's strength against its enemies, its prestige among its friends, and the opportunities it offered to its citizens. Those pledges have been fulfilled. The words spoken in Texas have been transformed into action in Washington, and we have America moving again.

Here in Austin, I pledged in 1960 to restore world confidence in the vitality and energy of American society. That pledge has been fulfilled. We have won the respect of allies and adversaries alike through our determined stand on behalf of freedom around the world, from West Berlin to Southeast Asia—through our resistance to Communist intervention in the Congo and Communist missiles in Cuba—and through our initiative in obtaining the nuclear test ban treaty which can stop the pollution of our atmosphere and start us on the path to peace. . . .

In Amarillo, I pledged in 1960 that the businessmen of this State and Nation—particularly the small businessman who is the backbone of our economy—would move ahead as our economy moved ahead. That pledge has been fulfilled. Business profits—having risen 43 percent in 2 years—now stand at a record high . . . We have stepped up the activities of the Small Business Administration, making available in the last 3 years almost $50 million to more than 1,000 Texas firms, and doubling their opportunity to share in Federal procurement contracts. . . .

In Grand Prairie, I pledged in 1960 that this country would no longer tolerate the lowest rate of economic growth of any major industrialized nation in the world. That pledge has been and is being fulfilled. In less than 3 years our national output will shortly have risen by a record $100 billion—industrial production is up 22 percent, personal income is up 16 percent. And the *Wall Street Journal* pointed out a short time ago that the United States now leads most of Western Europe in the rate of business expansion and the margin of corporate profits. Here in Texas—where 3 years ago at the very time I was speaking, real per capita personal income was actually declining as the industrial recession spread to this State—more than 200,000 new jobs have been created, unemployment has declined, and personal income rose last year to an all time high. This growth must go on. . . .

In Dallas, I pledged in 1960 to step up the development of both our natural and our human resources. That pledge has been fulfilled. The policy of "no new starts" has been reversed. The Canadian River project will provide water for 11 Texas cities. The San Angelo project will irrigate some 10,000 acres. We have launched 10 new watershed projects in Texas, completed 7 others, and laid plans for 6 more. A new national park, a new wildlife preserve, and other navigation, reclamation, and natural resource projects are all under way in this State. At the same time we have sought to develop the human resources of Texas and all the Nation, granting loans to 17,500 Texas college students, making more than $17 million available to 249 school districts, and expanding or providing rural library service to 600,000 Texas readers. . . .

In Wichita Falls, I pledged in 1960 to increase farm income and reduce the burden of farm surpluses. That pledge has been fulfilled. Net farm income today is almost a billion dollars higher than in 1960. In Texas, net income per farm consistently averaged below the $4,000 mark under the Benson regime; it is now well above it. And we have raised this income while reducing grain surpluses by one billion bushels. We have, at the same time, tackled the problem of the entire rural economy, extending more than twice as much credit to Texas farmers under the Farmers Home Administration, and making more than 100 million dollars in REA loans. . . .

In San Antonio, I pledged in 1960 that a new administration would strive to secure for every American his full constitutional rights. That pledge has been and is being fulfilled. We have not yet secured the objectives desired or the legislation required. But we have, in the last 3 years, by working through voluntary leadership as well as legal action, opened more new doors to members of minority group—doors to transportation, voting, education, employment, and places of public accommodation—than had been opened in any 3-year or 30-year period in this century. There is no non-controversial way to fulfill our constitutional pledge to establish justice and promote domestic tranquility, but we intend to fulfill those obligations because they are right. . . .

In El Paso, I pledged in 1960 that we would give the highest and earliest priority to the reestablishment of good relations with the people of Latin America. We are working to fulfill that pledge. An area long neglected has not solved all its problems. The Communist foothold which had already been established has not yet been eliminated. But the trend of Communist expansion has been reversed. The name of Fidel Castro is no longer feared or cheered by substantial numbers in every country. And contrary to the prevailing predictions of 3 years ago, not another inch of Latin American territory has fallen prey to Communist control. . . .

In Texarkana, I pledged in 1960 that our country would no longer engage in a lagging space effort. That pledge has been fulfilled. We are not yet first in every field of space endeavor, but we have regained worldwide respect for our scientists, our industry, our education, and our free initiative.

In the last 3 years, we have increased our annual space effort to a greater level than the combined total of all space activities undertaken in the 1950's. We have launched into earth orbit more than 4 times as many space vehicles as had been launched in the previous 3 years. We have focused our wide-ranging efforts around a landing on the moon in this decade. We have put valuable weather and communications satellites into actual operation. We will fire this December the most powerful rocket ever developed anywhere in the world. And we have made it clear to all that the United States of America has no intention of finishing second in outer space. Texas will play a major role in this effort. The Manned Spacecraft Center in Houston will be the cornerstone of our lunar landing project, with a billion dollars already allocated to that center this year. Even though space is an infant industry, more than 3,000 people are already employed in space activities here in Texas, more than $100 million of space contracts are now being worked on in this State, and more than 50 space-related firms have announced the opening of Texas offices. This is still a daring and dangerous frontier; and there are those who would prefer to turn back or to take a more timid stance. But Texans have stood their ground on embattled frontiers before, and I know you will help us see this battle through. . . .

Finally, I said in Lubbock in 1960, as I said in every other speech in this State, that if Lyndon Johnson and I were elected, we would get this country moving again. That pledge has been fulfilled. In nearly every field of national activity, this country is moving again—and Texas is moving with it. From public works to public health, wherever Government programs operate, the past 3 years have seen a new burst of action and progress—in Texas and all over America.

For this country is moving and it must not stop. It cannot stop. For this is a time for courage and a time for challenge. Neither conformity nor complacency will do. Neither the fanatics nor the faint-hearted are needed. And our duty as a party is not to our party alone, but to the Nation, and, indeed, to all mankind. Our duty is not merely the preservation of political power but the preservation of peace and freedom.

So let us not be petty when our cause is so great. Let us not quarrel amongst ourselves when our Nation's future is at stake. Let us stand together with renewed confidence in our cause—united in our heritage of the past and our hopes for the future—and determined that this land we love shall lead all mankind into new frontiers of peace and abundance.

Source: John F. Kennedy Presidential Library

THOUGHT QUESTIONS:

1. How did Kennedy try to use historic bonds between Texas and the Democratic Party to promote unity?

2. How did Kennedy incorporate Texas into his current administration's efforts to fulfill promises made during the 1960 campaign?

3. At the end of the speech, how did Kennedy attempt to lessen inter-party divisions?

Judge Sarah Hughes Describes Delivering the Oath of Office to Lyndon Johnson Following the Kennedy Assassination

As described previously, Sarah T. Hughes practiced law in Dallas before becoming one of first women elected to the Texas House of Representatives. In 1935, Governor James Allred appointed her to a vacancy on the Fourteenth District Court in Dallas, making her the first woman state district judge in Texas. Hughes continued to serve as district judge until 1961, when President John F. Kennedy named her to the federal bench. She became a national figure on November 22, 1963, when she administered the oath of office to Lyndon Johnson on Air Force One following the assassination in Dallas of President Kennedy. The following excerpt from an oral interview provides us with an account of her thoughts and actions on that terrible day.

Hughes: . . . On the way out [of the Dallas Trade Mart Luncheon where Kennedy was scheduled to speak], just as I got--stepping out of the door, someone in a car stopped and said that the President had died. I was with my secretary and court reporter--they had been sitting upstairs. My court reporter is Odell Oliver and my secretary is Gwen Graul. Actually they had known about it before we did, because someone had a transistor radio in the balcony and they had heard about what had happened before we knew anything about it. I said that there wasn't any use to go back to the office. Incidentally I was going down to Austin for the [Texas Democratic State Party Committee] dinner that night and had my things in the car. I was going with Jan and Barefoot [former state legislator Harold Barefoot Sanders Jr. – a U.S. attorney at the time, later to become a federal judge].

Interviewer: You were out there in your car?
Hughes: I was in my car, but I was going to transfer my things into their car. We went on home. They'd--

Interviewer: The three of you?
Hughes: The three went on to my house and they went on--left my house right away and went on home. And I immediately called the office to let them know that I was home. When I called the office, someone who answered said [that] Barefoot Sanders, who was then U.S. attorney, was in the office and wanted to speak to me. So he came to the phone and said the Vice-President is on the other line and wants you to go out to the airport and swear him in.

Interviewer: Had they been looking for you or did you just happen to hit it right at the moment they started looking?
Hughes: They had been looking for me. That was not the first call to my office. The first call was by an aide of the Vice-President, and my law clerk had answered the phone, and he had said that he didn't know where I was. Immediately after he hung up, the phone rang again and it was the Vice-President. He told John Spinuzzi, who was my law clerk--said that he wanted to find me, and John says, "Well, we'll find her." Just at that time Barefoot came in the office and at that time the phone rang and I was on the other end of the line.

Interviewer: Was Barefoot then with the President or the Vice-President at the time?
Hughes: No, the Vice-President had called him to--

Interviewer: Where was Barefoot, at home or in his office?
Hughes: No, he was in his office.

Interviewer: He wasn't going to the luncheon.
Hughes: Oh, yes, he had been to the luncheon, but then he went back to his office and the Vice-President had called him to try to find me. I presume you know that he likewise called Irving Goldberg, and Irving suggested he phone me.

Interviewer: Why you, may I ask?
Hughes: What's that?

Interviewer: Why you in particular?
Hughes: Well, the Vice-President wouldn't have called either of the other judges. I don't know whether you want me to explain why he wouldn't have, but I—

Interviewer: I would appreciate it if you would.
Hughes: Well, one of them was Joe Estes, who was a so-called Eisenhower Democrat and was appointed by Eisenhower, and the other one was T. Whitfield Davidson, who had enjoined the Democratic executive committee from certifying Johnson's name when he was nominated for the Senate. As a matter of fact on the way home, the three of us, Gwen and Odell and I, had been discussing where the Vice-President would be sworn in. Of course the plan had been for Kennedy to go to the Ranch with the Vice-President, and one of us suggested that possibly he would go on to the Ranch and be sworn in there. Then it was suggested, no, he'd fly back to Washington and immediately be sworn in there. No one even thought that he'd be sworn in in Dallas. So I told Barefoot "Yes," I would be glad to do it and he said "How long will it take you?" And I told him ten minutes. He said that he would look up the oath of office while I was on my way out. I asked him where the plane was and he described where it was.

Interviewer: It was at Love Field?
Hughes: It was at Love Field.

Interviewer: Now where do you live in Dallas?
Hughes: I live in Highland Park.

Interviewer: So you were on the right side of town.
Hughes: Yes, it does only take me about ten minutes to get there.
So on the way out I--everybody wants to know what I was thinking about. I was thinking first of all that I must not think about Kennedy; I must think about the country going on.

Interviewer: Were you driving your own car?
Hughes: Yes.

Interviewer: That gives you something to think about.
Hughes: Yes. And another thing I was thinking about was that I must get there in a hurry,

because Vice-President Johnson is always in a hurry and wants things done right now and I shouldn't delay. And the other thing that I was thinking about was what the oath of office was, in case Barefoot couldn't find it. I was brash enough to think that I could give the oath without having looked it up. You see I swear so many people--jurors—and I've given the oath of office to other public officials; I've sworn in many, many young lawyers and they always have to swear to perform the duties of the office and uphold and preserve the Constitution of the United States and I was quite sure that those were the two things that—

Interviewer: The oath is basically the same.
Hughes: Yes, the same. So when I got out there I saw the plane. It's a beautiful plane, as you know.

Interviewer: Where was it?
Hughes: It was on the right as you go out. Do you know that statue that is in the front of the airport, the figure holding out--it's a woman I guess--her arms?

Interviewer: Yes.
Hughes: Well, it was just about there. There was a little road that turned off to the right. There were some police officers stationed there. I had seen them and they knew me. Campaigning with police officers is always something you must do because you know they've got a vote. So I knew who they were. I told them what I wanted and one of them who was on the motorcycle went out to the plane to check and then led me in the car. I met--as I got out of the car--

Interviewer: You drove right up to the ramp?
Hughes: Close to it, yes. As I got out Chief [Jesse] Curry was there (he's the chief of police) and he said "Mr. Sanders wants you to call him." Well, I knew that Barefoot had the oath by then, but I said "Well, I know what the oath is." So in place of calling him I went on up the ramp. And somebody, I don't know who it was, met me and I then said "I don't need the oath of office; I know what to say." But in just a moment somebody handed me a copy of the oath. I understand that someone had telephoned to the Attorney General and had gotten a copy of the oath. I wasn't told that but anyway I was handed it.

Interviewer: Barefoot didn't dictate it to someone.
Hughes: No, he didn't dictate it. And then somebody handed me a book and said "This is a Catholic Bible." I walked on into the second compartment and there were a lot of people there; the Vice-President and Mrs. Johnson were there and neither--none of us said anything. I embraced both of them and then the Vice-President said, "Mrs. Kennedy wants to be here. We'll wait for her."

Interviewer: She hadn't come from the hospital?
Hughes: She had come from the hospital and was in the rear of the airplane. So we waited a few minutes and she did come out and he, Vice-President Johnson, told her to stand on his left and Mrs. Johnson on his right. And I leaned over to her and said "I loved your husband very much."

Mr. Johnson turned to her and told her who I was; that I was a district judge who had been appointed by her husband. Then I repeated the oath of office and the Vice-President repeated it after me, he had his hand up--one hand up, and the other on this book.

Interviewer: Did you do it in short phrases?

Hughes: Oh, yes, I have learned that under tense circumstances people don't do very well at remembering long sentences and it's better to make them short. Just as soon as--and the oath of office is in the Constitution, but it does not contain the words "So help me God!" Well, every oath of office that I had ever given ended up with "So help me God!" So it was just automatic that I said "So help me God!" He immediately leaned over and kissed his wife and Mrs. Kennedy, and I said something to him that the country was behind him and I knew that he would make a great President. He turned around and said to the pilot, "Let's be airborne." I hurried out and as I went out, I handed this book to someone and whoever it was I handed it to said, "Don't you want to keep it?" I said, "No, it doesn't belong to me." I got out and Senator Yarborough had just driven up and he got to the ramp too late. They had already pulled the ramp up. I went home.

Interviewer: Quite a day.

Hughes: Yes, it was.

Source: Lyndon B. Johnson Presidential Library

THOUGHT QUESTIONS:

1. Whose decision was it to have Sarah Hughes deliver the oath of office? Why was she chosen?

2. What did Hughes say she was thinking about during the ride over to the airport?

3. How did she describe the scene on the plane? Did she keep the Bible that Johnson used to swear the oath? Why or why not?

===============

Civil Rights Activist James Farmer Discusses Lyndon Johnson

===============

James Leonard Farmer, Jr. was an African American civil rights activist from Marshall, Texas who became one of the leading figures in the national civil rights movement. In 1942, Farmer and a group of students co-founded the Congress of Racial Equality (CORE), whose goal was to end racial segregation through nonviolent methods. Farmer was the orga- nization's first leader, serving as the national chairman from 1942 to 1944. Among other achievements, CORE was involved in organizing the Freedom Rides as well as the famous March on Washington. He also worked for the NAACP in the early 1960s. By mid-1960s, Farmer was growing disenchanted with the growing black nationalist ideas permeating CORE, so he resigned in 1966 to take a teaching position at Lincoln University. In 1968, newly elected President Richard Nixon offered him the position of Assistant Secretary of the Department of Health, Education, and Welfare – the position that he held when interviewed for the LBJ Library's Oral History Project. A portion of that interview appears below.

Interviewer: So we don't need to go into it here. Then, following chronologically, the next stage is the death of President Kennedy, late in 1963, and the accession of Mr. Johnson. He is known to have called a number of civil rights leaders soon after he became President and met with them. Were you in that group?
Farmer: Yes, he called me the Sunday after the assassination of President Kennedy, he called me at home. And I was astounded, I'd never been called by a President before! It was impressive.

Interviewer: I can imagine. What did he--
Farmer: Well first the operator said, "Mr. Farmer," and I said, "Yes," and she said, "Long distance call." And I said, "Who's calling operator," I was very tired, we'd just gotten back home.

And she said, "The President," and I was about to say "The president of what," when Mr. Johnson came on the phone. And he said, "Mr. Farmer, I just wanted to touch base with you, and I remember very well when we had that long talk when you were down in my office when I was Vice President, and Chairman of the President's Commission on Equal Employment Opportunity. That we asked for your help then and we got it. And we're going to need your help in the months that lie ahead, and I want you to know that, and I hope that we can count on you to help us. And I'd like to talk with you, so next time you are in Washington drop by to see me."

Well, I had no idea what "drop by to see me" means when the President of the United States calls! So I asked a politician friend of mine "What does it mean when the President of the United States says 'drop by to see me'." He said, "The President of the United States doesn't say drop by and see me!" And I said, "Well, he just did!" "Well then he means," said this party, "get in touch with his appointment secretary as soon as possible and set up an early appointment," which I did. I saw him then in the White House on December 6 of 1963.

Interviewer: A private meeting with you and he?
Farmer: Yes, just the two of us.

Interviewer: And what was discussed there, sir?
Farmer: Oh, I was with him for an hour and a half or two hours I guess, and we discussed many things, including the Civil Rights Bill, and he made countless phone calls and received countless phone calls from the Hill in the course of our conversation.

Interviewer: Most of them pertaining to the Bill?
Farmer: Pertaining to the Bill and he said he was running into great difficulty but he's got to get that bill through, he's got to get it through, it's of vital importance, and some of the Southerners tell him that they'll buy the bill if he will take out the public accommodation section. But he can't do that because that's the heart of the bill as far as he is concerned. . . .

Interviewer: Had you for example had any doubts immediately after the assassination for example, had you had any fear that perhaps a President from Texas might change the Civil Rights Bill?

Farmer: There were lingering fears but those fears were modified, moderated by the conversation with him while he was Vice President and the reaction then. Well, we discussed other things in that meeting. I suggested to the President that one of the things which was bugging me was the fact that we were opening up doors of opportunity, but that millions of people on whose behalf we were working might not be able to walk through those doors, because of inadequate education and everything else. He agreed, enthusiastically and asked what the solution was. I told him that I felt there was no one solution but one part of the solution was a massive campaign on adult illiteracy, that we ought to work on that, and there was sufficient technical knowledge to do it.

He expressed great interest, and as an old school teacher and former head of the NYA under Roosevelt, was very much interested in this, and asked me if I wouldn't submit a memorandum to him. He suggested a lengthy memorandum which would be gone over by his staff and a summary of that memorandum, which he personally would read. I agreed to do that. And he said, "When you go out and the press asks you what we talked about you can tell them this, that we talked about it and that I was enthusiastic about it because of my background."

Then as I was going out the President asked me what part of Texas I was from, and I told him Marshall. And he said, "Is that right! Do you realize that's Mrs. Johnson's hometown?" And I told him, "No, I wasn't aware of that," and he told me her father had owned a garage or filling station--

Interviewer: Grocery store I believe--
Farmer: Was it a grocery store, I thought he said a garage.

Interviewer: It may have been. I associated Mrs. Johnson's father with Karnack, which is also in that area but he may have--
Farmer: Maybe he said a garage, I think he did, but maybe not. And he told me where it was located in Marshall, the streets, and asked if I knew where that was and I did not. It's so long since I've been in Marshall the streets are vague.

Interviewer: He knew you were from Texas, you didn't mention it.
Farmer: No. He knew that I was from Texas. And after that meeting we had contact on a number of occasions. I called him several times, he told me to call at anytime, if we had a problem just to call him. . . .

Source: Lyndon B. Johnson Presidential Library

THOUGHT QUESTIONS:

1. What contact did Farmer have with Lyndon Johnson soon after the Kennedy assassination? What did the two men discuss?

2. Describe the initial doubts that Farmer had regarding Johnson's commitment to civil rights? Why did he have these doubts?

3. How was Johnson able to alleviate Farmer's doubts about him?

Excerpts from President Lyndon B. Johnson's Special Message to Congress Seeking Passage of the Voting Rights Act (March 15, 1965)

In this eloquent speech to the U.S. Congress, President Lyndon B. Johnson urged passage of sweeping federal voting rights legislation that would end remaining barriers to the vote. Johnson delivered his address a week after deadly racial violence erupted in Selma, Alabama, as state and local police attacked African Americans preparing to march to the state capital of Montgomery to protest voting rights discrimination in the form of literacy and knowledge tests administered solely to African Americans to keep them from registering to vote. Before a second march took place, Rev. James Reeb, a white Unitarian minister from Boston who planned to join the marchers, was attacked and killed in Selma by segregationists.

After delivering this speech, President Johnson federalized the Alabama National Guard and sent additional troops to ensure protection for the second march to Montgomery, which proceeded on March 21. After passing both houses of Congress, Johnson signed the Voting Rights Act of 1965 on August 6.

Mr. Speaker, Mr. President, Members of the Congress:

I speak tonight for the dignity of man and the destiny of democracy. I urge every member of both parties, Americans of all religions and of all colors, from every section of this country, to join me in that cause.

At times history and fate meet at a single time in a single place to shape a turning point in man's unending search for freedom. So it was at Lexington and Concord. So it was a century ago at Appomattox. So it was last week in Selma, Alabama. There, long-suffering men and women peacefully protested the denial of their rights as Americans. Many were brutally assaulted. One good man, a man of God, was killed.

There is no cause for pride in what has happened in Selma. There is no cause for self-satisfaction in the long denial of equal rights of millions of Americans. But there is cause for hope and for faith in our democracy in what is happening here tonight. For the cries of pain and the hymns and protests of oppressed people have summoned into convocation all the majesty of this great government -- the government of the greatest nation on Earth. Our mission is at once the oldest and the most basic of this country: to right wrong, to do justice, to serve man.

In our time we have come to live with the moments of great crisis. Our lives have been marked with debate about great issues -- issues of war and peace, issues of prosperity and depression. But rarely in any time does an issue lay bare the secret heart of America itself. Rarely are we met with a challenge, not to our growth or abundance, or our welfare or our security, but rather to the values, and the purposes, and the meaning of our beloved nation.

The issue of equal rights for American Negroes is such an issue.

And should we defeat every enemy, and should we double our wealth and conquer the stars, and still be unequal to this issue, then we will have failed as a people and as a nation. For with a country as with a person, "What is a man profited, if he shall gain the whole world, and lose his own soul?"

There is no Negro problem. There is no Southern problem. There is no Northern problem. There is only an American problem. And we are met here tonight as Americans -- not as Democrats or Republicans. We are met here as Americans to solve that problem. . . .

Every American citizen must have an equal right to vote.

There is no reason which can excuse the denial of that right. There is no duty which weighs more heavily on us than the duty we have to ensure that right.

Yet the harsh fact is that in many places in this country, men and women are kept from voting simply because they are Negroes. Every device of which human ingenuity is capable has been used to deny this right. The Negro citizen may go to register only to be told that the day is wrong, or the hour is late, or the official in charge is absent. And if he persists, and if he manages to present himself to the registrar, he may be disqualified because he did not spell out his middle name or because he abbreviated a word on the application. And if he manages to fill out an application, he is given a test. The registrar is the sole judge of whether he passes this test. He may be asked to recite the entire Constitution, or explain the most complex provisions of state law. And even a college degree cannot be used to prove that he can read and write.

For the fact is that the only way to pass these barriers is to show a white skin. Experience has clearly shown that the existing process of law cannot overcome systematic and ingenious discrimination. No law that we now have on the books -- and I have helped to put three of them there -- can ensure the right to vote when local officials are determined to deny it. . . .

Wednesday, I will send to Congress a law designed to eliminate illegal barriers to the right to vote. . . . This bill will strike down restrictions to voting in all elections -- federal, state, and local—which have been used to deny Negroes the right to vote. This bill will establish a simple, uniform standard which cannot be used, however ingenious the effort, to flout our Constitution. It will provide for citizens to be registered by officials of the United States Government, if the State officials refuse to register them. It will eliminate tedious, unnecessary lawsuits which delay the right to vote. Finally, this legislation will ensure that properly registered individuals are not prohibited from voting. . . .

There is no constitutional issue here. The command of the Constitution is plain. There is no moral issue. It is wrong -- deadly wrong -- to deny any of your fellow Americans the right to vote in this country. There is no issue of States' rights or national rights. There is only the struggle for human rights. I have not the slightest doubt what will be your answer. . . . But even if we pass this bill, the battle will not be over. What happened in Selma is part of a far larger movement which reaches into every section and State of America. It is the effort of American Negroes to secure for themselves the full blessings of American life. Their cause must be our cause too. Because it's not just Negroes, but really it's all of us, who must overcome the crippling legacy of bigotry and injustice.

And we shall overcome. . . .

As a man whose roots go deeply into Southern soil, I know how agonizing racial feelings are. I know how difficult it is to reshape the attitudes and the structure of our society. But a century has passed, more than a hundred years since the Negro was freed. And he is not fully free tonight.

It was more than a hundred years ago that Abraham Lincoln, a great President of another party, signed the Emancipation Proclamation; but emancipation is a proclamation, and not a fact. A century has passed, more than a hundred years, since equality was promised. And yet the Negro is not equal. A century has passed since the day of promise. And the promise is un-kept.

The time of justice has now come. I tell you that I believe sincerely that no force can hold it back. It is right in the eyes of man and God that it should come. And when it does, I think that day will brighten the lives of every American. For Negroes are not the only victims. How many white children have gone uneducated? How many white families have lived in stark poverty? How many white lives have been scarred by fear, because we've wasted our energy and our substance to maintain the barriers of hatred and terror?

And so I say to all of you here, and to all in the nation tonight, that those who appeal to you to hold on to the past do so at the cost of denying you your future.

This great, rich, restless country can offer opportunity and education and hope to all, all black and white, all North and South, sharecropper and city dweller. These are the enemies: poverty, ignorance, disease. They're our enemies, not our fellow man, not our neighbor. And these enemies too—poverty, disease, and ignorance: we shall overcome. . . .

The bill that I am presenting to you will be known as a civil rights bill. But, in a larger sense, most of the program I am recommending is a civil rights program. Its object is to open the city of hope to all people of all races.

Because all Americans must have the right to vote. And we are going to give them that right. All Americans must have the privileges of citizenship—regardless of race. And they are going to have those privileges of citizenship—regardless of race.

But I would like to caution you and remind you that to exercise these privileges takes much more than just legal right. It requires a trained mind and a healthy body. It requires a decent home, and the chance to find a job, and the opportunity to escape from the clutches of poverty.

Of course, people cannot contribute to the nation if they are never taught to read or write, if their bodies are stunted from hunger, if their sickness goes untended, if their life is spent in hopeless poverty just drawing a welfare check. So we want to open the gates to opportunity. But we're also going to give all our people, black and white, the help that they need to walk through those gates.

My first job after college was as a teacher in Cotulla, Texas, in a small Mexican-American school. Few of them could speak English, and I couldn't speak much Spanish. My students were poor and they often came to class without breakfast, hungry. And they knew, even in their youth, the pain of prejudice. They never seemed to know why people disliked them. But they knew it was so, because I saw it in their eyes. I often walked home late in the afternoon, after the classes were finished, wishing there was more that I could do. But all I knew was to teach them the little that I knew, hoping that it might help them against the hardships that lay ahead.

And somehow you never forget what poverty and hatred can do when you see its scars on the hopeful face of a young child. I never thought then, in 1928, that I would be standing here in 1965. It never even occurred to me in my fondest dreams that I might have the chance to help the sons and daughters of those students and to help people like them all over this country.

But now I do have that chance—and I'll let you in on a secret—I mean to use it. . . .

Above the pyramid on the great seal of the United States it says in Latin: "God has favored our undertaking." God will not favor everything that we do. It is rather our duty to divine His will.

But I cannot help believing that He truly understands and that He really favors the undertaking that we begin here tonight.

Source: Lyndon B. Johnson Presidential Library

THOUGHT QUESTIONS:

1. What justifications does Johnson use for the efforts to end voter discrimination?

2. How does Johnson attempt to let non-African Americans know that they would also benefit from granting full voting rights to blacks?

3. How did Johnson draw from his experiences as a teacher of Tejanos in the late-1920s to lay out his desires for the nation near the end of the speech?

Rev. Claude William Black Jr. Discusses the Impact of Racial Discrimination in San Antonio

The Rev. Claude William Black Jr., was an influential civil rights advocate in San Antonio, Texas. He was a pastor at Mount Zion First Baptist Church, the largest African-American church in the city. He led efforts against segregation and helped integrate San Antonio's parks, swimming pools, and department store lunch counters. During the 1970s, Black served on the San Antonio City Council and was its first black mayor pro tem. In this excerpt from an oral interview, Black describes growing up with discrimination in San Antonio and its impact on him and the local African-American community.

Interviewer: What was it like growing up black in San Antonio?
Black: It offered awfully limited experience interracially. I'm not sure that this was true of all. I began at fourteen working for an uncle who had a store with a delivery of ice and wood, as well as kind of a convenience store-a 7-11 of that generation, a neighborhood store. And I started driving a truck, delivering ice to a number of people in the summer for the old-fashioned icebox that held ice that was delivered to them. And I spent all of my time working for him through my college years. So I never had a real opportunity to work in the integrated community.

. . . I can remember going into the downtown area and recognizing that all of the fountains were marked. You either had a fountain for white or fountain for colored, as they put it. Your restrooms were marked: restroom for white or restroom for colored.

Then there were no major restaurants that you could enter in. I saw no [black] clerks in the major stores. There were no tellers in any of the banks. There were no black bus drivers. There were no black firemen. There were very few black policemen. In many instances, the black policemen that I saw operated in the black community.

There were always stories that were part of family conversations about hostility and about the unpleasant experiences of blacks-not only in San Antonio but in other areas. So you built up a kind of expectation that if the person was white, you would not expect fairness out of him. You would not expect him to treat you as he would treat others. And I think that was the product, also, of limited contact.

Interviewer: Could you tell some of the stories you heard as a child?

Black: Oh, I heard stories of some conflict that my father [a Pullman porter] would have with the conductor, who wanted him to do things that he felt were not appropriate in terms of his job. And that conductor had the power to simply tell him to go home and to report him to the superintendent, and he would be either grounded or be fired. And naturally any conflict that my father had with the conductor brought tension to the whole household, because we knew that if he was fired that meant that the whole economy of our family life was going to be changed. And we also knew that his recourse, or remedy for it, was not that good-that he could not simply take exception to the position of the man and then find himself reestablished on his job. So there was always tension in those stories that were told.

Then there were stories that were told from my family point of view of resentment that would arise even from customers. People who were on the railroad would sometimes give him a hard time. . . .

Interviewer: How does a man deal with tension like that when he doesn't have any real recourse?

Black: How do you survive in a hostile community? You started that early in your childhood-survival skills. I can remember if I saw a group of white guys coming towards me that I thought might want to start something just for the sake of starting something, then I sought to avoid them rather than confront them. If it meant crossing the street, I crossed the street. But a black person growing up at that period was always sensitive and could anticipate the kind of hostility he's likely to run into.

. . . I had an uncle who was a fairly dark man, who was married to an aunt who was a very, very fair woman. And, on one occasion, he was driving his car and his wife was seated in the back, and a policeman stopped him and was about to give him a ticket. And he simply said, "Well, you see, I'm driving for this lady. And I'm sorry that, you know, that I made this.."

"You drive for this lady?"

"Yeah."

"Okay, go ahead. Go ahead, boy."

You see, what he did was use the fairness of his wife, since the man could not tell whether she was white or black, and escaped at least paying a ticket. Now that's just one instance where individuals have used the strategy.

Another thing, I think (along with the fact that blacks were thrown into this position, there was also within the spirit of the white-maybe it's a human condition) is that to be able to rescue somebody, [you had to be able] to command a situation in which you had the power to determine. That attribute blacks used for their own survival. That is on the other side of that coin and what blacks have called "being an Uncle Tom." Because what he was doing was simply playing up to the pride and the sense of power that he knew this man wanted.

Interviewer: It's kind of like the Bre'r Rabbit tales-make a fool out of him.

Black: He was able to at least survive whatever he was facing. He used it as a strategy. As time went on, that [image] became very undesirable for many blacks. But I think, in many instances, as we look back over it, we get a better understanding of it as a strategy of survival. When you recognize, here's a man who cannot read very well; he's trying to buy property; he's afraid that somebody is taking advantage of him. So he goes to the man and says to him, "Well, I don't know much about this. I don't understand it. Would you read it to me and would you tell me what I ought to do?" Now that kind of humility from a man who maybe is older than the man he's talking to was resented by many of the younger blacks, you see. . . .

Interviewer: Did you use that strategy when you were growing up? Do you remember?

Black: I was sort of protected from this whole kind of experience because I worked for my uncle and I worked primarily in the black community. I didn't get too far out of the black community. I was not called upon to use the strategy. I'm not saying that if I had been caught up in some situations that I might not have felt that my survival was worth more than my pride at the time. . . .

I think if I had had greater contact with whites, I would have been able to distinguish or to make an evaluation based upon persons, rather than upon races. And I came to that ability to do that while I was in seminary in Newton Center, Massachusetts. The Andover Newton Theological Seminary provided me with the first opportunity to enter into an integrated situation, which allowed me to evaluate and to be able to measure whites, in terms of their conduct rather than in terms of their color.

I met a man from Virginia who came with the same kind of racial bias toward blacks that I carried in me toward whites. We were both very opinionated as to what we felt—what he felt a black man was, and I was very well informed on what I knew a white man was. And we, as a result of the class relationships, studying and that sort of thing, we got to know each other fairly well.

When you're absent, when you're separated from each other, a lot of myths gather. . . .

Source: Institute of Texan Cultures

THOUGHT QUESTIONS:

1. What forms of discrimination and negative attitudes toward himself, family members, and the African American community did Rev. Black recall from his childhood in San Antonio?

2. How did Rev. Black say that he and other blacks reacted to that discrimination and treatment?

3. When and why did Rev. Black begin to look at whites as individuals rather than simply members of the white race?

Texas Cotton, U.S.A.

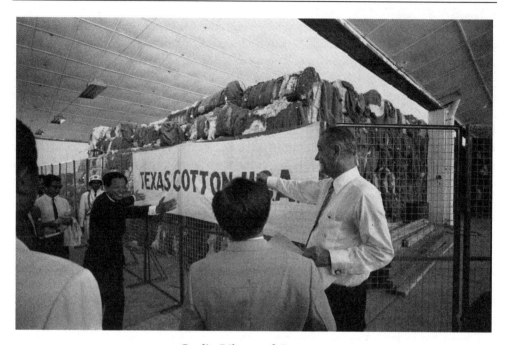

Credit: Library of Congress

On May 12 1961, Vice President Lyndon Johnson toured Saigon in South Vietnam. Here he is inspecting Texas cotton from the United States at a Saigon textile mill. While visiting South Vietnamese leader Ngo Dinh Diem, he assured Diem that he was crucial to U.S. objectives in Vietnam. When President Kennedy entered the White House, there were roughly 500 American military advisers in South Vietnam; by the time of Kennedy's death in November 1963, there were over 16,000 U.S. troops (allegedly still only serving as advisers) in that beleaguered country. Contrary to Kennedy's claim that American troops were not fighting, in reality they were, accompanying ARVN (Army of the Republic of South Vietnam) on "search and destroy" missions as well as fighting Viet Cong on their own initiative.

THOUGHT QUESTION:

How did U.S. involvement in Vietnam sidetrack LBJ's "Great Society" once he became president?

"Johnson Treatment"

The "Johnson Treatment" is displayed here with Louis Martin (top-L) at a reception for the Democratic National Committee delegates on April 20, 1966, in the Red Room of the White House, Abe Fortas (top-R), associate justice of the Supreme Court in July 1965, at the White House, and with Senator Richard Russell (bottom) on December 17, 1963, in the Cabinet Room of the White House.
Photo credit: LBJ Presidential Library

THOUGHT QUESTION:

Describe the "Johnson Treatment" and explain how Johnson used it to influence people.

BIOGRAPHIES

SARAH HUGHES (1896-1985). Sarah Tighman Hughes, the famous Texas judge and state politician, was born in Baltimore, Maryland on August 2, 1896. She attended public schools in Baltimore and graduated from Goucher College in 1917 with an A.B. in biology. After teaching science for two years in North Carolina, she enrolled in the George Washington University Law School, receiving her law degree in 1922. During this period she worked in the Washington, D.C. police force, working with juvenile offenders.

She married a classmate, George E. Hughes of Palestine, Texas, in 1922 and the couple moved to Dallas where her husband began a private law practice. Mrs. Hughes soon joined another law firm and practiced law for eight years before becoming one of the first women elected to the Texas state legislature after the granting of woman suffrage. She served three terms when Governor James Allred made her the first woman district judge in Texas in 1935 by appointing her to the bench of the Fourteenth District Court in Dallas. The next year, voters elected her to full terms for the next twenty-four years. During her tenure she played an important role in the construction of Dallas's first juvenile detention center and securing a Texas constitutional amendment allowing women to serve as jurors.

In 1946 Hughes was defeated in the Democratic primary when she ran for a congressional seat. She also failed in her bid to win a place on the Texas Supreme Court in 1958. Three years later, she asked Senator Ralph Yarborough and Vice President Lyndon Johnson to recommend her for the federal judgeship of the northern district of Texas. Along with the help of Speaker Sam Rayburn, they succeeded in overcoming opposition due to her age (she was sixty-five) to convince President John F. Kennedy to appoint her to the post. In October 1961, she became the first woman to serve as a federal district judge in Texas.

Known for her liberal views and impartial administration of justice, Hughes served the Fourteenth Judicial District of Texas for fifteen years until her retirement in 1975. She was a member of the three-judge panel that first heard the landmark Roe v. Wade abortion case in 1973. Among her other well-known decisions as a federal judge were Shultz v. Brookhaven General Hospital (equal pay for equal work for women) in 1969 and Taylor v. Sterrett (upgrading prisoner treatment in the Dallas County jail) in 1972. Hughes became a nationally-known figure as a result of John Kennedy's assassination in Dallas on November 22, 1963 after she was called to administer the oath of office to Lyndon Johnson aboard Air Force One at Love Field. The photo of her administering the oath of office to Johnson remains one of the indelible images of tragic event and its aftermath. Hughes is the only woman in American history to have sworn-in a president, a responsibility usually reserved for the Chief Justice of the United States. She died on April 23, 1985 and is buried in Dallas.

HENRY B. GONZÁLEZ (1916-2000). Henry Barbosa González, longtime Democratic congressman and civil rights advocate, was born on May 3, 1916 in San Antonio, one of six children of Mexican immigrants. Educated in San Antonio public schools, González graduated from Jefferson High School in 1935 and continued his education at the University of Texas at Austin and San Antonio College. He received his law degree from St. Mary's University in San Antonio in 1943. During World War II he served as a civilian cable and radio censor for military and naval intelligence. Upon his return he worked as an assistant juvenile probation officer, eventually becoming the chief probation officer of the Bexar County Juvenile Court. From 1947 to 1951 helped his father run a translation service in San Antonio.

In 1953 González became the first Tejano elected to the San Antonio City Council, serving as mayor pro-tempore for part of his first term. While serving on the council he spoke out frequently against segregated public facilities. In 1956 he was elected to the state senate, becoming the first Mexican American to serve in that body in over 100 years. The following year he and Senator Abraham Kazen undertook the longest filibuster in the history of the Texas Legislature (thirty-six hours) in order to successfully terminate eight of ten racial segregation bills designed to evade the U.S. Supreme Court's Brown v. Board of Education decision. González ran for governor in 1958, finishing third in the race behind Price Daniel and Pappy O'Daniel with 18.6 percent of the vote despite spending only $1,600 on his campaign. A strong supporter of John F. Kennedy, Gonzalez served as co-chairman of the national Viva Kennedy vote drive during the 1960 presidential campaign.

In 1961 González failed in his bid to be elected to the U.S. Senate, but later that year became the first Mexican American from Texas elected to the U.S. House of Representatives when he won a special election to fill a vacancy. He served in the House for the next thirty-seven years, known for his outspoken liberalism and run-ins with rival politicians and citizens who confronted him with their opposing views. In 1963 he shoved West Texas congressman Ed Foreman, who called him a "Pinko" on the House floor, and in 1986, he punched a man who called him a communist in a San Antonio restaurant. While serving on the House Banking and Currency Committee, González became an expert on the nation's banking system as well as public housing. During the Kennedy and Johnson years, he helped usher many bills through Congress including the Housing Act of 1964 and the Civil Rights Act of 1964. He campaigned to end the bracero program under which foreign workers harvested agricultural crops, but often under deplorable conditions. During the 1980s he drafted savings-and-loan bailout legislation and worked to expose the banking industry's excesses. After being elected committee chairman in 1989, he began to assail the Federal Reserve Board's policies, and opened investigations that led to the resignation of the government's chief thrift regulator and to the conviction of Charles Keating.

González's suffered from health problems during his last term. When he retired from Congress in 1998, his son Charlie, a former district judge, won the election to succeed him. González died on November 28, 2000 and is buried in San Fernando Cemetery II in San Antonio.

RALPH YARBOROUGH (1903-1996). Ralph Webster Yarborough, United States senator and leader of the liberal faction of the Democratic Party during the middle of the 20th century, was born in Chandler, Texas on June 8, 1903. He attended local schools and was appointed to the United States Military Academy at West Point in 1919. After dropping out the following year, he taught school while attending Sam Houston State

Teachers College, and worked various jobs to pay his way through law school at the University of Texas. Yarborough received his law degree in 1927 and practiced law in El Paso before being hired as an assistant attorney general in 1931. For the next four years the young lawyer gained recognition by winning several cases against various oil companies to establish the right of public schools and universities to oil-fund revenues. His work secured billions of dollars for public education in Texas.

In 1936 Governor James Allred appointed Yarborough to a state district judgeship in Austin, a position to which he was elected later the same year. His first attempt for statewide elective office occurred in 1938, when he ran for attorney general, ultimately coming in third place in the Democratic primary. During World War II, Yarborough served in the U.S. Army in both Europe and the Pacific, having attained the rank of lieutenant colonel by the war's end, earning a Bronze Star and a Combat Medal. He spent eight months with the military government of occupation in Japan then returned to Austin to resume the practice of law and pursue his political career. In the Democratic primary of 1952 Yarborough challenged incumbent governor R. Allan Shivers but lost. In the campaign, he rallied the liberal wing of the Democratic Party against Shivers who enjoyed wide support from conservatives. Yarborough lost twice more attempts to defeat conservatives for the governorship, in 1954 against Shivers again, then in 1956 to Price Daniel. When Daniel vacated his senatorial seat in 1957 to assume the governorship, however, Yarborough joined the field of twenty-one candidates and narrowly won. He won by solidifying the support of most liberal Texas Democrats.

In the Senate, Yarborough became a rarity among southern Democrats. He refused to support a resolution opposing desegregation and became one of only five southern senators to vote for the Civil Rights Act of 1957. Yarborough won a full term in 1958 when he defeated conservative Bill Blakley in the Democratic primary and Republican Ray Wittenburg in the general election. Yarborough defeated future president George H. W. Bush to win reelection in 1964. During Lyndon Johnson's presidency, he supported many Great Society measures in the realm of civil rights, education, public health, and environmental protection. The senator voted for the Civil Rights Act of 1964 and was one of only three southerners to support the Voting Rights Act of 1965. Yarborough sponsored or cosponsored the Elementary and Secondary Education Act, the Higher Education Act, the Bilingual Education Act, and the revised GI Bill of 1966. Meanwhile, he strongly advocated for such public-health measures as the Occupational Health and Safety Act and the Community Mental Health Center Act. A strong believer in preserving the environment, he co-authored the Endangered Species Act of 1969 and sponsored legislation establishing three national wildlife sanctuaries in Texas (Padre Island National Seashore, Guadalupe Mountains National Park, and Big Thicket National Preserve).

Because of his liberal stands on social issues during the 1960s, Yarborough continued to alienate himself from conservatives within the Democratic Party. In 1970 Lloyd Bentsen, Jr., defeated him in the primary, eventually replacing him in the Senate. Two years later, he made one last attempt at political office when he chose to run against John Tower for the latter's seat, but was defeated in the primary by Barefoot Sanders. Yarborough returned to private practice in Austin and pursued his lifelong hobby of collecting books. He died in Austin on January 27, 1996 and is buried in the State Cemetery.

BRUCE ALGER (1918–2015). The bombastic Far Right Republican congressman Bruce Reynolds Alger was born in Dallas on June 12, 1918. The eldest child of a bank representative, he grew up in a suburb of St. Louis, Missouri before attending Princeton University where he studied philosophy and art while playing center for the school's football team. Upon his graduation in 1940, he worked for the RCA Corporation as a field representative, demonstrating their new television division at the World's Fair in New York, and married his first wife Lucille Antoine. Soon after the birth of their first child, Alger joined the Army Air Corps after U.S. entry into World War II. After training at Kelly Field in San Antonio, he was deployed to the Pacific Theater as a bomber pilot and flew 23 bombing missions over Japan. After the war he returned to Dallas with his wife who gave birth to two more children as he started his own real estate company, beginning the Alger Park subdivision in the eastern side of the city.

Encouraged by local business and community leaders to seek an open seat in Congress, Alger ran as a Republican, which surprised many since no Texas Republican had been elected to Congress in twenty years, and never from Dallas. Portraying himself as a moderate supporter of President Eisenhower, the candidate tapped into growing Republican Party strength in the North Texas city. Alger pulled off the upset victory, winning over an unpopular former mayor with 53 percent of the vote, and soon shed moderation in favor of the Far Right politics held by H.L. Hunt and other Texas oil billionaires whose money drove the ultraconservative movement within the Republican Party during the 1960s. Over his ten years in Congress, Alger was often termed one of the least effective lawmakers for failing to sponsor any significant legislation and his refusal to compromise with Democrats and fellow Republicans alike. His belief in limited federal government action led him to vote against most White House proposals, whether pushed by Republican President Eisenhower or his Democratic successors John F. Kennedy and Lyndon B. Johnson, such as federal support for public housing, subsidized school lunches, Social Security benefit increases, the Civil Rights Act of 1964 calling for an end to public segregation, and the creation of the Medicare system. On foreign affairs, he echoed the sentiments of groups seeking the withdrawal of the United States from the United Nations and the end to formal recognition of all communist governments.

Alger became known to most Americans during the 1960 presidential campaign when he famously organized a demonstration of agitated wealthy Republican women against fellow Texan Lyndon Johnson when the Democratic vice-presidential nominee arrived in Dallas for a fundraiser at the Adolphus Hotel four days before the election. Carrying a large sign reading "LBJ SOLD OUT TO YANKEE SOCIALISTS," Alger led the angry group (dubbed the Mink Coat Mob by the local press due to the attire of choice worn by many of them) which proceeded to accost Johnson and his wife Lady Bird as they exited their car. One woman grabbed Lady Bird's white gloves and threw them in the gutter to approving cheers as the Johnsons entered the Baker Hotel located across the street from the Adolphus. When asked to control the crowd, he reportedly replied "I don't think it is rude to show a socialist and traitor what you think of him." Lyndon Johnson, however, held better political instincts, deciding (much to the chagrin of his wife) that the couple would reemerge and walk through the gauntlet of harassment to the lobby of the Adolphus knowing that local and national media would capture the entire scene. Enduring the ubiquitous jeers and occasional spittle from the overzealous crowd, the Johnsons made it to the fundraiser and the television images and general reporting of the incident subsequently damaged the Republican ticket of Richard Nixon and Henry Cabot Lodge, Jr. who carried Dallas by a two-to-one margin but narrowly lost Texas and the national Electoral College vote. Years later, Nixon lamented: "We lost Texas in 1960 because of that [expletive deleted] congressman from Dallas."

Alger was finally defeated when he was caught up in the 1964 Democratic wave election following the assassination of John F. Kennedy in Dallas. Though Kennedy's killer, Lee Harvey Oswald, was a Far Left extremist, memories of Johnson's rude treatment in 1960 and the vile rhetoric that many ultraconservatives in Dallas used against Kennedy prior to his visit, contributed to the congressman's defeat at the hands of former Democratic mayor Earle Cabell. He returned to the real estate business in Dallas, remarried (his first marriage had ended in 1961), and largely stayed out of politics except for occasional public appearances. After his retirement in 1990, he sold his home and spent ten years travelling the country with his wife in an RV. He died in an assisted living facility in Florida on April 13, 2015, at the age of 96. Though largely forgotten at the time of his death, Alger's rhetoric portraying all liberals as God-hating socialists, his tendency to exploit fears of the spread of communism, and to drive resentment among white, working-class Texas against minorities for political gain, his constant portrayal of the federal government as an omnipresent threat to liberty, and his near-dogmatic refusal to compromise foreshadowed much of the later rise of the Tea Party Republicans during the early twenty-first century.

Chapter 18

A Transitional Decade, 1972-1979

Barbara Jordan Reflects on Lyndon Johnson

Barbara Jordan became the first black woman to be elected to the Texas State Senate in 1966. In 1972 she became the first African American, man or woman, ever elected to the U.S. Congress from Texas. In this excerpt from an oral interview, she reflects favorably on Lyndon Johnson.

Interviewer: I think the first question I'd like to ask would be how did you meet LBJ and what were your experiences with LBJ?

Jordan: Of course, everyone in Texas knew that Lyndon Johnson was a premier political figure in Texas. But when I was in the Texas State Senate--I served in the senate from January of 1967 until 1972 when I went to the Congress--Lyndon Johnson was president of this country, and I received a telegram at my home in Houston from Lyndon Johnson. The telegram was to the effect "we are having a meeting at the White House" or having several people to discuss the future of a bill which was pending in the Congress. This bill was regarding changes in housing legislation to infuse that legislation with a civil rights component. And this telegram asked if I would meet at the White House to discuss this legislation, and it concluded, "Present this telegram at" some gate of the White House. Well, I was, of course, quite startled to receive a telegram from the President of the United States asking that I come to Washington to talk about anything! I said, "Well, I guess I will go." And I took the telegram--I was in Houston when I received the telegram--came back to Austin for the senate and showed it to my colleagues in the senate. I said, "You see, I've got an invitation to go to Washington." They were kind of excited about just the prospect. Now at the time, John Connally was governor of Texas, and I hadn't had very good relations with Mr. Connally, but here was this invitation to the White House, so I went. . . .

. . . . got a taxi and went to the White House, presented my telegram and got in, just like magic. I went up to what I now know was the Cabinet Room. There were other people assembled, people who were active in the civil rights movement. We sat and waited around a table for the President and the Vice President, Hubert Humphrey, to arrive. Well, as I sat there really at the far end of the table, I still said to myself, "Now, Lyndon Johnson probably doesn't know who I am or what I am about, and my name probably just slipped in somehow and got into that [list]." So the President came in, everybody stood up. He sat down, we all sat down, and we started to discuss this legislation, fair housing legislation. And the conversation was going around the table. The President would call on first one person for a reaction and then another person for a reaction. Then he stopped and he looked at my end of the table, he said, "Barbara, what do you think?" Well, I just . . . in the first place, I'm telling you, I didn't know the President knew me, and here he's looking down here saying "Barbara" and then saying, "What do you think?" So that was my first exchange with Lyndon Johnson. I'm startled. I got myself organized, of course, not so that I wouldn't stammer, since it is not my habit to stammer when talking, and I gave a response and then this conversation ensued. That was my first contact personally with Lyndon Johnson. . . .

Interviewer: The positive impression that you have of Johnson personally, was that feeling eminent in the Texas Legislature about Johnson while you were in it? Was there a ground swell with respect to Johnson?

Jordan: We all loved Lyndon Johnson as members of the Texas State Senate. We didn't know him very well. Most of us did not have one-to-one encounters or contacts with him, but he was certainly well respected and very highly regarded by my colleagues in the Texas senate, and he was our number-one Texan at all times. That was quite clear. . . .

Interviewer: You had a fund raiser or something in Houston and there's a picture of you and Lyndon Johnson embracing. I think he said if you ever need him to come to your aid, he would come.

Jordan: That is true.

Interviewer: So the friendship, from the point that you went to Washington for that meeting, grew from that.

Jordan: Well, it certainly did grow from that. On another occasion President Johnson called my house and asked me to serve on a presidential commission. He was establishing and did set up a commission on income maintenance programs, and he called my house one day, which upset my mother to no end. I mean, upset her in a good way; she just couldn't quite handle the President of the United States being on the telephone at her house. When I walked in from some place, and she said, almost breathlessly, "The Ranch is calling," I said, "The Ranch is calling?" She said, "The President is calling from the Ranch." And so I got on the phone and I said, "Hello, Mr. President," and that is when President Johnson asked if I would serve on the income maintenance commission. He told me who else would be on it, and it was, I thought, a worthy thing to do, and so I did serve on that commission. That was a second conversation that I had with the President, when he did establish that commission. . . .

The President was invited to Houston for a fund raiser--not a fund raiser--well, I think we were retiring a debt for Senator Ralph Yarborough, because Senator Ralph Yarborough always had a debt. And the President came to Houston to speak at a function to retire that debt. I was involved in the planning of this dinner, and there was great discussion of who will introduce Lyndon Johnson. And when the President was heard from, he said, "I want Barbara Jordan to introduce me," and that's what I did.

That was the occasion when, after that dinner, Lyndon Johnson held my hand in both of his as only he could do and said, "If ever you need anything from me, money, marbles or chalk"--I'll never forget it--"just call." So when I decided to run for the Congress I said, well, I'm going to call it in. I'm going to call it in because money is needed at this time. And that's when I called the President, who had left office at that time, and told him about my plans to run for Congress and asked if he would come for a fund raiser, and he said yes. I knew he would because he wouldn't have said that if he hadn't meant it. He didn't have a habit of just promising people things like that. That was a strong statement. So he did come to Houston to this fund raiser, which we had at the Rice Hotel, when I was raising money for my race for Congress. We had a hotel ballroom filled with people. We kept it quiet that the President was coming, but when the word got out that he would be there, the President's buddies thought they'd better ante up, and they did. . . .

Interviewer: So he was very accessible. You felt you could get to him pretty [easily], as accessible as a president could be to anybody, I guess.

Jordan: I never had any difficulty getting through to Lyndon Johnson. I can't say that about every public figure that I've tried to contact, but I can say that about Lyndon Johnson.

Source: Lyndon B. Johnson Presidential Library

THOUGHT QUESTIONS:

1. How well did Jordan know Lyndon Johnson before she was invited to her first visit to the White House? What was the purpose of that initial visit?

2. What was the occasion of Jordan's second conversation with Johnson?

3. Did Jordan find Johnson to be helpful and accessible even after he was no longer president? If so, in what ways?

Roe v. Wade and the "Right to Privacy"

*In January 1973, the U.S. Supreme Court issued its landmark ruling in the **Roe v. Wade** case involving a challenge to Texas's restriction against abortion in all cases except on medical advice to save the life of the mother. In early 1970, a single woman living in the Dallas area named Norma McCorvey (referred to as "Jane Roe" in the legal proceedings to protect her identity) was pregnant with her third child and filed the suit in U.S. District Court against Dallas County District Attorney Henry Wade. Though she won the case, the state of Texas appealed the decision, and she gave birth before the case was decided. In these excerpts from Harry Blackmun's now-famous majority opinion, the justice outlines his reasoning for ruling that Texas's abortion law was too restrictive but also why states do have a compelling interest to place limitations on the practice.*

MR. JUSTICE BLACKMUN delivered the opinion of the Court....

This Texas federal appeal and its Georgia companion, *Doe v. Bolton*, present constitutional challenges to state criminal abortion legislation. The Texas statutes under attack here are typical of those that have been in effect in many States for approximately a century. The Georgia statutes, in contrast, have a modern cast and are a legislative product that, to an extent at least, obviously reflects the influences of recent attitudinal change, of advancing medical knowledge and techniques, and of new thinking about an old issue.

We forthwith acknowledge our awareness of the sensitive and emotional nature of the abortion controversy, of the vigorous opposing views, even among physicians, and of the deep and seemingly absolute convictions that the subject inspires. One's philosophy, one's experiences, one's exposure to the raw edges of human existence, one's religious training, one's attitudes toward life and family and their values, and the moral standards one establishes and seeks to observe, are all likely to influence and to color one's thinking and conclusions about abortion.

In addition, population growth, pollution, poverty, and racial overtones tend to complicate and not to simplify the problem.

Our task, of course, is to resolve the issue by constitutional measurement, free of emotion and of predilection. We seek earnestly to do this, and, because we do, we have inquired into, and in this opinion place some emphasis upon, medical and medical-legal history and what that history reveals about man's attitudes toward the abortion procedure over the centuries....

I

The Texas statutes that concern us here are Arts. 1191-1194 and 1196 of the State's Penal Code. These make it a crime to "procure an abortion," as therein defined, or to attempt one, except with respect to "an abortion procured or attempted by medical advice for the purpose of saving the life of the mother." Similar statutes are in existence in a majority of the States. Texas first enacted a criminal abortion statute in 1854. This was soon modified into language that has remained substantially unchanged to the present time.... The final article in each of these compilations provided the same exception, as does the present Article 1196, for an abortion by "medical advice for the purpose of saving the life of the mother."...

II

Jane Roe, a single woman who was residing in Dallas County, Texas, instituted this federal action in March 1970 against the District Attorney of the county. She sought a declaratory judgment that the Texas criminal abortion statutes were unconstitutional on their face, and an injunction restraining the defendant from enforcing the statutes.

Roe alleged that she was unmarried and pregnant; that she wished to terminate her pregnancy by an abortion "performed by a competent, licensed physician, under safe, clinical conditions"; that she was unable to get a "legal" abortion in Texas because her life did not appear to be threatened by the continuation of her pregnancy; and that she could not afford to travel to another jurisdiction in order to secure a legal abortion under safe conditions. She claimed that the Texas statutes were unconstitutionally vague and that they abridged her right of personal privacy, protected by the First, Fourth, Fifth, Ninth, and Fourteenth Amendments. By an amendment to her complaint Roe purported to sue "on behalf of herself and all other women" similarly situated.

James Hubert Hallford, a licensed physician, sought and was granted leave to intervene in Roe's action. In his complaint he alleged that he had been arrested previously for violations of the Texas abortion statutes and that two such prosecutions were pending against him. He described conditions of patients who came to him seeking abortions, and he claimed that for many cases he, as a physician, was unable to determine whether they fell within or outside the exception recognized by Article 1196. He alleged that, as a consequence, the statutes were vague and uncertain, in violation of the Fourteenth Amendment, and that they violated his own and his patients' rights to privacy in the doctor-patient relationship and his own right to practice medicine, rights he claimed were guaranteed by the First, Fourth, Fifth, Ninth, and Fourteenth Amendments....

V

The principal thrust of appellant's attack on the Texas statutes is that they improperly invade a right, said to be possessed by the pregnant woman, to choose to terminate her pregnancy. Appellant would discover this right in the concept of personal "liberty" embodied in the Fourteenth Amendment's Due Process Clause; or in personal, marital, familial, and sexual privacy said to be protected by the Bill of Rights...or among those rights reserved to the people by the Ninth Amendment....

VIII

The Constitution does not explicitly mention any right of privacy. In a line of decisions, however, going back perhaps as far as *Union Pacific R. Co. v. Botsford*, (1891), the Court has recognized that a right of personal privacy, or a guarantee of certain areas or zones of privacy, does exist under the Constitution...

This right of privacy, whether it be founded in the Fourteenth Amendment's concept of personal liberty and restrictions upon state action, as we feel it is, or, as the District Court determined, in the Ninth Amendment's reservation of rights to the people, is broad enough to encompass a woman's decision whether or not to terminate her pregnancy. The detriment that the State would impose upon the pregnant woman by denying this choice altogether is apparent. Specific and direct harm medically diagnosable even in early pregnancy may be involved. Maternity, or additional offspring, may force upon the woman a distressful life and future. Psychological harm may be imminent. Mental and physical health may be taxed by child care. There is also the distress, for all concerned, associated with the unwanted child, and there is the problem of bringing a child into a family already unable, psychologically and otherwise, to care for it. In other cases, as in this one, the additional difficulties and continuing stigma of unwed motherhood may be involved. All these are factors the woman and her responsible physician necessarily will consider in consultation.

On the basis of elements such as these, appellant and some amici ["amici curiae," Latin for "friend of the court"— a legal term for someone not a party to a case who offers information bearing on the case though not solicited by any of the involved parties] argue that the woman's right is absolute and that she is entitled to terminate her pregnancy at whatever time, in whatever way, and for whatever reason she alone chooses. With this we do not agree. Appellant's arguments that Texas either has no valid interest at all in regulating the abortion decision, or no interest strong enough to support any limitation upon the woman's sole determination, are unpersuasive. The Court's decisions recognizing a right of privacy also acknowledge that some state regulation in areas protected by that right is appropriate. As noted above, a State may properly assert important interests in safeguarding health, in maintaining medical standards, and in protecting potential life. At some point in pregnancy, these respective interests become sufficiently compelling to sustain regulation of the factors that govern the abortion decision. The privacy right involved, therefore, cannot be said to be absolute. In fact, it is not clear to us that the claim asserted by some amici that one has an unlimited right to do with one's body as one pleases bears a close relationship to the right of privacy previously articulated in the Court's decisions. The Court has refused to recognize an unlimited right of this kind in the past....

We, therefore, conclude that the right of personal privacy includes the abortion decision, but that this right is not unqualified and must be considered against important state interests in regulation....

Although the results are divided, most ... courts have agreed that the right of privacy, however based, is broad enough to cover the abortion decision; that the right, nonetheless, is not absolute and is subject to some limitations; and that at some point the state interests as to protection of health, medical standards, and prenatal life, become dominant. We agree with this approach....

IX

The District Court held that the appellee failed to meet his burden of demonstrating that the Texas statute's infringement upon Roe's rights was necessary to support a compelling state interest, and that, although the appellee presented "several compelling justifications for state presence in the area of abortions," the statutes outstripped these justifications and swept "far beyond any areas of compelling state interest." Appellant and appellee both contest that holding. Appellant, as has been indicated, claims an absolute right that bars any state imposition of criminal penalties in the area. Appellee argues that the State's determination to recognize and protect prenatal life from and after conception constitutes a compelling state interest. As noted above, we do not agree fully with either formulation.

A. The appellee and certain amici argue that the fetus is a "person" within the language and meaning of the Fourteenth Amendment. In support of this, they outline at length and in detail the well-known facts of fetal development. If this suggestion of personhood is established, the appellant's case, of course, collapses, for the fetus' right to life would then be guaranteed specifically by the Amendment. The appellant conceded as much on reargument. On the other hand, the appellee conceded on reargument that no case could be cited that holds that a fetus is a person within the meaning of the Fourteenth Amendment.

The Constitution does not define "person" in so many words. Section 1 of the Fourteenth Amendment contains three references to "person." The first, in defining "citizens," speaks of "persons born or naturalized in the United States." The word also appears both in the Due Process Clause and in the Equal Protection Clause. "Person" is used in other places in the Constitution: in the listing of qualifications for Representatives and Senators; in the Apportionment Clause; in the Migration and Importation provision; in the Emolument Clause; in the Electors provisions; in the provision outlining qualifications for the office of President; in the Extradition provisions and the superseded Fugitive Slave Clause 3; and in the Fifth, Twelfth, and Twenty-second Amendments, as well as in [Sections] 2 and 3 of the Fourteenth Amendment. But in nearly all these instances, the use of the word is such that it has application only postnatally. None indicates, with any assurance, that it has any possible pre-natal application.

All this, together with our observation, supra, that throughout the major portion of the 19th century prevailing legal abortion practices were far freer than they are today, persuades us that the word "person," as used in the Fourteenth Amendment, does not include the un-born. This is in accord with the results reached in those few cases where the issue has been squarely presented....Indeed, our decision in United States v. Vuitch (1971), inferentially is to the same effect, for we there would not have indulged in statutory interpretation favorable to abortion in specified circumstances if the necessary consequence was the termination of life entitled to Fourteenth Amendment protection.

This conclusion, however, does not of itself fully answer the contentions raised by Texas, and we pass on to other considerations.

B. The pregnant woman cannot be isolated in her privacy. She carries an embryo and, later, a fetus, if one accepts the medical definitions of the developing young in the human uterus. The situation therefore is inherently different from marital intimacy, or bedroom pos-session of obscene material, or marriage, or procreation, or education, with which Eisenstadt and Griswold, Stanley, Loving, Skinner, and Pierce and Meyer were respectively concerned. As we have intimated above, it is reasonable and appropriate for a State to decide that at some point in time another interest, that of health of the mother or that of potential human life, becomes significantly involved. The woman's privacy is no longer sole and any right of privacy she possesses must be measured accordingly.

Texas urges that, apart from the Fourteenth Amendment, life begins at conception and is present throughout pregnancy, and that, therefore, the State has a compelling interest in protecting that life from and after conception. We need not resolve the difficult question of when life begins. When those trained in the respective disciplines of medicine, philosophy, and theology are unable to arrive at any consensus, the judiciary, at this point in the develop-ment of man's knowledge, is not in a position to speculate as to the answer.

It should be sufficient to note briefly the wide divergence of thinking on this most sensi-tive and difficult question. There has always been strong support for the view that life does not begin until live birth. This was the belief of the Stoics. It appears to be the predominant, though not the unanimous, attitude of the Jewish faith. It may be taken to represent also the position of a large segment of the Protestant community, insofar as that can be ascertained; organized groups that have taken a formal position on the abortion issue have generally re-garded abortion as a matter for the conscience of the individual and her family. As we have noted, the common law found greater significance in quickening. Physicians and their sci-entific colleagues have regarded that event with less interest and have tended to focus either upon conception, upon live birth, or upon the interim point at which the fetus becomes "viable," that is, potentially able to live outside the mother's womb, albeit with artificial aid. Viability is usually placed at about seven months (28 weeks) but may occur earlier, even at 24 weeks....

In areas other than criminal abortion, the law has been reluctant to endorse any theory that life, as we recognize it, begins before live birth or to accord legal rights to the unborn except in narrowly defined situations and except when the rights are contingent upon live birth....In short, the unborn have never been recognized in the law as persons in the whole sense.

X

In view of all this, we do not agree that, by adopting one theory of life, Texas may override the rights of the pregnant woman that are at stake. We repeat, however, that the State does have an important and legitimate interest in preserving and protecting the health of the pregnant woman, whether she be a resident of the State or a nonresident who seeks medical consultation and treatment there, and that it has still another important and legitimate interest in protecting the potentiality of human life. These interests are separate and distinct. Each grows in substantiality as the woman approaches term and, at a point during pregnancy, each becomes "compelling."

With respect to the State's important and legitimate interest in the health of the mother, the "compelling" point, in the light of present medical knowledge, is at approximately the end of the first trimester. This is so because of the now-established medical fact...that until the end of the first trimester mortality in abortion may be less than mortality in normal childbirth. It follows that, from and after this point, a State may regulate the abortion procedure to the extent that the regulation reasonably relates to the preservation and protection of maternal health. Examples of permissible state regulation in this area are requirements as to the qualifications of the person who is to perform the abortion; as to the licensure of that person; as to the facility in which the procedure is to be performed, that is, whether it must be a hospital or may be a clinic or some other place of less-than-hospital status; as to the licensing of the facility; and the like.

This means, on the other hand, that, for the period of pregnancy prior to this "compelling" point, the attending physician, in consultation with his patient, is free to determine, without regulation by the State, that, in his medical judgment, the patient's pregnancy should be terminated. If that decision is reached, the judgment may be effectuated by an abortion free of interference by the State.

With respect to the State's important and legitimate interest in potential life, the "compelling" point is at viability. This is so because the fetus then presumably has the capability of meaningful life outside the mother's womb. State regulation protective of fetal life after viability thus has both logical and biological justifications. If the State is interested in protecting fetal life after viability, it may go so far as to proscribe abortion during that period, except when it is necessary to preserve the life or health of the mother.

Measured against these standards, Art. 1196 of the Texas Penal Code, in restricting legal abortions to those "procured or attempted by medical advice for the purpose of saving the life of the mother," sweeps too broadly. The statute makes no distinction between abortions performed early in pregnancy and those performed later, and it limits to a single reason, "saving" the mother's life, the legal justification for the procedure. The statute, therefore, cannot survive the constitutional attack made upon it here....

XI

To summarize and to repeat:

1. A state criminal abortion statute of the current Texas type, that excepts from criminality only a life-saving procedure on behalf of the mother, without regard to pregnancy stage and

without recognition of the other interests involved, is violative of the Due Process Clause of the Fourteenth Amendment.

(a) For the stage prior to approximately the end of the first trimester, the abortion decision and its effectuation must be left to the medical judgment of the pregnant woman's attending physician.

(b) For the stage subsequent to approximately the end of the first trimester, the State, in promoting its interest in the health of the mother, may, if it chooses, regulate the abortion procedure in ways that are reasonably related to maternal health.

(c) For the stage subsequent to viability, the State in promoting its interest in the potentiality of human life may, if it chooses, regulate, and even proscribe, abortion except where it is necessary, in appropriate medical judgment, for the preservation of the life or health of the mother.

2. The State may define the term "physician," as it has been employed in the preceding paragraphs of this Part XI of this opinion, to mean only a physician currently licensed by the State, and may proscribe any abortion by a person who is not a physician as so defined.

In *Doe v. Bolton*, procedural requirements contained in one of the modern abortion statutes are considered. That opinion and this one, of course, are to be read together.

This holding, we feel, is consistent with the relative weights of the respective interests involved, with the lessons and examples of medical and legal history, with the lenity of the common law, and with the demands of the profound problems of the present day. The decision leaves the State free to place increasing restrictions on abortion as the period of pregnancy lengthens, so long as those restrictions are tailored to the recognized state interests. The decision vindicates the right of the physician to administer medical treatment according to his professional judgment up to the points where important state interests provide compelling justifications for intervention. Up to those points, the abortion decision in all its aspects is inherently, and primarily, a medical decision, and basic responsibility for it must rest with the physician. If an individual practitioner abuses the privilege of exercising proper medical judgment, the usual remedies, judicial and intra-professional, are available....

Source: Supreme Court of the United States, *ROE v. WADE, 410 U.S. 113* (1973)

THOUGHT QUESTIONS:

1. On what legal basis did Justice Blackmun find that an implied "right to privacy" led to the conclusion that the Texas state law outlawing abortion in all cases except those involving the life of the mother was unconstitutional? Do you agree or disagree? Why?

2. Though the justice stated that he would not attempt to answer the issue of when human life begins, on what basis did he say that an unborn fetus was not legally a person? Do you agree or disagree? Why?

3. On what basis did the justice make his determination that the state does have a compelling interest to regulate the practice of abortion at certain stages of human development? At what point does the state have that interest? At what stage of pregnancy could the state definitely not intervene from preventing an abortion, according to the justice? Do you agree or disagree with these determinations? Why?

Amado M. Peña, Jr. Discusses Changing Influences on His Art

*Amado Maurilio Peña, Jr. was born in Laredo, Texas in 1943. He studied art and educa-
tion at Texas A & I (now Texas A&M Kingsville). He began teaching art during the 1960s
in Laredo, Crystal City, and Austin. He continues to teach as part of the Studio Art League
program at Alexander High School in Laredo while also serving as an adjunct professor in the
College of Education at the University of Texas. He has been a successful professional artist for
more than 30 years. According to Pena, his art "celebrates the strength of a people who meet
the harsh realities of life in an uncompromising land," and his work is a "tribute to the Native
Americans who survive by living in harmony with an adversarial, untamed environment."*

*As Peña describes in this excerpt from an oral interview, the artist was actively involved in
the Chicano Movement during the 1960s and this participation was reflected in his art. Over
time, however, his art began to evolve as the times changed and as the artist himself changed.*

**Interviewer: Can you tell us something about what was going on in the school [in
Crystal City] at that time?**
Peña: If you are making reference to the reason I went to Crystal City, it in part had to do
with a restructuring of the entire system by the circumstances that had happened prior to
my going there. For the first time a community in the state of Texas actually took charge
of their own destiny. It started out through political means, with education. It started
with students wanting better education, and then it became a political issue. Through
the politics and the system, they were able to use that to restructure their school. So the
politics had made the changes in their educational system.

It so happened that the president of the school board was an old college friend of
mine that I went to school with. When he went to A&I to recruit, I was graduating with
my graduate degree, and he was looking for someone to set up an art program in his
school system. Prior to him going there, I was already involved. I was a student activist in
the art department. (laughter)

There was a period prior to my graduation, prior to 1968—well, 1970, between
1969 and 1970—where I returned to school. And in the process of returning to school,
my work, my art work had started to take a new twist. . . . I was doing imagery that was,
I guess you would say, radical but not in the sense of political radical. It was just radical
in the sense of art. It was just something I really felt very strongly about, imagery and
the color and design, so it was pretty abstract for an artist where I was located. It was extremely radical. But the struggle within myself as I was searching for something that had
some relevancy to being creative—I knew that I was creative as an artist, but I didn't have
content that was really making the impact that I really wanted, that I was looking for.

And so, when I went back to school as a grad student, through circumstances in the
department and the politics and the Chicano movement going on at the time, I became
involved with some groups and found the transition was very natural to politicize the
times through the art; record what the Chicano movement was about.

The participation in the movement for me was as an artist [through] the artist's role.
It's like everybody had a role in the movement—the politicians did the politics, the poets

did the poets, the musicians did the music, and the artists did the arts, and it went on and on. The historians did the history. (laughter) And so I kind of became a leader in that sense, because I was one of the few that was in the department at the time. There were a few others. [I] proceeded to bring out imagery in art, you know, in different mediums to portray what was going on with the movement.

Interviewer: Can you trace your identity and your evolution in terms of your own ethnicity, heritage, development, and identification with your ethnic background in the evolution of your art? I am looking at where you started [with] the first images [grounded] in the Chicano movement, to the images that you have now.

Peña: Through my art work, you can trace the start, which has to do with finally understanding who I am. Yeah. You can. And it's kind of flip-flop. For example, the first images have to do with the present times that not necessarily affected me directly, but affected all of us that were of Mexican descent. It was twofold. We all did the same thing. It was two things that the movement was saying: One is that you have to be proud of who you are and your culture; and we can trace our culture to Mexico, and we can trace our culture to all of the cultures that have come. So we handpicked. We handpicked the Aztecs. We handpicked— probably we didn't handpick the Spaniards—but we definitely handpicked the underdogs. We handpicked Zapata, and we handpicked Pancho Villa. We handpicked certain images that, to us, [had to do with] our birth. At the same time, we handpicked Che Guevara; we handpicked Corky Gonzalez, and Cesar Chavez, and the low-riders, and all of those things. And those were things that were happening "now." . . .

Interviewer: And you created new images.

Peña: We created images that recorded our history; where it hadn't happened before. I mean, where in any history book did you ever see Zapata being cited as a hero of Mexican people? Of Mexican-American people for that matter? Or Cesar Chavez, for example? Those were things; like I said, we went back and forth. We borrowed, and we kept on borrowing.

So there was a period. That was it. That was the start. That was an identity. That was saying, this is really who I really am. . . .

Interviewer: After that time period of the Chicano images that you were doing, was there another period? Or did you go right straight into the Indian images that I see you painting now?

Peña: What happened—because for so many years the intensity of what was going on at the time and my commitment to documenting the times and the images that were necessary—I reached the point where I was tired of doing them. I wanted to talk about us, about myself, about our people, and there were other ways of saying those things, of saying good things about our culture or bad things about our culture, that blood and guts were not the only thing that were required. You know, it seemed like that was what most of us were dealing with. And so I was tired.

I decided that I didn't want to do that anymore. It took one image, one specific image that really kind of just made me stop. I did a portrait of a little boy that had been shot through the head in Dallas, and the image was so powerful that it just made me sick. I decided that I had enough. I needed to find something else, some other way of talking about ourselves. So I stopped doing work.

I had made one trip to Mexico to see art, period. I came across some very simple Indian drawings that people from the Southern part of Mexico were doing through their craft [by] recording their everyday events in a very primitive way and very simple way. And I said, "There it is. Right there. They're talking about themselves, but there's no blood. I mean, they are telling us about what they do every day. They're telling us about what's in their backyard. They're telling us about, you know, how far they have to walk to get water. And it's a pretty picture." And so I said, "Hey, you know, that part of us we never really took time to talk about." So I came back and borrowed their approach to doing that. I threw away all of my academics and started looking in my backyard.

I started looking at the things that were part of our culture, part of me, part of my children, and started making pictures of them and the things that were so beautiful about us that we never really took time to record. It seemed like politics were the ones that were dominating the issues. So I did many, many, many pictures of things that were relevant to our people but not necessarily had to make an impact on anybody else—but a lot of it's on me. Everybody who saw it could see and understand that it was something that they lived. It was something that they knew, but they never saw it in pictures. So I went through a period of doing that.

I don't remember how long I spent doing that, but I had the opportunity to travel west, and as a result of going and doing a [an art] show on the road, I ended up in New Mexico. All this time, when we were doing this whole Chicano movement, it seemed like we were so isolated with our part of the world. Texas was very different than California. And Chicanos were different in California. They were different in New Mexico. They were different in Arizona, and they were different in Colorado. We knew that, but we never really came in contact with them that much, or at least I didn't.

When I went to New Mexico, through just being in the right place at the right time, I came across some things that I didn't understand too well. It was kind of like in that place it seemed like the mixture of the cultures was not just there, but it was also alive and moving around. And it made me wonder, are we any different than that? And we're not. . . .

And there's more to it than that. I had to really say, "Well, if I'm not, you know, what is? What is a Mexican American?" I mean really take and try to analyze that. What is it? . . .

And so I started looking and trying to make pictures; trying to make sense of this in the sense that I want to make pictures of it. So I start looking at where the two cultures, the native and Spanish, for a lack of a better word, "mixed," existing in this region. They intermarried, obviously; there's the mixed blood. But I'm looking for visuals; I'm looking for things that I can make some sense of. . . .

I tell people, I really don't paint Indians. When you think of Indians, [you think of them] with feathers and warbonnets and war shields and riding horses and bows and arrows. I don't. I do the mixture. I do the things that influence and what, to me, the both cultures have shared. . . .

Source: Institute of Texan Cultures

THOUGHT QUESTIONS:

1. How did the Chicano Movement influence Peña's art during the 1960s?

2. Why did he stop doing Chicano art? What type of art did he start doing instead?

3. How did his trip to New Mexico begin to influence his art in new directions?

Flaco Jimenez Discusses His Early Interest in Music and the Origin of Conjunto

Leonardo "Flaco" Jimenez is a Grammy Award-winning button accordionist, born and raised in San Antonio, whose family has done much to popularize Tejano "conjunto" (also known as norteño) music, which feels the heavy influence of polka music brought to Texas by German immigrants. In addition to his renowned solo work, Jimenez was a member of the 1990s supergroup "Texas Tornadoes" (with Doug Sahm, Augie Myers, and Freddy Fender) known for its fusion of rock, country, and Tejano music. In this excerpt from an oral interview, he describes his early interest in accordion music and the legacy of his father and grandfather.

Interviewer: Flaco, we in San Antonio, of course in Texas, know you as a fine accordion player. And the conjunto music and Flaco Jimenez is just number one in San Antonio and Texas. How did you become a musician and since when have you been playing, also?

Jimenez: Well, I started as a musician, when I was about seven years old. I started liking music about that time, being that my grandfather and my father were accordionists. And so I think it's in my blood as far as accordion playing is concerned. So I started liking the accordion when I was about seven years old. But I didn't really get to it until I was twelve. But, still, I knew I could learn, but being that I was seven years, pretty young. But, still, I got to learn the accordion by observing my Dad's teachings. He used to teach young kids from the neighborhood; used to teach accordion. So I caught on just by observing teachings.

Interviewer: And what kind of accordion is that?

Jimenez: It's a button accordion, it's called diatonic accordion. It's real different from a keyboard accordion or a piano accordion. It's very different—diatonic and piano. It's pretty different. The keys are different. I mean, if you play a key in one on the piano accordion, push and pull, it's the same note. And the diatonic, well, it's different, push and pull, it's different.

Interviewer: Your father, then, probably learned from his father to play the accordion?

Jimenez: Yes. My grandfather, Patricio Jimenez, was one of the first that started playing this type of accordion here, around the Texas area, around the San Antonio area. So he caught on, as far as playing the button accordion, because he used to go to German dances in the New Braunfels area here about thirty miles from here. So he used to go and dance and see how that kind of music was played—the polka and schottisch and whatever, you know. That oompah music.

So, then, he managed to buy one, buy a button accordion. So he started . . . this is the story that my Dad . . . because I didn't really get to know my Granddaddy. He died before I was born.

Interviewer: And then your father picked it up from your grandfather. Your father's name was Santiago, right?

Jimenez: Was Santiago Jimenez, uh huh. So my dad, Santiago, picked it up from my grandfather, Patricio. So he started playing, started recording in 1936, his first record. And, of course, my Granddaddy never got to record because there were no facilities for recording at that time. No studios, and all, so I didn't get to hear my granddaddy at all. But what I hear, my Dad used to tell me stories about him. He was a superb player. . . .

Interviewer: We know your father and you started music as a conjunto music. How was this term related or came about?

Jimenez: Okay. Conjunto music is really the origin of conjunto; the name conjunto, well, in my know-how, it means get together of musicians. Conjunto is . . . it's like conjunto of guitar, drums and a bajo sexto. So it's a conjunction of music. So that's why we call it conjunto.

Interviewer: Was your father the first person to name it this particular term?

Jimenez: Yes. Uh huh. [His group was called] "Santiago Jimenez and His Conjunto." So he used to call it conjunto. Then some other names were called this music, like norteño music.

Interviewer: That's probably because you're north of Mexico.

Jimenez: North of Mexico, yes, of the northern part of the border. So it has been called norteño music, which is north of the border music, which is Texas.

Source: Institute of Texan Cultures

THOUGHT QUESTIONS:

1. How old was Jimenez when he started as a musician? Who influenced his interest?

2. How did his grandfather, Santiago Jimenez, become exposed to German music?

3. According to Jimenez, who invented the term "conjunto"? How was the term derived?

Historian Felix Almaraz Discusses Changing Depictions of Hispanics in Film

A native of San Antonio, Felix D. Almaráz, Jr. is a distinguished Texas history professor specializing in Mexican American studies. The author of numerous published works on Texas, the Spanish Borderlands, and Colonial Latin America, Almaráz received a Ph.D. from the University of New Mexico in 1968 and began teaching at UT San Antonio in 1973, the first year the university offered classes. He has always had a strong interest in cinema. In the following excerpt from an oral interview in which he discusses his early life in San Antonio, focusing especially on the movie houses in his hometown, Dr. Almaráz comments on the changing representation of Hispanic film characters over the years.

Interviewer: What about in the films themselves? When did you start . . . that you did start to notice stereotypical ethnic depictions in the films themselves? Like in cowboy films, for instance.

Almaráz: Oh, yes. In those . . . in the early films I guess there was no attempt to build up, let's say, the role of a Mexican or the role of a black. Just let him be—play the stereotypical roles—and thus perpetuating an image for another generation. The change, I thought, occurred in the . . . when . . . in a film with Roy Rogers when he brought in Tito . . . from Mexico to appear in two movies with him. And Tito was a matinee idol in his country and so he found another generation of admirers over here. And he got equal billing. Roy Rogers always came out first and the horse and Tito. But they . . . and then Wild Bill Elliot started, in his big budget pictures. Then he started treating Hispanics as human beings. The role may have been one of animosity—not because of ethnicity but because of certain views about whatever the problem may have been. But toward the end they would talk about courage. And they would address them by a name rather than just, "Hey, Pancho or Jesus," where they would just kind of exaggerate the pronunciation.

But in the movies before World War II, a lot of them, they were just put together in a hurry and if it made sense, fine. They didn't . . . or in a let's say . . . let's just take the Alamo as a source . . . and a battery of these Alamo movies that came out. And Santa Anna was always depicted as some greasy kind of bearded type of individual—just low-down and high-smelling. But as you got into the John Wayne version of it, he's still a coyote, he's still depicted as a dictator, but they have J. Carroll Nash playing him in the Alamo John Wayne version. You get to the one at the IMAX ["Alamo: The Price of Freedom," released in 1988] when I had a chance to be an advisor to that movie, I said, "Well, if you're going to stick to the same story-line of Travis at the . . . inside of the Alamo defending, drawing a line you know in the sand, because you're going to make him the protagonist, then as we say in theater, then you have to have that antagonist to balance it off." And I said history couldn't have given you a better antagonist than Santa Anna. So Santa Anna is depicted by Enrique Sandino who was almost born in the saddle in Columbia. His family raised horses, to train them for the well-to-do. . . And, so when you see Sandino as Santa Anna coming out, he controlled that horse and reminded me so much of Wild Bill Elliot—you control the animal by the pressure of your legs. You don't jerk the animal this way, you guide this animal, but it has to be someone who knows the equestrian skill. And so here's Santa Anna, the caudillo, of course! But he's an eloquent. I'm sure, I mean he enjoyed . . . he loved the fancy clothes. So it's taken at least three generations in order to bring about some a revision of these stereotypical images. You wouldn't I don't think the public today would tolerate a black actor coming on a Bojangles, and just going through the motions and going on, "Yes, boss" and things like that.

Source: Institute of Texan Cultures

THOUGHT QUESTIONS:

1. When did Almaráz begin to notice a change in the manner in which Mexicans were portrayed in films?

2. What aspects made the new depiction noteworthy?

3. How did Almaráz advise the filmmakers about how Santa Anna should be portrayed for the IMAX film version of the *Alamo* that is currently played in Rivercenter Mall in San Antonio?

River Walk Jazz Musician Jim Cullen, Jr. Recalls His Club's Start, Describes the Stresses That Can Develop in a Band, and Reflects on Success and Happiness

As Jim Cullum, Jr. tells the story, one day he caught sight of an antique cornet in a hockshop window. He headed directly to his father's grocery business and begged for the money to buy it. After his father (a former jazz musician) relinquished the required seven dollars, Jim taught himself how to play. While attending Trinity University in San Antonio, he formed a seven-piece jazz ensemble, the Happy Jazz Band, and invited his father to play whenever he could. In 1963, Cullum and a group of local business leaders invested $1,000 to establish The Landing, a jazz club on the San Antonio River Walk, as a showcase for the group. Eventually, Jim's father retired from the grocery business to play regularly with his son.

Starting out in the basement of the current Joe's Crab Shack, The Landing had a brief stay in the space now occupied by The Original Mexican Restaurant before moving to the River Walk level of the Hyatt Regency Hotel in the fall of 1982. Over the past forty years under Cullum's direction, the band has become a River Walk fixture allowing the musician to pursue his lifelong passion of researching, preserving, and presenting traditional jazz to the public. In this excerpt from a 1980 oral interview, Cullum describes the downtown San Antonio tourist revival of the late-1960s that helped his band's notoriety and the inner tensions that can develop among musicians within a band.

Interviewer: All right. You opened [The Landing] in April of '73.
Cullum: '63.
Interviewer: '63. Gosh. 17 years ago. And it was a success.
Cullum: Well, it was a—let me just tell you about that. Jim Hayne was so smart about promoting it. And they got that group of people to work on it. Not just invest money, but everybody worked. I can remember 'em havin' meetings out at the country club. 'Course these were fancy people that, you know, most of 'em belonged to the country club anyway. But they'd have the meetings at the country club and they'd buy dinner for everybody and then they'd all sit around and address invitations to the opening and stuff. That was the kind of a spirit that—
Interviewer: You were open 3 nights a week. Thursday, Friday and Saturday.
Cullum: Well, no. When we first started, the opening nights were Thursday, Friday and Saturday. Thursday night was black tie. And Friday and Saturday dress was optional. But everybody wanted to come on the black tie night. And they were pullin' strings with these VIP investors to concede, you know. So it was a very good situation to be that in demand, you know. From the very outset. So it was a big success. But we found right away—we never had intended to play except on weekends, you know. The band was gonna play on weekends. But we brought Cliff Bruton down here from Dallas to play piano in the band, and he was supposed to play with a couple of other guys on weeknights to make about a 5 night a week deal. And it didn't work at all 'cause the weeknights would just fall flatter than a fritter. Nobody would come down there; on the weekends we would be jammed.

So it gradually worked around to where we were just open on weekends. . . .

But we tried to be open 5 days a week, you know. And it would just be like it was deserted, you know. You'd look on the river and there wouldn't be a soul. It was just—you'd stand out there for 30 minutes and not one person would walk by, you know.

Interviewer: And during all this time, you and your dad were still in the wholesale grocery business.

Cullum: Oh yeah. We were in the wholesale grocery business. And this was very much a thing—you know, when I think back about it, the time I wasted foolin' around. I would work hard in that grocery business and I wouldn't touch my horn from Saturday to the next Friday a lot of times. Wouldn't even touch it; wouldn't take it outta the case. And that's no way to play the trumpet. Go down there and struggle, go crazy tryin' to play, and sounded terrible, and you know. Never had any chops. So little by little we—you know, it's just a very gradual process. The first changes in the scene, well, after a couple of years it began to change. The audience became a little different. It became less a toy of these wealthy investors and more of a place for the tourists gradually. It started changing. At first it was all San Antonio people.

Interviewer: Right. I remember that.

Cullum: But little by little it started changing. The River Walk, within a short time, a couple of years, the Poco Loco opened next door. And the two places together had a sort of an attraction. But little by little it changed. And by 1968, of course, they built two big hotels.

Interviewer: HemisFair.

Cullum: HemisFair. And all these out-of-town people started comin', and convention facilities were built in '68. That's just 5 years later. And by that time the scene of the San Antonio people comin' had changed quite a bit. It was down to maybe 50/50 in our audience. 50% San Antonio, or even maybe less.

Interviewer: And now it's about 99% most of the time.

Cullum: Yeah. It's about somewhere between—it's about 10% local, I think, now. . . .

Interviewer: What year was it you moved? [from The Landing's original location]
Cullum: '74.

Interviewer: Yeah. I started to say '75.

Cullum: But we made it. And then after we got over there, we went through a couple of crisis points. And we're still not out of the woods yet, where I didn't know if we were gonna make it or not.

Interviewer: You went through it the winter of '78, '79 where it rained all winter. It was cold all winter and nobody came to the river.

Cullum: And I'll tell you that we made the first money that the Landing's ever made in 18 years in March and April, the first money that amounted to anything. And I'm still concerned about it. However, I feel that with all the development that's goin' on all around us, that ultimately we're gonna be, you know, able to survive and flourish and do okay.

Interviewer: Yeah. And another new hotel just up the river. Marriott is in and the river is extremely active. And as you say, your business is what? Ninety percent tourist now.

JC: Yeah. We should be all right now. I'm pretty confident about it.

Interviewer: Well, you ever had times when you say, "Hey, is it all worth it?" You know, "I'm bustin' my butt."

Cullum: No. Not really. Once in awhile I've thought about—day-dreamed. Everybody does this though, you know. I've thought about leavin' town and gettin' away from here and startin' over where I can just be a musician and not trying to be into all this stuff. But I don't wanna do that. If I did that I'd have to play some music I didn't like and stuff. And this way I can play exactly what I want and the band is great. So it suits me and it's worth it.

Interviewer: It's taken an enormous amount of will power and effort, I think, for you to hold everything together with some of the crises you've just described and the changes in personnel, or bringing personnel in who play the way you want 'em to play.

Cullum: It's been a hard thing to get. For one thing it's very hard to get seven people— and, we're just talking about strictly musically, and leaving all the business and stuff out. It's very hard to get seven people who want to all go exactly the same way. And you might be able to get seven guys who will go out and play casual—a one time thing—and listen to each other and kinda bend their styles and blend, and sound pretty good, you know, and do very good. But to have a continuing professional band, there are personalities there—their musical ideas come to the surface, you see. And a guy who's a very good player, he's got some musical ideas of his own that he wants to express his own thoughts. And it's hard to get seven guys whose basic thoughts, when they all surface, are gonna kinda go the same way. You get somebody who thinks that it's either too modern or it's not modern enough—we've had that a lot, you know. Or else it's, you know, you have all kinds of things about it's too loud or it's too—we've had guys on there that they didn't think it was he-manish enough, it was too sweet or—

Interviewer: Or this guy's gettin' in my way when I play.

Cullum: Yeah. You've got all kinds of things. So somebody has to kinda dictate in those situations exactly what's gonna happen as best you can, you know. And a lot of these things don't come up with casual bands or just jobbing bands or a group that'll go out and play occasionally—a weekend band. They'll never come up, see? Because the guys are not—it's a looser kind of thing there.

Interviewer: And your band plays six nights a week, and often on Sundays you're on the road or gigs. So there's just a lot of opportunity for frictions.

Cullum: To develop. And there's a lot of opportunity for differences of musical opinion. And sometimes they may be very minor, but they'll get to be like a grit of sand in between two guys, even though it's just a little minor—

Interviewer: Just a little rub.

Cullum: Yeah. And pretty soon, the guys'd come to me and they'd say, "I just can't stand the way so and so plays and such," you know. These little things drive me crazy. Hey man, come on, you know. And then sometimes it's a very inconsequential little thing. So I have to get the two of 'em together and say, "Now, look. What you're doin' on this kinda time here," maybe it's the drums or whatever it is, you know, "what you're doin' on this is botherin' so and so. On this chorus just—on this solo just play this. Just play 2-beat. That's what he wants. Do you mind doin' that?" "Well, I don't like to play 2-beat." "Well, then how 'bout half and half." (laughter) So you finally get—

Interviewer: You compromise.

Cullum: There's gotta be some give and take and compromise, yeah.

Interviewer: What do you think about the future of jazz. Obviously you're heavily invested in the future of your band and jazz as—

Cullum: Well see, I'm not doin' it because of—I have not done any of this like a typical business man. I have not done it because I expected to make a lot of money, although I sure wouldn't mind it, you know. I wouldn't mind makin' some money. But I haven't done anything—anything that I've done in this music—because I thought it was the smart way to make money or that it had a great, bright future, or that it was gonna bring me fame and fortune, or any of that kind of stuff. And I really don't care as much about prosperity, great tremendous success or anything. I'll be very satisfied with a modest degree of success and to be able to keep the band together and have a full career and do this. That will be—I will be very satisfied with that kind of result from this activity.

Of course, you want it to be as good as possible. But as to what the future is gonna be, I really don't even think about it, you know. I don't think about—sit there and well, jazz is gonna become a big rage and we're all gonna get rich or somethin'. I never even think about it. I don't frankly. I think it's not gonna ever be a real big time, super thing, you know. I don't think we're ever gonna be playing Hollywood Bowl or in arenas and things, around a 100,000 people and stuff like that. I don't think that jazz is gonna ever have that. It's kinda like classical music, you know. Classical music has a certain appeal, very definite, strong appeal to a certain audience, certain people whose tastes run that way and their educational situation—they know about it; they like it; they listen to it. And jazz music is kinda the same kinda thing. No doubt that it is becoming more popular as time goes by, you know. It's been a gradual—

Interviewer: The pendulum's coming back.

Cullum: Yeah. It's gradually becoming more and more and more popular. But I just personally can hardly see it becoming a big rage. I don't see any kinda thing about it. I really just don't care. I mean, I'm too occupied and concerned with day to day affairs of playing and practicing.

Source: Institute of Texan Cultures

THOUGHT QUESTIONS:

1. How did Cullum describe the original clientele of The Landing. How did that change starting in the late-1960s and why?

2. What types of musical difficulties did Cullum cite that he has had over the years in trying to keep a band together? How did Cullum say he tends to work out these types of problems within the group?

3. What did Cullum say with regard to success and happiness? Did he wish to make a huge sum of money playing in large stadiums someday or to release a hit jazz tune?

Texas Stadium's "Hole"

Originally planned as a domed sports arena, Texas Stadium could not support the weight of the entire roof, resulting in most of the stands being enclosed but not the playing field itself. This prompted Cowboys linebacker D. D. Lewis to make his now-famous quip: "Texas Stadium has a hole in its roof so God can watch His favorite team play." This was often paraphrased as the "hole" in the stadium's roof was there "so that God can watch His team." Coupled with NFL films' touting of the team as "America's Team" in promotional videos, the Cowboys became a "love them or hate them" enterprise. The playing surface installed in 1971 officially was labeled Texas Turf and was a form of AstroTurf. The Cowboys left Texas Stadium (located in Irving) after the 2008 NFL season for the new Cowboys Stadium in Arlington, which has a retractable roof system and, for nostalgia purposes, mimics the Texas Stadium's "hole."

THOUGHT QUESTION:

Do you think the popularity of D.D. Lewis's quote says anything about what many Texans like to think about themselves? Why or why?

BIOGRAPHIES

BARBARA JORDAN (1936-1996). Barbara Charline Jordan, African American politician and teacher, was born in Houston, Texas, on February 21, 1936. After attending public schools, her father, a Baptist minister and warehouse clerk, helped her to attend Texas Southern University, where she graduated *magna cum laude* in 1956. She received a law degree from Boston University in 1959 and passed bar exams in Massachusetts and Texas. After teaching for a year at Tuskegee Institute, Jordan returned to Houston and opened a law practice, working from her parents' home for three years until she could afford to open her own office.

Jordan's first involvement in politics involved registering black voters for the 1960 presidential campaign. She ran twice, unsuccessfully, for the state Senate until 1967 when redistricting and increased African American voter registration led to her election as the first black state senator in Texas since 1883. During the next six years she gained a reputation as a pragmatist working within the system rather than against it, earning the respect of her white male colleagues in the process as demonstrated by her unanimous selection as president pro tempore of the Senate in 1972.

In 1973, Jordan won the congressional seat from the Eighteenth Texas District, becoming simultaneously the first African American woman from a southern state and the first black Texan ever to represent Texas in Congress. A powerful public speaker, she gained national prominence for her role in the 1974 Watergate hearings as a member of the House Judiciary Committee, delivering the most memorable speech during the proceedings. In 1976, Democratic Party officials chose Jordan to become the first woman ever to deliver the keynote address at their national convention.

In 1979, Jordan retired after three terms to accept the Lyndon Baines Johnson Public Service Professorship at the LBJ School of Public Affairs, University of Texas at Austin where she taught courses on government, politics, and ethics. In that same year, she published her autobiography, *Barbara Jordan: A Self Portrait*. In 1992 she once again delivered the keynote address at the Democratic Party national convention. Two years later she received the Presidential Medal of Freedom. A number of ailments in her later years, including multiple sclerosis, confined her to a wheelchair. She finally died of pneumonia and leukemia on January 17, 1996 and is buried in the State Cemetery.

JOHN TOWER (1925-1991). John Goodwin Tower, Republican United States Senator, was born on September 29, 1925, in Houston, Texas. He grew up in East Texas communities where his father, a Methodist minister, preached. Upon graduating from Beaumont High School in 1942, he began to attend Southwestern University. In June 1943 he enlisted in the United States Navy and served during World War II as a seaman aboard an amphibious gunboat in the Pacific. He remained active in the naval reserve until 1989. After the war, Tower returned to Southwestern University, where he received a B.A. degree in political science in 1948. The next year he moved to Dallas in order to attend graduate school at Southern Methodist University. While in Dallas, he completed his coursework and started teaching political science at Midwestern University in Wichita Falls. In March of 1952, he married Lou Bullington in Wichita Falls. The couple had three daughters before they divorced in 1976. The next year, Tower married Lilla Burt

Cummings and remained married for ten years until they divorced in 1987. Tower received his M.A. in political science from SMU in 1953.

While in Wichita Falls, Tower became an active member of the Republican Party. In 1954 he lost a race for state representative from the Eighty-first District. In 1960 he received the Republican nomination to challenge Senate Majority Leader Lyndon Johnson. Though easily defeated by Johnson in the Senate race, a vacancy developed when Johnson was elected John Kennedy's vice president. Tower defeated William Blakely in a special election to fill out the term. With his election Tower became the first Republican to win statewide office in Texas since Reconstruction. His election and subsequent victories in 1966, 1972, and 1978 has often been seen as the symbolic beginning of the arrival of two-party politics in Texas.

During his Senate career, Tower proved to be influential on many domestic and foreign policy issues. He first served on two major Senate committees: Labor and Public Welfare, and Banking and Currency, but his favorite was Armed Services Committee, in which he landed a spot in 1965 and served until his retirement, including a stint as chairman from 1981 to 1984. While on the committee, he strongly supported the Johnson administration during the Vietnam War. Later, as chairman of the Armed Services Committee, Tower used his position to strengthen and modernize the country's military. He also assumed a state and national leadership role in Republican Party politics, giving his whole-hearted aid and support to all Republican candidates for president from Barry Goldwater to George H. W. Bush.

Tower retired from the Senate in 1985 and was soon appointed by President Ronald Reagan to serve as chief U.S. negotiator at the Strategic Arms Reduction Talks in Geneva, Switzerland. He then began to chair a Washington lobbying group while holding the title of distinguished lecturer in political science at Southern Methodist University. In 1986, President Reagan asked him to chair the review board created to study the National Security Council and its staff in the wake of the so-called Iran-Contra Affair. The Tower Commission's report criticized several Reagan administration officials and the National Security Council for their dealings with the Iranian government and the Nicaraguan Contras.

In 1989, President George H. W. Bush chose Tower to become his Secretary of Defense but the Senate refused to confirm the nomination, citing his ties to defense contractors, his conservative political views, and allegations of excessive drinking and womanizing. (Congressman Dick Cheney of Wyoming, then the House Minority Whip, later received confirmation as defense secretary.) On April 5, 1991, Tower and his daughter Marianne were both killed along with twenty-one others in the crash of a small commuter plane attempting to land at Brunswick, Georgia. He and his daughter are buried in a family plot in Dallas. His autobiography, *Consequences: A Personal and Political Memoir,* was published just a few months before his death.

MARY KAY ASH (1918-2001). Mary Kathlyn Wagner, businesswoman and founder of the Mary Kay Cosmetics empire, was born on May 12, 1918 in Hot Wells (Harris County), Texas. She attended Regan High School in Houston, graduating in 1934. She attended the University of Houston until she married in 1943. Ash had three children before divorcing her husband, leading to her employment with a direct sales firm, hosting parties to encourage people to buy various household items. In 1952, she was hired as a national training director for a Dallas direct-sales firm, World Gift Company, where she worked until 1963. When a man that she trained received a promotion and higher salary, Ash quit in protest and wrote a book to assist women in business.

Not happy with her unpleasant experiences in the traditional male-dominated workplace, she decided to start up her own business, Mary Kay Cosmetics, opening a small store in Dallas. The basis of the business, however, was similar to the previous direct-sales companies for which she worked—selling cosmetics through at-home parties and other sponsored events. Nevertheless, Ash wished her company to operate differently, in that she chose not to utilize sales territories for her representatives and developed incentive programs for her salespeople, such as the practice of making them buy products from the company at wholesale prices and then selling them at retail price to their customers as well as enabling salespeople to earn additional commissions for recruiting successful new employees. The company grew rapidly, especially after Ash's appearance in a profile piece on CBS's *60 Minutes* program. Her practice of giving pink Cadillacs to her top sales people displayed the company's success as well as serving as a highly visible promotional tool.

Her business strategies have attracted much interest over the years, popularized in three books she authored: *Mary Kay: The Success Story of America's Most Dynamic Businesswoman* (1981), *Mary Kay on People Management* (1984), and *Mary Kay: You Can Have It All* (1995). In 1987 she retired and became chairman emeritus of the company. By 2008, the company had over 1.5 million representatives worldwide with sales topping $2 billion. She died on November 22, 2001. Her son Richard continues to run the company that he helped her to create.

CAROL BURNETT (1933 –). Comedic icon Carol Burnett was born in San Antonio, Texas, on April 26, 1933. The alcoholism of both her father, a movie theater manager, and her mother, greatly impacted her childhood. Her parents divorced in the late 1930s and she was largely raised by her maternal grandmother. Though she moved out to California with her grandmother at age seven to live closer to her mother who got a job as a publicity writer for Hollywood movie studios, she always identified as a Texan. Her youthful memories, good and bad, growing up in San Antonio during the Great Depression would impact her later work.

After graduating from Hollywood High School in 1951, Burnett attended UCLA with plans of pursuing a career in journalism before focusing on theater arts and English with ideas of becoming a playwright. Because the playwright program included a required acting course component, she reluctantly signed up and was so thrilled with the laughter that she received from the audience to an improvised comedic line during a show that she was forever hooked on performing in front of a crowd. Despite her mother's desire for her to follow in her footsteps and become a writer, Burnett later reflected that the warmth and validation that the crowd gave her completely broke her out of her shell and led her no choice than to pursue her ambitions as an entertainer. She performed in several university comedic and musical productions before leaving college to pursue a career in New York City with her college sweetheart and future first husband Don Saroyan.

Burnett lived in a boarding house in Manhattan while working as a hat-check girl in between receiving bit parts on local television programs before catching on as an attention-getting entertainer on the New York night club cabaret circuit, eventually performing her feature parody number "I Made a Fool of Myself over John Foster Dulles" (then the Secretary of State for President Dwight Eisenhower) on *The Tonight Show*, hosted by Jack Paar, and *The Ed Sullivan Show*, both very popular nationally syndicated television shows. Her big break in show business took place in 1959 when she won the starring role of Princess Winnifred in the original Broadway production of the musical comedy *Once Upon a Mattress*, receiving a Tony Award nomination for Best Performance by a Leading Actress in a Musical. She became a regular performer for three years on *The Gary Moore Show*, a popular early 1960s variety show, earning an Emmy Award for her portrayal of an assortment of zany characters. After she and her first husband divorced in 1962, Burnett married television producer Joe Hamilton the following year. They had three daughters before divorcing in 1984.

The entertainer's star continued to rise during the mid-60s. Burnett became close friends with Jim Nabors and Lucille Ball, appearing often on their popular television shows *Gomer Pyle, U.S.M.C.* and *The Lucy Show,* before landing her own variety program on CBS in 1967, *The Carol Burnett Show.* For the next twelve years, the hour-long music and comedy show featuring Burnett, Harvey Korman, Vicki Lawrence, Lyle Waggoner, and Tim Conway became a staple of 1970s television, receiving consistently high ratings while earning Emmy and Golden Globe Award nominations every season of its production for its rousing mixture of musical numbers, movie and soap opera parodies, and sketch comedy. Among its most popular features was a recurring sketch, "The Family," inspired directly from Burnett's childhood in San Antonio. For the episodes, the show's writers originally envisioned a dysfunctional Midwestern family but she immediately transformed the main characters (an optimistic wife played by Burnet, a curmudgeonly husband payed by Korman, and a wisecracking grandmother played by Lawrence) into self-disruptive Southerners patterned after her own family members. Though the writers thought this might be seen as condescending to those from Dixie, Burnett felt that Southerners would love the depictions because it would remind them of someone they knew. While not completely autobiographical, the sketches were nevertheless cathartic experiences for the comedienne as she worked to derive humor from painful experiences from her youth. She closed every episode of her show with a tug on her left ear—a secret message of love to her grandmother that she had originally sent during her very first television appearance.

Burnett appeared in some films and other television programs during her variety show's run, most notably as the first guest on PBS's *Sesame Street* in 1969. After *The Carol Burnett Show* ended in 1978, she appeared in a steady stream of movies, including *The Four Seasons* (1981), *Annie* (1982), and *Noises Off* (1992), made guest appearances on several television comedy shows, and occasionally returned to the stage to perform in an assortment of theatrical productions, winning another Tony Award nomination in 1995 for her role as Charlotte Hay in the comedic play *Moon Over Buffalo.* The resilient entertainer continues to work into her eighties, occasionally touring with a popular nostalgia show entitled "Laughter and Reflection," while collecting an impressive list of well-deserved career awards, including a Kennedy Center Honor, the Presidential Medal of Freedom, the Mark Twain Prize for American Humor, the Screen Actors Guild Lifetime Achievement Award, and induction into the Texas Film Hall of Fame.

Chapter 19

Complex Times, 1980-1994

"Senator, You're No Jack Kennedy"

Though most remembered for delivering a devastating line during the 1988 vice-presidential debate, Lloyd Bentsen, Jr. enjoyed a long and successful political career representing Texas in Congress before that famous moment on the national stage. After serving as a bomber pilot in Europe during World War II, he returned to his native Rio Grande Valley and was elected to the U.S. House of Representatives in 1948. After serving three terms, he entered the private sector, eventually founding an insurance company and serving on the board of directors of Lockheed Corporation as well as several oil and gas companies. In the 1970 Democratic Party senatorial primary, Bentsen upset the incumbent, Ralph Yarborough, who led the party's liberal faction in Texas, by lambasting the senator for his votes in favor of the Civil Rights Act of 1964, the Voting Rights Act of 1965, and his opposition to the Vietnam War. Bentsen went on to win the general election against his Republican opponent, George H. W. Bush. Over time, Bentsen came to be viewed as an effective centrist Democrat, gaining re-election two more times before the Democratic presidential nominee in 1988, Governor Michael Dukakis of Massachusetts, asked the senator to be his running mate in his race against Bush, the Republican presidential nominee. Many pundits at the time (and since) have posited that Dukakis's choice of Bentsen was a mistake, not because of any liability on Bentsen's part, but because the elder statesman from Texas seemed to come across as more "presidential" in terms of his bearing and temperament than the governor.

Bentsen certainly registered a fine performance in his one and only televised vice-presidential debate on October 5, 1988, when he sparred with Bush's running mate, Dan Quayle, the 41-year-old junior senator from Indiana. Showing fine preparation, Bentsen and his aides noticed that when Senator Quayle was asked about his youth and relative inexperience at the national level, he frequently cited the fact that President John Kennedy had as much overall national experience as he did when running for president in 1960. If Quayle responded along those lines again during the debate, Bentsen would be ready. When his opponent did indeed fall into his familiar pattern, Bentsen, almost on cue, retorted with a seemingly improvised and heartfelt response: "Senator, I served with Jack Kennedy. I knew Jack Kennedy. Jack Kennedy was a friend of mine. Senator, you're no Jack Kennedy." Bentsen's partisans in the audience roared in approval and millions watching the event at home realized that it would be one of the unforgettable moments of the 1988 presidential campaign. Over time, the exchange (excerpted below) has become a classic in the history of modern American politics.

Ultimately, the debate did not affect the final outcome of the race—the Dukakis-Bentsen ticket lost the election overwhelmingly to Bush and Quayle. The Republican candidates also won handily in Texas by a 56-43 percent margin. The election news that year, however, was not all bad for Bentsen. Though disappointed at losing out on the vice presidency, state law allowed him to run concurrently for re-election to his Senate seat, and Bentsen won another term by garnering almost 60 percent of the vote. Texas voters still liked Lloyd Bentsen, and they continued to do so despite many political pundits pointing out that the senator and John Kennedy were never close friends.

MODERATOR, JUDY WOODRUFF: Brit Hume, a question for Senator Quayle.

BRIT HUME: Senator, I want to take you back to the question that I asked you earlier about what would happen if you were to take over in an emergency, and what you would do first and why. You said you would say a prayer, and you said something about a meeting. What would you do next? [Laughter]

DAN QUAYLE: I don't believe that it's proper for me to get into the specifics of a hypothetical situation like that. The situation is that if I was called upon to serve as the president of this country, or the responsibilities of the president of this country, would I be capable and qualified to do that? And I've tried to list the qualifications of twelve years in the United States Congress. I have served in the Congress for twelve years; I have served in the Congress and served eight years on the Senate Armed Services Committee. I have traveled a number of times - I've been to Geneva many times to meet with our negotiators as we were hammering out the INF Treaty; I've met with the western political leaders - Margaret Thatcher, Chancellor Kohl - I know them, they know me. I know what it takes to lead this country forward. And if that situation arises, yes, I will be prepared, and I will be prepared to lead this country, if that happens. [Applause] . . . .

JUDY WOODRUFF: Tom Brokaw, a question for Senator Quayle.

TOM BROKAW: Senator Quayle, I don't mean to beat this drum until it has no more sound in it. But to follow up on Brit Hume's question, when you said that it was a hypothetical situation, it is, sir, after all, the reason that we're here tonight, because you are running not just for Vice President [Applause]
And if you cite the experience that you had in Congress, surely you must have some plan in mind about what you would do if it fell to you to become President of the United States, as it has to so many Vice Presidents just in the last 25 years or so.

QUAYLE: Let me try to answer the question one more time. I think this is the fourth time that I've had this question.

BROKAW: The third time.

QUAYLE: Three times that I've had this question—and I will try to answer it again for you, as clearly as I can, because the question you are asking is what kind of qualifications does Dan Quayle have to be president, what kind of qualifications do I have and what would I do in this kind of a situation. And what would I do in this situation? I would make sure that the people in the cabinet and the people that are advisors to the president are called in, and I would talk to them, and I will work with them. And I will know them on a firsthand basis, because as vice president I will sit on the National Security Council. And I will know them on a firsthand basis, because I'm going to be coordinating the drug effort. I will know them on a firsthand basis because Vice President George Bush is going to recreate the Space Council, and I will be in charge of that. I will have day-to-day activities with all the people in government. And then, if that unfortunate situation happens - if that situation, which would be very tragic, happens, I will be prepared to carry out the responsibilities of the presidency of the United States of America. And I will be prepared to do that. I will be prepared not only because of my service in the Congress, but because of my ability to communicate and to lead. It is not just age; it's accomplishments, it's experience. I have far more experience than many others that sought the office of vice president of this country. I have as much experience in the Congress as Jack Kennedy did when he sought the presidency. I will be prepared to deal with the people in the Bush administration, if that unfortunate event would ever occur.

WOODRUFF: Senator Bentsen.

BENTSEN: Senator, I served with Jack Kennedy, I knew Jack Kennedy, Jack Kennedy was a friend of mine. Senator, you're no Jack Kennedy. [Prolonged shouts and applause] What has to be done in a situation like that is to call in the -

WOODRUFF: [to the audience] Please, please, once again you are only taking time away from your own candidate.

QUAYLE: That was really uncalled for, Senator. [Shouts and applause]

BENTSEN: You are the one that was making the comparison, Senator - and I'm one who knew him well. And frankly I think you are so far apart in the objectives you choose for your country that I did not think the comparison was well-taken.

WOODRUFF: Tom, a question for Senator Bentsen.

BROKAW: Since you seem to be taking no hostages on the stage, let me ask you a question—[Laughter]—about the American hostages, nine, still in brutal captivity in the Middle East….

Source: Commission on Public Debates

THOUGHT QUESTIONS

1. How did Senator Quayle's attempt to answer a question about his level of political experience by invoking the name of John Kennedy create an opening for Bentsen to exploit as he did? How well had the senator been doing up to that point?

2. What did you think about the way that the reporters (Hume and Brokaw) addressed the issue of Senator Quayle's experience? Were they fair in trying the clarify matters by following up with additional questions on the issue after not being satisfied with the answers they first received?

3. How important are televised political debates in helping you and people that you know well choose which candidate to support for president or governor? If important, how and why? If not, why not?

President George H. W. Bush Addresses the Texas State Legislature

George H.W. Bush took a long political road to becoming president, serving in numerous government posts—congressman, United Nations ambassador, envoy to China, and Director of the Central Intelligence Agency—before serving two terms as Ronald Reagan's vice president. Elected president in 1988, Bush's presidency continued the Republican success in national elections initiated by Reagan, experienced the end of the Cold War with the collapse of the Soviet Union, and culminated with the Persian Gulf War and a bruising economic recession that doomed Bush re-election bid. In these excerpts from remarks delivered to the Texas State legislature on April 26, 1989, the president reflects on his Texas experiences (though a Connecticut native he represented a Houston district in Congress for a time) and the greatness of the Lone Star State.

Thank you very, very much for that warm welcome. Mr. Speaker, thank you, sir, for presenting me to this esteemed body. And, Lieutenant Governor Hobby, my respects and thanks to you and to Bill Clements. It's a good thing it isn't his birthday. [Laughter] I'm not sure another plaid day in the Texas Legislature is in order. But a belated happy birthday, anyway.

I'm delighted to be back in Austin with so many friends. And I'll want to discuss a few issues facing Texas and all of America. But let me just say a few words about what it means to be a Texan. My credentials: I have my driver's license here, and I have my Texas hunting license here, and, somewhere, my voter registration slip. And it is true, I like Kennebunkport, but I am a Texan. And so, I just want to clear the air and say a few words about that.

You know, like the former kingdom of Hawaii, Texas is a nation that had to reconcile itself to being a State. But like Hawaii, we'll never reconcile ourselves to being ordinary. From the Pecos to the Pedernales, from the Rio Grande to the Red River, there is no place on Earth like Texas, nor is there another capitol in America quite like this one, built of this rose-tinged granite that blushes in the low sun. And this being Texas, we had to build a capitol that is exactly one foot taller than the one in Washington. And so, I hope it's not too much of a cliché to say that Texas stands tall in the heart of this President.

Perhaps for this reason, Larry McMurtry, who was at the White House the other day -- he's one of my favorite writers -- in ``Lonesome Dove" he describes the mythic Texas and conjures that sense of the place we all know so well. And I'm inspired by a man of letters who can convincingly adopt the voice of the cowboys and the outlaws, men whose only schooling was in dodging bullets, whose only lessons were in how to run or rustle cattle.

But unlike Davy Crockett, I first set out for Texas not on horseback from Tennessee but from Connecticut in a red Studebaker in June of 1948. And more than 40 years later, that trip is still a vivid memory: Highway 80, neon Pearl Beer signs appearing in the desert twilight -- and see, I've got a note here -- and stopping at a cafe -- I'll admit it I didn't know if chicken-fried steak was a chicken fried like a steak or a steak that tasted like a chicken, but I've learned. [Laughter]

And still, Bar [Barbara Bush, the president's wife] and I settled in Texas, as did many before us. We raised five kids and helped get into the business world -- helped start a business. And in that span of 40 years, I've watched with pride as this State has grown into even greater glory. And in my lifetime, I've seen the oil wealth of west Texas help finance the building of great cities, the expansion of great universities and colleges -- the origins of a Texas renaissance, if you will. The energy business helped make Texas what it is today: the third coast of the United States.

This Texas renaissance lasted for years, even decades. But you also know another more recent chapter of the Texas story: oil cheaper than some of this fancy mineral water, skylines of sometimes empty buildings, expensive homes to be had just for the monthly payments, and thousands of laid-off workers. Now, I'm no cowboy; I pitch horseshoes for a living, but I don't ride these broncos. I understand, though, that cowboys have a term for the most dangerous and cunning bronco of all, and they call it a sunfisher. And those broncos will rebel against a rider by adopting a motion not unlike the sunfish: a full-force leap into the air, back arched high, flank twisting the rider to the left, head and upper torso twisting the rider to the right in an attempt to tear him apart. And let me suggest that not so many months ago, the whole State of Texas, our State, felt like it had been on just such a ride. But strong men and women are challenged by adversity, and I believe Texas has proven that. And there may be a few more bumps and bruises ahead, but make no mistake: Texas is back -- back in the saddle, strong in every way.

State unemployment has dipped to its lowest level in 4 years, signaling, I think, the diversification of the Texas economy. In 1970 the energy sector accounted for nearly 25 percent of State output -- 25 percent. And last year it accounted for 11.4 percent. And yet Texas has more than regained the 208,000 jobs it lost from 1986 to 1987, with employment in plastics and aviation, electronics, space, and computer programming leading the way. More people are at work in Texas today than ever before in our history. And the Dallas-Fort Worth Metroplex leads in defense and aviation and technology; Houston in space and biomedical research; Austin, microelectronics. Another sign that Texas is becoming a world center of technology is the selection of Ellis County as the site of the Superconducting Supercollider. And when built, the SSC will enable us to study elemental particles with names like quarks and mesons and neutrinos -- sounds like a breakfast cereal that these grandkids of ours are into these days. . . .

Still, no matter how diversified and high tech that we become, a strong domestic energy industry is important, still important, to the future of this State and, in my view, to the future of all America. I find it disturbing that nearly 50 percent of America's oil is imported. This is not good for the national security of the United States of America. And now some are questioning the future of America's energy production in the aftermath of the wreck of the Exxon Valdez off Alaska. I am as concerned as anyone, as all Americans are, by the environmental tragedy in Prince William Sound. We're using Federal resources intelligently to clean it up. We're working with industry to develop an improved plan in the event of a future spill. But shutting down our domestic energy production is no answer and would merely increase our dependence on foreign oil. We must, and we will, maintain a strong domestic energy industry.

To reduce our dependence on foreign oil, we must return to high levels of exploratory drilling. I propose to stimulate domestic drilling with tax credits and other incentives. We need more research -- this isn't just a function of the Government, incidentally -- but we need more research to learn how to recover more of our secondary and tertiary oil. And I want to do something else. Texas has a 65-year supply of one of the cleanest forms of energy known to man: natural gas. And I call on the United States Congress, at long last, to fully decontrol natural gas. And I believe that's going to happen soon.

We need a national energy policy that relies not only on oil but on other sources as well. I believe we can and must use safe nuclear power. I believe that coal has a bright future. And you know my confidence in natural gas. As we all become increasingly concerned about the need for clean air, we must look more to natural gas and to nuclear power. We must press forward with clean-coal technology, and we must produce more of our corn crop to produce -- switch more of our corn crop to produce ethanol; more of our natural gas to produce methanol. And the greater use of these alternate fuels will rapidly improve the air quality of our most heavily polluted cities. And I'm talking about Los Angeles, Denver; I'm talking about Houston, Texas, and other heavily impacted areas. . . .

But the way is clear to a future as bright and promising as the blue Texas sky: a new reliance on a diversified economy and the technologies of the next century. And this is the secret of the Texas turn around, and its unfolding is a tribute not just to the entre-preneurial spirit of Texans themselves but to the leadership of Governor Clements, Sena-tors Gramm and Bentsen, the congressional delegation, and the men and women of the Texas legislature. Texas is starting to feel like its old self again. And there's a feeling now that anything is possible. I'm not standing here trying to underestimate the problems of education or health or urban blight, but there is a new feeling abroad. Who knows, the Astros might win in the National League, and, yes, under enlightened new leadership -- [laughter] -- the Texas Rangers might even win in the American League. Good luck!

Seriously, as we face our future in the White House, Barbara and I take with us mem-ories of people and places from a State that has been home for most of our lives -- all of my adult life, if you will. We remember those 12 years in west Texas. It's a dry heat. You don't feel it -- [laughter] -- my eye! We were there for 12 years. But the people -- I feel their strength and fierce independence to this very day. And I remember driving the kids across Texas. We moved down from west Texas down to the gulf coast, slowing down to take in the fields of the blue bonnets and Indian paintbrush. I don't think you can drive through that country without thinking of yourself as a naturalist or an environmentalist, or at least counting your blessings. And I remember the people of Houston, many of them mature and skeptical, but who nonetheless listened to a very green young man and sent him to Congress in 1966. And I remember Lyndon Johnson at his ranch back in 1969, when I went over there -- an elder Democrat, retired from the Presidency, giving neighborly advice to a young Republican, while his very special Lady Bird held out her hand in hospitality.

Barbara and I treasure these 41 years as Texans -- the sights and sounds of our adult lifetime, the trust of many friends, and the love of a family. And all this and more we remember when we think of home.

You know, I've been thinking about it. Ann Richards was right. [Laughter] Why do you think that I said we could cancer conquer? [Laughter] Look, I kept putting that silver foot in my mouth -- [laughter] -- all along the way. But the bottom line is when they ask, "Where's George?", say he's in Austin, among friends. And I'm very proud to be back. Thank you all. God bless you. And God bless the United States of America.

Source: George H. W. Bush Presidential Library

THOUGHT QUESTIONS:

1. What myths about Texas does Bush begin and conclude his remarks with in an attempt to connect with the audience of state lawmakers? How did Bush try to establish his "Texas credentials" with the crowd?

2. What was Bush's formula for reducing dependence on foreign oil? In what ways was his proposals "preaching to the choir," guaranteeing a warm reception?

3. Regarding Bush's energy proposals, do his arguments sound familiar to many proposals offered today, some twenty years later?

Excerpts from President George H. W. Bush's Remarks at a Fundraising Dinner Honoring Governor Bill Clements in Dallas, Texas (November 10, 1989)

In Texas, the late-1970s witnessed the election of the state's first Republican governor in 100 years with William Clements's 1978 victory. Though he was defeated in 1982, Clements won a second four-year term in 1986. In excerpts from the following speech given at a Republican fundraiser, President George H. W. Bush praises his friend Governor Clements, makes allusions to current state and national issues, and mentions Clements's eventual successor, Democrat Ann W. Richards.

Thank you very much, Governor, and thank all of you for that warm welcome. . . .

Bill, you and I do go back a long way—long before either of us got into politics. And we shared common goals in business and in politics. We also have a lot in common as public speakers. We've certainly been accused of making our share of verbal gaffes. But so what if we've been known to put our foot in our mouth from time to time? I just hope that your foot is as silver as mine. [Laughter]

At least you're a colorful character. I guess the whole country has heard of the story—at least it got widespread play up in Washington—of how the Governor, eating in a Dallas restaurant when a holdup took place—and how he just kept right on eating his hamburger through the whole ordeal. I'm not sure that was Texas courage, hunger, the need for new glasses or a hearing aid, but nevertheless—[laughter]—

I would not, nor Barbara [Bush, the president's wife]—we wouldn't have missed this affair for anything. Over the years, I have come to depend on Bill's steady friendship and his sound advice, and so have the people of Texas. And tonight's tribute is our way of letting you know just how much we appreciate you.

Your first term, Bill, was a glorious time for Texas and a memorable chapter in the political history of our State. They say in west Texas that a mile between fenceposts is a long distance, but a mile between towns is short. Well, Bill, the time between these two terms of yours was short enough to preserve the gains you had achieved, but it was long enough to prove just how right you were about what works for Texas. Of course, there are those cynics who still say that on the day Bill Clements returned as Governor that the Texas National Guard switched back to plaid fatigues. [Laughter]

But we all know that in the middle years of the decade humor was in short supply in our State. And when you hit the comeback trail, houses could be had for payments, and tens of thousands of blue-collar providers just couldn't provide. Bill, Texas was in trouble, and Texas needed a leader, and Texas needed you.

Now, optimism has returned to the most optimistic State in the Union. Texas employment is up. Construction permits are up. Retail sales are up. Once again, Texas is a magnet for business and for research projects like the superconducting supercollider. The space industry is starting to take off, and the eyes of Texas are once again on the stars. All this adds up to jobs, prosperity, and a decent shot at happiness for countless families. So, the comeback of Bill Clements has meant nothing less than the comeback of Texas.

And these have also been comeback years for America. True, we still do face some extraordinarily difficult national problems. But tough national problems require nothing less than national solutions. And that's why I'm pleased to work so closely with Bill Clements and the other 49 chief executives in the States.

Bill and I share a similar approach on many issues, starting with crime fighting. Thanks to him, prison sentences in Texas are again measured in years, not meted out by the available square feet. And I believe we need this same disciplined, tough approach in Washington, starting with my administration's crime control legislation to toughen Federal sentences. And I believe Congress should help us now by putting the handcuffs on the criminals and not on the courts. And I'd like to see them get moving on this anticrime legislation. . . .

And Bill and I also share a similar approach on education reform. At this Charlottesville summit that I'm sure you read about, the Governors joined me in an historic compact to give our schools all across the country greater flexibility in return for greater accountability. And I am pleased to note that this was exactly what Governor Clements is already doing: rewarding good schools through the Educational Excellence Program.

And finally, as a former Deputy Secretary of Defense, Bill shares my view that the best way to keep America and the West free is to keep the United States of America strong. Of course, we all look now with hope in our hearts at the amazing changes in Eastern Europe -- indeed, in the Soviet Union itself. We look at it with encouragement and with hope. . . .

We've touched on several issues here—many issues important to Texas and the Nation. But I must note that Texas is now at the threshold of a new era. In just a little more than one year, Texans will choose a new Governor. And when I consider the talented Republicans who are running to succeed Bill, I can't help but say that, with continued Republican leadership, Texas cannot lose. And I am proud to be on this platform with several of these very distinguished Texans who are in this race -- willing to roll up their sleeves, get into the public arena, and go to work to help our State.

As you would expect, a Texas Democratic friend of mine had his own ideas about the election. He offered me his prediction that the next Governor of this State would be that smart, silver-haired, feisty, outspoken Lone Star lady with a sharp sense of humor [Ann Richards]. And I said, no way, not possible -- Barbara is very happy in the White House. [Laughter]

But the election is a year away. Tonight, we're gathered here to honor this Governor who's still at work -- still building a safer legacy of safer streets and better schools, of good government, decency and honor, greater opportunity.

Governor, Texas is a mythic place, a land of heroes. And their very names are the stuff of legend: Davy Crockett and Sam Houston and Stephen Austin. And I predict that when some future historian writes the history of modern Texas, there will be room for another hero, another great Texas leader, and his name will be Bill Clements. Thank you, Bill, for your service to our great State. And may I ask you to join me in a toast. To Bill and Rita [Clements], to you, and to Texas. And God bless our wonderful State, and God bless the United States of America. To the Clements! Thank you all. It's a great pleasure to be with you.

Source: George H.W. Bush Presidential Library

THOUGHT QUESTIONS:

1. According to Bush, what were William Clements' accomplishments as governor?

2. How did the president link himself with Clements on various issues?

3. How did Bush deliberately try to connect with his audience by using folksy Texas sayings, evoking Texas myths, and mentioning legendary Texas figures?

Governor Ann Richards' Gridiron Club Speech

Founded in 1885, the Gridiron Club in Washington, D.C. is the oldest and most prestigious organization for journalists. The group's annual dinner has become a Washington tradition as members of the government's elite, including the president, members of Congress, governors, and other officials bear the brunt of the humorous jousting. The politicians also take part in the festivities by responding to the withering commentary. On March 28, 1992, Governor Ann Richards was able to draw upon her legendary wit to return the fire.

So this is what you all do up here on Saturday nights. I don't know why-y-y-y anyone would think you're out of touch.

But Mr. President [George H. W. Bush], distinguished guests and stuffed shirts I'm having a great time tonight. And what a good looking audience you are. As my mama would say, "You look as good as a new-scraped carrot."

In any event, I'm proud to be out with such [a] high-class crowd. But I've been wondering, Mr. President—to overcome the image of attending a white tie dinner like this, how many pork rinds do you have to eat?

And Mr. President, putting aside partisanship, I can say in all honesty that it will be hard to beat the kind of strength, energy and grace under pressure that we have in the White House today. You are really one of a kind, Barbara.

And Dan Thomasson [editor of the *Scripps Howard News Service*], honey, about your speech in the dark. Some of your jokes got good laughs. As for the rest of 'em, well, I haven't heard so much silence since Quayle and Clinton got together to trade war stories.

Besides Dan Tomasson, I see other familiar faces from the press tonight, like Evans and Novak [journalists Rowland Evans and Robert Novak]. Ever hear how Evans and Novak first got together? Very interesting. 35 years ago, they were both staying at a hotel when their eyes met at the same keyhole.

And I see Peter Jennings in the audience. I tell you, he's so handsome he makes my knees weak. I've had a crush on Peter Jennings longer than he has.

But you know, the thing that truly grates on the press is that they think they'd make better candidates than the rest of us. With their superior knowledge of the issues, their sense of history, their command of the language, they would elevate the level of political discourse . . . like Pat Buchanan has.

Anyway, moving on, I suppose I should also recognize the Republican speaker for the evening, Lamar Alexander. Which one is he?

But, I've been trying to think what I would possibly tell you Beltway insiders that you don't already know. So what I've decided to do tonight is to analyze the election and what's been going on out there, since you people obviously don't have a clue.

Ladies and gentlemen, the voters of America are looking for a candidate who's strong, someone who's solid, someone who won't bend. Like my hair.

And where we gonna find such a candidate? Let's begin by analyzing the Republican side. Mr. President, a few months ago the American people asked you to come home from overseas and get to work on the economy. Well, sir, they've seen your plan and you can go back now.

Now, I know the president has tried hard to turn things around. I know he's tried hard to end the recession. God love him. As I said to him earlier, it's a damn shame Arnold Schwarzeneggar doesn't know diddly about economics.

The only two who have bigger domestic problems than Bush and Quayle are Andrew and Fergie [Prince Andrew and Princess Sarah Ferguson of England].

I mean things are tough. Even the president's official residence at the hotel in Houston went bankrupt. Course, that's his own fault for letting Dick Darman [Director of the Office of Management and Budget] work weekends as a desk clerk.

But I'm not quite as negative about the economy as some people are. I figure if John Sununu can find a job, anybody can find a job.

Now, also on the Republican side we have Pat Buchanan. Pat really scared the President there in New Hampshire. He scares the rest of us everywhere else.

But people often say to me, "Ann, what about the Democratic candidates?" Well, I haven't taken sides in the Democratic primaries 'cause a lot of those guys came to Texas to campaign for me. But I won anyway.

You know Paul Tsongas is here tonight. Paul I'm sorry you had to drop out, but I wouldn't have voted for you anyway. I wouldn't vote for anyone who looks better in a bathing suit than I do.

The only candidates left, of course, are Clinton and Brown. I for one never believed those rumors about Bill Clinton. I figured anyone who talked as much as he did at the '88 convention wouldn't have time for an affair.

Clinton wired Ross Perot from New York the other day and promised to re-enroll in ROTC if Perot would smuggle Jerry Brown into Iran.

And I was told this afternoon that there's another Bill Clinton story about to break. I could have gone all day without knowing that Bill had a checking account at the House bank.

The press is really giving Congress [a] hard time over a few bounced checks. I don't think that's a story at all. I mean, what the hell. They just assumed they could run their checking accounts like they ran the country.

And of course, we have ET's older brother, Jerry Brown. Jerry has many things going for him with the electorate. For example, he doesn't own a Japanese car. He drives a Saturn, because that's where he thinks they're from.

Jerry was going to come tonight but they don't make UAW jackets with tails.

He's sure missed a good time. But, anyway, I know it's traditional to end these dinners on a more serious note. And I'll tell you one reason I came tonight was because I happen to like newspapers and reporters—warts and all. My attitude toward newspapers is like that of the columnist Lewis Grizzard. When he was asked why his newspaper wasn't more truthful and accurate, he said, "Damn, it don't cost but a quarter!"

I've never picked up a newspaper in this country where I didn't get my money's worth. Where else can you get a snapshot of history at such a bargain price.

I hope newspapers will thrive and prosper in the years ahead. I know the journalist's life is not an easy one, and I wish the best for each of you, too. And so let me close with a toast and a wish by the great political sage, Johnny Carson, that says it all. "Ladies and gentlemen, may you be as rich as Republicans and have the sexual prowess of a Democrat."

Thank you one and all.

Source: The Dolph Briscoe Center for American History, The University of Texas at Austin

THOUGHT QUESTIONS:

1. Comment on the governor's skillful dispersion of the biting comments rather than focusing too much on any one person in the room.

2. How does the speech highlight Governor Richards's legendary style as a humorous, "down-home" politician?

3. Which is your favorite line of all the zingers that Governor Richards delivered and why?

Governor Ann Richards Defends NAFTA

The North American Free Trade Agreement (NAFTA) is a commercial treaty signed by Canada, Mexico, and the United States in 1992 which ended most tariffs between these nations and called for the gradual elimination of remaining trade barriers after fifteen years. The trade deal also includes important labor and environmental provisions. Labor leaders have been very critical of the agreement, pointing to lost American manufacturing jobs as companies moved their plants to Mexico. Proponents of NAFTA say this job loss is offset by the jobs created by increased exports to Mexico and Canada.

Governor Ann Richards was a staunch supporter of NAFTA and took a leading role in persuading Congress to approve the agreement. She believed that NAFTA would benefit Texas on a range of issues from immigration to economic growth. These remarks to a business forum in Washington D.C. summarize her views in favor of the treaty.

I am delighted to be here with this distinguished group today.

We in Texas have understood for a long time that our border is not the back door to the United States, it is our front door to a new world of trade and opportunity.

You and I are here in Washington today to help others understand that, too. Because we know that there are a lot of myths surrounding NAFTA.

Myth number one [is] that Mexicans cannot afford to buy U.S. goods.

The facts are that Mexico is already the United States' second largest trading partner . . . that each Mexican spends $340 a year on U.S. products—more than the Europeans or Japanese. . . . and that with NAFTA, American goods will become even more attractive because the high Mexican tariffs will go away.

If you plug it in, drive it, or run it over a computer network or a fiber optic line, it can be sold in Mexico.

Myth number two is that NAFTA is bad for the environment. Those of us here from Texas and Arizona know this is one concern that is just plain wrong.

Environmental problems existed along the border long before anyone ever thought about NAFTA. Yes . . . . they are terrible problems . . . but it is only since the advent of NAFTA that the governments of the United States and Mexico have focused on the problems.

Mexico has passed comprehensive environmental protection laws . . . modeled on U.S. laws. They have begun to seriously crack down on polluters.

And they have pledged half a billion dollars to enforcement and clean-up.

Increased cooperation between our two countries is our best hope of improving environmental conditions along our common border.

NAFTA will help.

Now of course, I have saved the biggest myth for last.

Myth number three is that NAFTA will cost the United States jobs and destroy our manufacturing base. This myth is a lot like trying to put the blame for rain on the people who make umbrellas.

There is no question that during the eighties some American companies took manufacturing business overseas.

But when you buy clothes and VCR's and cars, you see more "made in Taiwan or Korea" than "hecho in Mexico."

And we do not have a free trade agreement with any of these countries.

The fact is that companies who want to go Mexico because of wages—or for any other reason—will do so without NAFTA.

As many have pointed out, if low wages were the key to profitability, Bangladesh would rule the business world.

But the question before the Congress is not one of numbers. . . or of arguing whose study is more accurate.

It is one of national interest and national honor . . . a question of what kind of hand we deal ourselves for the future.

Because no matter what we do about this treaty, our economic future is tied to this hemisphere.

With the European Economic Community and the Pacific Rim as competition, it is time for us to cement our friendships close to home.

We are never going to solve our common problems—the environment, immigration, all of it—until we deal from mutual respect and economic security.

This is not an easy vote for many Members of Congress.

They are scared . . . . They face the loss of long-time friends and allies. . . They face the loss of crucial financial and political support.

I honestly believe the well-intentioned people who oppose NAFTA have dumped their concerns about larger issues of the new international economy on this agreement.

The bottom line is this. . . We have been begging, badgering and bashing Japan to give us a level playing field, open markets and an opportunity for friendly competition and cooperation.

Now the Canadians and Mexicans are freely offering us the same thing.

Now our friends are willing . . . and we ought to take them up on the offer.

Source: Governor Ann Richards Papers, Dolph Briscoe Center for American History, University of Texas at Austin

THOUGHT QUESTIONS:

1. What "myths" did Governor Richards say have been associated with NAFTA?

2. How did Richards respond to each of these alleged myths?

3. What concluding points did the governor make to urge support for NAFTA?

"Did NAFTA Spur Texas Exports?"

In 2006, Anil Kumar, an economist in the Research Department of the Federal Reserve Bank of Dallas, published a report analyzing the North American Free Trade Agreement's impact on Texas exports. The following is an abridgement of that report which appeared in Southwest Economy, the bank's bi-monthly publication containing articles about economic conditions and business development in Texas, New Mexico and Louisiana.

The North American Free Trade Agreement unites the United States, Mexico and Canada—three nations with a combined population of 426 million, total output of more than $13 trillion and regional trade of $700 billion in goods and services.

Because of the North American market's sheer size, NAFTA has been repeatedly dissected. Most studies have sought to determine whether the pact fulfilled proponents' predictions of increased trade, lower prices and higher incomes or led to what critics warned would be a "giant sucking sound" of U.S. jobs going to Mexico.

On balance, researchers have found NAFTA a slight positive for the U.S. as a whole. For example, a 1996 study estimated that NAFTA had increased U.S. exports by $5 billion, or 12 percent, a figure projected to grow as more of NAFTA's phased-in trade liberalization took effect.

A lesser volume of research focuses on what NAFTA has meant to state and local economies, although theory and common sense suggest trade deals might have different impacts within countries. States' industrial mixes and workforces vary widely, leading to comparative advantages that influence the composition and destination of exports. Geography is another key factor. Firms may operate in one state rather than another to take advantage of proximity to newly opened markets. The results of national studies of NAFTA's effects may not apply uniformly to all states.

Texas is one of the more interesting lenses through which to assess NAFTA. The state lies near the center of NAFTA's economic space—about equidistant from Mexico City and Toronto, with a 1,200-mile frontier with Mexico and networks of highways and rail lines that lead to some of the world's busiest border crossings. Texas political and business leaders strongly supported NAFTA's ratification, an indication that many presumed it would benefit the state's economy.

Has NAFTA been good for Texas? Merely counting the truckloads passing through border checkpoints in the Lower Rio Grande Valley, Laredo and El Paso would make it seem so. A more definitive answer, though, involves distilling NAFTA's influence from factors responsible for overall increases in Texas exports over the past decade or so. . . .

A fresh look at the issue, using industry-level export data, shows that NAFTA did indeed increase Texas' sales to Mexico—and to Canada as well. Perhaps more interesting, NAFTA also helped raise Texas exports to Asia, Europe and Latin America, making a strong case for net trade creation.

Before and After NAFTA

NAFTA went into effect Jan. 1, 1994. In general, it mandated eliminating trade barriers by 2008. For many products, the agreement did away with tariffs and other restraints immediately. Agriculture and apparel were the main sectors scheduled to be liberalized over a longer period.

Pre-NAFTA Mexico had the more protected economy, so it committed to larger tariff cuts than the U.S. and Canada. Average Mexican duties on U.S. goods fell from 12 percent in 1993 to 1.3 percent in 2001, while U.S. tariffs on Mexican goods declined from 2.1 percent to 0.2 percent. The effect of NAFTA on U.S.–Canada trade restraints was minimal because the two countries operated under a free-trade agreement that took effect in 1989.

Trade has increased by leaps and bounds in the NAFTA years. U.S. exports to Mexico rose from $42 billion in 1993 to $111 billion in 2004, while imports from Mexico increased from $40 billion to $156 billion. Over the same period, U.S. sales to Canada grew from $100 billion to $189 billion, while imports from Canada to the U.S. climbed from $111 billion to $256 billion.

During the first six years of NAFTA, Texas gained ground in many foreign markets, allowing the state to grow faster than the nation in overall exports. Texas exports to Mexico also increased—but not by any more than the nation as a whole. From 1994 to 2000, the growth of Texas shipments across the Rio Grande mirrored that of U.S. exports, just as it did in the five years prior to NAFTA's taking effect. Indeed, both Texas and U.S. exports to Mexico grew steadily before and after NAFTA, except for a sharp decline in 1995, the year following the pact's implementation. An economic crisis in Mexico led to a steep devaluation of the peso vis-à-vis the dollar, making U.S. exports to Mexico more expensive.

Given Texas' proximity to Mexico, it might be surprising that the state didn't increase its market share under NAFTA. Interestingly, one of the expanding markets has been Canada, the NAFTA partner farther from Texas.

Although trade grew faster with Canada, there's no denying the importance of Mexico to the state's economy. In 1993, nearly 40 percent of Texas' exports went to Mexico, compared with less than 10 percent of overall U.S. exports. The state trailed the U.S. average in sales to Canada and all other regions except Latin America.

In the NAFTA years, Mexico has become even more dominant as a market for Texas. By 2000, Mexico received more than 45 percent of Texas' exports, and Canada also gained as a destination for Texas products.

Broad-based data on exports suggest continuity rather than change in the first years NAFTA was in effect. Texas and the U.S. sold more to Mexico and Canada in 2000 than they did in 1993, but general trade patterns didn't change all that much in the six-year period. NAFTA's impacts on the Texas economy emerge more clearly by looking at the changes in exports by industry.

Looking at Industry Data

For both the U.S. and Texas, the leading exports are largely the same—industrial machinery including computer equipment, transportation equipment, electronics, chemicals and instruments. They reflect America's comparative advantages in the global marketplace. Texas' mix differs from the rest of the country—electronics, for example, has emerged as a particular strength for the state. Even so, the same five categories were at the top before NAFTA in 1993 and after it in 2000.

In terms of overall exports, some major Texas industries show distinct breaks from their pre-NAFTA trends. Texas electronics companies, for example, saw their exports grow significantly faster after NAFTA went into effect. Chemicals, which were dropping prior to the trade deal, began to rise after its implementation. After an initial decline due to Mexico's peso crisis of 1994, transportation equipment experienced an uptick in its growth rate.

Not all sectors show rising exports. Texas sales of lumber and wood had been increasing before 1994 but declined after NAFTA. Furniture and fixtures shows a similar pattern.

Industry data suggest churning beneath the surface for Texas exports. How much of it can be attributed to NAFTA? The answer requires a model that takes into account other factors that might contribute to the state's expanding overseas sales. . . .

Controlling for incomes, a time trend, exchange rates, the EU opening, Mercosur [the Southern Common Market] and other industry- or country-specific factors allows us to isolate NAFTA's impact on 28 Texas industries. When it comes to exports to Mexico, 19 of these industries benefited from NAFTA, while nine saw sales decline. Texas exports to Canada rose for 18 industries and fell for 10. Half of the 28 industries gained in both countries, while six declined in both countries.

Industries with statistically significant gains in exports to Mexico as a result of NAFTA were rubber and miscellaneous plastic products (79 percent), printing and publishing (78 percent), textile mill products (75 percent), petroleum and coal products (69 percent), leather and leather products (71 percent) and electronic equipment (49 percent). Significant declines were found in lumber and wood products (89 percent) and furniture and fixtures (75 percent).

The statistically significant NAFTA winners in terms of exports to Canada were oil and gas exploration equipment (286 percent), furniture and fixtures (75 percent), industrial machinery including computers (70 percent), apparel (66 percent), instruments and related products (58 percent) and rubber and miscellaneous plastic products (54 percent). The only significant decline was in metal mining (88 percent).

The diversity in gains and losses of exports among industries suggests trade deals affect economic sectors differently. Lower tariffs no doubt gave some Texas industries an advantage over Mexican and Canadian companies. Export declines might signal an inability to compete, although they could simply reflect some firms' decisions to shift economic activity to other states. Because Texas had more winners than losers, though, we can conclude that NAFTA in general made Texas industries more competitive.

Overall, NAFTA had an export-weighted average effect of 28 percent on Texas exports to Mexico. Adjusted for inflation, the trade deal accounted for roughly a quarter of Texas' 111 percent increase in exports to Mexico between 1993 and 2000.

During the same period, Texas' NAFTA-related exports to Canada rose 47 percent, or about a third of the state's 131 percent gain in that market. Texas sells quite a bit more to Mexico than to Canada. Even if the percentage effect is smaller, the NAFTA-led increases in exports to Mexico are larger in dollar terms.

The results indicate that NAFTA stimulated Texas' exports. These findings are similar to those of a St. Louis Fed study. Using a different state-level database covering the years 1988 to 1997, they estimated that NAFTA increased Texas exports to Mexico by 14 percent and to Canada by 28 percent. . . .

More Texas exports are only half the story. NAFTA also operated at the industry level, prompting a reorganization consistent with the theory of comparative advantage. As North American barriers fell, such knowledge- and capital-intensive industries as electronics, chemicals, transportation equipment and industrial machinery received a stimulating jolt. Labor-intensive industries, like lumber and furniture, couldn't maintain their exports.

The data don't allow industry-specific assessment of NAFTA beyond 2000. However, the steady increase in overall Texas exports in recent years at least suggests that NAFTA continues to exert a positive effect on the state's economy.

Source: *Southwest Economy*, Issue 2, March/April 2006, Federal Reserve Bank of Dallas

THOUGHT QUESTIONS:

1. How high were American, Canadian, and Mexican tariff rates before NAFTA?

2. Which Texas industries were initial "winners and losers" as a result of NAFTA in terms of increased or decreased exports up to the year 2000?

3. According to the report, what overall effect did NAFTA have on Texas exports to Canada and Mexico?

Bringing America Back!

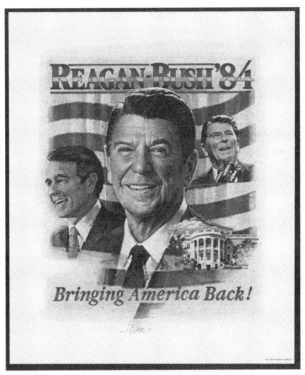

Credit: Library of Congress
Campaign Poster of Ronald Reagan and George H. W. Bush, 1984

In the election year of 1984, criticisms mounted about the immense foreign-trade gap and an unprecedented budget deficit. The administration's nuclear arms buildup alarmed many Americans. Re-election strategists were also well aware that a majority of the nation's minorities and women did not favor the president—that there existed a so-called "gender gap." Most dramatically, the president single-handedly destroyed the Professional Air Traffic Controllers Organization during their 1981 strike. This action was a major setback to the labor movement, signalling a significant change in government policy towards unions. Reagan and Bush relied on the president's popularity and slogans like "America is Back," and "It's Morning in America." The Republicans won a landslide victory. Bush served eight years as Reagan's loyal vice president—Bush ultimately remained much more moderate a Republican than either Reagan or his own son, George W. Bush.

THOUGHT QUESTION:

What benefits did Bush bring to the Republican ticket?

BIOGRAPHIES

H. ROSS PEROT (1930-). Billionaire businessman and former third-party presidential candidate Henry Ross Perot was born on June 27, 1930 in Texarkana, Texas. His father, an independent cotton buyer, entered his son into the U.S. Naval Academy in 1949 where he excelled. By 1955, however, he became unhappy with navy life and resigned his commission after fulfilling his four-year commitment.

After leaving the Navy, Perot became a salesman for International Business Machines (IBM). He noticed that business people often needed help in using electronic data-processing and computing systems. When management chose not to pursue his idea, he left IBM to form Electronic Data Systems (EDS) in 1962. Headquartered in Dallas, Perot first sought business from corporations for his data processing services, with the Frito Lay Corporation becoming his first big client. EDS profited from a nonstandard approach to the electronic data-systems market. Rather than agreeing to short-term contracts, EDS made five-year fixed-price contracts with its customers allowing its personnel to enter the customer's organization and establish a data-processing system leading to the client's employees to be assigned to other jobs. This helped reduce personnel costs for the customer and guaranteed a steady volume of business for EDS. Perot's company finally took off when EDS started receiving lucrative contracts from the U.S. government to computerize Medicare records. Eventually, this aspect of the business would account for 40 percent of the company's revenue. In 1984, General Motors (GM) purchased EDS for $2.4 billion. Two years later, GM bought out Perot for $700 million. In 1988, he founded Perot Systems based in Plano, Texas. His son, H. Ross Perot, Jr., eventually succeeded him as CEO.

During the 1980s, Perot began his involvement in politics by serving on a governor-appointed committee to study drug policy which resulted in five laws passed by the legislature designed to reduce illegal drug use. In 1983 he served on a committee studying ways to improve public education. The "No Pass, No Play" rule, under which students have to maintain passing grades in order to participate in school-sponsored extracurricular activities, passed by the legislature came from one of Perot's committee's proposals. Perot also became heavily involved in the Vietnam War POW/MIA issue.

Starting in the late 1980s Perot began openly criticizing the U.S. government for its alleged arrogance and ineptness. His criticisms of President George H.W. Bush, the Persian Gulf War, and massive government deficit spending set the groundwork for an eventual presidential run. In 1992 Perot shook up the presidential race with his personally-funded third-party campaign. His declared policies included balancing the federal budget, a firm pro-choice position on abortion, ending the outsourcing of jobs to foreign countries, opposition to gun control, and a protectionist trade policy. Perot's candidacy had a strong populist, anti-establishment bent to it allowing him to gain the support of independents and others generally upset with the status quo and not thrilled with the major party candidates, Republican President Bush and Democrat Bill Clinton. By the summer many polls showed Perot leading the race, but on July 16, Perot dropped out, citing alleged threats by Republican to unleash an assortment of dirty tricks designed to embarrass himself, his family, and his business. Many refused to believe him and some began to speak openly about Perot having a paranoiac streak within him. Despite his damaged reputation, when supporters succeeded in placing his name on all fifty state ballots, he reentered the race in

October. He made up for lost time by buying huge blocks of time on major television networks for infomercial-like campaign ads which garnered high ratings. His presidential debate performances also helped him build additional support, but far from enough to win. Ultimately, Perot received 19 percent of the national vote tally but no electoral votes.

After the 1992 election, Perot did not hastily disappear from politics. He was outspoken in his opposition to the North American Free Trade Agreement (NAFTA), at one point famously telling television viewers to listen for the giant "sucking sound" of jobs heading for Mexico if Congress ratified the trade deal. A poor debate performance on NAFTA against Vice President Al Gore further contributed to his political decline. In 1995, he founded the Reform Party and won its nomination for the 1996 presidential race, but this time he received only eight percent of the popular vote. In the 2000 Perot declined to run again. After refusing to get involved in the Reform Party rift over who would succeed him as their nominee, he reluctantly endorsed George W. Bush for president. Since then, Perot has largely avoided the political limelight, choosing to keep the subject of interviews to his business career. In 2008, *Forbes* estimated Perot's worth at 5 billion in 2008, ranking him the 72nd richest person in America.

SELENA (1971–1995). Singer and entertainer Selena Quintanilla Perez was born on April 16, 1971 in Lake Jackson, Texas. She attended public schools through the eighth grade in Lake Jackson and Corpus Christi, completing high school through the American School, a correspondence school for artists. Selena began performing when she was eight years old in the family group "Selena y Los Dinos" formed by her father who had played for several years with a Tejano band. He taught all of his children to sing and play music, teaching young Selena to sing in Spanish. They started performing at their family's restaurant and at weddings in the Lake Jackson area. In 1982 the group moved to Corpus Christi and played Tejano music at such venues as dance halls, nightclubs, weddings, and quinceañeras.

Selena recorded her first album in 1985, with her father selling the copies at their concerts. Within two years she became a star in the Tejano music world, winning the Tejano Music Award for Female Entertainer of the Year in 1987. Her popularity rising, she signed a contract with EMI Latin Records in 1989. Released in 1992, her album *Entre a Mi Mundo* became the first by a Tejana to sell more than 300,000 copies. In 1994 her album *Selena Live* won a Grammy for Best Mexican-American Album. She signed with SBK Records to produce an all-English album, but the bilingual *Dreaming of You* (released posthumously) would eventually appear instead.

Though her success remained largely within the Spanish-language market, by the early 1990s Selena's manager father sought to expose her to a wider audience. She appeared in advertisements for Coca-Cola, AT&T, Southwestern Bell, and the Dep Corporation. She also began to appear occasionally on a Mexican soap opera and had a cameo role in the film *Don Juan DeMarco*. She also began her own clothing line and opened Selena Etc., a boutique established in Corpus Christi and San Antonio with plans to expand into Monterrey and Puerto Rico. A new record deal with EMI Latin made Selena a millionaire. A 1994 Hispanic magazine stated her worth at $5 million.

Selena was at the height of her career in 1995, with signs of even greater notoriety if she could succeed in solidifying her crossover appeal to American mainstream audiences, but it was not to be. On March 31, she was shot in the back and killed in Corpus Christi by Yolanda Saldivar, after a dispute with the fan club founder and manager of Selena Etc. who Selena and her father correctly suspected was embezzling funds. Selena's death devastated her large fan base. Her tragic death, nevertheless, led to greater exposure for Tejano music. When *Dreaming of You* was finally released later that year, it became the first Tejano album to hit number one in the United States.

In the years after her death, Selena's popularity endures. In 1997, the film biography *Selena* told the story of the singer's life and has done much to keep her memory alive. The movie catapulted Jennifer Lopez to stardom for her honest portrayal of the entertainer. That same year, the city of Corpus Christi erected a memorial in her honor, which includes a life-sized bronze statue of the entertainer.

STEVIE RAY VAUGHAN (1954–1990). Legendary blues guitarist Stevie Ray Vaughan was born in Dallas on October 3, 1954. As a child, Vaughan grew up watching his older brother Jimmie play guitar and taught himself how to play, gravitating to the blues style that he most enjoyed. By his high school years, Vaughan stayed up all night playing in various clubs in Dallas's Deep Ellum district. For a while he enrolled in an experimental program for artistically gifted youth at Southern Methodist University, but he eventually dropped out of school in order to play music full time.

In 1972, at the age of seventeen, Vaughan moved to Austin to become a player on the city's music scene. Though achieving some local notoriety, his career did not take off until the late 1970s when he formed the band Triple Threat, later evolving into his most famous band Double Trouble, with Tommy Shannon and Reese Wynans. By the early 1980s the group gathered a large Texas following and began to receive acclaim from well-established music veterans. Though still not having signed a major record deal with a label, Double Trouble played the prestigious Montreux Jazz Festival in Switzerland. Their performance caught the attention of David Bowie, Jackson Browne, among others, who invited Vaughan to his Los Angeles studio to cut some demo recordings. Songs from that session later appeared on Vaughan's 1983 debut album, *Texas Flood*. Vaughan then played lead guitar on Bowie's popular album *Let's Dance*. Double Trouble soon signed a record contract with CBS/Epic Records.

Vaughan's fame rose dramatically in the early 1980s. A 1983 Guitar Player Magazine Reader's Poll voted Vaughan the Best New Talent and Best Electric Blues Guitarist. A track off *Texas Flood* received a Grammy nomination for Best Rock Instrumental performance. His follow-up albums were commercially successful and received positive reviews from music critics, receiving multiple Grammy nominations in the blues and rock categories.

In addition to his rapid fame, Vaughan's story during these years must also include his ongoing battle with alcoholism and drug abuse. He married Lenny Bailey in 1979, but they filed for divorce in 1987 when Vaughan hit a low point in his struggle with drug and alcohol abuse. After collapsing during a European tour, he checked himself into a rehabilitation center. When Vaughan left the clinic a sober man, he promised to commit to Alcoholics Anonymous' Twelve Step Program.

During the years after his rehab clinic stay, Vaughan's career resumed and continued to prosper. In 1990, he collaborated with his brother Jimmie, founding member of the Fabulous Thunderbirds, on *Family Style*. However, at the height of his resurgence,

Vaughan died in a helicopter crash on August 27, 1990 while en route to Chicago after a concert in Alpine Valley, East Troy, Wisconsin. Because the concert location was difficult to reach, many of the performers stayed in Chicago and flew in to participate in the show. Despite dense fog, helicopter flights continued to ferry performers in and out of the area. The copter containing Vaughan crashed into the side of a ski mountain, killing all aboard instantly. Over 1,500 people attended Vaughan's memorial service in Dallas.

After his death, Epic Records released *Family Style* (which earned Stevie and Jimmie a Grammy for Best Contemporary Blues Recording) plus two other Vaughan albums, *The Sky is Crying* and *In the Beginning*. In 1994, the city of Austin dedicated the Stevie Ray Vaughan Memorial Statue at Auditorium Shores on Lady Bird Lake, the site of many Vaughan concerts. It soon became one of Austin's most popular tourist attractions. In 2003, *Rolling Stone* ranked him the #7 Greatest Guitarist of All Time. Already a member of the Blues Hall of Fame, in 2008 Vaughan became eligible for induction into the Rock and Roll Hall of Fame.

NOLAN RYAN (1947 –). Hall of Fame pitcher Nolan Ryan was born in Refugio, Texas on January 21, 1947. He grew up in the Gulf Coast town of Alvin after his father moved the family there soon after his birth when he landed a job operating a delivery service for the *Houston Post*. After starring as a pitcher for Alvin High School, Ryan was drafted by the New York Mets in 1965 and spent less than a year in the minor leagues before appearing in his first big-league game for the Mets during the 1966 season. Injuries and illness caused him to miss most of the 1967 campaign. He returned to the Mets in 1968, serving primarily as a relief pitcher, a role that he continued during the 1969 "Miracle Mets" season when the New York club shocked the country by winning the World Series over the heavily-favored Baltimore Orioles. Despite his future long and illustrious career, it would prove to be Ryan's only World Series appearance.

The Mets traded Ryan to the California Angels after the 1971 season. Though the Angels only made the playoffs in his final year with the club, in 1979, his time with the Angles during the 1970s was the prime period of his career as he accomplished numerous individual pitching feats and established himself as the hardest-throwing pitcher in the major leagues. Though frequently plagued with wildness (he ended his career with more walked batters than any pitcher in baseball history), Ryan could be dominant on the days when his fastball and curveball were under his control. He struck out a record 383 batters during the 1973 season, a year in which he threw his first two no-hitters. In 1974, the fireballer twice struck out 19 batters in a game and had one of his pitches clocked at 100.8 miles per hour, the fastest baseball pitch ever recorded at the time. Ryan added a third no-hitter in 1974, and a fourth in 1975, tying the long-standing record held by Sandy Koufax.

When his contract with the Angles ended in 1980, Ryan returned to his home along the Texas Gulf Coast and signed a free agent deal with the Houston Astros, spending most of the 1980s with the club. In 1981, he broke Koufax's record by throwing his fifth no-hitter, and in early 1983, he struck out his 3,509th batter, breaking Walter Johnson's all-time record. Ryan went to the National League playoffs three times with the Astros, with the team losing each time.

After a contract dispute with the Astros, Ryan joined the Texas Rangers in 1989 for the first of his final four seasons and promptly posted a 16-win campaign in which he once again struck out more than 300 batters. He also struck out future Hall of Famer Rickey Henderson to become the only pitcher to ever record 5,000 strikeouts in a career (he ended his career with 5,714). In 1990, he surprised the baseball world by throwing his sixth no-hitter and further cemented his legendary status the following year by hurling an unbelievable seventh no-hitter at the age of 44. Ryan announced at the beginning of the 1993 season that he would retire at the end of the campaign. Though he could still throw over 95 miles per hour, the Texan would be playing in a major league-record 27 seasons. He tore a ligament in his pitching arm during his final game and completed the season with five more wins added to his total of 324 for his career. The most memorable moment of his last playing days, however, had occurred the month before when he engaged in a brawl with Robin Ventura of the Chicago White Sox after hitting the third baseman in the back with a fastball. Ventura, a skilled hitter with a low-key personality, believed Ryan deliberately tried to hit him (the two teams' pitchers had been hitting each other's batters intermittently for the past two years) and impulsively charged the mound. The tall Texan instinctively grabbed Ventura in a headlock (a move he later said he used when branding cattle on his ranch) and began punching him before a huge scrum of humanity overwhelmed both players, who eventually emerged bloody but with their pride intact. To this day, many Texans still try to make something uniquely "Texan" about the incident—how Ryan supposedly stood up to the challenge, while ignoring his role in precipitating the event. He was inducted into the Baseball Hall of Fame in 1999, his first year of eligibility, with 98.8 percent of the vote.

Upon his retirement, Ryan entered the private business world, expanding his existing ranching and beef distribution operations while purchasing two minor league baseball teams in Texas, the Corpus Christi Hooks and the Round Rock Express. He also began his career as a major league baseball executive in 2008 when he became the president of the Texas Rangers. The following year he joined businessman Chuck Greenberg in purchasing the Rangers, agreeing to remain serving as team president, later becoming CEO when Greenberg sold his interests in the club to Texas oil magnates Ray Davis and Bob Simpson. At the end of the 2013 season, Ryan stepped down as CEO and sold his minority stake in the Rangers, joining the Houston Astros as a special assistant to team owner Jim Crane, helping with the rebuilding of the team that culminated in 2017 with the Astros becoming the first Texas team to win the World Series.

Chapter 20

The Dawn of a New Century, 1995-2018

Excerpts from President George W. Bush's "Mission Accomplished" Speech aboard the *USS Abraham Lincoln*

On May 1, 2003, President George W. Bush famously landed (as a passenger) aboard the aircraft carrier **U.S.S. Abraham Lincoln** *in a Lockheed S-3 Viking aircraft in order to congratulate the ship's crew on their service during the Iraq War and to deliver a national television address. The publicity stunt would garner much criticism over the years, not so much for the overly macho image of Bush confidently strutting on the deck of the ship donning a pilot's flight suit, but for his bold statement at the beginning of his speech that "major combat operations in Iraq have ended" while a banner appeared behind him with the words "Mission Accomplished" emblazoned across the image of an American flag. Though the conventional phase of the war against the Iraqi military ended, the guerilla war that the Bush Administration did not anticipate against American occupation forces had already begun. By October 2008, over 98 percent of American casualties sustained since the start of hostilities occurred after Bush's speech. The following excerpt from that speech demonstrates the high hopes that Bush had for American success in the region after the war, his belief that most Iraqis would welcome the arrival of American forces as liberators, and the definite connection that the president made between operations in Iraq and the "war on terror" following the 9-11 attacks that he believed justified the war:*

Admiral Kelly, Captain Card, officers and sailors of the *USS Abraham Lincoln*, my fellow Americans: Major combat operations in Iraq have ended. In the Battle of Iraq, the United States and our allies have prevailed. And now our coalition is engaged in securing and reconstructing that country.

In this battle, we have fought for the cause of liberty, and for the peace of the world. Our nation and our coalition are proud of this accomplishment — yet it is you, the members of the United States military, who achieved it. Your courage — your willingness to face danger for your country and for each other — made this day possible. Because of you, our nation is more secure. Because of you, the tyrant has fallen, and Iraq is free.

Operation Iraqi Freedom was carried out with a combination of precision, and speed, and boldness the enemy did not expect, and the world had not seen before. From distant bases or ships at sea, we sent planes and missiles that could destroy an enemy division, or strike a single bunker. Marines and soldiers charged to Baghdad across 350 miles of hostile ground, in one of the swiftest advances of heavy arms in history. You have shown the world the skill and the might of the American Armed Forces. . . .

In the images of fallen statues, we have witnessed the arrival of a new era. For a hundred years of war, culminating in the nuclear age, military technology was designed and deployed to inflict casualties on an ever-growing scale. In defeating Nazi Germany and imperial Japan, Allied Forces destroyed entire cities, while enemy leaders who started the conflict were safe until the final days. Military power was used to end a regime by breaking a nation. Today, we have the greater power to free a nation by breaking a dangerous and aggressive regime. With new tactics and precision weapons, we can achieve military objectives without directing violence against civilians. No device of man can remove the tragedy from war. Yet it is a great advance when the guilty have far more to fear from war than the innocent.

In the images of celebrating Iraqis, we have also seen the ageless appeal of human freedom. Decades of lies and intimidation could not make the Iraqi people love their oppressors or desire their own enslavement. Men and women in every culture need liberty like they need food, and water, and air. Everywhere that freedom arrives, humanity rejoices. And everywhere that freedom stirs, let tyrants fear.

We have difficult work to do in Iraq. We are bringing order to parts of that country that remain dangerous. We are pursuing and finding leaders of the old regime, who will be held to account for their crimes. We have begun the search for hidden chemical and biological weapons, and already know of hundreds of sites that will be investigated. We are helping to rebuild Iraq, where the dictator built palaces for himself, instead of hospitals and schools. And we will stand with the new leaders of Iraq as they establish a government of, by, and for the Iraqi people. The transition from dictatorship to democracy will take time, but it is worth every effort. Our coalition will stay until our work is done. And then we will leave — and we will leave behind a free Iraq.

The Battle of Iraq is one victory in a war on terror that began on September the 11th, 2001, and still goes on. That terrible morning, 19 evil men — the shock troops of a hateful ideology — gave America and the civilized world a glimpse of their ambitions. They imagined, in the words of one terrorist, that September the 11th would be the "beginning of the end of America." By seeking to turn our cities into killing fields, terrorists and their allies believed that they could destroy this nation's resolve, and force our retreat from the world. They have failed.

In the Battle of Afghanistan, we destroyed the Taliban, many terrorists, and the camps where they trained. We continue to help the Afghan people lay roads, restore hospitals, and educate all of their children. Yet we also have dangerous work to complete. As I speak, a special operations task force, led by the 82nd Airborne, is on the trail of the terrorists, and those who seek to undermine the free government of Afghanistan. America and our coalition will finish what we have begun.

From Pakistan to the Philippines to the Horn of Africa, we are hunting down al-Qaida killers. Nineteen months ago, I pledged that the terrorists would not escape the patient justice of the United States. And as of tonight, nearly one-half of al-Qaida's senior operatives have been captured or killed.

The liberation of Iraq is a crucial advance in the campaign against terror. We have removed an ally of al-Qaida, and cut off a source of terrorist funding. And this much is certain: No terrorist network will gain weapons of mass destruction from the Iraqi regime, because the regime is no more.

In these 19 months that changed the world, our actions have been focused, and deliberate, and proportionate to the offense. We have not forgotten the victims of September the 11th — the last phone calls, the cold murder of children, the searches in the rubble. With those attacks, the terrorists and their supporters declared war on the United States. And war is what they got.

Our war against terror is proceeding according to principles that I have made clear to all: Any person involved in committing or planning terrorist attacks against the American people becomes an enemy of this country, and a target of American justice.

Any person, organization, or government that supports, protects, or harbors terrorists is complicit in the murder of the innocent, and equally guilty of terrorist crimes.

Any outlaw regime that has ties to terrorist groups, and seeks or possesses weapons of mass destruction, is a grave danger to the civilized world, and will be confronted.

And anyone in the world, including the Arab world, who works and sacrifices for freedom has a loyal friend in the United States of America. . . .

Our mission continues. Al-Qaida is wounded, not destroyed. The scattered cells of the terrorist network still operate in many nations, and we know from daily intelligence that they continue to plot against free people. The proliferation of deadly weapons remains a serious danger. The enemies of freedom are not idle, and neither are we. Our government has taken unprecedented measures to defend the homeland — and we will continue to hunt down the enemy before he can strike.

The war on terror is not over, yet it is not endless. We do not know the day of final victory, but we have seen the turning of the tide. No act of the terrorists will change our purpose, or weaken our resolve, or alter their fate. Their cause is lost. Free nations will press on to victory. . . .

Those we lost were last seen on duty. Their final act on this earth was to fight a great evil, and bring liberty to others. All of you—all in this generation of our military—have taken up the highest calling of history. You are defending your country, and protecting the innocent from harm. And wherever you go, you carry a message of hope—a message that is ancient, and ever new. In the words of the prophet Isaiah: "To the captives, 'Come out!' and to those in darkness, 'Be free!'"

Thank you for serving our country and our cause. May God bless you all, and may God continue to bless America.

Source: The White House

THOUGHT QUESTIONS:

1. What images of common Iraqis and their former leader, Saddam Hussein, did President Bush employ in the speech? How did these images color the argument he was trying to make?

2. What claims did Bush make in the speech with regard to the ability of modern technology to limit civilian casualties? Do you agree or disagree with his claims? Why or why not?

3. Most importantly, how did Bush directly link the war effort in Iraq with the 9-11 attacks and the "war on terror"? Cite with multiple examples.

A Texas Veteran of the Iraq War Discusses His Transition to Civilian Life

---

After the 9/11 attacks, President George W. Bush and members of his administration convinced a majority of both houses of Congress to authorize military action not only against the Taliban regime in Afghanistan that protected 9/11 mastermind Osama bin Laden, but also against Saddam Hussein's dictatorship in Iraq, claiming (incorrectly) that Hussein was developing "weapons of mass destruction" that could be used by terrorists for future attacks upon the United States. Though Hussein was toppled relatively easily, the invasion and occupation of Iraq (dubbed "Operation Iraqi Freedom" by the U.S. military) evolved into combat between U.S. forces and a slew of combatants ranging from anti-American militias to foreign terrorists running from March 2003 through December 2011, and eventually claimed the lives of 4,500 American soldiers, including over 400 Texans.

The American armed forces in the Iraq War consisted of a mixed group—career soldiers, sailors, and airmen; army, navy, and air reservists; and recent volunteers—similar to other wars, with the notable exception that draftees were not used and have not been used by the American military since the Vietnam War. As the case with previous wars, individuals joined the military for a variety of reasons and encountered a wide variety of experiences. They also display different reactions upon returning home once their tour of duty is up. While some veterans transition seamlessly to civilian life, others have more difficulty. In the following recent oral history, a North Texas veteran of Operation Iraqi Freedom, Christopher M. Gamblin, relates what motivated him to serve and some of the problems that he experienced trying to readjust to civilian life.

Interviewer: Ok, so where were you living whenever you enlisted?
Christopher M. Gamblin: Uh, in Allen, Texas. It was a couple of years after I graduated from high school. I just kind of bumped around, didn't really find anything I wanted to do, so, I just went up to the recruiter's office one day and signed up.

Interviewer: Did they promise you any specialty or anything?

Christopher M. Gamblin: I really wasn't looking for anything, I just I went in and talked to the recruiter and decided the reserve was the way I wanted to go, and went out and took the test and they offered me a list of jobs I qualified for, and this is what had the biggest bonus, so ...

Interviewer: Which one did you pick?

Christopher M. Gamblin: Uh, carpentry and masonry.

Interviewer: Ok.

Christopher M. Gamblin: At the time, it offered a bonus to do it and I figured, you know, I wasn't actually, uh, I guess, I wasn't actually thinking about going to war and getting deployed. So I was thinking it's just a weekend thing. And so, what's the difference, really, what I do? And they offered more money for that, so, I went ahead and took the money.

Interviewer: So you weren't thinking at all that you might have to go somewhere?

Christopher M. Gamblin: No, no, it just really didn't enter my mind.

Interviewer: OK

Christopher M. Gamblin: I probably would have chosen a different job if I would have had more time to think about it, but.

Interviewer: What do you think you would have picked?

Christopher M. Gamblin: Something with air conditioning. Pretty much anything with air conditioning (laughs) yeah….

Interviewer: Did you have a lot of down time [in Iraq]?

Christopher M. Gamblin: No, not really much at all. We, I mean at night, after we got off work there's not a whole lot we can do after the sun goes down….Our mission was to build a helicopter field, so we were working pretty much, we were leaving before the sun got up to go out to our job site, coming back after the sun went down and we couldn't work anymore. So we did that for the most part of the deployment.

Interviewer: So what kinds of things were you doing?

Christopher M. Gamblin: We were laying concrete.

Interviewer: Laying concrete?

Christopher M. Gamblin: Mm-hmm. Pretty much most of it, and we did, we built a couple of roads and did some renovations on some of their old barracks, some old Iraqi barracks so we could, so people could move into those so they could get out of tents and have somewhere to stay. We just pretty much kept busy….

Interviewer: Did you see any combat during your time?

Christopher M. Gamblin: No, most of the time, I mean other than convoys I was on post most of the time.

Interviewer: Were you, did you have a lot of mortars?

Christopher M. Gamblin: Um, fairly, I'd say on average probably once a week or so, once every two weeks, something like that. It all kinda blurs together now, but I guess I remember pretty frequently, mortars....

Interviewer: Alright. Um, what surprised you most about your time in Iraq?

Christopher M. Gamblin: How long it took. You think about a year, and a year's really not that long. But when you're counting the days, it just seemed like it took forever. That's pretty much, that was the worst part.

Interviewer: Did the war impact your relationship with your family?

Christopher M. Gamblin: I'd say so. We've worked it out, but I was a little different when I got home. A little more on edge, a little testier, a little quick to get angry, until I settled down and unwound. I've seen it in a lot of guys, you just get really tightly wound, and somebody'll be talking about something stupid that has no significance really on anything, and that's just ordinary talk for most people, and when you first get home it's just "Why are you talking about that? Shut up. Leave me alone." But it got better, it took a few months to settle down to where I wasn't just abrasive to everybody I talked to, but it's just a transition thing, as soon as you get off they just expect you to go home

Interviewer: Alright, so we were talking about coming back and readjusting to normal. Um, we've talked [with] several soldiers who mentioned being in country and pushing all their emotions in, and then when you get back having to readjust, and the difficulties of that. Did you experience that?

Christopher M. Gamblin: Yeah, like I said it's a transitioning period. You can't go from being on a, I guess you'd call it high alert, heightened sense of, cause you hear a bomb go off over here and you're like hey, I heard it go off, so I'm cool. But when you get home and nobody's trying to kill you. It's just kinda hard to relax at first, so. It's just weird. It's not something, it's not really easy to wrap your mind around, it's just something that takes time. There's nothing to do but just wait it out.

Interviewer: Did you ever talk to anybody about it?

Christopher M. Gamblin: No.

Interviewer: So were you stationed at just one place the whole time? Did you move at all?

Christopher M. Gamblin: No, I mean I went to a couple places and did a couple things, but for the most part I was in one place that whole time.

Interviewer: And how did you stay in touch with your family and friends?

Christopher M. Gamblin: E-mail, instant messaging, telephone.

Interviewer: And were you able to do that pretty regularly?

Christopher M. Gamblin: At least once a week or so. I kept pretty good contact....

Interviewer: Uh, so what did your experience in the Army teach you about yourself?

Christopher M. Gamblin: Um, I guess I really don't get as upset about stuff as often. I don't get negative thinking I can't do stuff. I mean after that, pretty much everything's doable after that. If I can sit through that, I can do pretty much anything I want. Some confidence building, so, it's just learning that somebody's, people think that their boundaries are a lot lower than they actually are. Your boundaries for human tolerance are pretty much anything is a lot higher than a lot of people are thinking they can do. Some people are thinking that looks really hard and disgusting, and I don't think I could ever do that, but if you have to you have to. It's all possible.

Interviewer: You mentioned not getting upset as much about things. What do you mean by that?

Christopher M. Gamblin: Well, like, um, let's say before, let's say you're at work, and something happens and there's nobody else around, and it's just nasty, and something's gotta get cleaned up. You know, before I mean you say "that's not my job, that's gross, I've gotta do that." Now I've cleaned up some pretty nasty stuff, so that's not as bad as some of the stuff I've seen. Or say you're at the fair, you're walking around and you have to go to the bathroom, and all there are some rank porta potties. I've seen some pretty rank porta potties, that really doesn't bother me that much anymore. It's just a, sometimes the boss tells you you've gotta come in Saturday night and work. I've had people order me to do a lot stupider stuff than that, so it's really no big deal, it's just life. And you can either get mad about it, or you can just deal with it and move on.

Interviewer: So kinda lowered your threshold for things bothering you?

Christopher M. Gamblin: Yeah, pretty much. I mean after some of the stupid shit I've seen, there's really no reason to get mad about some of the dumb stuff that goes on, when it's really just as easy to do it, and move on to the next thing.

Interviewer: So where did you go after you came back from Iraq?

Christopher M. Gamblin: I went home. I took, I made a mistake actually, I came home and I tried to start working probably a week or two after I got home. That actually was not a good idea. I ended up just getting really really pissed off at people. So after that I took a couple months off and just kinda decompressed, and then I got a job waiting tables, because it's just easy, low-stress, and I've actually been at the same job for the last couple years. It's easy, pays the bills, low stress, it's not bad. So I've been doing the same thing.

Interviewer: So how did you decompress, what did you do?

Christopher M. Gamblin: You know, I don't really know, it was just, it just kinda happened over a period of time. The people in my life just had a lot of patience for me, and eventually I just decided hey, I'm being a huge asshole to all of my friends. So, I just kinda took a little while and reevaluated, and just took a look at the way I was reacting to certain things, thought about it, and just kinda made it all work out....

Source: Veterans History Project, American Folklife Center, Library of Congress

THOUGHT QUESTIONS:

1. What were Gamblin's motivations for joining the military? How was his situation similar to people that you may know who consider making a similar choice?

2. In what ways did Gamblin state that he had difficulty transitioning back to civilian life after his deployment? Did he seek counseling or try to talk to anyone about how he was feeling? If not, should he have done so? Why?

3. How did Gamblin say that army life, serving in a war zone, and just being abroad taught him lessons about himself?

"Texas Transitions to Service Economy"

One of the important realities for Texas in the late-20th and early-21st centuries has been a dramatic shift from an economy based on farming, cattle raising, and oil production to one has kept these vital sectors but has become dominated by numerous vital service industries. In 2007, D'Ann Petersen, an associate economist in the Research Department of the Federal Reserve Bank of Dallas, analyzed this transition for Southwest Economy. An abridged version of her report appears below.

Texas has joined the nation in shifting its economy into services. Decade by decade, the state's service sector has expanded its share of employment and production in an economy traditionally known for cotton, cattle, crude oil and construction cranes.

While agriculture and goods industries remain vital to the state's economic health, the service sector today accounts for roughly 80 percent of jobs and 63 percent of output. Texas matches the U.S. in the share of employment in services. The state's share of output in services is less than the nation's 70 percent because of Texas' importance as an energy producer and growing role in manufacturing.

Measured by employment or output, services are expanding faster in Texas than in the U.S. The sector has emerged as the state's leading engine of job creation. Since 1990, it has added more than 2.4 million jobs on net and more than doubled the pace of employment growth in goods-producing industries.

For Texas as well as the U.S., the increasing importance of services reflects a long-term evolution, driven by the capacity of free enterprise economies to reinvent themselves. Agriculture's dominance faded with the rise of manufacturing, and today the factory era has given way to services. The transition shows the ability of businesses and workers to adapt to ever-changing circumstances, including rapid technological progress and an increasingly competitive world economy.

Sizing Up Services

Truckers making deliveries, technicians maintaining Internet sites, brokers selling insurance, architects designing shopping centers, managers running businesses, nurses caring for patients, waiters serving diners—all these and many others are service jobs.

To make sense of this sprawling sector, government agencies aggregate services into groups of related businesses. . . . The service sector's diverse members are grouped into seven private-industry categories and government. Texas' share of employment in each of them is at or below the nation's—with one notable exception. The state has 24.3 percent of its total employment in trade, transportation and utilities, compared with 22.9 percent for the U.S. as a whole.

This category owes its importance to Texas' strategic location on the Mexican border and in the center of the U.S. These attributes have spurred expansion of transportation networks, which have attracted firms in such industries as retail and wholesale trade, airlines, trucking, pipelines, rail and cargo transportation, and warehousing—all of which add to employment in this large sector.

Among the major transportation firms headquartered in Texas are Southwest Airlines, American Airlines, Continental Airlines and Burlington Northern Santa Fe Corp. The Port of Houston is the country's second-busiest deepwater facility, and Dallas/Fort Worth International Airport ranks sixth in the world for passenger traffic and 27th in the world for cargo volume. Houston's Bush Intercontinental Airport is the nation's ninth busiest in passenger traffic. Fort Worth's Alliance Airport, a purely industrial airport, is one of the country's largest intermodal facilities.

Job Engines

From 1990 through 2006—a period that includes vigorous expansion, recession and recovery—each of Texas' major service categories outperformed its U.S. counterpart in job growth.

Three industries stand out, not only doing better than the U.S. but growing faster than the state average of 2.7 percent.

Professional and business services lead expansion. The state's second-largest service category, with almost 15 percent of Texas jobs, is the top performer in job growth. Professional and business services include many knowledge-based positions in law, accounting, architecture, engineering, software design, management and consulting. The industry has added 655,900 jobs since 1990—an average annual pace of 5.7 percent, more than a percentage point faster than the nation. . . .

Growing population boosts education and health services. The second-fastest-growing service category includes private university and education workers, training center employees, doctors, nurses, medical technicians and social workers. It has added 571,900 jobs since 1990. Health care dominates the category, with about 1.1 million jobs, or 88 percent of the total and roughly 12 percent of Texas private employment.

Health care demand is rising nationwide as the population ages and new technology changes the delivery of medical services. In Texas, the rapidly growing population is another driver for health care employment. The second-most-populous state, Texas has been adding residents twice as fast as the nation, in part because of migration. Along the

Texas–Mexico border, health care-related jobs have been multiplying as many Mexicans cross the Rio Grande to meet their medical needs. . . .

Leisure and hospitality service employment increases. Texas boasts a wide range of attractions—the Alamo, Galveston and Padre islands, Space Center Houston, Big Bend National Park, the Fort Worth Stockyards, the State Capitol and the rolling Hill Country, to name just a few. Add in business travel and entertainment, and it makes for a healthy industry.

The leisure and hospitality category—which includes hotels, eating and drinking establishments, and recreation services—makes up 11.4 percent of Texas' economy and employs about as many workers as the state's factories.

Most leisure and hospitality industries have been adding jobs at a steady pace each year. Since 1990, job growth has averaged 3.8 percent, outpacing the nation's 2.7 percent. The lion's share of leisure and hospitality employment is concentrated in food-service and drinking establishments, which make up almost 80 percent of the total. This segment continues to add workers at a moderate pace, though job growth has slowed from the 1990s' pace.

The hotel industry makes up 10 percent of leisure and hospitality employment. While lodging employment dropped after the September 11 terrorist attacks, jobs have rebounded the past few years as demand picked up. Texas hotel construction is also on the rise, with the 2006 value of new construction contracts up 24 percent from a year earlier.

Weathering Downturns

Shifting the employment base from goods to services changes the way economies perform when hard times hit. Employment usually holds up better in services than in goods when economies slip into recession.

The high-tech and dot-com busts sent the country into recession in 2001, but Texas felt the impact longer than many areas, partly because of its large number of high-tech jobs. The 9/11 aftershocks that hurt the travel industry added to the tech crunch, prolonging Texas' recession through June 2003.

Overall, the Texas service sector weathered the storm, recording an annual employment decline only in 2001, when 67,100 jobs were lost. Texas' goods-producing sector lost over 188,000 jobs during the downturn, more than a quarter of them in high-tech manufacturing.

Consistent gains in education and health care, leisure and hospitality, and financial services buoyed Texas employment during the recession. These industries prospered in part because of relatively strong population growth and a healthy housing market, spurred by low mortgage rates.

Not all service industries sailed through the recession. Hardest hit was the information sector, with its high percentage of telecommunications service positions. Texas telecom firms shed slightly more than 29,000 jobs during the downturn. Productivity growth has since returned to this industry, yet new jobs remain elusive. Professional and business services also saw jobs decline considerably. Computer systems design, an industry that includes such companies as Plano-based EDS, lost about 18,000 jobs during the recession, accounting for almost 30 percent of the category's decline.

The trade, transportation and utilities industry was hurt by the post-9/11 drop in demand for air travel. Texas airline transportation employment fell by 12,200 during the downturn and continued to edge down through 2005, rebounding slightly in 2006. Other segments of trade, transportation and utilities, such as retail and wholesale trade, contracted during the downturn as consumer demand weakened across the U.S.

Once the Texas recovery began in mid-2003, employment growth swung back quickly in services while jobs continued to fall in goods-producing industries. In late 2004, however, goods joined services on an upward track, helping fuel the state's robust economic growth of the past few years. . . .

Plus or Minus for Texas?

The transition from goods to services often raises concerns about a possible decline in living standards if low-wage, low-skilled service jobs replace higher-paying jobs in the goods sector. Fortunately, this isn't the case for Texas. While labor churn creates hardships for some workers who lose their jobs, the service sector's overall expansion has coincided with rising prosperity in the state.

As services have taken a larger share of Texas' economy, productivity has grown in both the goods and service sectors, creating more job opportunities and leading to higher per capita income. Goods and services industries alike have benefited from the increased efficiency that comes from service firms' advances in business communications, financial innovations, and distribution and transportation networks. . . .

The expansion of industries rich in knowledge-based occupations has played a key role in pushing up Texas' productivity in services.

Since 1990, half of the state's service employment growth has been in the professional and business services and education and health industries. Many of these jobs require above-average education.

According to the Census Bureau, 68.3 percent of U.S. professional service workers age 25 to 64 had at least a bachelor's degree in 2006, compared with 33.2 percent of all workers in the age group. Workers with bachelor's degrees or greater held 39 percent of all service jobs, compared with 7 percent of general production occupations, including electrical equipment handlers, machinists, welders and print machine operators.

Knowledge-based service jobs tend to pay well. In Texas, average hourly wages in 2005 were $77.23 for internal medicine doctors, $44.81 for geological engineers, $39.53 for computer software engineers and $26.35 for registered nurses, according to the Bureau of Labor Statistics.

Of course, not all service jobs offer above-average pay. Industries such as retail sales, food preparation and household services pay relatively low wages. But low-wage positions are an important starting point for many of the state's younger, less experienced and less educated workers, including teens and some immigrants.

Overall, the transition from goods to services has benefited the Texas economy. The key to prospering as the economic base shifts lies in developing higher-end, knowledge-based services that offer better pay, greater productivity and global reach.

Texas has been able to do that over the past decade and a half. For the Texas economy to continue to expand its high-value-added service sector, however, it is essential that the state's education system continue to make progress on improving student achievement.

Source: *Southwest Economy,* Issue 3, May/June, Federal Reserve Bank of Dallas

THOUGHT QUESTIONS:

1. In terms of jobs and output, how large is the service sector to the Texas economy? How does this compare to the nation?

2. What are the leading categories of service jobs in the Texas economy? In these areas, how does Texas compare to the rest of the country?

3. How has the increasingly diversified Texas economy provided a stronger ability for the state to weather economic downturns?

Selected Texas Voting Statistics, 1970-2012

Year	Gubernatorial (Gov) or Presidential (Pres) Race in November	Percentage of Voting Age Population Registered	Percentage Turnout among All Registered Voters	Percentage Turnout among Voting Age Population
1970	Gov	57.75	53.89	31.12
1972	Pres	67.42	66.59	44.90
1978	Gov	60.63	41.71	25.29
1980	Pres	66.59	68.40	45.55
1994	Gov	66.09	50.87	33.62
1996	Pres	76.95	53.24	40.97
2010	Gov	70.62	37.53	26.50
2012	Pres	74.65	58.58	43.73

Source: State of Texas. Secretary of State's Office

THOUGHT QUESTIONS:

1. What factors play into a potential voter's decision to register to vote? What factors play into the decision to vote in a particular election?

2. Over the past 40 years, have Texans tended to vote more in governor's races than presidential races? Why or why not?

3. Over the past four decades, has the rate of voter participation in Texas gubernatorial and presidential elections (in terms of registration and actual voting) tended to increase, decrease, or remain roughly the same? Why do you think that is the case?

"Recession Arrives in Texas: A Rougher Ride in 2009"

The severe recession (a period of negative economic growth) that struck the United States near the end of the George W. Bush administration initially did not effect Texas nearly as much as the rest of the nation. Nevertheless, by the start of 2009 the economic downturn directly impacted the Lone Star State as business activity decreased and unemployment rose. In this excerpt from a Federal Reserve Bank of Dallas article appearing in the First Quarter 2009 edition of Southwest Economy, economists Keith R. Phillips and Jesus Cañas analyze the impact of what has become known as the "The Great Recession" upon the Texas economy.

Through much of 2008, the Texas economy continued to expand while the nation fell into recession. Growth in the energy and high-tech sectors and rising home prices were key factors in making Texas' economy one of the nation's strongest.

In the last half of the year, however, the state's economic conditions deteriorated rapidly. The weakening was primarily due to the deepening global financial crisis and sharp declines in energy prices, high-tech activity and exports.

Based on available data, Texas was in recession when 2009 began and was probably on the brink weeks or months before then. The state's last recession came during the 2001–03 tech bust.

The beginnings and ends of recessions take time to pinpoint because of data revisions and economic noise. This is especially true for state economies because performance measures are less reliable.

Evidence of the current recession comes from data on jobs and unemployment, composite gauges of current and future economic activity, various industry measures and anecdotal reports from Texas businesses.

These indicators suggest Texas trailed the official December 2007 start of the U.S. recession by at least six months. So far, the state's economic losses have been moderate compared with the rest of the country's, which means Texas is still faring better than the nation as a whole.

A Broad View

Texas' job growth of 0.4 percent in 2008 was greater than the U.S. decline of 1.9 percent and ranked eighth in the nation. However, the employment picture worsened toward the end of the year. At annual rates, jobs grew 1.5 percent through June, then declined 0.7 percent in the second half of the year.

Employment growth fell sharply in September, the month Hurricane Ike delivered a blow to the Texas coast. It bounced back in October, but cyclical economic factors likely caused declines of 0.7 percent in November and 2.1 percent in December.

As job growth weakened, the Texas unemployment rate rose sharply from 4.4 percent in June to 6 percent in December. This compares with the U.S. rate's increase from 5.6 percent to 6.8 percent.

The roots of the rising unemployment rates are different. In the U.S., much of the increase has been due to lost jobs. In Texas, the rate has climbed because of slower but still positive employment gains and faster labor force growth. . . .

A Sectoral View

Some key components of the Texas economy echo the broad measures in showing a sudden weakening in the second half of 2008.

Take exports. Aided by a falling dollar and strong energy industry, they were a bright spot the first six months of 2008, surging 12.4 percent. Compared with a year earlier, sales were up 15.2 percent to Europe, 13.2 percent to Latin America and 5.7 percent to Asia. However, slower growth overseas and the dollar's rising value have curtailed international demand, and Texas exports fell 16 percent from June to November.

Partly due to ebbing overseas sales, Texas manufacturers have experienced steep declines in business. Production, shipments, new orders and capacity utilization measures all fell sharply the final three months of the year, according to the Dallas Fed's Texas Manufacturing Outlook Survey. High-tech manufacturing output data aren't available at the state level, but national measures show this sector was hit hard the second half of 2008.

In the housing market, inventories, foreclosures and delinquencies all rose last year—but less in Texas than in the nation. Key to the divergence was home prices. They declined nationally but continued to rise in Texas on a year-over-year basis through the third quarter, according to the Federal Housing Finance Agency's measure of resold homes. Appreciation was broad based across Texas metro areas.

However, these price gains narrowed through¬out the year, fading to 0.45 percent from the second to third quarter. More broadly, the state's housing markets weakened, with new home construction falling sharply last year. Most likely, prices will dip slightly in 2009.

The energy industry was a key factor in the Texas economy's relative strength in the first half of 2008. Texas produces nearly a third of all U.S. natural gas, and it employs almost half the workers in the U.S. oil and gas extraction industry. Primarily because of high prices for natural gas, the Texas rig count by the middle of 2008 was at its highest level since the early 1980s.

The energy stimulus has deteriorated as oil and gas prices have plummeted. As a result, the Texas rig count fell by 410, or 50 percent, from the end of August to the first week of March.

The brunt of the decline has been borne by the land-based natural gas industry. The Beige Book, the Federal Reserve's anecdotal report on economic conditions, found that relatively expensive, nonconventional drilling in North Texas' Barnett Shale and the Permian Basin's tight sands led the upturn—and these areas will lead the downturn as well. Offshore and international activity have held up better and should continue to do so, largely because of the involvement of companies with longer-term perspectives and deeper pockets.

As drilling activity slows, layoffs are becoming widespread in the energy industry and are expected to grow in 2009. Related manufacturing activity is experiencing cutbacks, especially among producers of bits, pipe and tools.

Meanwhile, Texas' financial sector has expanded over the past several years, adding jobs while the industry has shrunk nationally. However, the current financial crisis will likely impact all regions significantly. Texas' financial-sector job growth has recently declined, and the trend is expected to continue.

In addition, troubled bank loans are increasing in the state, just as they are across the nation. Beige Book respondents continue to warn that a sharp tightening in lending will soon lead to a drop-off in commercial building. The Eleventh Federal Reserve District, which includes Texas and parts of New Mexico and Louisiana, has a high exposure to commercial real estate, at 29.4 percent of loans, compared with 13.9 percent for the nation.

A Metro View

According to the Dallas Fed's business-cycle indexes for Texas' major metro areas, the Austin and Dallas economies have slowed the most in recent months, while Houston has continued to grow.

In 2009, all the major metro areas in Texas will likely experience recessions. Their relative performance depends upon their industrial structures as well as local firms' competitiveness. . . .

Dallas has larger shares of jobs in the finance and insurance and real estate industries, which are at risk in the downturn. It also has large shares in such cyclically sensitive industries as wholesale trade, information, and professional and business services. Dallas has small shares in noncyclical industries such as health, leisure and government. Austin has large shares in such cyclically sensitive industries as construction, wholesale trade and information. . . . Dallas and Austin will probably be hurt the most this year. If energy prices drop much further, then Houston, with its heavy share of activity in natural resources and mining, will likely decline sharply as well.

The Forecast

The Texas Leading Index (TLI), the Dallas Fed's barometer of future economic activity, has weakened significantly in recent months. All but one of its eight indicators—new unemployment claims—declined the last three months of 2008.

The biggest negative contributors have been the slide in real oil prices, sharp decline in help-wanted advertising, increase in the Texas export-weighted value of the dollar and decline in the stock index of Texas-based companies.

The stock index tumbled 37 percent from June to January, compared with a 35 percent decline in the Standard & Poor's 500. The performance likely reflects the steep drop in energy stock prices, which have a heavier weight in the Texas index.

Based on TLI forecasts, Texas' nonfarm employment will decrease through March 2010—with the worst of it coming in the first six months of this year. The model estimates that jobs will recede at an annual rate of 3.9 percent through June, then improve to a 1.6 percent decline in the second half.

For all of 2009, the forecast is for employment to fall 2.8 percent, the equivalent of 296,000 jobs. Based on historical observation, this job loss is consistent with a rise in the unemployment rate to about 8 percent.

In sum, 2009 will be a difficult year in Texas as the state deals with the repercussions of the deep financial crisis plaguing the national and global economies.

Energy prices are hard to predict, and big movements could change the state's short-term outlook. At the same time, improvements in world financial markets and overall economic growth would enhance the state's growth prospects, particularly in the second half of the year.

While the short-term Texas outlook is weak, longer-term prospects remain healthy. Job growth, low business and living costs, and a young, fast-growing labor force remain positives that will help in recovery.

Source: *Southwest Economy*, First Quarter 2010 Issue, Federal Reserve Bank of Dallas

THOUGHT QUESTIONS:

1. How has the recession hit key sectors of the Texas economy?

2. What differences in local economic impacts did the economists identify when looking at different major metropolitan areas in Texas?

3. What reasons did the economists give to justify their cautiously optimistic outlook for the future of the Texas economy?

Actor Jaston Williams's Interesting Beginnings

The comedy play "Greater Tuna" began as a simple skit written by Jaston Williams, Joe Sears, and Ed Howard that they parlayed into a critically acclaimed production, debuting in 1981. The show is set in fictitious Tuna, Texas—"the third smallest town in Texas, where the Lions Club is too liberal and Patsy Cline never dies." The town's citizens (men, women, and children who are all played by Williams and Sears) provide the fodder for this satire on life in rural Texas. The demand for sequels became so great that Williams, Sears, and Howard created two holiday-themed shows entitled "A Tuna Christmas" and "Red, White, and Tuna," which are equally popular among fans.

In this excerpt from an oral interview, Jaston Williams humorously describes his life growing up in West Texas and his unlikely path to acting.

Interviewer: I'm at the Paramount Theater in Austin, Texas, to interview Jaston Williams, who is one of the performers in *Greater Tuna*. I'd like to start with- where you started in Texas, what your youth was about, and where you began.

Williams: I was born in El Paso on June 28, 1951. My father was a farmer and rancher. He came from very Western stock. My mother's family was much more Southern. So the children were kind of a mixed hybrid. We had kind of a "magnolia mother" and a "cowboy father." We lived on a farm outside of Van Horn, Texas—about twenty miles south of Van Horn. [We] lived there until I was about six years old, and then we moved up to the Panhandle. My father farmed there, and we lived in Overton, Texas, for nine years, which had been where my father was born in the early century. We were kind of an "old" family in the area. . . . I have more of an affection for far-West Texas where I lived before, when I was six years old. My mother lives in far-West Texas now. She lives in a little town called Dell City that's about 490 people, and it's at the base of the Guadalupe Mountains. . . . It really has kind of a "Tuna" atmosphere.

But it's that far-West Texas country; it's very, very independent; people are very, very independent. They may fight and squabble with each other greatly, but if anybody's broken down on the highway, they stop. I mean, they take care of each other. I think a lot of that has to do with a desert mentality. When you live in that kind of environment, if anybody needs help of any kind, there's no question about it, you just provide it. So I find something very wonderful about that part of the world.

We were Methodist; I loved it because you had to show up and you had to pay and you couldn't get real emotional! [laughter] So we were in church every time the lights were on. And, I look back on it now, my older brother resisted the religious background thing with every fiber of his being. He fought it every Sunday, and he never got to first base with my mother. He fought it every Sunday of his adolescent life, and he went to church every Sunday of his adolescent life. It never occurred to me to resist it. It was just something that you did. It was just a part of your life that was there.

I'm very grateful that my mother and my father had the religious background that they did, if, for no other reason, that it taught me social graces. It taught me that there are situations that you will be in as an adult where you're going to have to sit still, where you're going to have to be quiet, where you may have to listen to someone who's just boring the life out of you [laughter], but that you have to do this! And it taught you a sense of decorum.

The social lives of these communities were built entirely around churches and schools. I think that that kind of naturally came out in our plays when we write about the fictional town of Tuna, Texas. Everything is pretty much set around a church, a school, and a radio station. So I was very fortunate; I didn't realize what was out in the rest of the world. I, about halfway, thought that trees were something the Brothers Grimm had made up [laughter] because we hadn't seen very many of them. Forests were just out of the question and kind of frightening! Stuff could hide in there! [laughter] It's one thing in the Panhandle—if there's something violent, you can see it coming from a long way! [laughter]

Interviewer: Well, how did you leave? I mean, how did you leave that part of the country?

Williams: I graduated from high school on a Friday night in 1969, and I was gone Sunday morning. I came back briefly to go to Tech for a while, and I enjoyed it very much. Actually, I loved going to Tech. But I couldn't handle the sand, the weather. It's not as bad out there anymore, but there was a period there in the late 1960s, early 1970s, where it took on dust bowl proportions in the spring. The weather was more than I could deal with. It was very depressing. I came down to San Marcos right after high school and did a couple of semesters there, so I knew that there were trees and clean water and places where the toilets didn't freeze the first of December! [laughter] So, going back, I really loved Tech, and that's where I wanted to go to college, but the weather was just inhospitable. At a certain point I just thought—I can't . . . do this. Spring should be the most beautiful time of the year, and it was the worst time out there. So, another victim of the dust bowl.

I went to Houston. I was married at the time. Married very young, and my son was born on Mother's Day of 1971. He was about a month old when we moved to Houston. I was planning to go to the University of Houston, and I thought I would go by a junior college and pick up some electives. It was one of those moments where fate guided. You know, fate guides you somewhere and you think later, "How did I get here? What did I do to get here? And how wonderful this is." I decided to take some electives, and I thought, "Well, I'll wait. I'll go to U of H a semester, and I'll just go by a junior college not far from here."

I'd heard of a place called San Jacinto College in Pasadena—it's right across the street from Gilley's. I thought, "Well, this will be a great place to take biology, math, or whatever." And when I went in, they told me, "You have to declare a major." And I said, "Well, I, you know . . ." And they said, "Well, you have to." So I thought, "Well, I'll just be honest, and I'll major in theater." They said, "Well, you have to go talk to the Head of the Theater Department." I said, "But I don't want to take any theater." They said, "Well, you have to." They were big on the rules! [laughter] I thought, "I don't know if I'm going to like this *this* much."

I went to talk to the head of the Theater Department—his name is Jerry Rawlins Powell. He's been retired for a few years now, and he was a godsend for me. I talked to him for about an hour. Was absolutely fascinated by him. He was a real "no-bull" guy and was very direct. He said, "I don't know what we will do this year in terms of plays because I don't know who we've got. But we'll do four plays this season, and then we'll do some in the summer. I won't know until I see who shows up for the first audition what play we're going to do, but we'll do something." He had such a clear idea of what he liked, and he was very up-front with me about what he liked, and I took a liking to him immediately. During the first week of school, I dropped several courses and took pretty much a full load of his theater courses. He was literally a one-man theater department. So you had him for poetry [interpretation], for acting, for technical theater, and for lighting; he did it all.

It was the best thing that could possibly have happened to me for a couple of reasons. One was that at a certain point he told me, "You know, you're very good. We're going to use you; we're going to use you all year. And you really don't need to be in school," he said, "because you don't want to be in school. You don't want to do the things that students have to do in terms of all this other stuff you want to take. You want to be in theater. And I think you can do it."

He signed me up to audition for a theater company in San Antonio that I'd had the good fortune to see—I'd seen a performance of theirs when I was a student at San Marcos. It was the First Repertory Company of San Antonio. It's been defunct for a while, but [it was] an excellent, exciting, on-the-edge theater. I held them in high esteem, and it didn't occur to me to audition for them. I didn't know that they would open it up or anything. I didn't know how to get in the door with them. He told me, "You know, they're audition-ing next week, and I want you to go. You need to prepare a classic piece, and you need to prepare two contemporary pieces. Go to Rice University, and they'll see you there." And I did, and I got hired. They were hiring pretty much a new theater company; they were hiring about seven or eight actors. And I was the youngest person, I think, that they'd ever hired.

Interviewer: How old were you at that time?

Williams: I was not quite twenty-one. I was twenty when they hired me. They had to wait until my birthday for me to sign the contract, because you had to be twenty-one.

It changed my life. Again it was one of those things of "How did you get here?" It's something I love about life—that bizarre happenstance. The dust storm drove you away; you knew to get away from the storm. If nothing else, you're not going to get dust in your face! You end up across the street from Gilley's, studying theater with a one-man drama department who happens to be a genius. He pushes you toward San Antonio, and you're working what would have been, I guess, my senior year in college; I was working with the First Repertory Company, and it was like, "How in the hell did I get here?" I don't know how I got here, but I am so grateful and thankful. . . .

Source: Institute of Texan Cultures

THOUGHT QUESTIONS:

1. What part of Texas was Williams originally from? How did he feel about growing up there?

2. How does Williams feel about his early church-going experiences?

3. How did Williams get involved in acting?

San Antonio, Texas

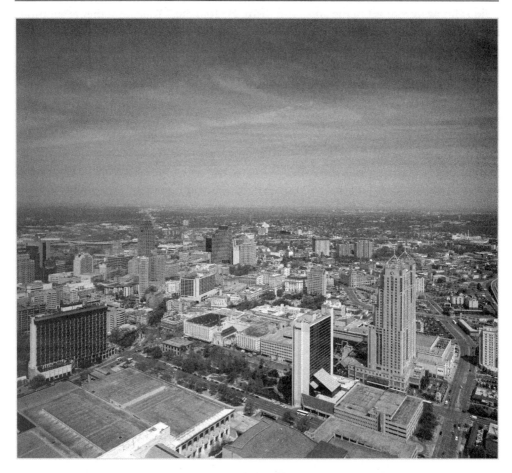

Credit: Library of Congress
March 17, 2005

A picture of San Antonio, the second largest city in Texas.

THOUGHT QUESTION:

Do the major cities in Texas, namely Houston, Dallas, San Antonio, and Austin, have unique characteristics and "personalities" or are they "all the same"? Explain.

BIOGRAPHIES

MOLLY IVINS (1944-2007). Mary Tyler Ivins, better known as Molly, the influential and iconic liberal political commentator, humorist, newspaper columnist, and author was born in Monterey, California on August 30, 1944. Her father was a conservative Republican who served as general counsel and later president of the Tenneco Corporation, an oil and gas company. Her homemaker mother had received a degree in psychology from Smith College. Ivins developed her liberal views partly from reading the *Texas Observer* at a friend's house. She graduated from St. John's School in Houston in 1962 and attended Smith College, receiving a B.A. in history in 1966. Ivins received a master's degree in journalism from Columbia University the following year and started working for *Houston Chronicle.* In the late-1960s she moved to the Minneapolis *Tribune* where she started as a police reporter and later covered local radicals for a regular feature labeled "Movements for Social Change." She then returned to Texas to become co-editor of the *Texas Observer.* In an effort to enliven their paper's writing style, the New York *Times* employed Ivins from 1976 to 1980, first as a staff writer, then later as head of the Denver Bureau. In 1982 she returned once more to Texas to write political commentary for the Dallas *Times Herald.* When that paper folded in 1991, she began writing for the Fort Worth *Star-Telegram.* Starting in 2001, Ivins became a successful syndicated writer with her column being run in hundreds of newspapers nationwide along with freelance pieces appearing in national political magazines.

Ivins's writings, including her books *Molly Ivins Can't Say That, Can She?, You Got To Dance With Them What Brung You: Politics in the Clinton Years, Shrub: The Short but Happy Political Life of George W. Bush*, and *Who Let the Dogs In? Incredible Political Animals I Have Known* all were characterized by her sharp wit and, despite her upper class background and New England collegiate education, an unapologetic liberal Texas populist style. She enjoyed lambasting the conservative political establishment in Texas, often seeming to reserve special venom for the state legislature and the Bush family (she is credited with first using the nickname "Shrub" for George W. Bush.)

In 1999, Ivins was diagnosed with breast cancer and waged a public battle against her illness. Chemotherapy treatments prolonged her life, but she frequently suffered from recurrences. She wrote her last columns in early January 2007 but died at her Austin on January 31. After her death, President George W. Bush issued a statement, noting: "I respected her convictions, her passionate belief in the power of words. She fought her illness with that same passion. Her quick wit and commitment will be missed." Ivins was a finalist for the Pulitzer Prize three times. She counted as her two greatest honors that the Minneapolis police force named its mascot pig after her and that her writings once led her to be banned from the Texas A&M University campus.

MICHAEL DELL (1965-). Michael Saul Dell, businessman and founder of the computer giant Dell, Inc., was born February 23, 1965, in Houston, Texas. The son of an orthodontist and a stockbroker, Dell's first business venture took place at age 12 when his parents allowed him to start up a direct marketing company offering a national stamp auction through the mail, earning him about $2,000. His first experience with computers reportedly occurred when, at age 15, his fascination with a new Apple II led him to take it apart and reassemble it, just to see if he could. While in high school Four years later, he sold *Houston Post* subscriptions through target marketing, earning $18,000 from which he bought a car and three new computers. .

Dell started his own computer company while a student at the University of Texas at Austin. Basing his business on providing custom-made computers to customers at a lower cost by the direct sales method rather than purchasing through retailers, Dell assembled computers from surplus parts made to the specifications relayed to him by his clients. Sales increased as Dell delivered computers to customers often at a 10 percent discount over other companies. With financial aid from his grandparents, he dropped out to devote full time to the company which eventually became the Dell Computer Corporation. The company saved money on storage costs and did not have to worry about unsold inventory by simply not beginning to assemble a computer, or even ordering necessary parts, until an order was placed. As the company grew, Dell eventually insisted that its parts suppliers maintain their warehouses close to Dell factories so orders could be assembled relatively quickly. He also improved sales by initiating practices that would later become industry standards, such as offering toll-free technical support over the phone, and later, online ordering. In 1992, Dell's skyrocketing success made him, at age twenty-seven, the youngest CEO ever of a Fortune 500 company.

Based in Round Rock, just north of Austin, Dell, Inc. continues to function on the same basic business premise as when it began: providing made-to-order computers directly to customers, though now doing so on a massive scale as it has become the largest PC manufacturer in the world with annual sales over $50 billion. In 2004, Dell temporarily stepped down for time as CEO while remaining chairman of the board, but resumed duties as CEO in 2007. While his salary is typically in the $1-$2 million range, he owns over 200 million shares of the company (about 10 percent of the total) and has an estimated net worth over $12 billion.

LARRY McMURTRY (1936 -). Acclaimed writer Larry Jeff McMurtry, best known for his Pulitzer Prize-winning novel *Lonesome Dove*, was born in Archer City, Texas on June 3, 1936. He worked on his family's cattle ranch until his early twenties, when he left to pursue his interest in writing, completing his undergraduate degree in English at North Texas State College in 1958 and earning an M.A. from Rice University in 1960. He then went to Stanford University on a fellowship to study fiction writing under Wallage Stegner before returning to Texas. Over the next several years McMurtry started writing his own fiction while teaching English and creative writing at Texas Christian University and Rice. He married Josephine Ballard, but the marriage did not last, leading McMurtry to raise their son James alone after the couple's divorce.

Published in 1961, McMurtry's first novel, *Horseman, Pass By*, was well received by the literary community. Set in the late-1950s, the novel centered on the generational clash between an old rancher, his stepson, and his teenage son. Hollywood adapted the book into the 1963 film *Hud*, starring Paul Newman. In 1966, McMurtry published *The Last Picture Show*, a novel based on the author's teen years growing up in a small Texas town. In 1971, McMurtry co-wrote the screenplay for a film version of the novel with director Peter Bogdanovich. The book and the movie version of the story gave McMurtry his first mainstream public notoriety outside of Texas.

Beginning in 1970, McMurtry began to set many stories within urban settings, publishing a series of novels using recurring characters to explore human relationships, including *Moving On, All My Friends Are Going to Be Strangers,* and, in 1975, the enormously popular *Terms of Endearment,* which he adapted for the 1983 blockbuster film version, which garnered numerous Academy Awards. He ended the series of related novels with *Evening Star,* a sequel to *Terms of Endearment.*

McMurtry's next major novel, *Lonesome Dove,* earned him the 1986 Pulitzer Prize for fiction. Set in the mid-1870s, the story concerns two aging Texas Rangers leading a cattle drive from South Texas to Montana. The novel was so well received, in part, because of its realistic portrayal of life in the Old West, avoiding many of the myths and stereotypes of the cowboy genre. In 1989, the novel was adapted for television and became an instant hit miniseries on CBS. He wrote two books related to *Lonesome Dove,* a sequel published in 1993 entitled *Streets of Laredo* and a prequel, 1995's *Dead Man's Walk* in addition to additional western novels, though none achieved *Lonesome Dove's* success. In the late-1980s and 1990s he also returned to characters created in some of his earlier works, publishing *Texasville* and *Duane's Depressed,* both sequels to *The Last Picture Show.*

Since the 1990s, McMurtry has made Archer City his primary residence. In late-1991 he underwent quadruple-bypass surgery and had a difficult recovery but continued to write and focus on establishing a huge rare and used bookstore in Archer City that by the early 2000s became the largest such establishment in Texas. McMurtry's most recent accolade came in 2006 when the film script that he co-adapted with Diana Ossana from E. Annie Proulx's 1997 short story "Brokeback Mountain" won the Academy Award for Best Adapted Screenplay.

BOB BULLOCK (1929–1999). Longtime Democratic politician Robert Douglas Bullock, Sr. was born in Hillsboro, Texas on July 10, 1929. The son of a Hillsboro city engineer and manager, Bullock attended Hillsboro High School and Hill College before serving as a supply clerk in the Air Force during the Korean War. In 1956, he graduated from Texas Tech University with a degree in business administration and two years later received a law degree from Baylor Law School. Bullock had been elected to the Texas state legislature while attending Baylor but resigned his office in October 1959 to practice law and serve as general counsel for the Texas Automobile Dealers Association. He was appointed to the Texas Historical Commission in 1963 and four years later was asked by Attorney General Martin Crawford to head his office's newly created Antitrust and Consumer Protection Division.

After supporting Preston Smith's successful 1968 gubernatorial bid, Bullock served as the governor's general counsel before being appointed secretary of state, the chief elections and records officer for Texas, in 1971. He quickly set about pushing popular reforms broadening campaign finance disclosures and modernizing voting procedures by establishing a computerized voter registration system before successfully challenging the long-serving incumbent comptroller of public accounts, Robert S. Calvert, in 1974.

For four terms, Bullock became a household name in Texas as he built a reputation as an attention-getting administrator pushing for modernized bookkeeping while being hell-bent on recovering long overdue money owed by recalcitrant taxpayers. To improve efficiency, he reduced the number of tax forms, set up the state government's first direct deposit system, demanded funds from the legislature to foster the implementation of computers in his office and updated accounting methods, and fired senior supervisors and staff who resisted the conversion. He also garnered media attention whenever "Bullock's Raiders" arrived to confiscate the inventory of businesses that were long delinquent in remitting collected sales taxes owed to the state government. In general, Bullock was credited with making the Comptroller's office an effective agency and a positive asset in managing the finances of the state government. As efficient as his tax office work may have been, Bullock's personal life was often a mess, largely due to the effects of his bipolar disorder. Bouts of his manic depression disorder led him to be a serial womanizer (he married five times in his life), an alcoholic, and a classic risk-taker who, among other questionable actions, scheduled frequent elaborate party trips on a taxpayer-owned private plane.

Bullock's personal limitations did not prevent him for seeking, or acquiring, higher office when he successfully ran for lieutenant governor in 1990. Because the lieutenant governor of Texas has such tremendous power as the presiding officer of the state Senate and control of the state government's budgeting process as leader of the Legislative Budget Board, all governors hoping for a successful term need to cultivate a positive working relationship with the individual holding that important post. Bullock served as lieutenant governor from 1991 through 1997 during the terms of Democratic governor Ann Richards and Republican governor George W. Bush, and worked together with each politician to pass numerous pieces of lasting legislation. During Richards's term, among other accomplishments, he secured creation of the Texas Performance Review to enable the State Comptroller to analyze state agency spending patterns and recommend cost-saving alternatives, aided in the consolidation of all state government environmental agencies into one department, and worked to establish Texas A&M International University at Laredo as the first South Texas school to offer doctoral programs. As the Texas legislature became Republican-dominated for the first time since Reconstruction during the governorship of George W. Bush, Bullock worked to advance some aspects of the governor's agenda while seeking successes of his own. While Bush received much, but not all, that he desired from the legislature (such as tougher juvenile crime and welfare reform measures, tort adjustments to benefit business, standardized testing requirements in the public schools, and a charter school program), Bullock secured legislation for creation of a state water management plan, tougher state regulations for long-term elder care facilities, and establishment of a Texas state history museum to be located in Austin.

In June 1997, Bullock announced that he would not seek re-election to another term as lieutenant governor and was retiring from politics. Though he gave up drinking in the early 1980s, the many years of hard drinking and chain smoking contributed to his early death from heart failure complicated by cancer on June 18, 1999. He was buried in the Texas State Cemetery in Austin, a site that he was instrumental in revitalizing after years of neglect by state authorities. Two years after his death, the new state history exhibition hall was opened to the public, officially named the Bullock Texas State History Museum in his honor.